# MILLER'S

# COLLECTABLES
# PRICE GUIDE 2008

MILLER'S COLLECTABLES PRICE GUIDE 2008

Created and designed by
Miller's Publications
The Cellars, High Street
Tenterden, Kent, TN30 6BN
Tel: +44 (0) 1580 766411
Fax: +44 (0) 1580 766100

First published in Great Britain in 2007
by Miller's, a division of Mitchell Beazley,
imprints of Octopus Publishing Group Ltd,
2–4 Heron Quays, London E14 4JP
Miller's is a registered trademark of
Octopus Publishing Group Ltd,
an Hachette Livre UK Company

ISBN-978 1 84533 345 4

A CIP catalogue record for this book is
available from the British Library

Set in Frutiger

Colour origination by Colour Wheel Ltd, Whitstable, Kent
Additional colour origination by Ian Williamson, Pevensey Scanning
Printed and bound: Rotolito Lombarda, Italy


Consultant Editor: Jonty Hearnden
General Editor: Katherine Higgins

Managing Editor: Valerie Lewis
Production Co-ordinator: Philip Hannath
Editorial Co-ordinator: Deborah Wanstall
Editorial Assistants: Melissa Hall, Joanna Hill, Maureen Horner
Production Assistants: Charlotte Smith, Mel Smith, Ethne Tragett,
Lizzie Winwood, Alexandra Lewis-Wortley
Advertising Executives: Michael Webb, Carol Woodcock
Advertising Co-ordinator & Administrator: Melinda Williams
Designer: Sam Ward
Indexer: Hilary Bird
Production: Peter Hunt
Jacket Design: Tim Foster, Victoria Burley
Photographers: Paul Harding, Jeremy Martin, Huw Merideth,
Shawn Miller, Dennis O'Reilly, Robin Saker

**Front cover illustrations:**
A pair of A. R. Sons leather platform boots, America, Los Angeles, 1970s. **£125–140 Clobber** ⊞
A Union Pacific Old Timers Club cloth badge, America, 4in (10cm) long. **£5–10 Antique Mystique** ⊞
An Orrefors glass Cyrano vase, by Gunnar Cyrén, engraved mark, Sweden, 1950s, 10¾in (27.5cm) high. **£400–460 Freeforms** ⊞
*Dennis the Menace* annual, 1964. **£25–30 phil-comics auctions** ⊞
A Tuscan bone china loving cup, limited edition, No. 213, 1953, 5in (12.5cm) diam. **£200–220 Hope & Glory** ⊞
A Corgi Toys Morris Mini Minor, No. 226, 1960–61, 3in (7.5cm) long, with box. **£60–70 J & S Haley** ⊞
A pair of sunglasses, France, c1960, 14in (35.5cm) wide. **£25–30 Clobber** ⊞


Photographs of Jonty Hearnden and Katherine Higgins by Adrian Pope
Introduction photograph of Katherine Higgins courtesy of the BBC *Homes & Antiques* magazine

# MILLER'S

# COLLECTABLES
# PRICE GUIDE 2008

### KATHERINE HIGGINS *GENERAL EDITOR*

## JONTY HEARNDEN
### *CONSULTANT EDITOR*

# HOW TO USE

To find a particular item, consult the contents list on page 5 to determine it can be found under the main heading – for example, Decorative Arts. You will find that larger sections have been sub-divided into more focused collecting areas. If you are looking for a particular factory, designer or craftsman, consult the index which starts on page 457.

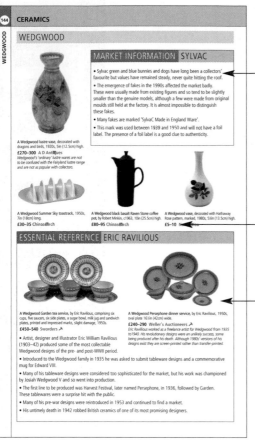

**Market Information**
What's hot, what's not – up to date buying and selling information, revised each year, on all the major collecting fields.

**Price guide**
this is based on actual prices realized. Remember that Miller's is a price guide not a price list and prices are affected by many variables such as location, condition, desirability and so on. Don't forget that if you are selling it is quite likely you will be offered less than the price range. Price ranges for items sold at auction tend to include the buyer's premium and VAT if applicable.

**Essential Reference**
information on design styles, makers, timelines, designers, types of wares, decoration, marks etc.

**Expert's Eye**
a detailed focus on an item, pointing out component parts and/or specific areas of interest and craftsmanship.

**Source code**
refers to the Key to Illustrations on page 446 that lists the details of where the item was photographed. The icon indicates the item was sold at auction. The icon indicates the item originated from a dealer.

**Detail**
this will either be a close-up of an interesting detail or an alternative view of the item.

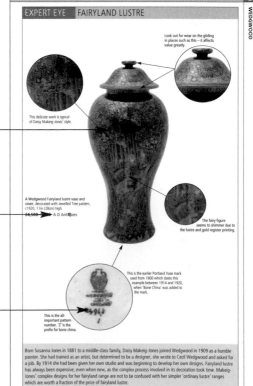

# contents

# MEET THE EXPERTS

The publishers would like to acknowledge the great assistance given by our consultants. We would also like to extend our thanks to all auction houses and their press offices, as well as dealers and collectors, who have assisted us in the production of this book.

**GENERAL EDITOR: Katherine Higgins** is an author, writer and broadcaster specializing in collectables. Current TV and radio credits include BBC TV's *Antiques Roadshow* (currently filming the 30th series) and ITV's *Christmas Show*. Katherine writes for *Woman & Home* magazine, *BBC Homes & Antiques* as well as the *Sunday Times*, *Daily Mail*, the *Express*, *The Times* and the *Daily Telegraph*. She has also worked extensively for Sky News. Katherine started her career in antiques as a Press Officer for Christie's and was antiques correspondent at the *Express*. She is passionate about modern collectables, especially Whitefriars glass, vintage fashion and all things plastic. Her first book, *Are You Rich?* was published by Andre Deutsch/Carlton Books in 1999.

www.higginsworld.co.uk
katherine@higgins-world.co.uk

**AERONAUTICA & SHIPPING: Geoff Pringle** has had a lifelong interest in all aspects of aeronautica, sailing and maritime history. After a career in industry he began his own business trading in nautical and aeronautical memorabilia. The company, Oldnautibits, has a worldwide customer base and deals predominantly from an informative and interesting website. The business recently won an award for the innovative use of the internet and was profiled in the *Financial Times*. Geoff also attends specialist and general antiques and collectors' fairs.

www.oldnautibits.com

**BOOKS: Justin Croft** is a specialist dealer in rare books and manuscripts. He is a member of BBC TV's *Antiques Roadshow* team and lives and works in Faversham, Kent.

www.justincroft.com

**CERAMICS: Steven Moore's** passion for collecting started as a child, beginning with curios begged or borrowed from his grandmother's attic. By the age of 16, he had curated his first exhibition at Newcastle's Laing Art Gallery and he had written his first book by 21. After studying to be an archaeologist he moved into antique dealing and writing. He is curator for CT Maling & Sons and Chairman of the Maling Collectors Society. He currently works as a freelance arts and antiques consultant, writer and broadcaster. Steven is a member of the *Antiques Roadshow* experts team and is currently filming the 29th season of the programme.

**FILM & ENTERTAINMENT: Stephen Lane** has been an avid collector of movie props and costumes for over 15 years and in 1999 set up the The Prop Store of London. Operating predominantly through a web site, The Prop Store is recognized as one of the world's leading vendors of film memorabilia. Stephen's opinion is often sought for TV shows, books, magazines, newspapers and web articles. He has also acted as an adviser to some of the world's leading auction houses.

www.propstore.com

**GLASS: Andy McConnell** appears on the BBC's *Antiques Roadshow* and has written for *The Times*, *Country Life* and BBC's *Homes & Antiques*. He has written *The Decanter, An Illustrated History of Glass from 1650*, and *20th Century Glass*.

Glass Etc 18–22, Rope Walk, Rye, East Sussex TN31 7NA
Tel: 01797 226600  www.decanterman.com

**MODERN TECHNOLOGY: Pepe Tozzo** has a background in healthcare and financial IT systems. His career started with the National Blood Transfusion Service as a medical scientist, after which he moved into IT in healthcare and financial markets. His interest in technology dates back to the early 1970s when the brilliance of Clive Sinclair's early jewel-like calculators fired his imagination. The technology explosion that followed heightened this interest. Pepe is the author of *Collectable Technology*, published by Carlton Books in 2005, and appears on both television and radio.

www.tozzo.co.uk

**ROCK & POP: Garry Shrum's** education in recorded music started early – when just five years old he was listening to his brother's records and in 1964 he was playing in his first band and attending his first rock concert (The Rolling Stones). After a stint in the corporate world, Garry started his own successful record store, Blue Meanie Records, in 1976. Attending many record shows in the United States and Europe over the years, Garry has become an expert on imports, especially those of the 1960s. He has been providing expertise for Heritage's Music and Entertainment Auctions since 2004.

Heritage Auction Galleries,
3500 Maple Ave, 17th Floor, Dallas,
Texas 75219-3941, USA
www.heritageauctions.com

**STAINLESS STEEL: Will Farmer** is a Director and valuer with Fieldings Auctioneers, based in Stourbridge, which he established six years ago with his business partner Nick Davies. A graduate silversmith and jewellery designer, Will specializes in 20th-century Decorative Arts with a keen passion for Art Deco ceramics and 20th-century glass. Will has featured as a ceramics expert on BBC TV's *Going for a Song*, *20th Century Roadshow* and is currently filming his fourth season for the *Antiques Roadshow*.

Fieldings Auctioneers, Mill Race Lane, Stourbridge, West Midlands DY8 1JN

**SPORT: Graham Budd** worked for Sotheby's for 25 years where he was a Deputy Director and Head of Sporting Memorabilia. High profile auctions he curated include the Lester Piggott Collection and the auction for the late Sir Stanley Matthews. In 2004 he founded his own company, Graham Budd Auctions, a specialist firm of auctioneers in the sporting memorabilia market. Graham Budd Auctions and Sotheby's still maintain a close association and the auctions are held at Sotheby's Olympia in London. Graham Budd is the author of two books, *Racing Art and Memorabilia, A Celebration of the Turf* (Philip Wilson, 1997) and *Soccer Memorabilia, A Collectors' Guide* (Philip Wilson, 1999). He is also a regular contributor to television and radio, including BBC TV's *20th Century Roadshow*.

gb@grahambuddauctions.co.uk
Tel: 020 8366 2525

**CULT TOYS: Andrew Kitchen & Alex Beasley** met at university in 1995 and discovered they shared a passion for late 20th-century toys that had never really left them since childhood. Although they originally specialized in the first release *Star Wars* toy line (by Kenner 1977–85), their knowledge has grown to cover a diverse array of cult children's toys originating from film and television. Many of the toys Andrew and Alex collect featured on the BBC TV's *Antiques Show*, filmed on location at the National Exhibition Centre in Birmingham. Their specialist knowledge is regularly called upon for contributions to print and internet articles. Over the past few years both have appeared as experts on BBC TV's *Antiques Roadshow* and *20th Century Roadshow*. Andrew and Alex run the online store www.toydreams.co.uk, which sells a large array of toys from this period.

**Katherine Higgins
General Editor**

This year is a very special one as we celebrate the 20th published edition of *Miller's Collectables Price Guide*. To mark our anniversary you'll notice we've gone big. For 2008 we've produced this larger format book, with bigger pictures, whole page expert analyses and more grass-roots information than you can imagine. It's a fitting celebration of two decades at the top – as a key barometer of the collectables marketplace.

And how things have changed in 20 years. Back in the 1980s 'collectables' (a term slapped on anything other than traditional antiques) were sidelined in general auction sales. Car boot sales were very much a novelty and the thought of buying a Pez sweet dispenser on the internet was little more than a pipe dream.

It wasn't until 1983 that the first teddy bear tentatively appeared in an international saleroom. Ten years later the gamble paid off when the same venue held their first all bear auction and triumphed with a record £110,000 for a Steiff. Now in any one day over 6,500 teddy bears are up for sale on eBay alone. The two decade ascent of the humble teddy is an example of how the collectables market has boomed and metamorphosized into the broadest collecting category we know.

A Kenner *Star Wars* Chewbacca doll, with bandolier strap and bowcaster, 1978, 14in (35.6cm) high.
**£70–85 Toydreams** ⊞

The rise in internet trading has certainly eroded the exclusivity of auctions and simultaneously opened up a global collectables arena. You don't need to spend a fortune to access this area and as our 2008 edition of the Price Guide proves the options are multifarious – from action figures to Zambezi Ware, the choice is yours.

This year we spotlight a number of hot categories. Cult toys from the 1970s, 1980s and 1990s are the lifeblood of memorabilia fairs and the internet. The level of interest from nostalgia-ridden twenty- and thirty-somethings has pushed the prices of their plastic childhood favourites steadily upwards. Similarly we take a close look at kitchenalia – particularly post-WWII pieces like Tupperware and 1950s Pyrex.

A stainless steel condiment bowl set, marked Rostfritt Stal, Sweden, 1960s–70s, 9in (23cm) long.
**£15–20 ModCats.com** ⊞

Vintage fashion, stainless steel and groovy 1960s and '70s glass and ceramics have equally extended coverage.

Our featured areas show you just how much we've moved on with collectables in 20 years. Here at Miller's we keep our ears to the ground and reflect the current trends so you can benefit. Of course, buying is all about spotting and to help you we have introduced a really focused look at key collectables. With my help and that of some of my fellow experts from BBC TV's *Antiques Roadshow*, you can pick up tips on exactly what to look for when you handle a would-be purchase for the first time. Armed with this knowledge you'll be able to tackle your collecting with confidence.

Anniversaries may be the perfect time to reflect but they're also a time to look ahead. This 2008 Guide gives you tips on Future Collectables like the high street fashions designed by Kate Moss, not forgetting Sainsbury's shopping bags. They're just one thought about where the collectables market will be 20 years from now. The certainty, of course, is that whatever happens, Miller's will still be there to guide you!

**Katherine Higgins**

A pair of Leslie Designs sandals, 1960s.
**£40–45 First Call** ⊞

# ADVERTISING & PACKAGING

## CERAMICS & GLASS

A J. W. Lawrence & Co baking dish, ceramic, early 20thC, 9in (23cm) diam.
**£30–35 Wenderton Antiques** ⊞

A Harris's Sausages advertising plate, ceramic, marked 'Burslem', c1910, 10in (25.5cm) diam.
**£90–100 Skip & Janie Smithson** ⊞

A Pepsi-Cola glass, by Continental Can Co, America, 1950s, 5in (12.5cm) high.
**£1–5 My Gigi's Treasures** ⊞

A Dr Pepper glass, by Continental Can Co, triple 'C' mark, America, 1950s, 5in (12.5cm) high.
**£1–5 My Gigi's Treasures** ⊞

A 7-Up glass, by Continental Can Co, America, 1950s, 5in (12.5cm) high.
**£1–5 My Gigi's Treasures** ⊞

A Butlin's glass, early 1960s, 2¾in (7cm) high.
**£1–5 John Smart** ⊞

A set of two Lurpak eggcups, ceramic, 2002, 3¾in (9.5cm) high.
**£1–5 Carol Woodcock** ⊞

# COCA-COLA

## ESSENTIAL REFERENCE COCA-COLA TRAYS

A Coca-Cola serving tray, depicting Coca-Cola's Summer Girl, lithographed by H. D. Beach Co, slight damage, America, Ohio, 1921, 10½ x 13¼in (26.5 x 33.5cm).

**£30–35 Heritage** ⚒

A Coca-Cola serving tray, lithographed by the American Art Works, slight damage, America, Ohio, 1939, 10½ x 13¼in (26.5 x 33.5cm).

**£120–150 Heritage** ⚒

A Coca-Cola serving tray, slight damage, America, 1950s, 10½ x 13¼in (26.5 x 33.5cm).

**£65–75 Heritage** ⚒

• Tin trays were supplied to soda fountains and drug stores as a means of furthering brand loyalty. The earliest recorded example dates back to 1897.

• Images from Coca-Cola calendars were adapted for printing onto the trays by lithographic specialists such as Chicago-based Charles W. Shonk & Co and the Ohio firms  American Art Works and H. D. Beach Co.

• Early serving and change trays were decorated with beauties. Coca Cola's first 'personality' face was actress Hilda Clark. In the 1930s Olympic champion swimmer Johnny Weissmuller and film-star Maureen O'Sullivan appeared on a metal serving tray.

• Coca-Cola employed well-known graphic artists such as Hamilton King, Haddon Sundblom (synonymous with the jolly Coca-Cola Santa Claus) and even Norman Rockwell to illustrate their merchandising, including trays.

• Condition is crucial to value – a tray can be worth £1 in very poor condition or £1,200 in mint condition. Scratches across the main image spell bad news. If there is damage it's far better to have light wear at the edge.

• Many reproductions have been made since the 1970s, so beware.

A Coca-Cola wall clock, by the Baird Clock Co, papier-mâché and wood with a metal dial and spring-driven pendulum, inscribed 'Coca-Cola, The Ideal Brain Tonic, Delightful Beverage, Specific for Headache, Relieves Exhaustion', America, New York, 1890s 13in (33cm) high.

**£3,750–4,250 Schmidt Museum** ⊞

A Coca-Cola Tiffany-style lamp shade, leaded-glass, the brass band inscribed 'Property of the Coca-Cola Company to be returned on demand', America, c1920, 18in (45.5cm) diam.

**£4,500–5,000 Schmidt Museum** ⊞

A sheet of 25 Coca-Cola bingo marker cards, 1940s, 5¾in (14.5cm) square.

**£1–5 Don & Chris' Old Stuff** ⊞

A Coca-Cola delivery truck promotional toy, metal, together with bottles and working lights, 1933, 11in (28cm) long.

**£600–700 Schmidt Museum** ⊞

A Coca-Cola advertising sign, enamel, 1950, 28in (71cm) wide.

**£200–230 Junktion** ⊞

A Coca-Cola advertising sign, 1950s, 36in (91.5cm) diam.
**£450–500 Schmidt Museum** ⊞

A Coca-Cola cup, waxed paper, 1950s, 3½in (9cm) high.
**£1–5 Don & Chris' Old Stuff** ⊞

A Coca-Cola glass, by the Continental Can Co, with triple 'C' mark, America, 1950s, 5in (12.5cm) high.
**£1–5 My Gigi's Treasures** ⊞

A Coca-Cola sign, enamel, Belgium, c1950, 54 x 24in (137 x 61cm).
**£115–125 Cobwebs** ⊞

A Coca-Cola and Pops-Rite popcorn bag, America, 1950s, 8½in (21.5cm) high.
**£1–5
Don & Chris' Old Stuff** ⊞

A Coca-Cola uniform tag, cloth, America, 1950s–60s, 2in (5cm) wide.
**£1–5 Don & Chris' Old Stuff** ⊞

A full page Coca-Cola magazine advertisement, America, 1964.
**£1–5
My Gigi's Treasures** ⊞

A Coca-Cola World Cup football polar bear, c1998, 6in (15cm) high.
**£1–5 M&C Cards** ⊞

## ENAMEL SIGNS

A Van Houten's Cocoa sign, enamel, c1900, framed, 6 x 15½in (15 x 39.5cm).
**£425–475** Ad-Age ⊞

A Fry's Cocoa sign, enamel, 1910, 36in (91.5cm) wide.
**£350–380** Junktion ⊞

A Vigil sign, enamel, 1920, 16in (40.5cm) wide.
**£25–30** Dantinman ⊞

A Smith's Newspapers Delivered sign, enamel, 1920, 22in (56cm) high.
**£220–250** Junktion ⊞

A National Telephone Service double-sided sign, enamel, c1920, 19 x 18in (48.5 x 45.5cm).
**£200–225**
Peter Campbell ⊞

A Brasso sign, enamel, France, c1921, 18in (45.5cm) high.
**£160–180** Dantinman ⊞

A Thornycroft Marine Motors sign, enamel, 1920s–30s, 20in (51cm) wide.
**£1,000–1,200** Cobwebs ⊞

A Cadbury's Bourneville Cocoa sign, enamel, 1930s, 13in high.
**£720–800** Ad-Age ⊞

A Técalémit Station Officielle sign, enamel, France, 1950s, 47in (119.5cm) wide.
**£250–280** Junktion ⊞

# PACKAGING

## ESSENTIAL REFERENCE  REPLICA FOOD

A Toms Milk Chocolate dummy bar, c1955, 5½in (14cm) wide.
**£10–15 David Huxtable** ⊞

Three Tobler shop window samples, tin, France, late 1950s, 6½in (16.5cm) wide.
**£10–15 David Huxtable** ⊞

- In the early days of shopping, way before branded packaging and colour photography existed, all products were behind the counter and customers were served by the shopkeeper.
- Realistic coloured wax and plaster models of fruit and vegetables played a key role in enticing customers to buy products at the turn of the 20th century.
- As branding took a foothold, food manufacturers relied on dummy wrappers to promote their products on the shelf and in shop windows.
- The most collectable replica foods are the Victorian and Edwardian wax models. Wrapped dummies relating to well-known brands are also sought after.
- Look at the condition thoroughly. Items displayed in shop windows are often heavily faded on one side.

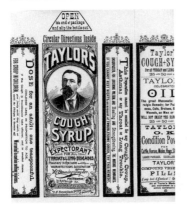

A Taylor's Cough Syrup box wrapper, America, c1885, 11in (28cm) high.
**£15–20 Kit Barry Ephemera** ⊞

A Fry's Shilling Chocolate box, wood, 1920, 9in (23cm) wide.
**£10–15 Dantinman** ⊞

A Mitre Dessert Fruits box, cardboard, c1930, 6in (15cm) diam.
**£1–5 M&C Cards** ⊞

A packet of Boots Primrose Household Soap box, c1960, 6in (15cm) long.
**£1–5 M&C Cards** ⊞

An ERA moth cartridge, 1950s, 2in (5cm) high.
**£1–5 Rin Tin Tin** ⊞

An Anco Macaroni bag, paper, Belgium, 1950s, 11 x 4¾in (28 x 12cm).
**£1–5 Twinkled** ⊞

An advertising fan, paper and bamboo, Thailand, c1980, 8in (20.5cm) high.
**£1–5 Postcard Club** ⊞

## PREMIUMS & GIVEAWAYS

A set of four Kellogg's plastic models of Bluebird cars, 1964, 2½in (6.5cm) wide.
**£50–60  Geoff Holden** ⊞

A Kellogg's plastic Golly figure, c1960, 2in (5cm) high.
**£30–35  collectorsworld** ⊞
*This figure was also made in other colours.*

A set of 16 Nabisco plastic *Magic Roundabout* figures, 1968, largest 1¼in (3cm) high.
**£40–45  Magic Toy Box** ⊞

A collection of Kellogg's plastic *Magic Roundabout* figures, c1970, largest 2in (5cm) high.
**£10–15 each  Magic Toy Box** ⊞

A Kellogg's plastic Mr Plod figure, 1960s, 2in (5cm) high.
**£20–25  collectorsworld** ⊞

Six Sainsbury's plastic Mr Men figures, 1990, 1½in (4cm) high.
**£1–5  John Smart** ⊞

## MARKET INFORMATION  ADVERTISING PREMIUMS

- The internet has opened up the market for premium trading in a major way. On any one day, eBay typically advertises over 6,000 fast-food premiums for sale – although the majority carry a price tag of less than £2 per set.

- McDonald's giveaways are among the most widely exchanged premiums today. They first appeared in the 1970s in the USA (1985 in the UK). For these to have any real value in the current market they must be sealed in their original packaging.

- Today's premiums are well-constructed pieces that often incorporate a mechanical element, but a century ago things were far more basic. Giveaways were typically cardboard figures, puzzle books, postcards and small tinplate toys – similar to those inside boxes of Cracker Jack popcorn, whose slogan was, not surprisingly, 'A-prize-in-every-package'.

- The scope of premium collecting is enormous and the key to success in this marketplace is to focus on a clear-cut area. For instance it could be Radio and TV premiums, fast food, cloth dolls, comic premiums or even character toys.

- Vintage premiums need to be in good condition and rare colour variants always attract attention. Vectis recently sold an unusually coloured Dumpty Doo duck from Cadbury's Cocoa Cubs series (1934) for close to £100. Average figures in the series sell for around £10.

- One of the most unusual premiums has to be the square inch plots of land in the Yukon, USA, which were given to all those who collected their Quaker Oats coupons in the 1950s.

# SHOWCARDS & PAPER ADVERTISING

A Hearts of Oak Benefit Society advertising postcard, c1908.

**£20–25** Memories ⊞

A Fry's Cocoa advertising postcard, c1910.

**£20–25** Memories ⊞

A Robin Starch advertising card, c1930, 22in (56cm) high, framed.

**£230–250** Dodo ⊞

A Cadbury's Chocolates Xmas Club show card, 1930s, framed and glazed, 13½ x 9in (34.5 x 23cm).

**£225–250** Ad-Age ⊞

A Schweppes advertisement, tin, c1950, 14in (35.5cm) wide.

**£50–55** M&C Cards ⊞

A Krementz magazine advertisement, America, 1971, 10 x 7in (25.5 x 18cm).

**£1–5** My Gigi's Treasures ⊞

*This advertisement depicts an assortment of jewellery with 'a heavy overlay of 14ct gold that gives these pieces much of the wearing quality and all of the rich beauty of solid Karat gold.' Material like this is useful to collectors as it shows the original selling prices and also helps to precisely date items (see also page197).*

*George Krementz started making gold jewellery for women and dress sets for men in America in 1866. In the 20th century a line of costume jewellery was added to the firm's repertoire.*

A Ramon dishcloth advertising display, cardboard, 1950s, 18in (45.5cm) high.

**£35–40** Clobber ⊞

Cans. Bad Guys or Good Guys?

A Can people magazine advertisement, America, 1971, 10 x 7in (25.5cm x 18cm).

**£1–5** My Gigi's Treasures ⊞

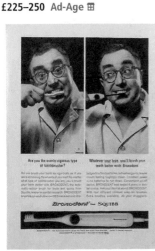

A Squibb Broxodent Automatic-Action Toothbrush magazine advertisement, 1963, 10 x 7in (25.5 x 18cm).

**£1–5** My Gigi's Treasures ⊞

A Huntley & Palmer's Fire Brigade biscuit tin, c1892, 6½in (16.5cm) high.
**£270–300 Michael Saffell** ⊞

A Huntley & Palmer's Showman biscuit tin, c1893, 6in (15cm) high.
**£220–250 Michael Saffell** ⊞

A Peek Frean's biscuit tin, in the form of a Royal Mail horse-drawn cart, 1904, 5in (12.5cm) wide.
**£270–300 Dantinman** ⊞

A MacFarlane Lang's biscuit tin, in the form of a bird's nest, c1910, 5½in (14cm) diam.
**£200–230 Michael Saffell Antiques** ⊞

A McVitie & Price's biscuit tin, c1924, 3in (7.5cm) diam.
**£15–20 Michael Saffell** ⊞

A Huntley & Palmer's biscuit tin, in the form of a kitchen range, 1926, 5in (12.5cm) wide.
**£180–200 Michael Saffell** ⊞

A Lyons Gala Night Biscuit Assortment tin, c1930, 4in (10cm) diam.
**£20–25 Michael Saffell** ⊞

A Gray Dunn & Co biscuit tin, in the form of a Wheel of Fortune, c1935, 5in (12.5cm) diam.
**£170–190 Michael Saffell** ⊞

A Weston's Tavern Bleu Cheese Biscuits tin, c1950, 8in (20.5cm) high.
**£5–10 Ann Lingard** ⊞

A Huntley & Palmer's biscuit tin, decorated with violets, slight damage, 1961, 4in (10cm) wide.
**£5–10 Retro2Go** ⊞

## EXPERT EYE BISCUIT TINS

Take a close look at the quality of the decoration here. Aside from the highly detailed scenes on the front, top and sides of the tin there's a wonderful decorative border, that anchors the whole design.

Considering its age this tin is in acceptable condition – if it was more modern then the obvious wear would reduce its value. The main image on the front is reasonably unspoilt, although you can see bare areas here and on the folded sides at the back where the ink has been worn away.

A Huntley & Palmer's Indian biscuit tin, c1894, 6⅛in (15.5cm) high.
**£270–300**
**Michael Saffell** ⊞

This tin's curved outline shows it was made to be a decorative object in its own right. The idea was that it would find a home in the parlour long after the biscuits had been eaten. Although machines were used for printing, this tin would have required many man-hours to finish.

The fact that their name is woven into a complex ornamental design on the back shows that Huntley & Palmer's were clearly proud of their work.

Read any printed information carefully, it can be a big clue to dating. Here it makes reference to `The Queen', which means it must pre-date Queen Victoria's death in 1901.

British–based Huntley & Palmer's began as a small bakery in 1822. The firm's growth was rapid and by 1900 it was the largest biscuit manufacturer in the world. The idea of making tins as a means of extending the shelf life of their biscuits and aiding their distribution came from Joseph Huntley's son. Large 10lb tins were the first to be used and grocers sold directly from these. Today it's the more elaborate lithographed tins like this that collectors vie for. Prices are very strong in US auctions as American collectors snap up British pieces on their home territory to avoid poor exchange rates. Morphy's recent sale in Pennsylvania saw a Huntley & Palmer's tin from the 1920s sell for £900. But this was topped by a Crawford's bus from the same era, which made £1,600. Both were in superb original condition with minimal pitting, fading or scratches.

TINS – CANDY/SWEETS

A Lovell's Devon Cream Toffee tin, c1914, 6¼in (16cm) high.
**£40–45 Dantinman** ⊞

A Heinrich chocolate tin, in the form of a tiled cottage, with a hinged lid, Germany, Nuremberg, 1920s–30s, 7in (18cm) high.
**£150–180**
**Penrith Farmers' & Kidd's** 🪓

A Rexall Pharmacies Peppermint Buttons tin, c1925, 3½in (9cm) wide.
**£10–15 Michael Saffell** ⊞

A Thorne's Extra Super Crème Toffee tin, 1920s, 4¼ (10.5cm) wide.
**£25–30 Tin Shop** ⊞

A sweet tin, printed with a fairy, 1930, 7in (18cm) wide.
**£45–50 Dodo** ⊞

A Pascall Weekly Assortment tin, 1930s, 6in (15cm) wide.
**£5–10 Rin Tin Tin** ⊞

A Crosse & Blackwell Starboard Lights Creme-de-Menthe sweet tin, 1930s, 6in (15cm) wide.
**£15–20 Rin Tin Tin** ⊞

A Thorne's Halloween Children Assorted Toffees tin, slight damage, 1930s, 6¾in (17cm) wide.
**£20–25 Tin Shop** ⊞

A Bensons toffee tin, c1950, 9in (23cm) high.
**£10–15 M&C Cards** ⊞

A Walters' Palm Toffee tin, c1950s, 11½in (29cm) high.
**£30–35 Ann Lingard** ⊞

A Café Espresso Candy Drops tin, France, c1960, 3in (7.5cm) diam.
**£5–10 Martin's** ⊞

# TINS – PROVISIONS

A Colman's Mustard tin, c1900, 9in (23cm) wide.
**£70–80 Michael Saffell** ⊞

A Mazawattee Tea tin, 1900, 7in (18cm) wide.
**£100–115 Dodo** ⊞

A Keen, Robinson & Co mustard tin, c1900, 7in (18cm) wide.
**£115–125 Michael Saffell** ⊞

A Moss, Rimmington & Co mustard tin, produced for *Exposition Universelle*, Paris, 1900, 9in (23cm) wide.
**£135–150 Michael Saffell** ⊞

A Lyons Tea tin, 1920, 5in (12.5cm) high.
**£15–20 M&C Cards** ⊞

A Mazawattee Tea Old Folks at Home tin, c1920s, 8½in (21.5cm) wide.
**£30–35 Rin Tin Tin** ⊞

A Te Sol tea tin, 1930s–40s, 6½in (16.5cm) wide.
**£20–25 Rin Tin Tin** ⊞

A Blue Ribbon Red Label tea tin, with a hinged lid, slight damage, Canada, 1930s, 8¾in (22cm) high.
**£35–40 Tin Shop** ⊞

A National Household Dried Milk tin, America, 1950s, 5in (12.5cm) high.
**£5–10 Twinkled** ⊞

A Ty-phoo Tea tin, 1970s, 6¼in (16cm) high .
**£5–10 Tin Shop** ⊞

## TINS – MISCELLANEOUS

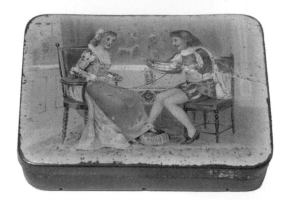

A Crescent hair pins tin, c1895, 4in (10cm) wide.

**£15–20** Michael Saffell ⊞

A souvenir tin, depicting a view of Port Erin, c1900, 3in (7.5cm) diam.

**£10–15** Michael Saffell ⊞

A Peps Coughs, Colds, Bronchitis and Lung, Throat and Chest Troubles tin, with a hinged lid, 1900s, 4¾in (12cm) high.

**£20–25** Tin Shop ⊞

A G.B. metal polish tin, c1910, 5in (12.5cm) high.

**£15–20** Dantinman ⊞

A Kayser sewing machine accessories tin, Germany, c1910, 5½in (14cm) wide.

**£40–45** David Huxtable ⊞

A Lilac Wax Polish tin, slight damage, 1910–20, 3¾in (9.5cm) diam.

**£5–10** Tin Shop ⊞

A Cherry Blossom Toilet Powder tin, c1930, 4in (10cm) high, with contents.

**£10–15** M&C Cards ⊞

A Mothak Powder bug killer tin and card, c1950, 4in (10cm) high.

**£5–10** M&C Cards ⊞

A Perma Nips lighter fuel tin, 1950s, 6in (15cm) wide.

**£10–15** Beaulieu Autojumble ⊞

A Durex Surgeons' Fingercots tin, slight damage, 1950s, 1½in (4cm) diam.

**£10–15** Tin Shop ⊞

# AERONAUTICA

## GROUND & CREW EQUIPMENT

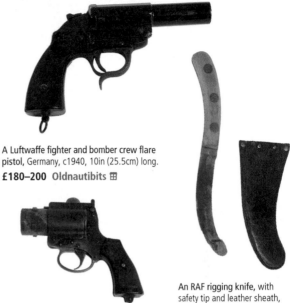

A Luftwaffe fighter and bomber crew flare pistol, Germany, c1940, 10in (25.5cm) long.
**£180–200** Oldnautibits ⊞

An RAF station bell, 1940, 13¼in (33.5cm) high.
**£800–900** Aeroclocks ⊞
*This is also known as a scramble bell. A recent auction saw a similar item, the Air Ministry fire bell from the Fighter Command Air Station at Biggin Hill, sell for £5,750, nearly ten times the estimate.*

An RAF aircraft flare pistol, c1943, 8in (20.5cm) long.
**£100–120** Oldnautibits ⊞

An RAF rigging knife, with safety tip and leather sheath, c1944, 11in (28cm) long.
**£35–40** Oldnautibits ⊞
*This knife was designed to cut parachute cords in an emergency.*

A USAAF bombardier's equipment case, Type E-1, c1943, 21in (53.5cm) wide.
**£90–100** Oldnautibits ⊞

An RAF ceramic wall plaque, 1940s, 11in (28cm) high.
**£120–140** Cobwebs ⊞

## ESSENTIAL REFERENCE SECTOR CLOCKS

An RAF sector clock, with winged crest, c1937, 18in (45.5cm) diam.
**£4,500–5,000 Aeroclocks** ⊞
*Note light pre-war colour to case.*

A WWII Royal Observer Corps electric Slave sector clock, c1937, 18in (45.5cm) diam.
**£1,800–2,000 Aeroclocks** ⊞

A Type I RAF sector clock, with laurel wreath, c1939, 18in (45.5cm) diam.
**£3,500–4,000 Aeroclocks** ⊞

A Type II RAF sector clock, restored, c1943, 18in (45.5cm) diam.
**£1,800–2,000 Aeroclocks** ⊞

• Sector Clocks were used for 50 years to control British military aircraft and monitor enemy aircraft. The colour of the segment below the minute hand was used to colour-code the time a sighting was received. The technique was introduced in 1917–18 by the Royal Flying Corps to track German aircraft that were bombing London.

• The first examples were called colour-change clocks. The coloured segments were red, yellow and green. Examples of these clocks remained in service with the RAF until well into WWII. RAF sector clocks (as opposed to those from the RFC) were probably made from 1935 onwards and had red, yellow and blue segments.

• Early examples of RAF clocks have winged crests until around 1937 when replaced by the laurel leaf crest. All RAF clocks until 1942 were built to an excellent standard with solid mahogany cases and high-grade fusee movements. The Royal Observer Corps also used an electric version with an 18in (45.5cm) dial, probably from 1935.

• From 1935 to mid-1939 sector clocks had a natural mahogany finish. During the war these were made with toned-down dark finishes. Most sector clocks were made by Elliott in 1939 and 1941. They were used by the Royal Air Force, the Royal Observer Corps and Navy and Army units working under RAF direction such as anti aircraft commands.

• From 1942 onwards an austerity sector clock was introduced. Made of oak with a small Smiths platform-escapement movement these clocks are of a poorer standard.

• After WWII, clocks were made by Elliott using their standard post-war oak office clock. To cope with the huge numbers of Russian aircraft which were likely to attack Britain in the Cold War, the coloured segments were further subdivided.

• Be careful when buying a sector clock. There are many fakes around, several of which have appeared on eBay. The original dials were printed with a smooth finish. A clock with a repainted dial might be a fake.

**Bob Gardner, Aeroclocks**

## TIMELINE PROPELLORS

An SE5A propeller, 95in (241.5cm) long.
**£2,500–2,800 Aeroclocks** ⊞

A Fokker D VII propeller, Germany, 108¼in (275cm) long.
**£2,500–2,800 Aeroclocks** ⊞

An FE8 propeller, 96in (244cm) wide.
**£3,700–4,100 Aeroclocks** ⊞

# MODELS & PLAQUES

A chrome model of two Lancaster bombers, 1930, 8in (20.5cm) high.

**£160–180  Hardy's Collectables** ⊞

A chrome model of a racing plane, 1930s, 6in (15cm) high.

**£75–85  Cobwebs** ⊞

A brass plaque, decorated with a Spitfire, inscribed 'Never have so many owed so much to so few. Winston Churchill', 1941, 12in (30.5cm) wide.

**£35–45  Cobwebs** ⊞

*This statement was used during a speech made by Winston Churchill when he addressed the House of Commons on 20 August 1940 at the height of the Battle of Britain.*

A WWII RAF mechanic's brass and aluminium model of a Supermarine Spitfire, 5in (12.5cm) high.

**£75–85  GB Military Antiques** ⊞

An aluminium model of a Supermarine Swift, on a wooden base, c1950, 10in (25.5cm) high.

**£65–75  Cobwebs** ⊞

A chrome-plated-brass model of a Supermarine Spitfire, 1960, 6in (15cm) wide.

**£35–40  Oldnautibits** ⊞

A laminated mahogany propeller tip, c1920, 41in (104cm) high.

**£135–145
Oldnautibits** ⊞

A Savoia Marchetti seaplane propeller, Italy, 1930s, 90½in (230cm) wide.

**£3,500–3,900  Aeroclocks** ⊞

A Hurricane propeller, 1939, 135½in (344cm) long.

**£4,000–4,500  Aeroclocks** ⊞

A Supermarine Seafire propeller blade, c1944, 54in (137cm) high.

**£320–350
Oldnautibits** ⊞

# PHOTOGRAPHS & POSTCARDS

A WWI Sanke card of Max Immelmann, signed 'Leutnant.', Germany, 4½ x 7in (11.5 x 18cm).

**£1,000–1,300 Aeroclocks** ⊞

A WWI printed photograph of Freiherr Manfred von Richthofen, sitting in his Fokker Dr 1, signed, Germany, 9 x 5in (23 x 12.5cm).

**£1,500–1,700 Aeroclocks** ⊞

A WWI Sanke card of Kurt Wolff, signed, Germany, 4½ x 7in (11.5 x 18cm).

**£1,000–1,300 Aeroclocks** ⊞

A postcard, signed by Werner Voss, Germany, 1917, 6 x 4in (15 x 10cm).

**£2,000–2,300 Aeroclocks** ⊞

A photograph of the airship R101, c1930, 10 x 12in (25.5 x 30.5cm).

**£30–35 David Huxtable** ⊞

A photograph of *Oberstleutnant* Adolf Galland, signed, dated 1940, 15 x 10in (38 x 25.5cm).

**£220–250 Aeroclocks** ⊞

*This is a rare autograph as Adolf Galland only held this rank for one month before promoted to Oberst.*

A Luftwaffe postcard of *Leutnant* Kurt Dix, by Binz, Germany, 1943, 6 x 4in (15 x 10cm).

**£25–30 S&D Postcards** ⊞

A postcard of the airship LZ129 *Hindenburg*, Germany, 1930s, 6 x 4in (15 x 10cm).

**£15–20 Cobwebs** ⊞

# PROGRAMMES & PRINTED EPHEMERA

A souvenir programme, from the first aeronautical meeting in Great Britain, 1909.
**£500–550  Aeroclocks** ⊞

*Flight, First Aero Weekly in the World*, November 1909, 12in (30.5cm) high.
**£8–10  Symes of Bristol** ⊞

A National Aviation Day Display flight ticket, 1933, 6in (15cm) high.
**£6–8  Symes of Bristol** ⊞

A National Aviation Day Display souvenir programme, Sir Alan Cobham, 1933, 10in (25.5cm) high.
**£10–15  Symes of Bristol** ⊞

A C. W. A. Scott's flying display programme, 1934, 10in (25.5cm) high.
**£5–10  Symes of Bristol** ⊞

*Battle of Britain*, booklet, 1940, 10in (25.5cm) high.
**£5–10  Tussie Mussies** ⊞

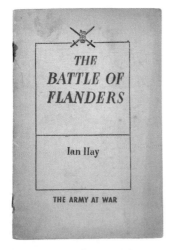

Ian Hay, *The Battle of Flanders, The Army at War*, 1940, 8in (20.5cm) high.
**£1–5  Tussie Mussies** ⊞

A propaganda booklet, *Bomber Command Continues*, 1942, 9½in (24cm) high.
**£1–5  Tussie Mussies** ⊞

A B.O.A.C. message card, 1950s, 5in (12.5cm) wide.
**£5–10  Cobwebs** ⊞

## UNIFORM – DRESS ACCESSORIES

An RFC mahogany walking stick, made from pieces of an aeroplane, initialled 'HFC', c1917, 29in (73.5cm) long.

**£160–175** Oldnautibits ⊞

An RAF officer's leather and cloth visor cap, c1940.

**£115–125** Oldnautibits ⊞

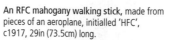

A chrome-plated cigarette case, with engine-turned decoration and RAF motif, 1940, 5in (12.5cm) high.

**£10–15** Tussie Mussies ⊞

An RAF officer's visor cap, with King's crown and Air Force badge, 1942.

**£90–100** Oldnautibits ⊞

An RAF service dress uniform, worn by Squadron Leader Thorburn, c1943.

**£200–220** Oldnautibits ⊞

An RAF pilot's battle dress tunic, complete with pilot's brevet (RAF wings) and DFC ribbon, 1943.

**£200–230** Oldnautibits ⊞

An RAF tropical issue uniform, comprising tunic, trousers and visor cap, worn by Air Chief Marshall Sir William MacDonald, with King's Crown buttons, pilot's brevet (RAF Wings) and medal ribbons , c1952.

**£400–450** Oldnautibits ⊞

## MARKET INFORMATION   UNIFORMS

- WWII uniforms and equipment relating to the RAF, Luftwaffe, USAAF and the Japanese Air Force are in strong demand. Scarcity is forcing up prices, with collectors being prepared to pay top money for good to excellent unrestored condition.

- Items with known provenance, such as a named airman or specific action, will also command a significant premium.

- The Battle of Britain continues to have a strong following, while the remake of the film *The Dam Busters* will undoubtedly rekindle interest in Guy Gibson, 617 Squadron and aeronautica in general.

- Flight clothing that was issued to air crew on operational sorties is a key area of interest with flying suits, helmets, parachute harnesses and Mae West lifejackets being very popular. Demand is outstripping supply with a resulting increase in prices. The RAF Irvin, together with the USAAF equivalent B-3 and the A-2 flight jacket favoured by fighter pilots have shown significant price rises over the last 12 months – a trend that is set to continue.

**Geoff Pringle, Oldnautibits**

# UNIFORM – FLYING

An RFC leather and cloth Warren flying helmet, 1900s.

**£580–650 Oldnautibits** ⊞

A leather flying helmet, 1930s.

**£135–160** ⚒ **Mastro Auctions**

A Luftwaffe LKpN101 net and leather flying helmet, complete with microphone and wiring, Germany, c1941.

**£300–350 Oldnautibits** ⊞

A pair of RAF 1941 pattern suede flying boots, with sheepskin lining, 1941.

**£200–220 Oldnautibits** ⊞

*Ankle straps were introduced in an attempt to prevent the boot falling off when bailing out and hanging from the parachute.*

A Luftwaffe bomber crew flying suit, with original rank badge, Germany, c1934.

**£450–500 Oldnautibits** ⊞

An RAF 1941 pattern 'Mae West' air crew life jacket, with rubber bladder, c1941.

**£300–350 Oldnautibits** ⊞

A Luftwaffe cloth flying jacket, with fur lining, Germany, c1942.

**£430–480 Oldnautibits** ⊞

An RAF Observer's parachute harness, with original back pad, c1943.

**£380–430 Oldnautibits** ⊞

A USAAF B-29 parker bomber jacket, with Talon zip, 1940s.

**£135–150 Rokit(B)** ⊞

A sheepskin flying jacket jacket, c1950.

**£135–150 Cobwebs** ⊞

# AMUSEMENT & SLOT MACHINES

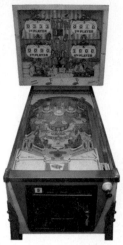

An Argyle Automatic Co fortune teller, 'The Automatic Astrologer', in an oak case, 1910, 32in (81.5cm) high.

**£900–1,000  PennyMachines** ⊞

*Fortune telling machines were popular in the Edwardian era and Argyle specialized in this area.*

A cast aluminium slot machine, paying cigarettes as prizes, operating on a penny, 1930s, 15in (38cm) high.

**£180–200  PennyMachines** ⊞

A Chicago Coins pinball machine, 'Festival', America, 1966, 53in (134.5cm) long.

**£450–500  Gazza's Pinballs** ⊞

*The Festival is thought to be the first game with a rotating carrousel target on the playboard. It was also Chicago Coins' first use of flipper return lanes.*

A Minisoccer electro-mechanical table football game, on four legs, 1966, 41in (104cm) wide.

**£350–400 PennyMachines** ⊞

A D. Gottlieb & Co pinball machine painted back glass, 'Top Score', America, c1975, 21½ x 26in (54.5 x 66cm).

**£40–45 Robert Mills** ⊞

A Sega three-reel mechanical one-armed bandit, 'Continental Grand Prix', America, 1970s, 30 x 15in (76 x 38cm).

**£135–150 PennyMachines** ⊞

A Bally Manufacturing Corp pinball machine, 'Mr & Mrs Pac Man', America, 1982, 53in (134.5cm) long.

**£720–800 Gazza's Pinballs** ⊞
*Cashing in on the popularity of the Pac Man character, over 10,500 of these pinball machines were sold. However, examples in pristine condition are hard to find today.*

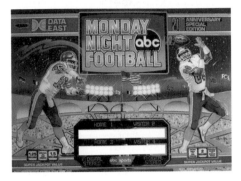

A Data East pinball machine back glass, 'Monday Night', America, 1989, 21 x 28in (53.5 x 71cm).

**£135–150 Gazza's Pinballs** ⊞
*The fantastic artwork by Kevin O'Connor makes this back glass a sought-after collectable.*

A Bell Fruit fruit machine, 'Dr Who The Time Lord', 1995, 69in (175.5cm) high.

**£135–150 Williams Amusements** ⊞

A Sega pinball machine, 'Batman Forever', America, 1995, 53in (134.5cm) long.

**£1,200–1,300 Gazza's Pinballs** ⊞

# ANIMATION

A Fleischer Studios ink and hand-painted animation cel, for *Popeye the Sailor*, c1930, 9 x 11in (23 x 28cm).

**£550–650 Heritage** 🔨

A Walter Lantz Productions ink and hand-painted animation cel, for *Woody Woodpecker*, c1950, 13 x 9in (33 x 23cm).

**£200–250 Heritage** 🔨

A Walt Disney animation cel, for *Peter Pan*, 1953, 9½ x 12in (24.5 x 30.5cm), framed.

**£330–400 Heritage** 🔨

An animation cel, for *Peter Pan*, 1953, 11 x 13in (28 x 33cm).

**£1,200–1,450 Wonderful World of Animation** ⊞

An animation cel, for *Sleeping Beauty*, 1959, 11 x 13in (28 x 33cm).
**£2,900–3,500 Wonderful World of Animation** ⊞

An animation cel, for *Sleeping Beauty*, 1959, 8 x 6½in (20.5 x 16.5cm).
**£550–650**
**Wonderful World of Animation** ⊞

A Schulz-Melendez animation cel, Snoopy and Charlie Brown, hand-painted with a facsimile background, America, 1960s, 8 x 12½in (20.5 x 32cm), matted and framed, together with a certificate of authenticity.

**£340–400 Heritage**

A United Artists Pictures animation cel, by Friz Freleng, The Pink Panther and the Inspector, limited edition of 300, America, 1988, 9½ x 11¾in (24 x 30cm), framed.

**£100–125 Heritage**

A Kodansha animation cel for *Akira*, Japan, 1988, 9 x 14 in (23 x 35.5cm).

**£160–290 Heritage**

A Kodansha animation cel, for *Akira*, Japan, 1988, 9 x 14in (23 x 35.5cm).

**£100–125 Heritage**

A Walt Disney animation cel, for *Who Framed Roger Rabbit*, hand-painted on a photographic print background, America, 1989, 8 x 13½in (20.5 x 34.5cm), with certificate of authenticity.

**£450–550 Heritage**

A Warner Bros animation cel, for *Bugs Bunny*, hand-painted and taken from the television commercial, America, 1989, 9 x 11½in (23 x 29cm), matted and framed, together with certificate of authenticity.

**£50–60 Heritage**

## ESSENTIAL REFERENCE COURVOISIER CELS

A courvoisier cel, for *Snow White and the Seven Dwarfs*, restored, 1937, 6½ x 5½in (16.5 x 14cm).

**£3,800–4,300 Wonderful World of Animation**

A courvoisier cel, for *Pinocchio*, light damage, 1940, 15 x 15½in (38 x 39.5cm).

**£2,200–2,500 Wonderful World of Animation**

A courvoisier cel, for *Dumbo,* slight damage, 1941, 14 x 15½in (35.5 x 39.5cm), framed.

**£2,300–2,600 Wonderful World of Animation**

• Soon after the general release of *Snow White and the Seven Dwarfs* (1937), Walt Disney Studios realized the potential of their production material.

• The Courvoisier Gallery in San Francisco presented Disney's animation cels as 'art' in their own right. Prices ranged from $5 to $75 a piece (equivalent to £250 – £2,500 today).

• Each cel was set against a background and often trimmed to the character. An entry level piece was a single cel with a plain background. A top budget piece was a multi-cel set up (where several cels were overlaid, although not necessarily in film order), set against an illustrated background. Each piece was then covered with a protective matt cel and usually framed.

• Genuine Courvoisier set ups nearly always have the character name or film title pencilled on the front with a WDP stamp and a label indicating the production name on the back.

• Originally Courvoisier were simply retailers but in the 1940s they made up and packaged the cels themselves before handing back their exclusive rights to Disney in 1946.

• The fragile nature of the nitrate cels and the mounting method have resulted in relatively few surviving. Those that do exist today are avidly collected.

• Subject matter and condition are two key factors. In cases where cels have lifted from their backgrounds you're likely to see paint cracking, which is costly to repair. The protective matt cels can also become discoloured and speckled over time.

# ART DECO

A brass frame, c1920, 11½in (29cm) high.

**£220–250  Hayman & Hayman** ⊞

A pair of chrome and Bakelite bookends, c1925, 5in (12.5cm) wide.

**£250–300  Durham House Antiques** ⊞

A set of rosewood dining chairs, with later hide seats, France, Paris, 1920.

**£630–700  Swan at Tetsworth** ⊞

A spelter figure of a woman, on an alabaster base, c1929, 15in (38cm) high.

**£300–350  Muir Hewitt** ⊞

A spelter figure of a dancer, by Lorenzl, on a marble base, 1920s, 11in (28cm) high.

**£300–350  Mike Weedon** ⊞

A spelter table lamp, in the form of a female dancer holding a globe, on an onyx base, c1925, 19¾in (50cm) high.

**£650–750**
**Andrew Hartley** 🔨

A pair of frosted glass wall lights, with cast-brass mounts in the form of cobras' heads, signed 'Viame', France, 1920s–1930s, 16in (40.5cm) wide.

**£380–450**
**Canterbury Auctions** 🔨

A *pochoir* postcard, by Max Ninon, depicting a masquerade love scene in Venice, signed, France, c1930, 5¾in (14.5cm) square.

**£45–50  VicMart.com** ⊞

*Max Ninon – a pseudonym for Vittorio Accronero – won the gold medal at the Paris Exhibition in 1925.*

A bronze bust of a woman, by Hagenauer, c1930, 10in (25.5cm) high.

**£800–900  James Strang** ⊞

## EXPERT EYE  DECO STYLE

Matching the Deco mood of emancipation a female huntress, after the Roman goddess Diana, replaces the age-old theme of a male hunter. Look how the pose exudes strength and control, yet remains cutting-edge modern in its outline. The sculptor has achieved this by exaggerating the sculpture's limbs to create a powerful yet flowing form.

Although obvious decoration is kept to a minimum this figure's facial features are still nicely detailed. The hair is sculpted into a plait, which is wrapped round to resemble the day's most fashionable cloche hat. Small details like this reveal casting quality.

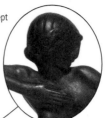

A hallmark of Deco sculpture is female nudity, which reveals a pared down elongated body, particularly evident when you look at this piece from behind. Taking a look from the back gives you a chance to see how well finished this sculpture is all the way round.

A bronze figure of a girl, signed 'I. Bartoli', probably France, 1929, 7in (18cm) high.
**£550–650  Top Banana** ⊞

The sculptor's signature appears on the back rather than beneath the base. This could point to the fact that it was part of a clock garniture but the overall quality suggests it was a stand-alone piece.

Look how thick and solid the base is – another mark of a quality piece. There's no sense of skimping on materials here. The decoration is influenced by pre-Columbian art and motifs like this were well used during the Art Deco era.

The fact that this is a signed and dated piece is a real bonus. If there is a downside it's that there is little recorded history about its sculptor, Bartoli. He is believed to have worked in France, a nation known for its quality casting thanks to its love of the lost-wax process. Bartoli doesn't rank in the top league of collectable names like Demêtre Chiparus or Josef Lorenzl, who are thoroughly researched and this influences the overall price tag. If it was by a better known sculptor, this piece could be worth at least twice as much. However it does offer a buyer plenty of scope to find out more, enhance the provenance and so increase the value. All that said – this is a quality item that shouts Art Deco the moment you see it and those factors alone stand for enduring collector appeal.

# AUTOGRAPHS

**Marilyn Monroe,** a signed programme for the original stage production of *The Seven Year Itch*, mounted with a photograph of Monroe from the film version, dated 1955, 6½ x 9in (16.5 x 23cm), framed.

**£3,000–3,500  Fraser's** ⊞

*The Seven Year Itch was originally performed at the Fulton Theatre, New York, running from 21 March 1955. The front cover features a black and white photograph of the play's stars Tom Ewell and Louise King. It also has a clear signature from Marilyn Monroe, who starred to great acclaim in the film version, in blue ink across the white border above the photograph. This is a very desirable piece.*

**Ginger Rogers,** an autograph, mounted with a photograph, 1970s, 12 x 16in (30.5 x 40.5cm).

**£70–80  Signature Connection** ⊞

*This is a later signature – her early autographs were more defined.*

**James Stewart,** an autograph, mounted with a studio portrait, 20thC, 20 x 16in (51 x 40.5cm).

**£85–95  Signature Connection** ⊞

**James Stewart,** a signed and titled drawing of Harvey the rabbit, c1950, 9¾ x 7¼in (24.5 x 18.5cm).

**£700–780  Fraser's** ⊞

**Elvis Presley,** a signed photograph, signed on both sides, c1960, 5 x 3in (12.5 x 7.5cm).

**£1,100–1,250**
**Autograph Collectors Gallery** ⊞

---

## ESSENTIAL REFERENCE  GETTING THE BEST AUTOGRAPH

- Contemporary star signatures are big business in the autograph world but they vary enormously in quality.

- Consider the backdrop – a signature set against a polished publicity photograph is more desirable than the same autograph written on an unflattering snap of the star.

- Look at where it is signed – top price tags go on signatures that are clear and easy to read. On a photograph, a dark pen signature that runs across the star's face is not as sought after as a well signed name in the pale background area.

- Ask about dating – signatures that are contemporary to the star's photograph have more cachet than later signings. Always find out when and where a signature was obtained – a reputable source will never shy away from telling you.

- Quality counts – if an autograph looks rushed and a little incomplete this will be reflected in its value. Equally, an autograph with a few extras like a quick sketch or catchphrase is like gold-dust to a collector.

**Mahatma Gandhi,** a signed postcard photograph, c1900, 6 x 3½in (15 x 9cm), mounted and framed.

**£4,000–4,500 Fraser's** ⊞

**Benito Mussolini and Victor Emanuel III,** a signed military document, dated 23 October 1927, 14½ x 9in (37 x 23cm).

**£900–1,000 Fraser's** ⊞

**Winston S. Churchill,** a signed photograph, inscribed 'Our Skipper', slight restoration, 1941–50, 16 x 12in (40.5 x 30.5cm), framed.

**£5,800–6,500**
**Peter Harrington** ⊞
*This photograph, taken late in 1941, was revived by the Conservative Party as a poster for the 1950 general election and the above item is probably contemporaneous with that. This is a rare and charismatic portrait of Churchill and it is extremely unusual to find one that is signed.*

**Clement Atlee,** a typed letter to Lt Col Thomas Moore, 16 March 1944, 9½ x 7½ in (24 x 19cm).

**£135–150 Argyll Etkin** ⊞

**Dr Seuss,** a signed leaf from *How the Grinch Stole Christmas*, 1950–60, 7¾ x 11in (19.5 x 28cm).

**£230–280 Heritage** 🔨

**Jack Brabham,** a signed photograph, c1950s, 6 x 4in (15 x 10cm).

**£35–40 Worcester Antiques** ⊞

**Michael Collins,** a photograph of the Apollo 11 crew signed by Michael Collins across his image, photo 1969, 8 x 10in (20.5 x 25.5cm), mounted and framed.

**£900–1,000 Fraser's** ⊞

**Margaret Thatcher,** an autograph, mounted with a newspaper cutting showing Thatcher holding a large image of Edward Heath, dated 4 May 1976, 6 x 4in (15 x 10cm).

**£150–175 Fraser's** ⊞

**Ayrton Senna,** a signed photograph, 1980s–90s, 10 x 8in (25.5 x 20.5cm).

**£1,100–1,250 Fraser's** ⊞

**Muhammad Ali,** a signed poster showing Ali lighting the Olympic flame at Atlanta in 1996, 1990s, mounted and framed, 44 x 33in (112 x 84cm).

**£550–650 Signature Collection** ⊞

**Caprice,** a signed photograph, 2003, 10 x 8in (25.5 x 20.5cm).

**£35–40**
**Autograph Collectors Gallery** ⊞

# AUTOMOBILIA

A Kayes tin and brass oil can, early 20thC, 4in (10cm) high.

**£15–20  Frank Scott-Tomlin** ⊞

A Joseph Lucas No 40 brass oiler , made for Rolls Royce, 1920s–30s, 8in (20.5cm) long.

**£90–100  R B Farley** ⊞

A Castrol motor oil glass bottle, 1920–30, 13½in (34.5cm) high.

**£15–20  R B Farley** ⊞

A BP Energol motor oil glass bottle , with original label, c1930s, 11in (28cm) high.

**£20–25  Below Stairs** ⊞

A bronze car mascot, in the form of an eagle, 1930s, 10in (25.5cm) wide.

**£180–195  Top Banana** ⊞
*This mascot was commonly used on Alvis cars.*

A Colonial Esso *Road News* promotional newspaper, containing articles about many tourist attractions and activities in New York state, with full New York state map showing road construction statewide and suggested detours, 1941.

**£10–15  Kit Barry Ephemera** ⊞

An Express Coach Services enamel advertising sign, showing Britain's motorways, 1956, 30in (76cm) high.

**£500–550  Junktion** ⊞

A motor fuel ration book, for cars with 100cc engines, 1973, 5in (12.5cm) wide.

**£1–5  Books Afloat** ⊞

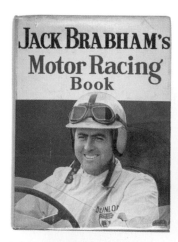

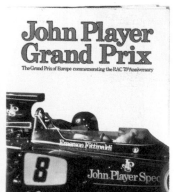

*Jack Brabham's Motor Racing Book*, published by Frederick Muller, London, 1960, 1st edition, 10in (25.5cm) high.

**£20–25 Worcester Antiques** ⊞

A John Player Grand Prix Brands Hatch programme, 1972, 11in (28cm) high.

**£10–15 Worcester Antiques** ⊞

A Silverstone Formula One motor racing programme, autographed by F1 driver Maria Pena De Filippi, 2001, 9in (23cm) high.

**£30–35 Comic Connections** ⊞

Fernando Alonso, a signed photograph, 2003, 6in (15cm) wide.

**£135–150 Comic Connections** ⊞

Jensen Button, a signed photograph, 2003, 6in (15cm) wide.

**£65–75 Comic Connections** ⊞

A 1/6th scale model of a Ferrari 156 (shark nose ), by Javan Smith, signed, 2005, 17in (43cm) long.

**£2,700–3,000 Racing Stuff** ⊞
*This is a large-scale, hand-built model, and each component, including the wheels and tyres, is made in the workshop. Each model is usually constructed from start to finish by one person.*

A Renault F1 cap, signed by Jean Carlo Fisichella and Fernando Alonso, 2005.

**£180–200 Comic Connections** ⊞

A driving suit, worn by Tony Kanaan during the Texas 500, June 11 2005.

**£370–440 Heritage** ⚒

An enamel Price's Motorine Motor Oil advertising sign, 1920, 24in (61cm) high.
**£120–135** Junktion ⊞

A tin Castrol advertising sign, 1920, 21in (53.5cm) high.
**£160–175** Junktion ⊞

A metal Humble Oil Rest Rooms sign, printed 'Property of Humble Oil & Refining Co.', America, early 1960s, 30in (76cm) high.
**£110–125** Kingston Antiques ⊞

An enamel Bus Stop Request sign, 1960, 18in (45.5cm) high.
**£40–45** Junktion ⊞

A cast iron and tin road sign, by IRS, 1930, 55in (139.5cm) high.
**£300–350** Junktion ⊞

An Esso Ethyl jerry can, 1930s, 5¼in (13.5cm) high.
**£60–65** Beaulieu Autojumble ⊞

A steel Ovoline motor oil cannister, 1930, 19½in (49.5cm) high.
**£65–75** Dantinman ⊞

A Shell X100 motor oil can, by Valor, 1960s, 13in (33cm) high.
**£65–75** R B Farley ⊞

# BADGES/PINS

A celluloid Waterbury's Metabolized Cod Liver Oil pin, America, Iowa, c1900.

**£30–35**
**Kit Barry Ephemera** ⊞

A celluloid Pepsin Gum Co pin, by Whitehead & Hoag, America, New Jersey, c1900.

**£10–15**
**Kit Barry Ephemera** ⊞

An Australian Imperial Force badge, Australia, 1919.

**£25–30  Quay Centre** ⊞

A Shirley Temple badge, marked 'Fox Film Corp', America, 1935, 2½in (6.5cm) diam.

**£15–20  VicMart.com** ⊞

An enamel Butlin's Margate badge, 1958, 1in (2.5cm) diam.

**£35–40  Worcester Antiques** ⊞

A metal Space badge, 1950s, 2½in (6.5cm) wide.

**£5–10  Rin Tin Tin** ⊞

A BOAC cap badge, 1960, 1in (2.5cm) wide.

**£5–10  Tenterden Antiques** ⊞
*This badge is in the shape of the tail fin of the BOAC 707 Speedbird G–APFE, which broke up over Mt Fuji, Japan, on 5 March 1966, killing 124 people.*

A brass and enamel Corgi Model Club badge, 1960s, 1in (2.5cm) high.

**£5–10  John Smart** ⊞

A Cuban Communist propaganda pin, Cuba, c1970, 1in (2.5 cm) wide.

**£5–10  VicMart.com** ⊞

A silver and enamel London Fever Hospital badge, 1975, 1½in (4cm) wide.

**£25–30  Malcolm Welch** ⊞
*The London Fever Hospital was founded in 1802, treating typhus, smallpox and scarlet fever, and had just 15 beds. By 1842 it was admitting 1,500 patients a year and in 1849 it moved to a site with 200 beds in Liverpool Road, Islington, London, remaining there until the site was closed in 1974.*

A diecast Lone Star Rider badge, 1960s, 2¼in (5.5cm) wide.

**£1–5  John Smart** ⊞

A brass and enamel BT Busby Badge, c1980, 1¼in (3cm) diam.

**£1–5  John Smart** ⊞

# ROBERTSON'S

A brass and enamel Robertson's Golden Shred golly badge, by Graham Products, Cricketer, 1930s, 1½in (4cm) high.

**£110–125 Worcester Antiques** ⊞

A brass and enamel Robertson's golly badge, Bagpiper, 1930s–50s, 1½in (4cm) high.

**£25–30 Tenterden Silver Vaults** ⊞

A brass and enamel Robertson's golly badge, Tennis Player, 1930s–50s, 1½in (4cm) high.

**£25–30 Tenterden Silver Vaults** ⊞

A brass and enamel Robertsons's Silver Shred badge, 1950s, 1in (2.5cm) high.

**£25–30 Tenterden Antiques** ⊞

A brass and enamel Robertson's Golden Shred golly badge, Skater, 1950s, 1¼in (3cm) high.

**£20–25 Worcester Antiques** ⊞

A brass and enamel Robertson's golly badge, Motorcyclist, 1970s, 1½in (4cm) high.

**£25–30 Worcester Antiques** ⊞

A brass and enamel Robertson's golly badge, Car Driver, c1980, 1in (2.5cm) high.

**£10–15 Malcolm Welch** ⊞

A brass and enamel Robertson's golly badge, Skier, c1980, 1in (2.5cm) high.

**£25–30 Malcolm Welch** ⊞

A brass and enamel Robertson's golly badge, Lollipop Man, 1980s, 1in (2.5cm) high.

**£35–40 Malcolm Welch** ⊞

A brass and enamel Robertson's Golden Shred golly badge, Ice Skater, 1930–50s, 1½in (4cm) high.

**£25–30 Tenterden Silver Vaults** ⊞

A fake brass and enamel Robertson's golly badge, Ice Skater, c1980, 1in (2.5cm) high.

**£1–5 Malcolm Welch** ⊞

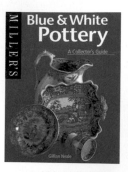
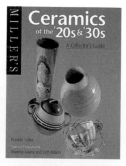
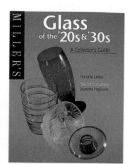
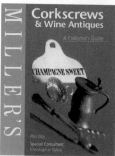
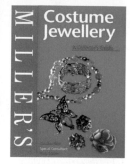

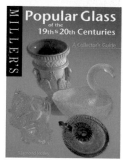
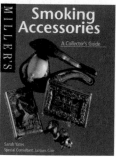

# BICYCLES

A bicycle and bicycle parts catalogue, France, 1912, 14½in (36.5cm) wide.
£270–300 Early Technology ⊞

An Excelite Cycle Burning Oil tin, for bicycle lights, 1910, 5in (12.5cm) high.
£20–25 Dantinman ⊞

An enamel Raleigh Cycles advertising sign, 1910, 23in (58.5cm) high.
£170–190 Junktion ⊞

A Selbach bicycle, with a treble taper tube, Chater Lea chain set and pedals, Constructor brakes and rims, Brooks saddle and Highgate handlebars, 1930.
£340–380 Alexander von Tutschek ⊞

A Lucas battery cycle lamp, model 79, with a japanned finish, c1936, 4in (10cm) high, in original box.
£70–75 ⊞ Alexander von Tutschek

A Rudge bicycles cardboard sign, c1950, 26in (66cm) wide.
£50–60 Murrays' Antiques ⊞

A Carminargent alloy touring cycle, France, 1946.
£450–500 Alexander von Tutschek ⊞

An Elephant bicycle tyre repair outfit tin, 1960s, 4½in (11.5cm) long.
£5–10 R B Farley ⊞

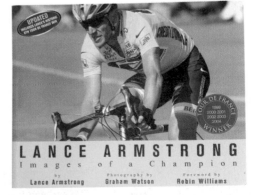

Lance Armstrong, Lance Armstrong: Images of a Champion, signed, 2005, 9½ x 11½in (24 x 29cm).
£1,800–1,950 Fraser's ⊞

# BLACK MEMORABILIA

A slave Petition for Freedom, for 'Negro Wilson' vs. Robert Hammott , America, Frederick County Maryland, 1790, 7½in (19cm) wide.

**£670–770 Black History Store** ⊞

A commemorative coin, inscribed 'We Are All Brethren, Slave Trade Abolished by Great Britain', 1807, 1½in (4cm) diam.

**£90–100 Black History Store** ⊞

*The Genius of Universal Emancipation* newspaper, No.6 Vol 1, September 1830, 23½ x 14¾in (59.5 x 37.5cm).

**£50–55 Black History Store** ⊞

An Emancipation Certificate, for William, a Negro Boy slave, America, Missouri, Ray County, 1852, 9 x 7in (23 x 18cm).

**£700–800 Black History Store** ⊞

*Walter Browning, The Slave's Protector,* published by the American Reform Tract and Book Society, Cincinnati, 1856, 1st edition, 88 pages, embossed cloth, 7 x 5in (18 x 12.5cm), slight damage.

**£300–350 Black History Store** ⊞

A Freedman's Bureau Labour Contract, an agreement with a former slave to work on the China Grove Plantation for one year, America, Mississippi, 1866, 14 x 8½in 35.5 x 21.5cm).

**£1,400–1,550 Black History Store** ⊞

A coin, inscribed 'Liberty and No Slavery', America, 1863, ¾in (2cm) diam.

**£110–125 Black History Store** ⊞

*National Anti-Slavery Standard* newspaper, published by the American Anti-Slavery Society, America, New York, 2 April 1870, 29½ x 23½in (75 x 59.5cm).

**£80–90 Black History Store** ⊞

A Black Maria tobacco tag, 1920s, 1in (2.5cm) high.

**£1–5 Don & Chris' Old Stuff** ⊞

A grape label, America, California, 1930s, 13¼in (33.5cm) wide.
**£1–5 Don & Chris' Old Stuff ⊞** ·

A Waverley Grower's Co-operative crate label, America, Florida, 1930s, 9in (23cm) wide.
**£5–10 Don & Chris' Old Stuff ⊞**

A Longwood Plantation syrup label, America, Lousiana, 1930s, 11in (28cm) long.
**£1–5 Don & Chris' Old Stuff ⊞**

A Kwango Rum label, 1930s, 5½in (14cm) high.
**£1–5 Don & Chris' Old Stuff ⊞**

A Ruby Porto Rican Sweet Potatoes crate label, America, 1940s, 9in (23cm) wide.
**£5–10 Don & Chris' Old Stuff ⊞**

A pair of rubber keychain figures, with a brass rings in ears, America, 1960s, 2in (5cm) high.
**£5–10 Don & Chris' Old Stuff ⊞**

A plastic and metal Afro Styling Rake, America, late 60s, in original packaging, 10in (25.5cm) long.
**£1–5 Don & Chris' Old Stuff ⊞**

A flicker disc, flickers between 'United We Shall Overcome' and black and white hands shaking, American, late 1960s, 1½in (4cm) diam.
**£1–5 Don & Chris' Old Stuff ⊞**
*This was the famous slogan of the American Civil Rights movement in the 1960s.*

# BOOKS

**M**ODERN FIRST EDITIONS by Ian Fleming, Grahame Greene, John Grisham, John Le Carré, J. K. Rowling, Dr Seuss, Evelyn Waugh and Virginia Woolf are eagerly sought after by collectors and command good prices in the sale rooms. So, if you want to collect modern firsts where should you start and what should you be looking for before parting with your money?

My advice is always to collect what you really enjoy – perhaps favourite books from childhood or favourite recent authors. You are more likely to build a satisfying collection if you appreciate the books you buy. It is hard not to be impressed by the huge prices achieved at auction by the stars, but many authors are much more affordable and can make a handsome collection.

Collecting modern first editions is an enjoyable, rewarding and occasionally profitable activity. You do, however, need to look carefully at what you buy to be sure that it is a first edition, that it retains its original dust-jacket if issued with one and that the condition is as fine as you can afford.

As in so many collecting fields, condition is everything. This is especially true of collectable children's books. We all remember colouring in a black-and-white illustration, writing our name on all our books when we'd learnt how to, or even throwing away a crumpled dust-jacket. Children read books with little hands and sometimes grubby fingers, so children's books in really fine condition are quite rare. As a result, they are sought after and sometimes expensive. The Ladybird books have become very collectable in recent years, a development fuelled by our thirst for nostalgia.

Choosing a field to collect is not hard. Crime and science fiction are popular, as are animal stories, thrillers and adventures. Books that have recently been made into films, such as *Harry Potter* and *Lord of the Rings*, for example, tend to be especially sought after, so you could look for books which are going to be filmed in the future. If you enjoy a gamble, spotting future best-sellers can be rewarding. Those who spotted Harry Potter as a superstar and bought the first volume on publication were soon smiling. 'Hyper-modern' or contemporary firsts by popular authors such as Sebastian Faulks, Joanne Harris, Ian McKewan and Terry Pratchett will be collectable for a good while to come, but try spotting the literary stars of the future before they get to the Booker Prize listings.

Finally, since many modern firsts are not intrinsically rare, it's worth finding copies that are in some way unique. Signed copies, personally inscribed copies and 'association' copies, ie owned by someone interesting or famous, will always carry an extra cachet.

**Justin Croft**

## MODERN FIRST EDITIONS

## ESSENTIAL REFERENCE | SEXTON BLAKE

• The fictional character Sexton Blake was the creation of Harry Blyth. He first appeared in 1893 in *The Halfpenny Marvel*, and was subsequently part of at least 4,000 stories by 200 different authors until 1978.

• Initially a star of boys' weekly magazines, Blake later had an entire series devoted to his adventures. *The Man Who Knew Too Much* is from the Sexton Blake Library, which ran from 1915 to 1963 and comprised thousands of issues – a remarkable achievement.

• Although later issues are not uncommon, the earlier examples are sought after by collectors, especially those in fine condition.

• Blake's creator modelled him on his famous forebear, Sherlock Holmes, but Blake was frequently updated and reinvented. His first film appearance was in 1907, followed by several silent films. However, his best-known screen appearance was in the 1960s cult television series.

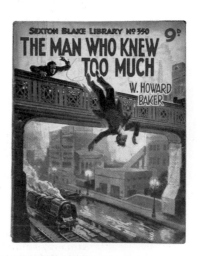

W. Howard Baker, *The Man Who Knew Too Much*, published by Amalgamated Press, 1955, series No 350, 7 x 5in (18 x 12.5cm).
**£5–10** Addyman Books

Liam O'Flaherty, *Mr Gilhooley*, published by Jonathan Cape London, 1926, 1st edition, 8 x 5in (20.5 x 12.5cm).
**£100–120 Biblion** ⊞
*Anglo-Irish author Liam O'Flaherty wrote* Mr Gilhooley *a year after his celebrated novel* The Informer, *which was made into an Academy Award-winning film by John Ford in 1935.*

Salman Schneour, *Noah Pandre's Village*, published by Chatto & Windus, London, 1938, 1st edition, 7½ x 5in (19 x 13cm).
**£50–60 Barter Books** ⊞
*This is the first edition in English, translated from the original Yiddish.*

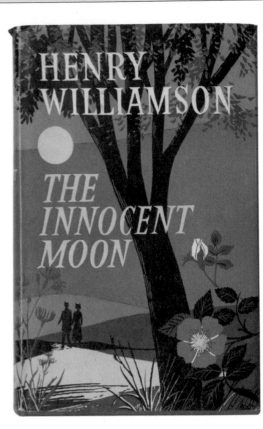

Henry Williamson, *The Innocent Moon*, published by MacDonald, London, 1961, 1st edition, 8 x 5in (20.5 x 12.5cm).
**£50–60 George Bayntun** ⊞
*This is a good example of a classic pictorial dust jacket.*

Walter Unsworth, *The Devil's Mill*, published by Victor Gollancz, London, first edition, signed by the author, 1968, 8¼ x 5½in (21 x 14cm).
**£55–60 Barter Books** ⊞

Michael Moorcock, *The Oak & The Ram*, 2nd volume of *The Chronicle of Prince Corumk*, published by Alison & Busby, London, first edition, 1973, 8¾ x5½in (22 x 14cm).
**£35–40 Barter Books** ⊞

P. G. Wodehouse, *The Head of Kay's*, published by Souvenir Press, London, 1974, 1st edition, 8 x 5in (20.5 x12.5cm).
**£30–35
Nigel Williams Rare Books** ⊞
*The very first edition, by A & C Black, was published in 1922.*

Carol Shields, *The Stone Diaries*, published by Random House, Canada, 1993, 1st edition, 7½in (19cm) high.
**£90–100
George Bayntun** ⊞
*Issued in very small numbers prior to the author's mainstream success,* The Stone Diaries *was a Pullitzer prize-winner in America and shortlisted for The Booker Prize in the UK.*

## CHILDREN'S BOOKS

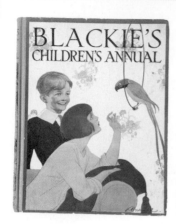

*Blackie's Children's Annual*, 1920s, 11 x 9in (28 x 23cm).
**£35–40 J & J's** ⊞
*This annual is highly collectable in fine condition, which is surprisingly rare. Issues include illustrations by Cicely Mary Barker and Ernest Aris.*

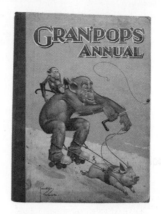

Arthur Groom, *Gran'pops Annual*, illustrated by Lawson Wood, published by Dean & Son, London, 1930, 10¼ x 7in (26 x 18cm).
**£30–35 Barter Books** ⊞

J. F. Horrabin, *The Japhet & Happy Annual*, illustrated by J. F. Horrabin, published by News Chronicle Publications, 1933, 8 x 7in (20.5 x 18cm).
**£20–25 George Bayntun** ⊞

*Hobbies New Annual*, edited by F. J. Camm, published by George Newnes, 1934, 10 x 8in (25.5 x 20.5cm).
**£10–15 J & J's** ⊞

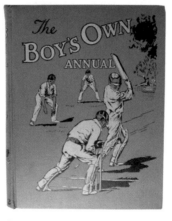

*The Boy's Own Annual*, Vol 62, edited by Robert Harding, published by Dean & Co, London, 1939–40, 11 x 8¾in (28 x 22cm).
**£45–50 Barter Books** ⊞
*Look for early issues. The annual was first published in 1879.*

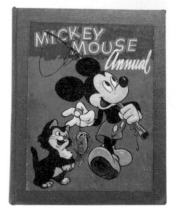

Walt Disney, *Mickey Mouse Annual*, published by Dean & Son, London, 1948, 9 x 6in (23 x 15cm).
**£40–45 Barter Books** ⊞
*Walt Disney's Mickey Mouse is always a favourite among collectors.*

*Playbox Annual*, 1955, 11 x 8in (28 x 20.5cm).
**£1–5 Heanor Antiques** ⊞

*Japhet & Happy's Annual*, published by News Chronicle Publications, London, 1966, 12 x 8in (30.5 x 20.5cm).
**£10–15 Upstairs Downstairs** ⊞

*Dr Who Annual*, published by the BBC, 1980.
**£1–5 Steve Blackham** ⊞
*The first annual appeared in 1966, three years after the television series. Some of the early issues can still be found.*

Dr Seuss, *The 500 Hats of Bartholomew Cubbins*, published by Vanguard, New York, 1938, 11¾ x 9in (30 x 23cm).
**£80–100 P B A Galleries** 🔨
*This is one of the earliest and rarest Dr Seuss titles, particularly sought after in its dust jacket, which is not present here.*

Dr Seuss, *If I Ran the Zoo*, published by Random House, New York, 1950, 1st edition, 12 x 9in (30.5 x 23cm).
**£400–500 P B A Galleries** 🔨

Dr Seuss, *Horton Hears a Who!*, published by Random House, New York, 1954, 1st edition, 11 x 8in (28 x 20.5cm).
**£630–750 P B A Galleries** 🔨
*20th Century Fox Animation and Blue Sky Studios' recent collaboration has brought the character of Horton to the big screen. The 2008 release of their animated film promises to set alight collectors' interest in first edition copies such as this.*

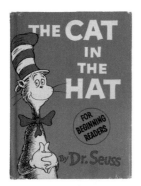

Dr Seuss, *The Cat in the Hat*, published by Random House, New York, 1957, 1st edition, 9 x 6½in (23 x 16.5cm).
**£1,900–2,250 P B A Galleries** 🔨

Dr Seuss, *If I Ran the Circus*, published by Random House, New York, 1956, 1st edition, 11 x 8in (28 x 20.5cm).
**£240–280 P B A Galleries** 🔨

Dr Seuss, *How the Grinch Stole Christmas!*, Random House, New York, 1957, 1st edition, signed, 11 x 8in (28 x 20.5cm).
**£1,800–2,150 Sotheby's (NY)** 🔨
*With the* How the Grinch Stole Christmas!, *Dr Seuss created a Mr. Scrooge for the 20th century.*

Dr Seuss, *Happy Birthday to You!*, published by Random House, New York, 1959, 1st edition, 10¾ x 8in (27.5 x 20.5cm).
**£175–215 P B A Galleries** 🔨

Dr Seuss, *Dr Seuss's Sleep Book*, published by Random House, New York, 1962, 1st edition, 11 x 8in (28 x 20.5cm).
**£65–75 P B A Galleries** 🔨

Dr Seuss, *The Cat in the Hat Comes Back*, published by Random House, New York, 1958, 1st edition, 9 x 6½in (23 x 16.5cm).
**£85–100 P B A Galleries** 🔨

## MARKET INFORMATION                    DR SEUSS

- Dr Seuss was the pen-name of Theodor Seuss Geisel, the American author and cartoonist beloved by children throughout the English-speaking world. His hilarious rhymes and outlandish characters have appealed to several generations of children and adults.

- *The Cat in the Hat* (1957) and *Green Eggs and Ham* (1960) are among the top ten best-selling children's books of all time.

- Film adaptations such as *The Grinch Who Stole Christmas!* (2000) and *Horton Hears a Who!* (for release 2008) have brought new demand for first editions of Dr Seuss books. Prices for fine copies of true first editions remain strong at auction.

- Almost all Dr Seuss books were first printed in New York, so true first editions must state that. Editions printed in England are more common in the UK and far less valuable.

Beatrix Potter, *The Story of Miss Moppet*, published by Frederick Warne & Co, New York and London, c1906, 1st American edition, 4¼ x 3in (11 x 7.5cm).

**£125–150 P B A Galleries** 🔨

*The publisher, Warne and Co, experimented with this wallet binding in 1906–07. Beatrix Potter considered it too fragile for children, and later issues were printed in standard book format.*

Beatrix Potter, *The Story of a Fierce Bad Rabbit*, published by Frederick Warne & Co, New York and London, c1907, 1st American edition, 4¼ x 3½in (11 x 9cm).

**£155–190 P B A Galleries** 🔨

Beatrix Potter, *The Tale of Jemima Puddle-Duck*, published by Frederick Warne & Co, New York and London, 1908, first edition, 5½ x 4in (14 x 10cm).

**£220–260 P B A Galleries** 🔨

Beatrix Potter, *The Tale of the Flopsy Bunnies*, published by Frederick Warne & Co, London, 1909, 1st edition, 5½ x 4¼in (14 x 11cm).

**£280–340 P B A Galleries** 🔨

Beatrix Potter, *The Tale of Mrs. Tittlemouse*, published by Frederick Warne & Co, London, 1910, 1st edition, 5½ x 4¼in (14 x 11cm).

**£125–150 P B A Galleries** 🔨

Beatrix Potter, *The Tale of Timmy Tiptoes*, published by Frederick Warne & Co, London, 1911, 1st edition, 5½ x 4in (14 x 10cm).

**£95–115 P B A Galleries** 🔨

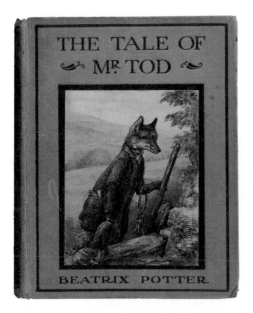

Beatrix Potter, *The Tale of Mr. Tod*, published by Frederick Warne & Co, London, 1912, 1st edition, 5½ x 4in (14 x 10cm).

**£155–190 P B A Galleries** 🔨

Beatrix Potter, *Appley Dapply's Nursery Rhymes*, published by Frederick Warne & Co, London, 1917, first edition, 5 x 4in (12.5 x 10cm).

**£190–225 P B A Galleries** 🔨

## EXPERT EYE    BEATRIX POTTER'S PETER RABBIT

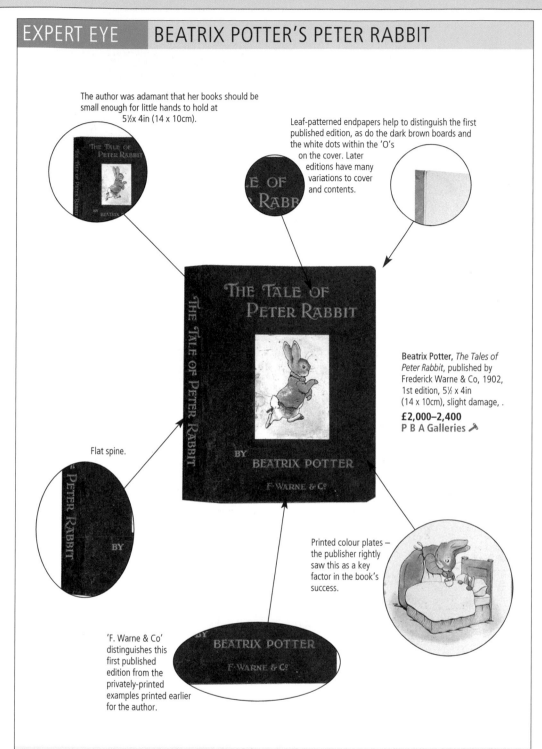

The author was adamant that her books should be small enough for little hands to hold at 5½ x 4in (14 x 10cm).

Leaf-patterned endpapers help to distinguish the first published edition, as do the dark brown boards and the white dots within the 'O's on the cover. Later editions have many variations to cover and contents.

Beatrix Potter, *The Tales of Peter Rabbit*, published by Frederick Warne & Co, 1902, 1st edition, 5½ x 4in (14 x 10cm), slight damage, .

**£2,000–2,400**
**P B A Galleries**

Flat spine.

Printed colour plates – the publisher rightly saw this as a key factor in the book's success.

'F. Warne & Co' distinguishes this first published edition from the privately-printed examples printed earlier for the author.

Like all books associated with hit films, Beatrix Potter's books have seen strong demand in the wake of *Miss Potter*. Such demand doesn't always last after the excitment of a film dies away, but Beatrix Potter's legendary children's books look set to remain highly collectable.

Identifying first editions of a Beatrix Potter title is not always straightforward, especially since they do not usually contain printed dates. The copy of *The Tale of Peter Rabbit* shown here is the first published edition. It is preceded by the exceptionally rare edition, printed in 1902 on the instruction of Miss Potter herself, after her manuscript was rejected by several publishers. Warnes took the book on and the edition pictured was printed in 1902, although it is undated. Look for the colour of the covers, the dots in the 'O's on the cover. If there is a printed date anywhere on the book or if it has a dust jacket listing other Potter titles, then it is a later edition.

As always, condition is everything in collectors' children's books. This copy has been carefully restored, and is therefore worth around half the value of a good, unrestored copy.

*Smoke and Fluff*, published by Ladybird, c1941, 7 x 4¾in (18 x 12cm), dust jacket.
**£120–130 Robert Mullin** ⊞

*Downy Duckling*, published by Wills & Hepworth, c1946, 7 x 4½in (18 x 11.5cm), dust jacket.
**£100–120 Robert Mullin** ⊞

*The Flower Show*, published by Wills & Hepworth for Ladybird, c1953, dust jacket.
**£150–165 Robert Mullin** ⊞

*Julius Caesar and Roman Britain*, published by Ladybird, c1959.
**£30–35 Robert Mullin** ⊞

*The Lord's Prayer and other prayers for children*, published by Ladybird, c1961.
**£25–30 Robert Mullin** ⊞

*Magnets, Bulbs and Batteries*, published by Ladybird, c1962, 7 x 4¾in (18 x 12cm), matt boards.
**£15–20 Robert Mullin** ⊞

*Look at this*, Key Words Reading Scheme, 1b, published by Ladybird, c1964, 7 x 4¾in (18 x 12cm), matt boards.
**£20–25 Robert Mullin** ⊞

*Well-Loved Tales, The Elves and the Shoemaker*, published by Ladybird, c1965, 7 x 4¾in (18 x 12cm), matt boards.
**£30–35 Robert Mullin** ⊞

*Learning about Heraldry*, published by Ladybird, c1974, 7 x 4¾in (18 x 12cm).
**£15–20 Robert Mullin** ⊞

## MARKET INFORMATION                    LADYBIRD BOOKS

• The familiar pocket-sized Ladybird books first appeared in 1940 and were an immediate success. The first series included animal characters such as Bunnikins and Downy Duckling.

• Because Ladybirds were first issued during WWII, price was a key to their success. Each book was priced at half a crown (about 12 pence in today's money) and the price was held for a remarkable 30 years.

• The appeal of Ladybird books to collectors is based on nostalgia. We all enjoy rediscovering books from our childhood and Ladybirds were often the first books we saw.

• Early editions from pre-1960 are the most sought after, provided their original dust jackets are still present and in good condition. Editions from the 1960s and '70s with illustrations by artists such as Martin Aitchison are also favourites. The various fairytales series continue to be popular. The later series are still very affordable, while earlier series are becoming more expensive.

• Spotting a first edition is not easy, since many reprints bear the dates of the originals. Look on the dust jacket (if it has one) and on the back cover and check to see if your book is the last one listed on the rear flap. If so, it may be a first.

Kenneth Grahame, *The Wind in the Willows*, illustrated by Nancy Barnhart, published by Methuen & Co, London, 1922, 1st illustrated edition, 7½in (19cm) high.

**£60–75 George Bayntun** ⊞
*The very first edtion of this title was published in 1908.*

Hugh Lofting, *Doctor Doolittle's Zoo*, illustrated by Hugh Lofting, published by Jonathan Cape, 1928, 1st edition, 8 x 6in (20.5 x 15cm).

**£35–40 George Bayntun** ⊞
*This first edition is missing its dust jacket, which could increase value to as much as £200.*

Racey Helps, *Tippetty's Treasure*, published by Collins, London, 1949, first edition, 7 x 6in (18 x 15cm).

**£20–25 J & J's** ⊞

Walter De La Mare, *The Lord Fish*, illustrated by Rex Whistler, published by Faber & Faber, London, 1933, 1st edition, 8in (20.5cm) high.

**£35–40 George Bayntun** ⊞
*This book features illustrations and a dust jacket designed by Rex Whistler, the dazzlingly talented artist who died on his first day in action in WWII.*

Richmal Crompton, *William the Bold*, illustrated by Thomas Henry, published by George Newnes, London, 1950, 1st edition, 8 x 5in (20.5 x 12.5cm).

**£135–150**

**Nigel Williams Rare Books** ⊞

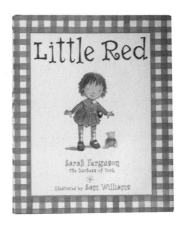

Sarah Ferguson, the Duchess of York, *Little Red*, published by Simon & Schuster UK, 2003, 1st edition, signed.

**£10–15 Katherine Higgins** ⊞

## ESSENTIAL REFERENCE    TOLKIEN

J. R. R. Tolkien, *The Hobbit*, published by George Allen & Unwin, London, 1937, 1st edition, 5¾ x 6¾in (14.5 x 17cm).

**£4,500–5,000**
**Peter Harrington** ⊞

J. R. R. Tolkien, *The Lord of the Rings*, comprising: *The Fellowship of the Ring*, *The Two Towers* and *The Return of the King*, published by George Allen & Unwin, London, 1954–55, 1st editions, 7¾ x 9¾in (19.5 x 25cm).

**£7,700–8,500 Peter Harrington** ⊞
*Further interest in the work of Tolkien is likely to be generated by the 2007 stage adaptation of* The Lord of the Rings *at London's Theatre Royal in Drury Lane. It marks 50 years since writing on the series first began.*

J. R. R. Tolkien, *Tree and Leaf*, published by George Allen & Unwin, London, 1964, 1st edition, 7¾ x 9¾in (19.5 x 25cm).

**£200–220**
**Peter Harrington** ⊞

• The year 2007 saw the 70th anniversary of *The Hobbit*, and with it came another wave of interest in collecting the works of Tolkien, with *The Hobbit* and *The Lord of the Rings* being the most sought after.

• Tolkien prices have been upwardly mobile since the first of the recent film adaptations, and prices asked or achieved at auction are sometimes excessive. Whether they will retain these levels over the coming years remains to be seen.

• Fine copies of first editions of *The Hobbit* or *The Lord of the Rings* retaining their original dust wrappers in excellent state, are rarely encountered. Most people read their copies, just as Tolkien had hoped, and condition suffered accordingly.

• Copies with genuine inscriptions by the author (forgeries are not unknown) command exceptional prices.

# BOTTLES

## MILK BOTTLES

Two glass milk bottles, with cardboard tops, 1920–30, larger 10in (25.5cm) high.
**£10–15 each  Houghton Antiques** ⊞

A Tilly Bardin Guernsey Farms glass milk bottle, America, c1951, 9½in (24cm) high.
**£10–15  Jim Call** ⊞

A Footman Hillman Dairies glass milk bottle, America, Maine, 1950s, 5½in (14cm) high.
**£5–10  Jim Call** ⊞

A McKinstry Dairy glass milk bottle, America, Michigan, Sheldon, 1950s, 8¾in (22cm) high.
**£10–15  Jim Call** ⊞

A Weiss Farm glass milk bottle, America, Massachusetts, Stoneham, 1950s, 7¼in (18.5cm) high.
**£10–15  Jim Call** ⊞

A Hillside Dairy glass milk bottle, America, Long Island, c1967, 9½in (24cm) high.
**£10–15  Jim Call** ⊞

A J. V. Holden Dairy glass milk bottle, Lancashire, Darwen, 1970s, 8½in (21.5cm) high.
**£10–15  Jim Call** ⊞

A Unigate glass advertising milk bottle, 1980s, 7¼in (18.5cm) high.
**£5–10  Jim Call** ⊞

A Dairy Crest glass advertising milk bottle, 1980s, 7¼in (18.5cm) high.
**£5–10  Jim Call** ⊞

# ASSORTED BOTTLES

A glass spirit bottle, 1890, 9in (23cm) high.

**£1–5  Old Ironmongers** ⊞

*The four-sided tapering bottle was the most popular vessel for Dutch gin.*

A Harrrogate Spa glass mineral water bottle, c1890, 10in (25.5cm) high.

**£10–15  Old Ironmongers** ⊞

*Harrogate in North Yorkshire was Britain's first spa water town. The well was discovered in 1571. By the 1920s, Harrogate was the UK's largest exporter of mineral water.*

A Laycocks of Chester glass bottle, with original ball stopper, c1895, 9in (23cm) high.

**£1–5  Old Ironmongers** ⊞

A stoneware stout bottle, with transfer-printed label, 1900, 8½in (21.5cm) high.

**£120–135  Below Stairs** ⊞

A stoneware ginger beer bottle, with transfer-printed label, c1920, 7in (18cm) high.

**£10–15  Jam Jar** ⊞

A glass two-pint beer bottle, embossed 'Gibbs Mew & Co, Anchor Brewery, Salisbury', 1920s, 13in (33cm) high.

**£5–10  Below Stairs** ⊞

# BREWERIANA

A John Haig & Co Special Old Scotch Whisky pub mirror, by H. B. Macphail, Scotland, Glasgow, c1890, 36in (91.5cm) wide.

**£720–800  Georgian Antiques** ⊞

An O. H. B. Scotch Whisky jug, c1910, 5in (12.5cm) high.

**£35–40  David Huxtable** ⊞

A Russells' Ales tin advertising sign, 1920, 28in (71cm) high.

**£180–200  Dodo** ⊞

Two copper ashtrays, advertising Worthington beer and Ross's Ginger Ale, 1925, 4½in (11.5cm) diam.

**£5–10 each  David Huxtable** ⊞

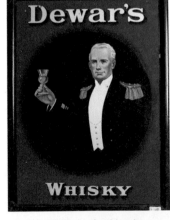

A Dewar's Whisky tin advertising sign, 1930, 28in (71cm) high.

**£270–300  Dodo** ⊞

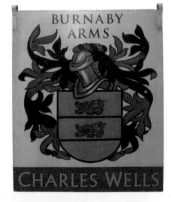

A metal public house sign, inscribed 'Burnaby Arms' and 'Charles Wells', c1940, 36in (91.5cm) high.

**£150–165  Piccadilly Antiques** ⊞

A set of four dummy Mercier Champagne shop display bottles, c1950, largest 25in (63.5cm) high.

**£145–160  M&C Cards** ⊞

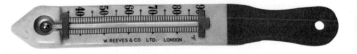

A malthouse ceramic brewery thermometer, by W. Reeves & Co, London, 1950, 14in (35.5cm) long.

**£10–15  Early Technology** ⊞

A Haig Scotch Whisky Insulex ice bucket,
1950s, 7in (18cm) diam.

**£20–25  Twinkled** ⊞

A Casanis ceramic water jug, France, 1950s,
6½in (16.5cm) high.

**£50–55  David Huxtable** ⊞

*This jug would have accompanied a measure
of Pastis, traditionally served as an apéritif.*

A wooden public house sign, inscribed 'The
Chequers' and 'Greene King', c1960,
44in (112cm) high.

**£200–250  Piccadilly Antiques** ⊞

A plastic ice bucket, in the form
of a brandy bottle, 1970s,
11in (28cm) high.

**£10–15  Twinkled** ⊞

A Carlton Ware Guinness cruet set, comprising salt, pepper and mustard pots, 1950s,
pepper pot 3¾in (9.5cm) high.

**£55–60  Tenterden Antiques** ⊞

A Guinness for Strength advertising
poster, by Edward Ardizzone,
printed by John Waddington,
1953, 59¾in (152cm) high.

**£250–300
Onslow Auctions** ⚒

A Guinness advertising showcard,
1960, 5in (12.5cm) high.

**£35–40  Dodo** ⊞

A goatskin bodhrán, by Waltons of Dublin, 'Guinness Extra Stout',
on a birchwood frame, Ireland, 1980s, 18¼in (46.5cm) diam.

**£70–80  Tenterden Antiques** ⊞

# CAMERAS

## 35MM CAMERAS

An Argus metal and leather camera, with 35mm Cintar lens, America, 1939–66, 5in (13cm) wide.

**£30–35 Otford Centre ⊞**
*This camera was nicknamed 'The Brick'.*

A Clarus MS-35 camera, America, 1946–52, 5in (12.5cm) wide.

**£55–65 Arundel Photographica ⊞**

A Voigtlander Prominent leather and steel camera, with interchangeable Ultron lens and 35mm range finder, Germany, c1953, 5in (13cm) wide.

**£220–250 Otford Centre ⊞**

A Wrayflex II Unilite metal and leather camera, with Wray lens, 1950s, 5in (13cm) wide.

**£500–550 Otford Centre ⊞**

An Agimatic metal and leather camera, with Agilux lens, c1956, 4¼in (11cm) wide.

**£50–60 Otford Centre ⊞**

A Canon Dial 35 camera, Japan, 1960s, 5½in (14cm) high.

**£55–60 Antique Photographic ⊞**
*This 35mm half-frame camera was made famous by being used by Number 6 in the episode 'Many Happy Returns' from The Prisoner TV series. The telephone dial is used to set the filmspeed and, unlike most 1960s' half frames, the film runs top to bottom so the photograph is still in landscape format.*

A Haiou Seagull DF single lens reflex camera, China, c1970, 6in (15cm) wide.

**£75–85 Arundel Photographica ⊞**

A Kiev 4A F2 Jupiter 8N Rangefinder camera, Russia, c1974, 8in (20.5cm) wide.

**£70–80 Arundel Photographica ⊞**

A Canon AE-1 single lens reflex camera, Japan, 1976, 13in (33cm) wide.

**£90–100 Antique Photographic ⊞**

A Nikon FE2 camera, No. 2235382, with a Nikon Nikkor f/2.8 24mm lens No. 629869, 1983–89, 5¼in (13.5cm) wide.

**£120–145 Skinner ⚒**

# CINE CAMERAS

A Kodak model B 16mm camera, with100ft spools, c1925, 10in (25.5cm) wide.

**£35–40 Arundel Photographica** ⊞

A Pathé 9.5mm motocamera, c1928, 5in (12.5cm) high.

**£45–50 Arundel Photographica** ⊞

A Coronet B 9.5mm camera, c1932, 5in (12.5cm) high.

**£45–50 Arundel Photographica** ⊞

A Kodak Model K clockwork 16mm camera, with Anastigmat 1.9/25 lens, 1930–46, 10in (25.5cm) wide, with case.

**£35–40 Camera House** ⊞

A Paillard Bolex B8L 8mm camera, with 13mm and 36mm lenses, Switzerland, c1958, 9in (23cm) high.

**£60–70 Arundel Photographica** ⊞

A VEB Pentaflex 8 standard 8mm camera, with magazine load, Germany, c1960, 8in (20.5cm) wide.

**£45–50 Arundel Photographica** ⊞

A Canon Super 8 camera, Model Zoom 518 with f1.8/9.5-47.5 C-8 zoom manual lens, trigger grip 4 and wrist strap, c1968, 6in (15cm) wide.

**£55–65 Camera House** ⊞

A Bolex Paillard Model H16 RX-5 reflex camera, triple turret flat base, turret handle, reflex viewfinder, saddle for 400ft magazine, Switzerland, c1972, 9in (23cm) high.

**£580–660 Camera House** ⊞

A Sankyo Super 8 camera, Model XL-600S Sound with f1.2/7.5-45mm macro zoom lens, microphone and headset, c1977, 10in (25.5cm) wide.

**£110–130 Camera House** ⊞

A Canon auto zoom 1014 electronic Super 8 camera, c1980, 12in (30.5cm) wide.

**£220–250 Arundel Photographica** ⊞

A Kodak Hama Gamma-Series Digital Camera 40, c1995.

**£45–50 Pepe Tozzo** ⊞

## FOLDING CAMERAS

A Shew and Co ¼-plate Eclipse camera, 1890s, 5½in (14cm) high.

**£270–300** Arundel Photographica ⊞

An Eastman Kodak pocket box camera, America, 1899, 4in (10cm) wide.

**£110–120**
Antique Photographic ⊞

A Kodak No. 3A model B2 folding pocket camera, with Rapid Rectilinear f4-f128 lens, pneumatic shutter, red bellows, mahogany/leather-covered 122 film and plate back adapter with focusing screen, 1902, 10in (25.5cm) high.

**£40–45** Camera House ⊞

An Eastman Kodak No 3A folding Brownie camera, America, 1910, 8¾in (22cm) wide.

**£45–50**
Antique Photographic ⊞

An Eastman Kodak pocket camera, America, 1915, 4¾in (12cm) high.

**£15–20**
Antique Photographic ⊞

An Eastman Kodak Beau Brownie box camera, America, c1930, 4in (10cm) wide.

**£70–80**
Antique Photographic ⊞

A Kamera Werkstätten Pilot reflex camera, Germany, 1930s, 4¾in (12cm) high.

**£135–150**
Antique Photographic ⊞

A Kodak No. 2 Hawkette Bakelite camera, 1930s, 7in (18cm) high.

**£45–50**
Antique Photographic ⊞

A Supersport Certo camera, with Trioplan 7.5cm/f2.9\Compur shutter and uncoupled Rangefinder, 1935–41, 5in (12.5cm) wide.

**£60–70** Camera House ⊞

A Zeiss Ikon Nettar camera, Germany, c1949, 5in (12.5cm) wide.

**£20–25** Old Ironmongers ⊞

A Houghton Ensign Selfix 420 camera, c1950, 7in (18cm) high.

**£35–40** Old Ironmongers ⊞

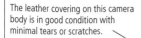

## EXPERT EYE   A FOLDING CAMERA

The leather covering on this camera body is in good condition with minimal tears or scratches.

Check the bellows for wear. In well-used cameras they can become detached from the camera body where the original adhesive has deteriorated.

Some Ikon models have a circular metal tag on the side of the body, which was positioned by the retail outlet. This can add to the camera's provenance.

**A Zeiss Ikon Ideal folding plate camera,** with Tessar f4.5/155mm lens set in a Compur dial-set shutter, with five slides and leather case, Germany, c1927, 6in (15cm) high.

**£115–135 Worcester Antiques** ⊞

For absolute precision and the perfect shot Ikon's double extension bellows were capable of rise and fall as well as shift. Discrete clips were neatly positioned on the outside to avoid sagging when they were fully extended.

A typical carrying case (not shown) would have been black leather embossed with the Zeiss logo on the back. Having this and a range of slides as accessories adds to this camera's value.

The dial-set Compur shutter, which mimics an iris, is beautifully engineered with a mechanism that is similar to a watch movement. It was widely used at the time even by Leica for a version of the Leica I. The FD monogram at the top denotes the shutter's manufacturer, Friedrich Deckel. To help with dating, Compur replaced their dial-set shutter with a rim-set version around 1928.

Zeiss Ikon used a number of lenses for their 'Ideal' range with Tessar being the best quality. The fact that's it's not anti-reflection coated is a marker of its pre-WWII date.

Zeiss Ikon was the result of a mass merger of German camera firms in 1926. The resulting output was prolific and appealed to customers across the board. Pre-WW II was the firm's boom period and plate cameras such as this were highly regarded. By 1938 the Ideal line was discontinued. Today a new breed of photographers recognize the sheer quality of cameras like this and many are bought to be used. Look out for Zeiss Ikon's helpful numbering system that precisely aids model identification. It is usually written like a fraction – the top part being the model number and the bottom showing the format. In this case it's 250/3.

# CERAMICS

I T IS NO COINCIDENCE that the ceramics tables at each BBC TV's *Antiques Roadshow* are so busy — collecting ceramics remains as popular as ever. The popularity of online trading has transformed collecting ceramics, but savvy collectors are always looking for something new, something up and coming.

A Jasba dish, with metallic oxides, marked, Germany, 1970s, 9¾in (25cm) diam.

**£35–40 Outernational** ⊞

So what do I see in my crystal ball? Well that would be telling, but here are a few ideas. Last year I suggested that West German post-war ceramics would be on the up, and they are. The 'Lava'-type glaze examples are now gaining popularity, but what of the other West Germans? Firms such as Thomas, KPM, Hutschenreuther and Meissen produced amazing white porcelain pieces in the late 1960s and '70s that remain undervalued. Only last week I picked up two pieces in a charity shop for 50p each. The same shop had three West German stoneware pieces at £15 plus.

A Saxbo stoneware vase, by Leon Galleto, with impressed marks, Denmark, 1956, 12¼in (31cm) high.

**£540–600 Freeforms** ⊞

Still looking to Europe, most Scandinavian potteries are now being recognized but only the well-known names are expensive, although certain lines by Upsala Ekeby and Jie Gantoffa are still affordable and printed designs such as Rörstrand's 'Picknick' can still occasionally be found.

Aldo Londi's great designs for Bitossi are underpriced, as are almost all Italian post-war ceramics, many of which were distributed by Raymor in the US. Londi's 'Rimini Blue' and the less common 'Rimini Red' can still be bought online for a fraction of what they should be worth, but for how much longer? Great 1950s Italian pots can still be picked up for a few pounds if you are lucky, especially when they are often just marked 'Foreign'. As Europe extends east and more people travel, should we be looking to Poland and further afield for the next hot thing?

A Myott Fan vase, pattern No. 8600, 1930s, 8½in (21.5cm) high.

**£230–250 Myott Collectors Club** ⊞

So what's big in the UK right now? Clarice Cliff still seems unstoppable. Lower down the price scale Myott's fab'n'funky so-British Art Deco pots are creeping up in value, and about time too. Already a slim volume entitled *The Mystery of Myott* has been published (see page 112). There is still a lot of scope for collectors of post-war ceramics.

In The US post-war American wares are now getting the recognition they deserve, as are post-war European works. As these pieces get pricier firms that are still in business are bringing out copies of their original ranges, such as Homer Laughlin's Fiesta line and one wonders what effect this will have on the originals.

**Steven Moore**

# ART POTTERY

A **C. H. Brannam jug,** with fish-head spout, decorated with fish and seaweed, incised marks, 1900, 13in (33cm) high.

**£300–330 Ruskin Decorative Arts** ⊞

A **Bretby Rocket vase,** with *sang-de-boeuf* glaze, c1900, 15in (38cm) high.

**£330–370 Country Seat** ⊞

## ESSENTIAL REFERENCE CANDY WARE

A **Candy Ware vase,** with drip glaze, shape No. 203, stamped 'C14' to base, 1930s, 6in (15cm) high.

**£40–45 Decorative Antiques** ⊞

A **Candy Ware vase,** with splash glaze, 1930s, 9in (23cm) high.

**£40–45 Decorative Antiques** ⊞

• Candy Ware was produced between 1936 and 1950 by tile manufacturers Candy & Co at Newton Abbot, Devon.

• Unlike their earlier 'Westcontree Ware', which was moulded, Candy Ware was hand thrown.

• Known for its experimental crystalline glazes, Candy Ware is a very up-and-coming collectable.

A **George Clews Chameleon Ware vase,** 1920s, 7in (18cm) high.

**£100–115 Beth** ⊞
*Chameleon Ware was developed in 1914 by George Clews works manager David Clapper who wanted to provide an affordable alternative to the hand-thrown wares of Ruskin Pottery. Chameleon Ware was slip cast, but used similar glazes and thus was less expensive. The name is said to derive from the fact that the colour of the ware changes in the kiln. Clapper went on to introduce a range of animals in the 1930s, including a chameleon, much desired by Chameleon Ware collectors.*

A **George Clews Chameleon Ware vase,** 1920s, 10in (25.5cm) high.

**£145–160
Worcester Antiques** ⊞

A **Devonmoor vase,** with gloss glaze, impressed mark, 1930s, 3½in (9cm) high.

**£20–25
Decorative Antiques** ⊞
*Devonmoor pottery is quite difficult to date. It opened in 1913, closed the following year, reopened in 1922 and finally closed in the 1980s. Their 'art' pieces, such as this vase, tend to date from 1922 to 1939.*

A Collard Honiton vase, decorated with Islamic Arches pattern, shape No. 91, 1920s, 3½in (9cm) high.

**£30–35 Decorative Antiques** ⊞

A Collard Honiton jug, 1920s–30s, 5in (12.5cm) high.

**£55–65 Decorative Antiques** ⊞

A Pilkington's Royal Lancastrian vase, incised mark, date code for 1909, 5¼in (13.5cm) high.

**£150–165 Country Seat** ⊞
*The impressed version of the Pilkington 'P' supported by the Burton bees mark often includes Roman numerals beneath it. These designate the date. This piece is marked 'IX' for 1909.*

A Pilkington's Lancastrian vase, impressed mark, c1904, 6in (15cm) diam.

**£135–145 Country Seat** ⊞
*This piece bears the first registered trademark of the firm and capital 'P' supported by bees, as well as the impressed 'P' used from 1897. Printed on early pieces from the 1903–04 period, the same design was impressed from 1905.*

A Pilkington's Royal Lancastrian jar, designed by William S. Mycock, incised mark, c1930, 6in (15cm) high.

**£360–400 Country Seat** ⊞

A Watcombe Pottery Torquay two-handled vase, c1905, 10in (25.5cm) high.

**£85–95 Country Seat** ⊞

## ESSENTIAL REFERENCE UPCHURCH POTTERY

An Upchurch Pottery baluster vase, by Edward Spencer, incised mark, c1910, 12in (30.5cm) high.

**£420–470 Country Seat** ⊞

An Upchurch Pottery bowl, incised mark, c1930, 7½in (19cm) diam.

**£60–70 Country Seat** ⊞

• Upchurch Pottery was founded in 1909 to make bricks, pipes and tiles.

• Art wares were added in 1913, designed by Edward Baker.

• These art wares became popular and were patronized by Queen Mary.

• Edward Spencer, who had worked with the Martin Brothers, worked with Baker to develop glazes.

• Baker ran the pottery until his death in 1955.

• His son, William, took over running the pottery until 1963.

An Arequipa pottery bowl, decorated in trail slip with leaves, signed, America, California, dated 1912, 5½in (14cm) wide.
**£1,250–1,500 Rago Arts** ⚒
*Frederick Hurten Rhead, son of Frederick Alfred Rhead and brother of Charlotte, worked for a number of American potteries, notably Roseville (1902–11) and Arequipa (1911–18). Arequipa ware was produced as occupational therapy by patients at the Arequipa Sanitorium, north of San Francisco.*

A Marblehead pottery vase, possibly by Arthur Baggs and Hanna Tutt, decorated with seven tree trunks, America, 1904, 4½in (11.5cm) high.
**£2,000–2,500 Skinner** ⚒

## ESSENTIAL REFERENCE NEWCOMB COLLEGE

A Newcomb College desk set, decorated by Roberta Kennon, comprising quill pot, inkwell with cover and sponge holder, stamped mark, slight damage, America, c1902, quill pot 4¼in (11cm) high.
**£5,000–6,000 Rago Arts** ⚒
*This desk set was originally a wedding gift for Beverly Randolph, a decorator for Newcomb from 1895 to 1903.*

A Newcomb College candlestick, decorated by Leona Nicholson with frogs and crescent moons, America, c1902, 11½in (29cm) high.
**£9,000–11,000 Rago Arts** ⚒
*This is an unusual design, executed with great panache by Leona Nicholson.*

A Newcomb College vase, decorated by Mazie Ryan with wisteria, slight damage, marked, America, 1904, 8½in (21.5cm) high.
**£23,000–28,000 Rago Arts** ⚒
*This piece is out of the ordinary. It was exhibited at the Louisiana Purchase Exhibition of 1904 and this provenance, combined with its striking design, makes this vase a highly important example sought after by collectors.*

• Operating between 1895 and 1940, the pottery was part of Newcomb College, the women's section of Tulane University, Louisiana.

• Initially a decorating studio, professional potters were employed to create pieces to be decorated by students.

• Pieces in subtle blues, greens and yellow inspired by the southern landscape are now highly sought after.

• Its most famous design is 'Moon and Moss', depicting trees hung with Spanish moss, typical of the deep south.

• Abstract designs inspired by the locale were introduced in the 1920s and '30s and included waves and the architecture of the New Orleans Spanish quarter.

A Rookwood vase, painted by F. Rothenbusch with nasturtiums, flame mark, America, c1907, 10½in (26.5cm) high.
**£560–670 Rago Arts** ⚒

A Rookwood vase, painted by Elizabeth Lincoln with birds and flowers, flame mark, America, 1925, 17¼in (44cm) high.
**£2,700–3,200 Rago Arts** ⚒

A Rookwood vase, painted by Louise Abel with a floral wreath, flame mark, America, c1923, 4¼in (11cm) high.
**£800–1,000 Rago Arts** ⚒

## ESSENTIAL REFERENCE PAUL REVERE

A Paul Revere Saturday Evening Girls bowl, slight damage, signed, America, 1914, 11½in (29cm) diam.

**£2,400–3,000 Skinner** ⚒

A Paul Revere Saturday Evening Girls bowl, with incised landscape design, initialed 'S. G.', probably for Sarah Galner, America, 1916, 8½in (21.5cm) diam.

**£1,200–1,450 Skinner** ⚒

- Usually marked 'SEG', these pieces were produced by the Paul Revere pottery in Boston, Massachusetts.

- The Saturday Evening Girls were poor girls from immigrant families and profits from the sale of their work was used to establish a fund for their education.

- The pottery was best known for its motto and nursery wares.

- Other popular motifs include sensitive depictions of animals, usually in simple outline form.

A Roseville creamer, moulded with magnolia, slight damage and repair, signed, America, 1943–44, 3in (7.5cm) high.

**£20–25 Heritage** ⚒
*The slight damage to the spout has reduced the value of this item by around one third.*

A Roseville console bowl, moulded with zephyr lilies, signed, America, 1946, 17in (43cm) wide.

**£100–120 Heritage** ⚒

A Van Briggle vase, moulded with jonquils, marked, America, 1905, 10½in (26.5cm) high.

**£1,000–1,250 Rago Arts** ⚒

A Van Briggle vase, moulded with peacock feathers, minor damage, America, 1904, 10¾in (27.5cm) high.

**£720–860 Rago Arts** ⚒

A Van Briggle vase, moulded with peacock feathers, America, 1908–11, 9¼in (23.5cm) high.

**£850–1,000 Rago Arts** ⚒

A Van Briggle jardinière, moulded with stylized morning glories, slight damage, marked, America, 1905, 6½in (16.5cm) high.

**£600–700 Rago Arts** ⚒

A Weller vase, mouded with Blossom pattern, glaze drip to foot, impressed mark, America, c1935, 8in (20.5cm) high.

**£25–30 Heritage** ⚒

# BELLEEK

A Belleek Ivy sugar bowl, Ireland, Second Period, 1891–1926, 4in (10cm) diam.
**£90–100  Bac to Basic** ⊞

A Belleek Hexagon teapot, knop damaged, Ireland, Second Period, 1891–1926, 7in (19cm) wide.
**£120–135  Tenterden Antiques** ⊞
*The fragile nature of Belleek means that undamaged examples are highly valued. In perfect condition, this teapot would be worth at least £100 more.*

A Belleek Hexagon sugar bowl, Ireland, Second Period, 1891–1926, 2¼in (5.5cm) high.
**£40–45
Tenterden Antiques** ⊞

A Belleek Aberdeen jug, Ireland, Second Period, 1891–1926, 6in (15cm) high.
**£230–260
Delphi Antiques** ⊞
*A collectable shape, Aberdeen is either plain, like this example, or applied with flowers. These jugs were made in three sizes and collectors try to find all three as full sets are rarely found.*

A Belleek Leaf plate, Ireland, Second Period, 1891–1926, 5in (12.5cm) wide.
**£50–60  Scottish Antique & Arts** ⊞

A Belleek Hexagon cup and saucer, Ireland, Second Period, 1891–1926, cup 2¼in (5.5cm) high.
**£90–100
Tenterden Antiques** ⊞

A Belleek Harp Shamrock bowl, Ireland, Second Period, 1891–1926, 3¼in (8.5cm) wide.
**£45–50
Tenterden Antiques** ⊞

A Belleek Heritage Collection Shamrock honey pot and cover, limited edition, Eleventh Period mark, dated 2005, 6in (15cm) high.
**£55–65  Bentley's** 🔨
*These limited edition pieces are expensive to buy and often retain little value although they are an inexpensive way of obtaining examples of rare items. Collectors prefer to seek original examples, not copies. If this were an original First Period example it would be worth several hundred pounds.*

A Belleek Shamrock biscuit barrel, Ireland, Fourth Period, 1946–55, 6½in (16.5cm) high.
**£150–165
Tenterden Antiques** ⊞

A Belleek Shamrock cream jug, Ireland, Seventh Period, 1980–92, 2½in (6.5cm) high.
**£35–40  ReMemories** ⊞

# BESWICK

A Beswick model of a bulldog, 'Bashford British Mascot', by Arthur Gredington, 1941–90, 5¼in (13.5cm) high.

**£90–100**
**Tenterden Antiques** ⊞
*A matt version was produced between 1987 and 1989 and is available in a brindle colourway.*

A Beswick model of an Alsatian, 'Ulrica of Brittas', by Arthur Gredington, 1942–94, 5¾in (14.5cm) high.

**£25–30** **ReMemories** ⊞
*A matt version was produced from 1970.*

A Beswick model of a springer spaniel, by Arthur Gredington, damaged, 1946–67, 4in (10cm) high.

**£20–25** **ReMemories** ⊞
*Arthur Gredington's running spaniel was also produced in a rare blue colourway between 1947 and 1954.*

A Beswick model of a collie, 'Lochinvar of Ladypark', by Arthur Gredington, 1961–94, 7in (18cm) high.

**£45–50** **Tenterden Antiques** ⊞

A Beswick model of a St Bernard, 'Corona Garth Stroller', by Arthur Hallam, 1968–89, 4in (10cm) high.

**£50–55** **ReMemories** ⊞

A Beswick model of a bulldog, 'Bosun', c1980, 3in (7.5cm) high.

**£30–35**
**Tenterden Antiques** ⊞

A Beswick model of a boxer, by Alan Maslankowski, 1970–89, 5¾in (14.5cm) high.

**£50–60** **Tenterden Antiques** ⊞
*A latecomer in the dogs series, this model was introduced in 1988 and produced in both gloss and matt. The latter gives a more natural look, but gloss is generally favoured by collectors.*

A Beswick model of a boxer, 1999–2001, 5½in (14cm) high.

**£45–50** **ReMemories** ⊞
*This is the later 'D' series model, produced when Beswick was part of Royal Doulton.*

A Beswick model of golden labrador, by Arthur Gredington, c1989, 3¼in (8.5cm) high.

**£35–40** **Tenterden Antiques** ⊞

A Beswick model of a springer spaniel, by Amanda Hughes-Lubeck, c1989, 5½in (14cm) high.

**£50–60** **ReMemories** ⊞

A Beswick model of a cocker spaniel, 'Horseshoe Primula', by Arthur Gredington, c1993, 3in (7.5cm) high.

**£20–25** **ReMemories** ⊞

## EXPERT EYE  A BESWICK DOG

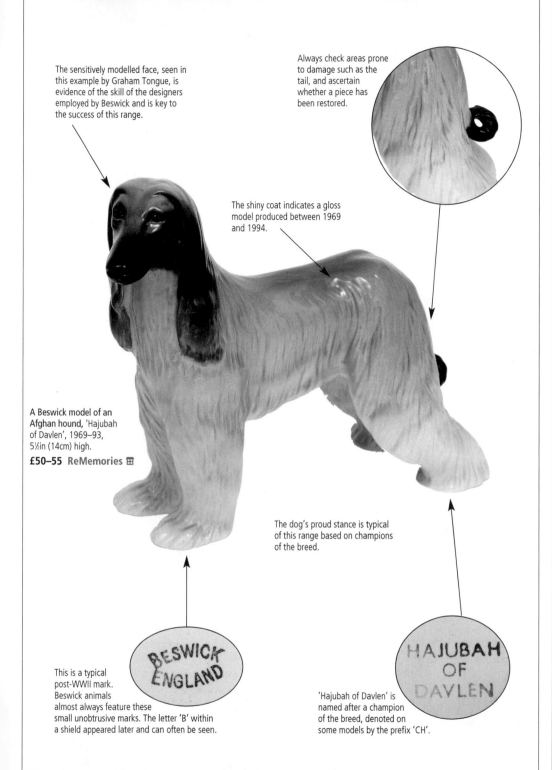

The sensitively modelled face, seen in this example by Graham Tongue, is evidence of the skill of the designers employed by Beswick and is key to the success of this range.

Always check areas prone to damage such as the tail, and ascertain whether a piece has been restored.

The shiny coat indicates a gloss model produced between 1969 and 1994.

A Beswick model of an Afghan hound, 'Hajubah of Davlen', 1969–93, 5½in (14cm) high.

**£50–55 ReMemories** ⊞

The dog's proud stance is typical of this range based on champions of the breed.

This is a typical post-WWII mark. Beswick animals almost always feature these small unobtrusive marks. The letter 'B' within a shield appeared later and can often be seen.

'Hajubah of Davlen' is named after a champion of the breed, denoted on some models by the prefix 'CH'.

Britain is said to be a nation of dog lovers, so it is not surprising that these Beswick dog models are very popular with collectors. Produced from 1933, the early Beswick dogs are generally of the novelty type which was very much in vogue at that time. The big breakthrough came in 1941 when Arthur Gredington introduced his champions series. Modelled in show stance, these life-like models were based on real champions, the first being the Dalmatian 'Arnoldene', number 961. After Gredington's retirement, the tradition was continued by Albert Hallam, who also produced many fine models.

A Beswick model of a Hereford cow, by Arthur Gredington, shape No. 1384, 1954–97, 4¼in (11cm) high.

**£120–145  Penrith Farmers' & Kidd's** 🔨

*This is the later version with small horns. The matt version is worth twice as much as the gloss model.*

A Beswick model of a Guernsey calf, designed by Arthur Gredington, shape No. 1249A, 1954–97, 2¾in (7cm) high.

**£130–160  Penrith Farmers' & Kidd's** 🔨

A Beswick model of a dairy shorthorn cow, 'Chamption Eaton Wild Eyes 91st', shape No. 1510, 1957–73, 4¾in (12cm) high.

**£800–950  Gorringes (L)** 🔨

A Beswick model of a Galloway bull, 'Silver Dunn', shape No. 1746C, 1962–69, 4½in (11.5cm) high.

**£900–1,080  Gorringes (L)** 🔨

*All of the Galloways are collectable, but be aware of colour variations: the fully black version is worth slightly more, whereas the 'belted' version (black with a white middle) is a further £1,500.*

A Beswick model of a dairy shorthorn bull, 'Champion Gwersylt Lord Oxford 74th', shape No. 1504, 1957–73, 5in (12.5cm) high.

**£600–720  Gorringes (L)** 🔨

A Beswick model of a Friesian bull, 'Champion Coddington Hit Bar', 1997, 8in (20.5cm) long.

**£180–200  Box of Porcelain** ⊞

A Beswick model of a Jersey bull, 1997, 7in (18cm) long.

**£180–200  Box of Porcelain** ⊞

A Beswick model of a boy on a pony, 'Palomino', by Arthur Gredington, shape No. 1500, slight damage, issued 1957–76, 5½in (14cm) high.

**£120–145 Penrith Farmers' & Kidd's** 🔨

A Beswick model of a huntsman on a horse, shape No. 868 (second version), 1952–94, 9¼in (23.5cm) high.

**£120–145 Locke & England** 🔨
*The first version of this model, in which the rider's coat is cut away at the waist, is worth over £200 more, whereas in this version the coat covers the thigh. The horses' heads also differ, this one having a more Arab profile, dished between the forelock and muzzle.*

A Beswick model of a palomino's head, by Arthur Gredington, shape No. 1384, 1955–69, 4in (10cm) high.

**£70–85 Penrith Farmers' & Kidd's** 🔨

A Beswick model of a Shire horse, c1960, 8½in (21.5cm) high.

**£65–75 ReMemories** ⊞

A Beswick model of a horse, 'Spirit of the Wind', on a wooden base, 1980s, 7in (18cm) high.

**£100–110 Tenterden Antiques** ⊞

A Beswick group of a horse and foal, 'First Born', c2002, 10in (25.5cm) wide.

**£160–175 Box of Porcelain** ⊞

A Beswick model of a palomino pony, 1999–2002, 6¾in (17cm) high.

**£110–120 Tenterden Antiques** ⊞

A Beswick model of a horse, 'Hunter', c2002, 10in (25.5cm) high.

**£85–95 Box of Porcelain** ⊞

A Beswick model of a horse, 'Spirit of Wisdom', c2002, 10in (25.5cm) high.

**£160–175 Box of Porcelain** ⊞

A Beswick model of a doe, 1940s, 6in (15cm) high.

**£20–25 ReMemories** ⊞

A Beswick model of a fish, 'Golden Trout', by Arthur Gredington, shape No. 1246, 1952–70, 10in (25.5cm) long.

**£200–250 Era Antiques** ⊞

A Beswick model of a kitten, by Colin Melbourne, shape No. 1436, marked, 1956–89, 3¼in (8.5cm) high.

**£20–25 Mary's Memories** ⊞
*With the closing of the Beswick factory in September 2002, such items are increasing in value and becoming sought after. This particular colourway was produced between 1962 and 1973.*

A Beswick model of a barn owl, with foil label, c1946, 4¼in (11cm) high.

**£45–50 Tenterden Antiques** ⊞
*This early version with split tail feather is worth more than the later closed tail version.*

A Beswick model of a seated fox, by Graham Tongue, shape No. 2348, 1970–84, 12in (30.5cm) high.

**£260–320 Penrith Farmers' & Kidd's** 🔨

A Beswick model of Winnie the Pooh, from the Winnie the Pooh series, 1990, 2½in (6.5cm) high.

**£100–110 Box of Porcelain** ⊞

A Beswick model of a grey wagtail, c1973, 4in (10cm) wide.

**£25–30
Tenterden Antiques** ⊞

## TIMELINE  BESWICK MARKS

Although established in 1884, most early Beswick wares are unmarked. The impressed mark 'Beswick England' was introduced in 1936 and is usually seen on pre-WWII items, often on pieces designed by Hallam or Symcox. A number refers to the shape.

The circular printed mark is critical in dating examples to the post-WWII period. In use from 1948 to 1954, it is found in gold on Beatrix Potter figures.

The oval mark was in use from 1954 to 1972 and is also found in gold on Beatrix Potter figures.

Beswick often received commissions from individual firms to make special products. The name was always worked into the design.

1969–1971

A Beswick model of Beatrix Potter's Mrs Rabbit, first version with umbrella sticking out, 1951–74, 4in (10cm) high.

**£135–150 Box of Porcelain** ⊞

A Beswick model of Beatrix Potter's Pickles, gold backstamp, 1971–82, 4½in (11.5cm) high.

**£450–500 Box of Porcelain** ⊞

A Beswick model of Beatrix Potter's Miss Moppet, BP-3b stamp to base, 1974–85, 3in (7.5cm) high.

**£40–45 Mary's Memories** ⊞

A Beswick model of Beatrix Potter's Foxy Whiskered Gentleman, brown backstamp, c1978, 5in (12.5cm) high.

**£75–80 ReMemories** ⊞

A Beswick model of Beatrix Potter's Benjamin Bunny, brown backstamp, 1970s, 3½in (9cm) high.

**£45–50 ReMemories** ⊞

A Beswick model of Beatrix Potter's Poorly Peter Rabbit, brown backstamp, 1970s, 3½in (9cm) high.

**£70–75 ReMemories** ⊞

1971–1982

1970s

1979

This mark from the 1990s has been redesigned to fit the base of this Winnie the Pooh figure.

This is the very last Beswick Beatrix Potter mark used between c2000 and 2002.

A Beswick model of Beatrix Potter's Johnny Town-Mouse, brown backstamp, 1980s, 4in (10cm) high.

**£200–220  ReMemories** ⊞

A Beswick group of Beatrix Potter's Goody and Timmy Tiptoes, by David Lyttleton, BP-3c backstamp, 1986–96, 4in (10cm) high.

**£80–100  Penrith Farmers' & Kidd's** 🔨

A Beswick model of Beatrix Potter's Tom Kitten with a butterfly, Royal Albert stamp, 1987–94, 3½in (9cm) high.

**£145–160  Box of Porcelain** ⊞

A Beswick model of Beatrix Potter's Little Pig Robinson spying, by Ted Chawner, BP-3c backstamp, issued 1987–93, 3½in (9cm) high.

**£70–85  Penrith Farmers' & Kidd's** 🔨

A Beswick model of Beatrix Potter's Thomasina Tittlemouse, BP-3b backstamp, discontinued in 1989, 3½in (9cm) high.

**£50–55  Mary's Memories** ⊞

A Beswick model of Beatrix Potter's Peter Rabbit, brown backstamp, 2002, 4½in (11.5cm) high.

**£90–100  ReMemories** ⊞
*This model has the unusual satin glaze produced between 2002 and 2003.*

## ESSENTIAL REFERENCE  THE VALUE IN VARIATION

A Beswick model of Beatrix Potter's Tommy Brock, first version with spade handle above paw, brown backstamp, 1970s, 3½in (9cm) high.

**£160–175  ReMemories** ⊞
*This first version was found to be vulnerable to damage so is rarely found in good condition, hence the price.*

A Beswick model of Beatrix Potter's Tommy Brock, second version with spade handle in paw, brown backstamp, 1970s, 3½in (9cm) high.

**£45–50  ReMemories** ⊞
*This second version is easily identified by the spade handle in rather than above the paw, and is worth a fraction of its rarer counterpart.*

A Beswick model of Beatrix Potter's Tommy Brock, by Graham Orwell, second version, BP-3b backstamp, issued from 1975, 3½in (9cm) high.

**£45–55  Penrith Farmers' & Kidd's** 🔨
*The change in jacket colour has added a few pounds.*

• The manufacture of ceramics is a unique business, with the potential for disaster at every stage in the process.

• Whether breakages or misfirings, all variations add greatly to the overall cost of an item. Consequently shapes and figures in particular are often altered to make them more commercially viable.

• The canny collector can make a killing by looking out for variations in design – it's where the money is.

# ESSENTIAL REFERENCE    MR SYMCOX

A Beswick dish, decorated with mallards, 1939–69, 2in (5cm) high.

**£30–35  Tenterden Antiques** ⊞

A pair of Beswick two-handled Thistle vases, by Mr Symcox, shape No. 94/2, 1934, 8in (20.5cm) high.

**£75–80  Decorative Antiques** ⊞

A Beswick Art Deco Vase, designed by Mr Symcox for the Trentham range, shape No. 90, with satin matt glaze, 1933–40, 7½in (19cm) high.

**£45–50  Decorative Antiques** ⊞

• Mr (John) Symcox was a modeller at the Beswick Pottery between 1933 and 1942.

• Mr Symcox was also responsible, with Arthur Hallam, for the new range of Art Deco shapes introduced in 1933.

• He designed the Trentham range under licence for the firm Hardy's in Nottingham.

• These pieces are always marked 'Trentham Art Ware' and were made from 1934 to 1941.

A Beswick jug, decorated with palm trees, 1940s, 7¼in (18.5cm) high.

**£30–35  Bentley's** 🔨

A Beswick hand-painted cheese dish, surmounted by a strawberry, 1930s, 8in (20.5cm) wide.

**£70–80  Beth** ⊞

A Beswick lipped globular vase, by Albert Hallam, shape No. 1352, 1954, 4in (10cm) high.

**£70–80  retroselect** ⊞

A Beswick hand-painted vase, by Albert Hallam, decorated with Houses pattern, shape No. 13441, 1954, 9¾in (25cm) high.

**£45–55  Anthony Welling** 🔨

A Beswick pot, decorated with Houses pattern, black interior, 1950s, 5in (12.5cm) diam.

**£90–100  Beverley** ⊞

A Beswick freeform vase, by Colin Melbourne, 1956, 11¾in (30cm) high.

**£70–80  retroselect** ⊞

# CARLTON WARE

A Carlton Ware lustre bowl, decorated with Swallow and Cloud pattern, 1925, 8in (20.5cm) diam.

**£270–300 Beverley** ⊞

A Carlton Ware Gondola bowl, decorated with Devil's Copse pattern, gilded handles and feet, 1920s, 13in (33cm) wide.

**£1,000–1,200 Design Gallery** ⊞
*This is a very desirable pattern and the bowl is in excellent condition. Gilded wares are especially prone to wear.*

A Carlton Ware tea caddy, decorated with Red Devil pattern, 1930s, 6in (15cm) high.

**£3,000–3,500 Design Gallery** ⊞
*This item is highly sought after.*

A Carlton Ware cruet set, c1930, tray 9in (23cm) wide.

**£40–45 Beth** ⊞

A Carlton Ware hand-painted jampot, in the form of a cottage, c1930, 4½in (11.5cm) high.

**£60–70 Beth** ⊞

A Carlton Ware vase, c1930, 10in (25.5cm) high.
**£180–200 Tenterden Antiques** ⊞
*This piece is an unfinished and therefore would be classed as a 'second'.*

A Carlton Ware hand-painted sugar shaker, in the form of a cottage, c1930, 5in (12.5cm) high.

**£100–115 Beth** ⊞

A Carlton Ware Handcraft vase, with geometric design, c1930, 5in (12.5cm) high.

**£150–165 Beverley** ⊞
*The Handcraft range was introduced in 1929 and ran for a decade. This example, called Chevron, is typical of the more stylized pieces in this range.*

A Carlton Ware cocoa/chocolate mug and cover, decorated with Clematis pattern, 1930–40, 5in (12.5cm) high.

**£270–300 Scherazade** ⊞
*Mugs are rare, and one with the original undamaged cover raises the price dramatically. Covers are often chipped and damaged.*

A Carlton Ware Blue Max teapot, 6½in (16.5cm) high.

**£60–70 Locke & England** ⚒

A Carlton Ware cress dish, decorated with Waterlily pattern, 1930s, 9in (23cm) wide.

**£25–30 ReMemories** ⊞

*This piece is not marked, either because they simply forgot, or more likely the pierced holes left no space for a mark.*

A Carlton Ware ginger jar and cover, decorated with Temple pattern, No. 2880, black printed mark, 1894–1927, 12¼in (31cm) high.

**£180–220 Dreweatt Neate** 🔨

A Carlton Ware vase, decorated with New Mikado pattern, 1920s–30s, 4in (10cm) high.

**£80–90 Ferguson & Evans** ⊞

A Carlton Ware hand-painted Bleu Royale trinket box, 1950s, 5in (12.5cm) wide.

**£135–150 Beth** ⊞

A Carlton Ware posy holder, 1930s, 2½in (6.5cm) high.

**£45–50 Tenterden Antiques** ⊞

A Carlton Ware John Peel musical mug, 1930s, 5in (12.5cm) high.

**£70–80 Beverley** ⊞

## ESSENTIAL REFERENCE   CARLTON WARE DOWN UNDER

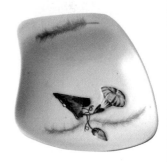

A Carlton Ware salad bowl and servers, one salad server restored, c1930, 3½in (9cm) high.

**£35–40 Tenterden Antiques** ⊞

A Carlton Ware butter/jam dish, decorated with Buttercup pattern, 1960s, 4½in (11.5cm) diam.

**£20–25 ReMemories** ⊞

A Carlton Ware butter/jam dish, decorated with a convolvulus, c1960s, 4in (10cm) high.

**£5–10 ReMemories** ⊞

• Many Carlton Ware pieces from the mid-1930s up to the early 1960s include the words 'Registered Australian Design' alongside the Carlton Ware mark. However, it is a popular misconception that these pieces were made especially for the Australian market.

• During the 1930s, Japanese manufacturers copied much good British pottery, including Carlton Ware, and the copies could be sold for much lower prices than the originals.

• At this time there was no copyright protection, but Carlton Ware's owner Frederick Cuthbert Wiltshaw found a novel way around the problem. He discovered a clause in the South East Asian Treaty that protected designs registered in Australia, thus preventing them from being copied by the Japanese.

• Wiltshaw took advantage of this situation by registering many Carlton Ware designs in Australia.

A Carlton Ware butter/jam dish, decorated with Redcurrants pattern, 1930s, 4in (10cm) diam.

**£15–20  ReMemories** ⊞

A Carlton Ware jam pot, in the form of a a blackberry, 1940s, 3in (7.5cm) high.

**£85–95  Beverley** ⊞

A Carlton Ware Wellington vase, impressed No. 2973/1, gold script backstamp, 1971, 11¾in (30cm) high.

**£25–30  retroselect** ⊞

A Carlton Ware hand-painted toast rack, in the form of a house, 1930s, 4in (10cm) wide.

**£110–125  Beth** ⊞

A Carlton Ware hand-painted Rouge Royale vase, decorated with a flying duck, 1950s, 7in (18cm) high.

**£230–250  Beverley** ⊞

*The mark on this vase was in use between 1952 and 1962. Duck, pattern No. 4455, is part of the Rouge Royale range, introduced after WWII.*

A Carlton Ware jam pot, in the form of a pear, 1960, 4¼in (11cm) high.

**£20–25  Halcyon** ⊞

A Carlton Ware Walking Ware sugar bowl, 1970s, 4in (10cm) high.

**£15–20  Brackley Antiques** ⊞

A Carlton Ware biscuit barrel, in the form of a house, registration mark No. 779973, repaired, 1930s, 8½in (21.5cm) high.

**£70–80  Tenterden Antiques** ⊞

A Carlton Ware teapot, in the form of an apple, 1968–90, 5in (12.5cm) wide.

**£45–50  Halcyon** ⊞

A Carlton Ware Pineapple dish, foil label, 1960s, 5in (12.5cm) long.

**£15–20  ReMemories** ⊞

*Items with original labels are popular with collectors as they have probably been rarely used.*

A Carlton Ware Denimware teapot, with wicker handle, c1978, 4¼in (11cm) diam.

**£25–30  retroselect** ⊞

## EXPERT EYE — HUMPTY DUMPTY

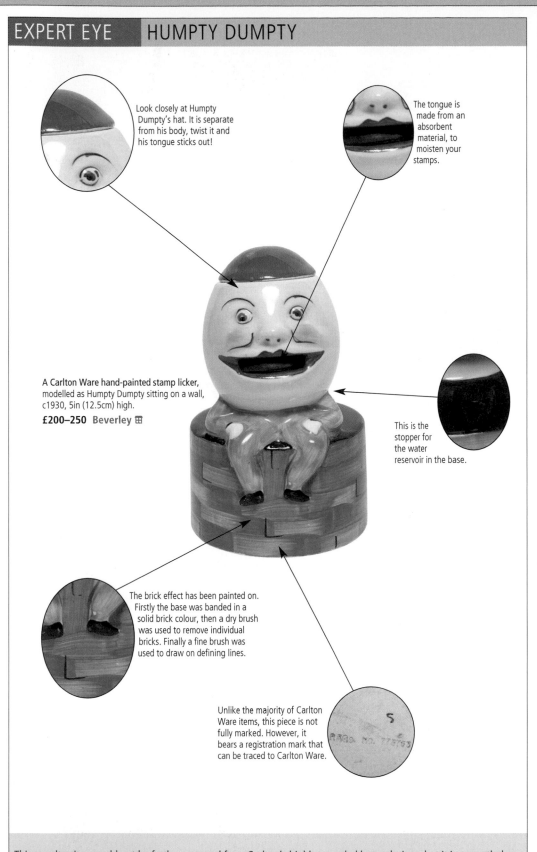

Look closely at Humpty Dumpty's hat. It is separate from his body, twist it and his tongue sticks out!

The tongue is made from an absorbent material, to moisten your stamps.

A Carlton Ware hand-painted stamp licker, modelled as Humpty Dumpty sitting on a wall, c1930, 5in (12.5cm) high.

**£200–250  Beverley** ⊞

This is the stopper for the water reservoir in the base.

The brick effect has been painted on. Firstly the base was banded in a solid brick colour, then a dry brush was used to remove individual bricks. Finally a fine brush was used to draw on defining lines.

Unlike the majority of Carlton Ware items, this piece is not fully marked. However, it bears a registration mark that can be traced to Carlton Ware.

This novelty piece could not be further removed from Carlton's highly regarded lustre designs, but it is, nevertheless, a popular item. Part of Carlton's appeal is the huge diversity of designs and sometimes the more wacky an item is, the more desirable it is to collectors. It is possible that not many of these Humpty Dumpty stamp lickers were made – lack of popularity when new is often a good thing for collectors as it means few will have survived, thus increasing value. So look out for ugly ducklings, they may become swans!

**CHINTZ WARE**

**A Royal Winton teapot stand,** decorated with Cotswold pattern, c1930, 6½in (16.5cm) diam.

**£20–25 Tenterden Antiques** ⊞

**A Crown Ducal fruit set,** comprising six dishes, transfer-printed with Florida pattern, c1930, large dish 9in (23cm) wide.

**£170–185 Beverley** ⊞

*Although not specifically for the American market, Florida was exported in great quantities to the US. Initially made as tea ware, more functional pieces like this fruit set and dinner ware, were introduced at the request of Crown Ducal's American agents.*

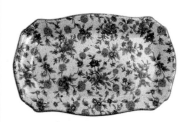

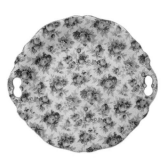

**A Royal Winton pin tray,** decorated with Old Cottage Chintz pattern, 1930s, 8in (20.5cm) wide.

**£20–25 Tenterden Antiques** ⊞

**A Royal Winton cake plate,** decorated with Evesham pattern, c1930, 9½in (24cm) diam.

**£115–130 Beverley** ⊞

**A Royal Winton Norman teapot for two,** decorated with Wellbeck pattern, 1930s, 9in (23cm) high.

**£200–250 Beverley** ⊞

**A Barker Bros Royal Tudor ware cake stand,** 1930s, 3in (7.5cm) high.

**£30–35 Tenterden Antiques** ⊞

**A James Kent cup and saucer,** decorated with Du Barry pattern, 1930s, cup 3in (7.5cm) high.

**£50–55 Tenterden Antiques** ⊞

**A Royal Winton bowl,** decorated with Sweet Pea pattern, 1930s, 7½in (19cm) wide.

**£50–60 Tenterden Antiques** ⊞

**A James Kent cheese dish and cover,** decorated with Du Barry pattern, 1930s, 7in (18cm) wide.

**£170–185 Beverley** ⊞

*Individual pieces such as a cheese dish or teapot are always highly coveted collectables. After all, there is often only one such item per family as opposed to numerous cups, plates and saucers.*

**A James Kent tea set for one,** c2003, tray 10in (25.5cm) wide.

**£180–195 Tenterden Antiques** ⊞

*This is a faithful reproduction of the original set and was produced for the centenary year. It is very difficult to determine if these exact reproductions will become collectable. Although collectors are keen to buy them, reproductions often undermine the value of the originals, and rarely hold their prices long term.*

# EXPERT EYE   TREFOIL DISH

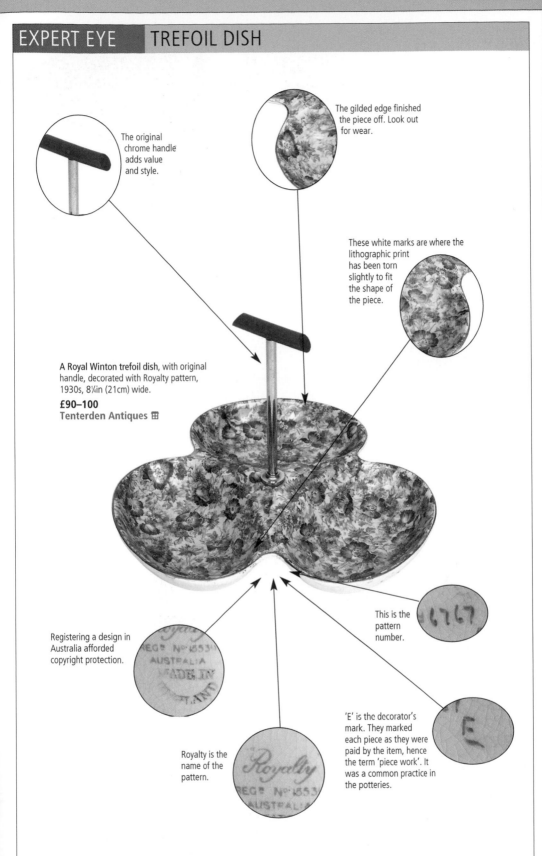

The original chrome handle adds value and style.

The gilded edge finished the piece off. Look out for wear.

These white marks are where the lithographic print has been torn slightly to fit the shape of the piece.

**A Royal Winton trefoil dish**, with original handle, decorated with Royalty pattern, 1930s, 8¼in (21cm) wide.
**£90–100**
**Tenterden Antiques** ⊞

Registering a design in Australia afforded copyright protection.

This is the pattern number.

Royalty is the name of the pattern.

'E' is the decorator's mark. They marked each piece as they were paid by the item, hence the term 'piece work'. It was a common practice in the potteries.

What could be more redolent of the 1930s than this dish? With its trefoil shape, chintz design and, to top it off, a chrome and Bakelite handle it is true 'thirties style. Royalty was a popular design. It was also available on a black ground, known as 'Majestic'. Chintz wares were a great success in their day – cheap to produce and packed full of colour, they were just what every aspiring young married couple wanted.

## CLARICE CLIFF

A Clarice Cliff Bizarre coffee cup and saucer, decorated with Gayday pattern, c1930, cup 2¼in (5.5cm) high.
**£200–220 Tenterden Antiques** ⊞

A Clarice Cliff Conical coffee cup and saucer, decorated with Coral Firs pattern, 1933–38, cup 2¼in (5.5cm) high.
**£430–480 Beverley** ⊞

A Clarice Cliff Bizarre cup and saucer, decorated with Blue Chintz pattern, 1932, saucer 5¾in (14.5cm) diam.
**£200–250 Andrew Muir** ⊞

A Clarice Cliff Conical cup and saucer, decorated with Delicia Pansies pattern, c1932, cup 2½in (6.5cm) high.
**£360–400 Banana Dance** ⊞

A Clarice Cliff cup and saucer, decorated with Crocus pattern, 1930s, cup 2½in (6.5cm) high.
**£270–300 Banana Dance** ⊞

A Clarice Cliff Bizarre cup and saucer, decorated with Coral Firs pattern, 1930s, cup 2½in (6.5cm) high.
**£360–400 Banana Dance** ⊞

A Clarice Cliff Blinton coffee cup and saucer, decorated with Crocus pattern, 1930s, cup 3in (7.5cm) high.
**£250–280 Banana Dance** ⊞

A Clarice Cliff Bizarre Tankard coffee pot and cover, c1928, 8½in (21.5cm) high.
**£630–700 Andrew Muir** ⊞

A Clarice Cliff Bizarre Lynton coffee pot, decorated with Viscaria pattern, 1934, 7½in (19cm) high.
**£270–300 Tenterden Antiques** ⊞

A Clarice Cliff Rooster teapot, c1930s, 8in (20.5cm) high.
**£35–40 Beverley** ⊞

A Clarice Cliff Bizarre Lotus jug, decorated with Sliced Circle pattern, 1929, 12in (30.5cm) high.

**£4,000–4,500  Andrew Muir** ⊞
*Both shape and pattern greatly influence the value of Clarice Cliff items. Here the ever-popular Lotus jug is combined with the desirable Sliced Circle pattern – a commercially unstoppable combination.*

A Clarice Cliff Bizarre Lotus jug, decorated with Coral Firs pattern, 1933–38, 12in (30.5cm) high.

**£1,350–1,500  Andrew Muir** ⊞

A Clarice Cliff Bizarre Lotus jug, decorated with Sandon pattern, printed mark, c1935, 8in (20cm) high.

**£250–300  Bearnes** 🔨

A Clarice Cliff milk jug, decorated with Crocus pattern, 1928–41, 3½in (9cm) high.

**£270–300  Banana Dance** ⊞

A Clarice Cliff Bizarre Lotus jug, decorated with Windbells pattern, 1933, 9in (23cm) high.

**£2,000–2,200  Banana Dance** ⊞

A Clarice Cliff jug, decorated with Celtic Harvest pattern, 1937–41, 11¼in (28.5cm) high.

**£115–125  Tenterden Antiques** ⊞

## ESSENTIAL REFERENCE  VALUABLE SHAPES

A Clarice Cliff Trieste milk jug, decorated with Crocus pattern, 1928–41, 2½in (6.5cm) high.

**£360–400  Banana Dance** ⊞

A Clarice Cliff milk jug, decorated with Tree and House pattern, 1929, 3¼in (8.5cm) high.

**£410–450  Banana Dance** ⊞

A Clarice Cliff Conical milk jug, decorated with Solomon's Seal pattern, 1930s–40s, 4in (10cm) high.

**£410–450  Banana Dance** ⊞
*Unlike most of Clarice Cliff's designs of this date, Solomon's Seal is hand enamelled over a lithographic print.*

- The right shape can make or break the value of a Clarice Cliff item.
- Collectors can be very choosy and prefer certain shapes.
- Some designs work better on certain shapes, and this will fetch a premium.
- Some shapes are always in fashion.
- Look out for named shapes such as Bon Jour, Stamford, Trieste or anything in Conical, especially sugar sifters.
- Numbered shapes such as the 380 double vase and 379 yo-yo are always in demand.
- Large plaques and Lotus jugs are also very popular, as are the sabots.
- Top of the tree has to be the Age of Jazz figures.

A Clarice Cliff Bizarre plate, decorated with Ravel pattern, c1929, 10in (25.5cm) diam.

**£65–75** Tenterden Antiques ⊞

*Ravel is a simple, freehand-painted design that, due to its simplicity, does not afford great value, especially on simple shapes like this plate. However, the same design on an item such as a Stamford teapot would be worth much more.*

A Clarice Cliff Fantasque plate, decorated with Melon pattern, 1930, 8½in (21.5cm) diam.

**£270–300** Tenterden Antiques ⊞

A Clarice Cliff plate, decorated with Latona Dahlia pattern, 1929–30, 9in (23cm) diam.

**£450–500** Worcester Antiques ⊞

A Clarice Cliff plate, decorated with Summerhouse pattern, 1932, 10in (25.5cm) diam.

**£450–500** Worcester Antiques ⊞

A Clarice Cliff plate, decorated with House and Bridge pattern, 1931, 10in (25.5cm) diam.

**£900–1,000** Banana Dance ⊞

*The House and Bridge pattern dates to 1932 and is an archetypal Clarice Cliff design that is always sought after. However, despite the name, not all examples feature a house and a bridge. This plate shows both and this is reflected in the price.*

A Clarice Cliff Bizarre plate, decorated with Nasturtium pattern, c1932, 7in (18cm) diam.

**£150–165** Tenterden Antiques ⊞

A Clarice Cliff plate, decorated with Idyll pattern, 1933, 6½in (16.5cm) wide.

**£480–530** Banana Dance ⊞

A Clarice Cliff Fantasque plate, decorated with Berries pattern, 1930, 6¾in (17cm) diam.

**£400–450** Banana Dance ⊞

Clarice Cliff plate, decorated with Islands pattern, 1936, 10in (25.5cm) diam.

**£40–45** Tenterden Antiques ⊞

*Islands pattern dates to 1936 and is a hand-coloured lithograph. This, along with its plain and non-typical design, makes it unpopular with collectors.*

A Clarice Cliff Circus plate, designed by Laura Knight, c1934, 8in (20.5cm) diam.

**£200–250** Beverley ⊞

A Clarice Cliff plate, decorated with Crocus pattern, 1928–41, 8in (20.5cm) diam.

**£20–25** Kingston Antiques ⊞

A Clarice Cliff jam pot and cover, decorated with Berries pattern, c1930, 3½in (9cm) high.

**£450–500 Banana Dance** ⊞

A Clarice Cliff Lynton honey pot, decorated with Autumn Crocus pattern, backstamp, 1928–41, 3¼in (8.5cm) high.

**£220–240 Moorcroft Antiques** ⊞

A Clarice Cliff Bon Jour jam pot, decorated with Crocus pattern, 1928–41, 4¼in (11cm) high.

**£450–500 Banana Dance** ⊞

A Clarice Cliff honey pot, decorated with Newlyn pattern, 1935, 3in (7.5cm) high.

**£540–600 Banana Dance** ⊞

A Clarice Cliff Bizarre mustard pot, decorated with Autumn Crocus pattern, 1928–41, 2in (5cm) high.

**£200–250 Moorcroft Antiques** ⊞

A Clarice Cliff jam pot, decorated with Autumn Crocus pattern, 1928–41, 3½in (9cm) high.

**£200–220 Moorcroft Antiques** ⊞

A Clarice Cliff Fantasque Bizarre jam pot and cover, decorated with House and Bridge pattern, 1932, 3in (7.5cm) high.

**£630–700 Gazelles** ⊞

A Clarice Cliff Bizarre jam pot, decorated with Delecia dripware pattern, marked, 1929–30, 3½in (9cm) high.

**£320–350 Moorcroft Antiques** ⊞

*Following on from her Original Bizarre range, Delecia was an early hit for Clarice Cliff. A simple, yet ever-changing design of running colours, it is often seen on its own (as in this example), or combined with other designs. It was also seen on old stock designs such as this shape from Wilkinson's Pottery.*

CLARICE CLIFF

A Clarice Cliff Bizarre Conical sugar sifter, decorated with Windbells pattern, c1933, 5½in (14cm) high.

**£500–600** Charterhouse ⚒

A Clarice Cliff sugar sifter, decorated with Nasturtium pattern, c1932, 5in (12.5cm) high.

**£700–780** Banana Dance ⊞

A Clarice Cliff Conical sugar sifter, decorated with Autumn Crocus pattern, 1928–41, 6in (15cm) high.

**£480–530** Beverley ⊞

## ESSENTIAL REFERENCE COLOURIFIC

A Clarice Cliff Daffodil toast rack, decorated with Melons pattern, 1930, 6in (15cm) wide.

**£400–450** Banana Dance ⊞

- Clarice Cliff is all about colour.
- The bolder, the brighter, the more Clarice it is, the better.
- Vivid clashing colours are what it's all about – but these need to be clearly defined.
- Collectors avoid fussy designs that look too crowded.

A Clarice Cliff Lynton sugar sifter, decorated with Crocus pattern, 1928–41, 5in (12.5cm) high.

**£340–380** Tenterden Antiques ⊞

A Clarice Cliff Lynton sugar shaker, decorated with Crocus pattern, 1935, 6in (15cm) high.

**£480–530** Beverley ⊞

A Clarice Cliff Bizarre toast rack, decorated with Crocus pattern, 1928–41, 5in (12.5cm) wide.

**£340–380** Tenterden Antiques ⊞

A Clarice Cliff toast rack, decorated with Jonquil pattern, 1933, 6in (15cm) wide.

**£360–400** Beverley ⊞

A Clarice Cliff vase, decorated with Delecia Nasturtium pattern, 1932, 8in (20.5cm) high.

**£900–1,000 Banana Dance** ⊞

A Clarice Cliff vase, decorated with Rhodanthe pattern, c1930, 12in (30.5cm) high.

**£450–500 Banana Dance** ⊞

*Clarice Cliff's habit of naming different colourways of the same design with individual names can lead to confusion among collectors. Rhodanthe is a typical example. Introduced in 1934, this orange, brown and yellow combination is Rhodanthe, whereas the same in mainly green with pink and yellow is called Aurea. Mainly green with navy blue added is also called Aurea and mainly pink with grey and yellow is called Pink Pearls.*

A Clarice Cliff vase, decorated with Autumn pattern, 1930–34, 6in (15cm) high.

**£900–1,000 Banana Dance** ⊞

A Clarice Cliff vase, decorated with Melons pattern, c1930, 9in (23cm) high.

**£1,800–2,000 Banana Dance** ⊞

A Clarice Cliff Archaic vase, decorated with Melons pattern, c1930, 9in (23cm) high.

**£1,800–2,000 Banana Dance** ⊞

A Clarice Cliff Indian Tree vase, 1934–39, 8in (20.5cm) high.

**£80–90 ReMemories** ⊞

A Clarice Cliff Isis vase, decorated with Alton pattern, c1934, 9¾in (25cm) high.

**£470–570 Rosebery's** 🔨

A Clarice Cliff Fantasque vase, decorated with Melons pattern, 1930s, 9½in (24cm) high.

**£1,800–2,000 Banana Dance** ⊞

A Clarice Cliff Aster vase, decorated with Inspiration pattern, 1929–31, 6in (15cm) diam.

**£540–600 Worcester Antiques** ⊞

A Clarice Cliff Isis vase, decorated with Rhodanthe pattern, 1934, 9¾in (25cm) high.

**£160–195 Rosebery's** 🔨

## EXPERT EYE  BROTH

Freehand painting within banding and lines is so typical of Clarice Cliff. In reality, the orange outline would have been painted by highly-skilled paintresses, then passed on to less skilled workers to be filled in.

A Clarice Cliff Fantaque vase, decorated with Broth pattern, shape No. 362, c1930, 8in (20.5cm) high.
**£1,200–1,350**
**Worcester Antiques** ⊞

362 is the shape number.

This gold mark was only used in that year.

Lawleys were pottery retailers and their name can often be found on pieces made for them.

Broth was based on a design by John Butler, who taught Clarice Cliff to paint.

Fantasque was introduced in 1928.

Although much of Clarice Cliff's output was freehand painted, the factory did find ways around this expensive technique. Training painters took time and with the run-away success of her pottery Clarice Cliff needed to speed up production. Many collectors do not realize that these pieces were often painted by more than one person. This Broth pattern vase would have had the outline of the design painted on first, probably by Fred Salmon. After this a less skiller painter would fill in the colours. By using this form of 'cheating', Cliff ensured the that quality remained high while the production was quick and cost-effective.

## CONTINENTAL

A Gouda Poppy bowl, Holland, c1926, 9in (23cm) diam.

**£670–750 Art Nouveau Originals** ⊞

A Gouda dish, marked, Holland, 1930s, 4in (10cm) diam.

**£20–25 ReMemories** ⊞

A Gouda miniature vase, marked, Holland, c1930s, 3in (7.5cm) high.

**£60–70 Beverley** ⊞

A Goldscheider figure of a dancer, by Stefan Dakon, impressed factory mark and designer's facsimile signature, restored, c1930, 15½in (39.5cm) high.

**£550–660 Gorringes (L)** ⚒

A Goldscheider figure of a dancer, 1930s, 11in (28cm) high.

**£1,200–1,400 Andrew Muir** ⊞

A Goldscheider figure of a harem girl, 1930s, 19in (48.5cm) high.

**£2,000–2,400 Andrew Muir** ⊞

## ESSENTIAL REFERENCE    WALL MASKS

A Goebel wall mask, Germany, 1930s, 7in (18cm) high.

**£300–350 Muir Hewitt** ⊞

A Goebel pottery wall mask, Germany, 1930s, 8in (20.5cm) high.

**£270–300 Muir Hewitt** ⊞

A Goebel wall mask, Germany, 1930s, 7in (18cm) high.

**£150–165 Beverley** ⊞

• Wall masks, so typical of the 1930s Art Deco period, were inspired by African wall masks. They were made by many European and British firms.

• A notable names to look out for is Cope & Co, who closed in 1947. Their examples are fairly basic and marked 'C & Co', but look out for unmarked later copies.

• Czechoslovakian firm Royal Dux produced a good number of face masks, including some men.

• William Goebel is well know for its wide range of well-made masks. Founded in 1871 the firm has operated in the Thungarian town of Oeslau ever since.

• Many examples were based on glamorous film stars of the period.

• The mask on the left is said to be Dorothy Lamour.

• Top of the facemask tree is Goldscheider. Made from red terracotta their style and modelling puts them out in front. Look out for damage or restoration on these pieces as terracotta is a soft material prone to damage.

# EXPERT EYE  GOUDA SOFIA VASE

These are the typical colours associated with the Gouda style. The combination of deep earth tones like the orange set on cream, combined with more drab shades like olive give a stunning effect.

Gouda pieces are hand painted. Look at how the design is not perfectly 'mirrored' here – this adds to the appeal and style of these pieces.

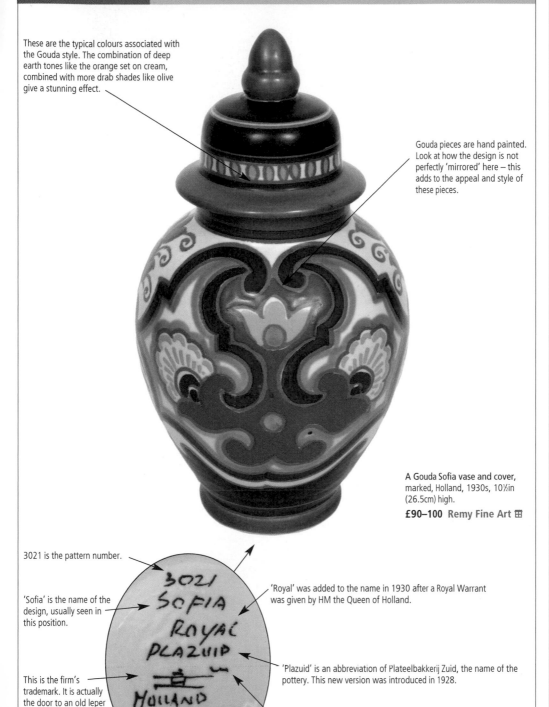

A Gouda Sofia vase and cover, marked, Holland, 1930s, 10½in (26.5cm) high.

**£90–100 Remy Fine Art** ⊞

3021 is the pattern number.

'Sofia' is the name of the design, usually seen in this position.

This is the firm's trademark. It is actually the door to an old leper hospital in Gouda dating to 1603. It is not known why it was chosen to represent the pottery.

'Royal' was added to the name in 1930 after a Royal Warrant was given by HM the Queen of Holland.

'Plazuid' is an abbreviation of Plateelbakkerij Zuid, the name of the pottery. This new version was introduced in 1928.

This is the artist's mark, showing who decorated this example

Gouda, pronounced 'how-da', is more than just cheese, it's a delicious-looking style of Dutch pottery that is greatly undervalued. The main style, typified by this example, combines strong earth tones with great shapes and strong floral designs. This type of pottery was produced by a number of firms based in and around the Dutch city of Gouda. The main factory was the Plateelbakkerij Zuid-Holland pottery who were in business from 1898 to 1964. From 1928 the name Plateelbakkerij was shortened to Plazuid and from 1930 the word 'Royal' added to the name after the warrant was granted by the Queen of Holland.

# SUSIE COOPER

A Susie Cooper teapot, hand-painted with Cubist pattern, c1930, 9in (23cm) wide.

**£580–650  Beverley** ⊞

*This simple yet stylish design is typical of Susie Cooper's work during this period and is always in demand with collectors.*

A Susie Cooper cream jug, decorated with Dresden Spray pattern, c1935, 2½in (6.5cm) high.

**£40–45**
**Tenterden Antiques** ⊞

A Susie Cooper tureen, decorated with Dresden Spray pattern, c1935, 7in (18cm) high.

**£60–70  Tenterden Antiques** ⊞

A Susie Cooper Kestrel teapot, decorated with Dresden Spray pattern, 1935, 4½in (11.5cm) high.

**£155–175  Banana Dance** ⊞

A Susie Cooper Kestrel coffee pot, decorated with Dresden Spray pattern, 1935, 6½in (16.5cm) high.

**£100–110  Banana Dance** ⊞

A Susie Cooper gravy boat, decorated with Patricia Rose pattern, 1938, 6in (15cm) wide.

**£40–45  Banana Dance** ⊞

A Susie Cooper trio, decorated with Tiger Lily pattern, late 1930s, 2½in (6.5cm) high.

**£80–90  Banana Dance** ⊞

## TIMELINE                    SUSIE COOPER

This is a variant of Susie Cooper's first mark used at her own factory. Dating to 1930–32, it was sometimes seen with Burslem underneath. An earlier example marked with 'Tunstall' dates to 1929–30 and is quite rare.

Perhaps the most famous of her marks, this was in use between 1932 and 1964. Printed in many colour variations, it often includes a pattern name. The best way to date a piece with this mark is by pattern and pattern number.

In production from 1932 to 1964, this is the same mark as before but without the leaping deer. Note the box beneath the mark – it was designed for the pattern number but is occasionally seen empty.

**A Susie Cooper tea plate,** decorated with Patricia Rose pattern, 1938, 7in (18cm) diam.
**£50–55  Banana Dance** ⊞

**A Susie Cooper plate,** 1938–39, 9in (23cm) diam.
**£70–80  Banana Dance** ⊞

**A Susie Cooper plate,** decorated with Cockerel pattern, 1938–39, 6½in (16.5cm) diam.
**£45–50  Beverley** ⊞

**A Susie Cooper tea cup and saucer,** decorated with sgraffito Crescents pattern, 1936, cup 3½in (9cm) diam.
**£50–60  Beverley** ⊞

**A Susie Cooper cheese dish,** decorated with Sea Anemone pattern, 1938–39, 8½in (21.5cm) wide.
**£100–115  Beverley** ⊞

**A Susie Cooper Quail tea service for two,** decorated with Wild Strawberry pattern, 1950s, teapot 5in (12.5cm) high.
**£250–280  Beverley** ⊞

**A Susie Cooper part dinner service,** comprising 31 pieces, decorated with Whispering Grass pattern, c1960, milk jug 4in (10cm) high.
**£90–100  Tenterden Antiques** ⊞
*Part services were never popular before the Internet age. Collectors can now buy a part set to obtain a particular piece, then sell the rest on line, hopefully making a good profit.*

Bearing her facsimile signature, this mark was used between 1932 and 1956. Note the pattern number – always the best clue to more accurate dating.

This simpler version of the signature mark was used between 1932 and 1964.

Dating to the post-WWII period and in use from 1950 to 1966, this mark often includes (as here) the pattern name.

In 1966, Susie Cooper Pottery was taken over by Wedgwood. This mark dates to that period and tends to be seen on items made between 1966 and 1968.

# COTTAGE WARES

A Royal Caledonia model of John Knox's house, c1910, 4in (10cm) high.

**£110–125 Scottish Antique & Arts** ⊞

A Harlow model of Ye Old Village Shop, by A. Saalheimer, c1910, 5in (12.5cm) wide.

**£120–135 Scottish Antique & Arts** ⊞

A Leadbeater model of Stokesay Castle gatehouse, c1920, 5in (12.5cm) wide.

**£80–90 Scottish Antique & Arts** ⊞
*Edwin Leadbeater produced ceramic wares at the Drury Place pottery between 1920 and 1924.*

A Lilliput Lane model of Greenstead Church, 1989, 4in (10cm) high.

**£25–30 Heirloom Antiques** ⊞

A David Winter model of The Rectory, by John Hine, English Village Collection, 1993, 3½in (9cm) high.

**£25–30 British Collectibles** ⊞

A David Winter model of Mr Turner's Cottage, by Enesco, 1999, 9in (23cm) high.

**£15–20 British Collectibles** ⊞

A Hazle Ceramics model of Nancy Kell, Amersham, 1999–2005, 6¼in (16cm) wide.

**£175–210 Hazle Ceramics** ⚒

A Hazle Ceramics model of African Crafts, Out of Africa series, issued 2004, 6¼in (16cm) high.

**£340–380 John English** ⊞

A Hazle Ceramics model of Marks & Spencer, 1999–2005, 4in (10cm) wide.

**£200–230 John English** ⊞
*This mould was based on the Liverpool branch of Marks & Spencer in 1903.*

A Hazle Ceramics model of The Village Newsagent, 2001–04, 4¼in (11cm) wide.

**£180–200 John English** ⊞

# CRESTED CHINA

An Albion China model of a Salisbury kettle, with Derby crest, early 20thC.
**£5–10 ReMemories** ⊞

An Arcadian model of a cockerel, with Eynsham Abbey crest, early 20thC, 4in (10cm) high.
**£35–40 Tenterden Antiques** ⊞

An Arcadian jug, with Lewes crest, early 20thC, 3¾in (9.5cm) high.
**£5–10 Tenterden Antiques** ⊞

An Arcadian model of a sailor winding a capstan, with New Milton crest, 1914–18, 4¼in (11cm) high.
**£125–140 Goss & Crested Club** ⊞

An Arcadian model of Shakespeare's house, with City of London crest, c1920, 3in (7.5cm) wide.
**£15–20**
**Scottish Antique & Arts Centre** ⊞

A Goss jug, with Dundee crest, early 20thC, 3in (7.5cm) high.
**£15–20 Tenterden Antiques** ⊞

A Norfolk Crest China model of a Red Cross van, with Canterbury crest, c1919, 2in (7cm) high.
**£60–70 J & M Collectables** ⊞

A Goss wall vase, with Shoreham crest, early 20thC, 3in (7.5cm) long.
**£15–20 Tenterden Antiques** ⊞

A model of a teapot, with Cork crest, Czechoslovakia, early 20thC, 3in (7.5cm) long.
**£15–20 Tenterden Antiques** ⊞

A model of a swan, with Skegness crest, marked 'Gemma', Czechoslovakia, early 20thC, 3¼in (8.5cm) high.
**£5–10 ReMemories** ⊞

A model of a jug, with Ramsgate crest, marked 'Gemma', Czechoslovakia, early 20thC, 2¾in (7cm) high.
**£15–20 Tenterden Antiques** ⊞

# CROWN DEVON

A Crown Devon biscuit barrel, with hand-painted decoration, 1930, 6in (15cm) high.
**£80–90 Beverley** ⊞

A Crown Devon vase, c1930, 7in (18cm) high.
**£15–20 Tenterden Antiques** ⊞

A Crown Devon Grounger jug, shape No. 900, hand-painted with a leaf design, 1930s backstamp, 4½in (11.5cm) high.
**£30–35 Decorative Antiques** ⊞

A Crown Devon jug and saucer, marked, 1930s, jug 3in (7.5cm) high.
**£5–10 New 2 You** ⊞

A Crown Devon vase, shape No. 371, pattern No. M238, 1930s, 5in (12.5cm) high.
**£15–20 Swan at Tetsworth** ⊞

A Crown Devon vase, decorated with Fairy Castle pattern, 1920s, 8in (20.5cm) high.
**£1,000–1,200 Design Gallery** ⊞

A Crown Devon Mattajade vase, decorated with Fairy Castle pattern, c1930, 8in (20.5cm) high.
**£1,000–1,100 Gazelles** ⊞
*Mattajade, launched in 1932 at the British Industries Fair, must be Crown Devon's most sought-after range. It was introduced by Enoch Boulton and the style of his previous employers, Carlton Ware, is self evident.*

A Crown Devon Mattajade vase, decorated with Fairy Castle pattern, 1930s, 8in (20.5cm) high.
**£850–950 Beverley** ⊞

A Crown Devon vase, 1940s, 3½in (9cm) high.
**£100–115 Beth** ⊞

# DENBY

A Denby stoneware bowl, 1920s, 7in (18cm) diam.

**£50–55 ReMemories** ⊞

A Denby model of a terrier, c1935, 3in (7.5cm) long.

**£85–95 Steven Bishop** ⊞

A Denby Danesby ware model of a French bulldog, 'Byngo', 1930s, 6in (15.5cm) high.

**£30–35 Anthony Welling** 🔨
*Byngo, the French bulldog, is a popular character in Denby's Danesby range. He is available in a number of colourways and always has one dark ear.*

A Denby Danesby ware rabbit, 1930s, 3¼in (8.5cm) high.

**£20–25 ReMemories** ⊞
*Danesby was Denby's tradename for its decorative wares.*

A Denby vase, 1930s, 10½in (26.5cm) high.

**£40–45 ReMemories** ⊞

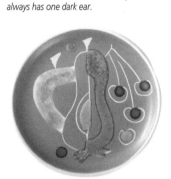

A Denby cloisonné coaster, by Glyn and Albert Colledge, 1957, 3½in (9cm) diam.

**£15–20 retroselect** ⊞

A Denby cruet set, by Glyn Colledge, marked, 1957, tray 8¾in (22cm) long.

**£35–40 retroselect** ⊞

Two Denby Burlington vases, by Glyn and Albert Colledge, 1959, larger 14½in (37cm) high.

**£30–35 Kevin Ward** ⊞
*The smaller vase is 9in (23cm) high and worth less, at around £10.*

A Denby trio, decorated with Gypsy pattern, marked, c1972, cup 2¼in (5.5cm) high.

**£5–10 New 2 You** ⊞
*Gypsy, designed by Trish Seal, was launched as an export range in 1971 and appeared in Britain a year later. Look out for the colour-co-ordinating 'Touchstone' cutlery by Gill Pemberton and husband Neil Harding, which was made to complement the range.*

A Denby milk jug, decorated with Falling Leaves pattern, c1984, 4in (10cm) high.

**£15–20 Chinasearch** ⊞

## T. G. GREEN

A T. G. Green Cornish Ware jug, 1920,
8in (20.5cm) high.

**£55–65 Jane Wicks** ⊞

A T. G. Green Cornish Ware jar, inscribed
'Ground Almonds', black shield backstamp,
c1930, 6½in (16.5cm) high.

**£135–150 cornishware** ⊞

A T. G. Green Cornish Ware fireproof dish,
Church Gresley backstamp, 1920s–40s,
10½in (26.5cm) diam.

**£180–200 Cornishware Search** ⊞

A T. G. Green Cornish Ware teapot, green
shield backstamp, c1950, 4½in (11.5cm) high.

**£125–140 cornishware** ⊞

A T. G. Green Cornish Ware cruet set and tray,
green shield backstamp, c1950, 6in (15cm) diam.

**£80–90 cornishware** ⊞

A T. G. Green Cornish Ware box, green shield
backstamp, 1930s–50s, 5½in (14cm) square.

**£270–300 Cornishware Search** ⊞

A T. G. Green Cornish Ware Melior
Cafétière, green shield backstamp, c1950,
5in (12.5cm) high.

**£250–280 cornishware** ⊞

A T. G. Green Cornish Ware vinegar bottle,
1950s–60s, 8¾in (22cm) high.

**£450–500 Cornishware Search** ⊞
*This item was produced for the
Continental market.*

A T. G. Green Cornish Ware Dreadnought
jug, green shield backstamp, c1950,
4½in (11.5cm) high.

**£25–30 cornishware** ⊞

A T. G. Green Cornish Ware butter dish and
cover, Church Gresley backstamp, c1980,
7½in (19cm) diam.

**£15–20 cornishware** ⊞

A T. G. Green Cornish Ware double egg cup,
c1980, 3¼in (8.5cm) high.

**£60–70 Cornishware Search** ⊞

A T. G. Green Cornish Ware butter dish and cover, c1950, 6in (15cm) high.

**£50–60   cornishware** ⊞

A T. G. Green Cornish Ware mixing bowl, 1950s–60s, 10½in (27cm) diam.

**£60–70   Cornishware Search** ⊞

A T. G. Green Cornish Ware Dreadnought jug, c1967, 3¼in (8cm) high.

**£45–50   Cornishware Search** ⊞
*This is one of the earliest gold Cornish Ware pieces.*

A T. G. Green Cornish Ware coffee pot, green shield backstamp, 1967, 7½in (19cm) high.

**£100–120   Cornishware Search** ⊞

A pair of T. G. Green Cornish Ware salt and pepper pots, target backstamp, c1970, 4¾in (12cm) high.

**£360–400   cornishware** ⊞
*Black Cornishware is very rare.*

A T. G. Green Cornish Ware Country Road utensils jar, Cloverleaf backstamp, c1990, 5½in (14cm) high.

**£20–25   cornishware** ⊞

A T. G. Green storage jar, late 1990s, 6¼in (16cm) high.

**£45–50**
**Cornishware Search** ⊞
*This storage jar was made as a trial piece.*

A T. G. Green Cornish Ware tureen, decorated with Grassmere pattern, c1935, 10in (25.5cm) diam.
**£25–30 cornishware** ⊞

A T. G. Green Blue Domino toast rack, marked, 1930s–60s, 6¼in (16cm) long.
**£60–70 Cornishware Search** ⊞

A T. G. Green trio, decorated with Safari pattern, 1960s–70s.
**£25–30 Pineapple Ice Bucket** ⊞

A T. G. Green Easimix mixing bowl, 1960s, 10in (25.5cm) diam.
**£15–20 Quay Centre** ⊞
*The flat panelled side allowed the bowl to be tilted forward to rest on the table, which made mixing and whisking far easier.*

A T. G. Green Gripstand mixing bowl, marked, 1970s, 13in (33cm) diam.
**£10–15 New 2 You** ⊞

## ESSENTIAL REFERENCE STREAMLINE

A T. G. Green Streamline storage jar, inscribed 'Baking-Powder', 1930s, 4in (10cm) high.
**£75–85 Scherazade** ⊞

A T. G. Green Streamline storage jar, inscribed 'Lump Sugar', 1935–49, 6¼in (16cm) high.
**£100–120 Cornishware Search** ⊞

A T. G. Green Streamline storage jar, inscribed 'Bread Crumbs', 1935–49, 5in (12.5cm) high.
**£145–160 Cornishware Search** ⊞

Apart from the famous Cornish blue range, T. G. Green produced many other lesser known designs. Streamline was produced from the mid-1930s up to the mid-'50s. Its matt glaze and 'streamlined' shape and decoration perfectly evoke the period in which it was made. Long overlooked, it is now commanding the attention of collectors.

# HORNSEA

A Hornsea Studio slipware dish, 1955–56, 4in (10cm) wide.

**£5–10 20th Century Marks** ⊞

*In the 1950s, the government increased purchase tax on leisure goods, which included ashtrays. Hornsea and other potteries came up with a line of bonbon dishes to avoid the surcharge.*

A Hornsea fawn and log posy vase, from the Fauna range, 1956–59, 5½in (14cm) wide.

**£5–10 Tenterden Antiques** ⊞

A Hornsea Studio jardinière, mould No. 376, with flower holder, 1960–62, 13in (33cm) wide.

**£30–35 Hemswell Antique Centre** ⊞
*This jardinière originally sold for 17s 6d.*

A Hornsea Summit butter/cheese dish, marked, 1962–65, tray 17¾in (45cm) wide.

**£20–25 20th Century Marks** ⊞

*Summit was launched in 1960 and remained in production for many years. The simple shapes were inspired by designer John Clappison playing with sheets of cartridge paper and making simple forms. These experiments lead to the basic range of functional items. The ridged surface was produced in the mould and the coloured 'inlay' was, in fact, produced by spraying the piece then wiping off the excess, the colour remaining in the grooves.*

A Hornsea White Wedding vase, mould No. 828, 1962–66, 8in (20.5cm) high.

**£25–30 Hemswell Antique Centre** ⊞

A Hornsea Gaiety pot, slight damage, 1964–65, 5in (13cm) high.

**£25–30 retroselect** ⊞

A Hornsea pepper pot, by John Clappison, decorated with Fish pattern, 1977, 2¼in (5.5cm) high.

**£15 retroselect** ⊞

A Hornsea Love mug, by Ken Townsend, 1977, 3¼in (8.5cm) high.

**£25–30 retroselect** ⊞

*These were marketed as Young Lovers' mugs in the US. Value varies depending on who happens to be looking for a particular month at any given time.*

A set of four Hornsea Coral teacups and saucers, marked, 1980, cup 2¼in (5.5cm) high.

**£15–20 New 2 You** ⊞

A pair of Goebel figures, 'Umbrella Boy' and 'Umbrella Girl', Germany, 1950s, 12in (30.5cm) high.

**£100–125 Locke & England** 🔨

A Goebel Hummel figure of a girl in a tree, 'Apple Tree Girl', Germany, c1960, 6in (15cm) high.

**£100–120 ReMemories** ⊞

A Goebel Hummel wall vase, Germany, c1960, 4½in (11.5cm) high.

**£55–65 ReMemories** ⊞

A Goebel Hummel figure, 'School Boy', Germany, c1970, 5¼in (13.5cm) high.

**£75–85 Tenterden Antiques** ⊞

A Goebel Hummel figure, 'Star Gazer', c1970, 5¼in (13.5cm) high.

**£55–65 ReMemories** ⊞

A Goebel Hummel figure, 'Wayside Harmony', Germany, c1970, 4¼in (11cm) wide.

**£50–55 ReMemories** ⊞

A Goebel Hummel figure, 'Chick Girl', Germany, c1970, 4in (10cm) high.

**£40–45 ReMemories** ⊞

A Goebel Hummel figure, 'Little Goat Herder', Germany, c1970, 4¾in (12cm) high.

**£70–80 ReMemories** ⊞

A Goebel Hummel figure, 'Little Helper', Germany, c1970, 4¼in (11cm) high.

**£30–35 ReMemories** ⊞ ⊞

A Goebel Hummel figure, 'Singing Lesson', c1970, 3¼in (8.5cm) high.

**£35–40 ReMemories** ⊞

A Goebel Hummel plaque, 'Merry Wanderer', 1964–72, 6in (15cm) wide.

**£170–185 Tenterden Antiques** ⊞

# EXPERT EYE  A HUMMEL FIGURE

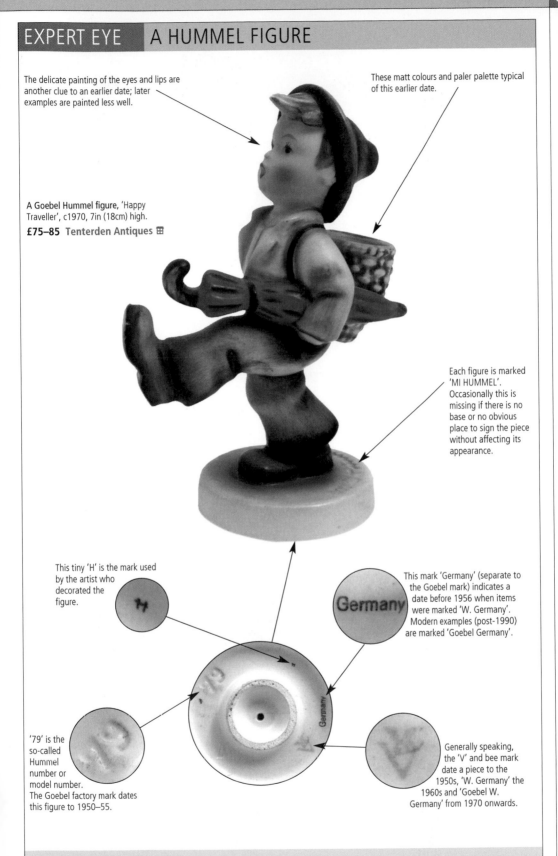

The delicate painting of the eyes and lips are another clue to an earlier date; later examples are painted less well.

These matt colours and paler palette typical of this earlier date.

A Goebel Hummel figure, 'Happy Traveller', c1970, 7in (18cm) high.
**£75–85 Tenterden Antiques** ⊞

Each figure is marked 'MI HUMMEL'. Occasionally this is missing if there is no base or no obvious place to sign the piece without affecting its appearance.

This tiny 'H' is the mark used by the artist who decorated the figure.

This mark 'Germany' (separate to the Goebel mark) indicates a date before 1956 when items were marked 'W. Germany'. Modern examples (post-1990) are marked 'Goebel Germany'.

'79' is the so-called Hummel number or model number. The Goebel factory mark dates this figure to 1950–55.

Generally speaking, the 'V' and bee mark date a piece to the 1950s, 'W. Germany' the 1960s and 'Goebel W. Germany' from 1970 onwards.

Born in 1909, Bertha Hummel became Sister Maria Innocenta Hummel on entering the Franciscan Convent of Siessen in 1931. A skilled artist, she continued to draw pictures of country children after entering the convent. She was approached by the firm of W. Goebel in 1935 to design an exclusive range of figures which were launched at the Leipzig Spring Fair in 1935. These figures were instantly successful and although Sister Hummel died in 1946 production continued. They are still popular today.

LENCI

# LENCI

A Lenci figure of a woman, 'Nudino', by Elena König Scavini, Italy, c1930, 7in (18cm) high.
**£1,500–1,700 Muir Hewitt** ⊞

A Lenci figural group of a peasant girl and rabbit, 'Ave Maria', by Elena König Scavini, Italy, c1932, 13in (33cm) high.
**£4,000–4,500 Andrew Muir** ⊞

A Lenci figure, 'Maternita', Italy, 1930s, 13in (33cm) high.
**£2,000–2,200 Andrew Muir** ⊞

A Lenci model of a fish, by Elena König Scavini, Italy, 1930s, 11in (28cm) high.
**£2,700–3,000 Andrew Muir** ⊞

A Lenci figure of a reclining woman, 'Nudino Disteso', by Elena König Scavini, Italy, c1932, 16in (40.5cm) long.
**£4,500–5,000 Andrew Muir** ⊞

A Lenci figural group, 'Nudino su Ippopatamo', by Elena König Scavini, Italy, 1935, 11in (28cm) high.
**£4,500–5,000 Andrew Muir** ⊞

## MARKET INFORMATION COLLECTING LENCI

- Lenci's distinctive figures have been growing in popularity with discerning collectors for a number of years. Today, partly due to increased availability outside Italy owing to the internet, they are fast becoming a very hot collectable.

- The company had become famous for its remarkable and well-made felt dolls. Ceramic production began in Turin from 1928, and a vast range of ceramics was made up to 1964.

- Many of the best of these were designed by the owner of the company Elena König Scavini, known as 'Madame Lenci'. The name Lenci originates from the time when Scavini lived in Germany, where she was known as Helenchen to her friends. Lenci is the Italianized version of this name.

- Later Lenci was said to stand for 'Ludus Est Nobis Constanter Industria', a Latin phrase meaning 'play is our constant work'.

- Both the meticulous attention to detail and sense of play give Lenci's models the character that makes them so appealing. Two other factors are their latent sexuality and Art Deco spirit.

- Nudity, a sense of Art Deco style and a dash of fun are all factors that add value to Lenci figures.

- Almost all Lenci figures have an incised signature and are carefully marked 'Lenci Turino' with a date.

- Abele Jacopi is another name that collectors look for. Her figures tend to be a bit more naturalistic, with slightly more rounded, less stylized bodies. Other artists of note are Giuseppe Ronzan, the head decorator from 1930 to 1939, who went on to open his own pottery, and Sandro Vachetti, a skilled modeller who also left to set up a rival firm in 1933. These pieces are marked 'Essevi, Torino' and are collectable in their own right.

# LLADRO

A Lladro figural group of a prince and princess on horseback, model No. 90090, Spain, c1970, 18in (45.5cm) high.

**£170–190 Heritage** ⚒

A Lladro model of a dog in a basket, by Juan Huerta, No. 1128, Spain, 1971–85, 7½in (19cm) high.

**£150–165 KCS Ceramics** ⊞

A Lladro model of a poodle, No. 1259, stamped, Spain, 1975–85, 5½in (14cm) high.

**£160–180 Mary's Memories** ⊞

A Lladro figure, entitled 'Sporting Billy Footballer', model No. 5135, limited edition, Spain, 1982, 9in (23cm) high.

**£200–220 KCS Ceramics** ⊞
*This figure was made for the American market and commissioned for the sports-oriented cartoon Sport Billy. Lladro made a series of different poses, both boy and girl.*

A Lladro figure, by Vincente Martinez, entitled 'Balloons for Sale', model No. 5141, Spain, 1982–96, 10½in (26.5cm) high.

**£150–165 KCS Ceramics** ⊞

A Lladro Figure of a boy holding a book, Spain, 1980s, 8¼in (21cm) high.

**£150–175 Tenterden Antiques** ⊞

A Lladro model of a lion, model No. 5436, marked, Spain, 1987–89, 2¼in (5.5cm) high.

**£110–125 Mary's Memories** ⊞

A Lladro figure of a leaning girl, Spain, 1980s–90s, 7½in (19cm) high.

**£60–70 Tenterden Antiques** ⊞

A Lladro figure, entitled 'Angel Praying', Spain, 2006, 5½in (14cm) high.

**£55–65** Box of Porcelain ⊞

A Lladro figural group of Pierrot with puppy and ball, Spain, 2006, 5in (12.5cm) high.

**£90–100** Box of Porcelain ⊞

A Lladro figure, entitled 'Female Physician', Spain, 2005, 14in (35.5cm) high.

**£165–180** Box of Porcelain ⊞

A Lladro porcelain group, entitled 'Romantic Feeling', Spain, 2007, 12½in (32cm) high.

**£1,800–2,000** Box of Porcelain ⊞

A Lladro group of a boy and a goat, entitled 'Natural Freedom', Spain, 2007, 12in (30.5cm) high.

**£450–500** Box of Porcelain ⊞

## ESSENTIAL REFERENCE  COLLECTING NAO

A Lladro Nao figure of a boy with a football, Spain, 1980s, 9½in (24cm) high.

**£35–40** Tenterden Antiques ⊞

A Lladro Nao figure of a girl, Spain, 1980s–90s, 9½in (24cm) high.

**£35–40** Tenterden Antiques ⊞

A Lladro Nao figure of a young woman, Spain, 1980s–90s, 8½in (21.5cm) high.

**£40–45** Tenterden Antiques ⊞

- Established as a separate brand by the famous Lladro company in 1968 to offer an entry-level collection inspired by the more expensive Lladro figures.
- Originally called Rosal but changed to Nao during the 1970s.
- The name is from a type of sailing ship called a 'Nao'.
- Although very similar in subject and design, Nao figures do not have the hand-finished work of the main Lladro ranges.

# MIDWINTER

A Midwinter Stylecraft milk jug, by Jessie Tait, decorated with Red Domino pattern, 1950, 6in (15cm) high.

**£25–30  Jane Wicks** ⊞

A Midwinter Stylecraft Fashion coffee service, with six cups and saucers, 1950s, coffee pot, 7½in (19cm) high.

**£40–45  Luna** ⊞

A Midwinter vase, marked, 1950s, 10¾in (27cm) high.

**£25–30  retroselect** ⊞

A Midwinter coffee service, by David Queensbury, with six cups and saucers, 1962–78, coffee pot 8½in (21.5cm) high.

**£35–40  Luna** ⊞

A Midwinter Stonehenge teapot, by Eve Midwinter, decorated with Spring Blue pattern, 1974, 7in (18cm) high.

**£40–45  Chinasearch** ⊞

*Born in 1926 Eve Midwinter was married to Roy Midwinter. She produced a small range of designs for the firm from 1960, but is best remembered for her striking patterns of the 1970s and 80s. Her 'Creation' glaze, shown here, was a revolution. Formulated with tiny specks in the glaze it was a great success.*

## ESSENTIAL REFERENCE  JESSIE TAIT

A Midwinter Savanna vase, by Jessie Tait, c1950, 7in (18cm) high.

**£120–135  Beth** ⊞

A Midwinter Magic Moments cup and saucer, by Jessie Tait, 1960, cup 3in (7.5cm) diam.

**£10–15  retroselect** ⊞

A Midwinter plate, by Jessie Tait, decorated with Simple Stripe pattern, 1965.

**£10–15  retroselect** ⊞

• Born Dorothy Jessie Tait in 1928, she was always known as 'Jessie'.

• After studying at the famous Burslem School of art she began working for Charlotte Rhead, but soon joined Midwinter as a designer in 1947.

• She is principally remembered for her innovative designs for Midwinter's Stylecraft range launched in 1953.

• Jessie continued as principle designer at Midwinter until the 1960s.

MOORCROFT

# MOORCROFT

A Moorcroft Macintyre Florian Ware vase, handles restored, painted signature and printed mark, early 20thC, 9½in (24cm) high.

**£380–460 Gorringes (L)**

A Moorcroft Macintyre Florian Ware vase, decorated with a landscape design, printed marks and signature to base, c1903, 11¾in (30cm) high.

**£2,800–3,400 Gorringes (L)**

A Moorcroft sugar bowl and cover, decorated with Eventide pattern, original paper label, c1925, 4in (10cm) diam.

**£1,500–1,650 Fountain Antiques** ⊞

A Moorcroft bowl, decorated with Spanish pattern, 1920s, 10in (25.5cm) wide.

**£1,000–1,200 Andrew Hartley**

A Moorcroft baluster vase, decorated with Freesia pattern, impressed mark and painted signature, 1935–40, 12½in (32cm) high.

**£700–850 Bearnes**

A Moorcroft perfume bottle and stopper, decorated with Spring Flowers pattern, 1939–49, 6in (15cm) high.

**£630–700 Glazed Over** ⊞

A Moorcroft vase, decorated with Hibiscus pattern, impressed mark, original paper label, 1930–50, 12½in (32cm) high.

**£200–260 Maxwell's**

A Moorcroft vase, decorated with Leaves and Fruit pattern, 1950–58, 5½in (14cm) high.

**£300–330 Glazed Over** ⊞

A Moorcroft vase, decorated with Anemone pattern, impressed mark, original paper label, 1930–50, 8½in (21.5cm) high.

**£240–290 Maxwell's**

A Moorcroft bowl and cover, decorated with Hibiscus pattern, impressed mark, paper royal warrant, c1953, 10¼in (26cm) diam.

**£220–270 Rosebery's**

A Moorcroft Rarotonga vase, painted and impressed marks, dated 1998, 3½in (9cm) high.

**£175–195 ReMemories ⊞**
*This lizard vase was designed by Emma Bossons as part of the Dateline series to mark the Millennium.*

A Moorcroft Cleopatra Blues vase, by Sian Leeper, shape No. 62/4, impressed with maple leaf mark, 2000, 4¼in (11cm) high.

**£115–130 Moorcroft Antiques ⊞**

A Moorcroft Wanderer's Sky vase, by Emma Bossons, painted and printed marks, 2003, 7¼in (18.5cm) high.

**£300–360 Penrith Farmers' and Kidd's** ⚒
*A year later, designer Emma Bossons replaced the vibrant turquoise sky with dark blue and the range was renamed Evening Sky.*

A Moorcroft Knypersley vase, marked, 2004, 4¼in (11cm) high.

**£75–90 Bentley's** ⚒

A Moorcroft Ragged Poppy vase, by Nicola Slaney, from Midsummer Surprise collection, octagon year stamp, 2004, 14in (35.5cm) high.

**£300–350 Box of Porcelain ⊞**

A Moorcroft Plevriana vase, marked, 2004, 7½in (19cm) high.

**£150–180 Bentley's** ⚒
*The Plevriana vase was named after a small village in Crete.*

A Moorcroft The Gardeners vase, by Kerry Goodwin, limited edition, 2006, 14in (35.5cm) high.

**£500–550 Box of Porcelain ⊞**
*With its decoration of black scarab beetles, this vase was known at the factory as 'the beetles pot'. Despite initial fears that the beetle would affect sales, it sold out instantly.*

A Moorcroft Shimba Hills jug, by Sian Leeper, limited edition, 2006, 12in (30.5cm) high.

**£840–930 Box of Porcelain ⊞**

# KEITH MURRAY

A Wedgwood earthenware vase, by Keith Murray, shape No. 3820, printed mark, 1930s, 6¾in (17cm) high.
**£450–540 Woolley & Wallis** 🔨

A Wedgwood black basalt vase, by Keith Murray, signed, c1930, 9in (23cm) high.
**£2,000–2,200 Gazelles** ⊞

A Wedgwood earthenware vase, by Keith Murray, shape No. 4325, printed and impressed marks, facsimile signature, 1930s, 10¼in (26cm) high.
**£350–420 Woolley & Wallis** 🔨

A Wedgwood vase, by Keith Murray, shape No. 3802, 1933, 6½in (16.5cm) high.
**£360–400 Beverley** ⊞

A Wedgwood mug, by Keith Murray, signed, c1930s, 5in (12.5cm) high.
**£90–100 Beverley** ⊞

A Wedgwood bowl, by Keith Murray, 1930s, 5in (12.5cm) high.
**£270–300 Beverley** ⊞

A Wedgwood vase, by Keith Murray, printed marks, 1930s, 7½in (19cm) high.
**£500–550 Beverley** ⊞

A Wedgwood vase, by Keith Murray, shape No. 3801, printed marks, 1933, 6in (15cm) high.
**£360–400 Beverley** ⊞

A Wedgwood mug, by Keith Murray, c1930s, 5½in (14cm) high.
**£100–115 Beverley** ⊞

# MYOTT

A Myott Persian jug, with hand-painted decoration, pattern No. 8301c, 1930, 6¾in (17cm) high.

**£35–40 Tenterden Antiques** ⊞

A Myott Persian jug, pattern No. 8679, 1930s, 8in (20.5cm) high.

**£40–45 Myott Collectors Club** ⊞

A Myott Persian jug, crown mark, pattern No. 8387, 1930s, 7in (18cm) high.

**£50–55 Moorcroft Antiques** ⊞

A Myott Round jug, pattern No. BG98, 1930s, 6¾in (17cm) high.

**£200–250 Myott Collectors Club** ⊞

A Myott jug, with hand-painted decoration, the handle modelled as a cat, 1930s, 8½in (21.5cm) high.

**£1,100–1,300 Gale & Sons** ⊞

A Myott Trumpet jug, pattern No. 9732, 1930s, 8½in (21.5cm) high.

**£130–145 Myott Collectors Club** ⊞

A Myott Egyptian jug, pattern No. 9811, 1930s, 7½in (19cm) high.

**£130–145 Myott Collectors Club** ⊞

A Myott Bow Tie jug, pattern No. 9764, 1930s, 7½in (19cm) high.

**£200–250 Myott Collectors Club** ⊞

A Myott Torpedo vase, pattern No. 8979, 1930s, 8½in (21.5cm) high.
**£450–500** Myott Collectors Club ⊞

A Myott Overflow vase, with ceramic insert, pattern No. P9469, 1930s, 6½in (16.5cm) high.
**£250–280** Myott Collectors Club ⊞

A Myott Overflow vase, pattern No. P9652, ceramic insert missing, 1930s, 6½in (16.5cm) high.
**£155–175** Myott Collectors Club ⊞

A Myott Torpedo vase, pattern No. 9114, 1930s, 8½in (21.5cm) high.
**£360–400** Myott Collectors Club ⊞
*Collectors love the funky – so British – shapes of Myott's 1930s wares. New research is discovering the original names of shapes, but some are just known by nicknames given to them by collectors. This is known as a Torpedo vase and is one of the most desirable shapes.*

## ESSENTIAL REFERENCE DECO SHAPES

A Myott Moderne vase, pattern No. 8669, 1930s, 6½in (16.5cm) high.
**£110–125** Myott Collectors Club ⊞

A Myott Diamond planter, with ceramic insert, pattern No. 8945, 1930s, 10½in (26.5cm) wide.
**£135–145** Myott Collectors Club ⊞

A Myott Fan vase, pattern No. 9111, 1930s, 8½in (21.5cm) high.
**£260–290** Myott Collectors Club ⊞

A Myott Bow Tie vase, with ceramic insert, pattern No. 9761, 1930s, 8in (20.5cm) high.
**£200–230** Myott Collectors Club ⊞

A Myott Square jug, pattern No. 8697, 1930s, 8¼in (21cm) high.
**£200–250** Myott Collectors Club ⊞

• Myott are beginning to be recognized for their quirky and very Art Deco shapes and designs.

• Quite different to their competitors, the style and distinctive patterns developed at Myott & Sons Alexander Pottery stand out from the crowd.

• For many years little was known about this factory but new research is finally bearing fruit. The real names for some shapes are known, but others are named after collector's nicknames.

• The so-called Pinch Neck jug was originally known as a Persian jug, said to have been designed after a Persian jug in the collection of Ashley Myott, one of the founders of the pottery.

• The publication in 2003 of *The Mystery of Myott* by Anne Myott and Philip Pollitt will no doubt help the prices of Myott to rise even further.

PENDELFIN

# PENDELFIN

**A Pendelfin Lucy Pocket model,** by Jean Walmsley Heap, 1960–67, 3½in (9cm) high.

**£125–135** ReMemories ⊞

*Pendelfins are made from 'stonecraft', a type of plaster. It is very vulnerable to damage, so check carefully for restoration.*

**A Pendelfin Rambler model,** by Doreen Noel Roberts, 1991–2003, 3½in (9cm) high.

**£15–20** ReMemories ⊞

**A Pendelfin Rolly model,** by Jean Walmsley Heap, discontinued 1997, 3½in (9cm) high.

**£10–15** ReMemories ⊞

**A Pendelfin Chuck model,** by Doreen Noel Roberts, 2000–04, 3½in (9cm) high.

**£15–20** ReMemories ⊞

**A Pendelfin Tripper model,** by Jean Walmsley Heap, No. 2065144, introduced 1997, 3½in (9cm) high.

**£15–20** Tintern Antiques ⊞

**A Pendelfin Blazer model,** No. 2062099, 1996–2004, 3½in (9cm) high.

**£20–25** Tintern Antiques ⊞

**A Pendelfin Busker model,** No. 2062542, 1997–2004, 4¼in (11cm) high.

**£20–25** Tintern Antiques ⊞

**A Pendelfin Picnic Midge model,** 1965–99, 4in (10cm) high.

**£5–10** Kingston Antiques ⊞

**A Pendelfin Casanova model,** 3½in (9cm) high.

**£25–30** ReMemories ⊞

*Different colourways can make a big difference to the price. This model of Casanova was also produced with a blue and a red cap.*

# POOLE

A Poole Pottery Aegean charger, designed and painted by Ross Sommerfelt, 1970s, 13in (33cm) diam.

**£260–300 KCS Ceramics** ⊞

*This is a one-off piece and consequently very sought after.*

A Poole Pottery Aegean charger, 1974–75, 12½in (32cm) high.

**£100–120 KCS Ceramics** ⊞

*This charger is a trial piece.*

A Poole Pottery Aegean Vase, by Alan White, decorated by Julia Wills, 1972–78, 9in (23cm) high.

**£95–105 KCS Ceramics** ⊞

A Poole Pottery Aegean vase, with sgraffito decoration, 1970s, 12½in (32cm) high.

**£135–150 KCS Ceramics** ⊞

A Poole Pottery Aegean dish, by Leslie Elsden, decorated by Janet Abury, 1970s, 7in (18cm) long.

**£15–20 ReMemories** ⊞

*Aegean was designed by Leslie Elsden as a replacement for the popular Delphis range. Launched in the 1970s, its dark colour palette was in vogue until the 1980s.*

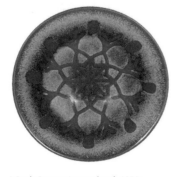

A Poole Pottery Aegean bowl, 1970s, 10¾in (27.5cm) diam.

**£60–70 ReMemories** ⊞

A Poole Pottery Atlantis vase, by Jennie Haigh, 1973–76, 7in (18cm) high.

**£135–150 Poole Room** ⊞

A Poole Pottery Atlantis vase, by Carol Kellet (Cutler), 1976–78, 7in (18cm) high.

**£145–160 KCS Ceramics** ⊞

A Poole Pottery sylvan slipware Atlantis ginger jar, by Guy Sydenham, 1970s, 6in (15cm) high.

**£200–230 KCS Ceramics** ⊞

A Poole Pottery Aegean dish, 1970s, 10½in (26.5cm) diam.

**£55–65 ReMemories** ⊞

A Carter, Stabler & Adams vase, painted by Eileen Prangnell, 1924–37, 6in (15cm) high.

**£160–175 KCS Ceramics** ⊞

A Carter, Stabler & Adams plate, painted by Eileen Prangnell, 1924–37, 8in (20.5cm) diam.

**£110–125 KCS Ceramics** ⊞

A Carter, Stabler & Adams vase, by Truda Adams, painted by Ann Hatchard, 1926–29, 8½in (21.5cm) high.

**£200–220 KCS Ceramics** ⊞

A Carter, Stabler & Adams fruit stand, by Truda Adams, painted by Grace Burge, 1927–29, 4½in (11.5cm) high.

**£80–90 KCS Ceramics** ⊞

A Carter, Stabler & Adams candlestick, 1930s, 9½in (24cm) high.

**£70–80 ReMemories** ⊞

A Carter, Stabler & Adams plate, decorated with a tortoise, c1945, 8¾in (22cm) diam.

**£15–20 ReMemories** ⊞

A Carter, Stabler & Adams vase, decorated with a flower sprig, 1950s, 5in (12.5cm) high.
**£25–30 ReMemories** ⊞

A Carter, Stabler & Adams plate, decorated with CS pattern, 1950s, 9¼in (23.5cm) diam.
**£15–20 ReMemories** ⊞

A Carter, Stabler & Adams dish, 1950s, 4in (10cm) diam.
**£1–5 ReMemories** ⊞

A Carter, Stabler & Adams ring posy vase, 1950s, 5in (12.5cm) diam.
**£20–25 Tenterden Antiques** ⊞

A Carter, Stabler & Adams jam pot and cover, decorated with YO sprig, 1950s, 4½in (11.5cm) high.
**£35–40 ReMemories** ⊞

A Poole Pottery posy trough, decorated with KN sprig, 1960s, 6¼in (16cm) long.
**£10–15 Tenterden Antiques** ⊞

A set of three Poole Pottery egg cups and stand, decorated with a floral design with a bird, 1967–72, cup 2in (5cm) high.
**£20–25 ReMemories** ⊞

A Poole Pottery vase, decorated with a floral design with a bird, 1960s, 5in (12.5cm) high.
**£25–30 ReMemories** ⊞

A Poole Pottery jug, 1970s, 4in (10cm) high.
**£20–25 Tenterden Antiques** ⊞

A Poole Pottery Delphis dish, painted by Jean Millership, 1966–69, 5in (12.5cm) diam.

**£35–40 Poole Room** ⊞

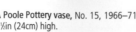

A Poole Pottery vase, No. 15, 1966–71, 9½in (24cm) high.

**£30–35 retroselect** ⊞

A Poole Pottery carved Delphis vase, painted by Josephine Wall, 1967–68, 6in (15cm) high.

**£85–95 Poole Room** ⊞

A Poole Pottery Delphis vase, late 1960s, 8in (20.5cm) high.

**£190–210 KCS Ceramics** ⊞

A Poole Pottery Delphis dish, by Anita Lawrence, 1970s, 5in (12.5cm) diam.

**£20–25 ReMemories** ⊞

A Poole Pottery Delphis dish, 1970s, 12in (30.5cm) diam.

**£30–35 Remy Fine Art** ⊞

## ESSENTIAL REFERENCE — POOLE IN THE 1950S

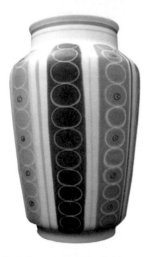

A Poole Pottery vase, painted by Gwen Haskins with PLC pattern, c1959, 9in (23cm) high.

**£150–170 Poole Room** ⊞

A Poole Pottery vase and flower bowl, by Alfred Read, decorated with PQC pattern, 1953–54, 10¾in (27cm) high.

**£360–400 retroselect** ⊞

• Whereas much of Poole's pre-WWII designs had a traditional look, even when the designs were dramatic, the post-war free-form range breaks away from the past entirely.

• New colours and designs painted onto new shapes give this range a strong 'new look'.

• The patterns were designed by Alfred Read who also designed shapes alongside Guy Sydenham.

A Poole Pottery free-form vase, decorated with PJB pattern, 1955, 7½in (19cm) high.

**£135–150 KCS Ceramics** ⊞

A Poole Pottery dish and cover, decorated with a peacock design, c1990, 5in (12.5cm) wide.

**£30–35** Halcyon ⊞

A Poole Pottery planter, decorated with a peacock design, c1990, 5in (12.5cm) high.

**£35–40** Halcyon ⊞

A Poole Pottery vase, decorated with a peacock design, c1990, 10in (25.5cm) high.

**£100–110** Halcyon ⊞

A Poole Pottery charger, decorated with a peacock design, c1990, 16in (40.5cm) diam.

**£100–110** Halcyon ⊞

A Poole Studio Viking charger, by Karen Brown, limited edition of 100, 1998, 16in (40.5cm) wide, boxed.

**£270–300** KCS Ceramics ⊞

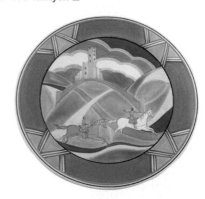

A Poole Pottery Corfe Castle charger, by Karen Brown, limited edition of 100, 1999, 16in (40.5cm) wide, boxed.

**£270–300** KCS Ceramics ⊞

A Poole Pottery Harry Rocks charger, by Karen Brown, limited edition, 1999, 16in (40.5cm) wide, boxed.

**£270–300** KCS Ceramics ⊞

A Poole Pottery Peacock charger, by Anita Harris, factory mark, c2000, 15¾in (40cm) diam.

**£85–105** Rosebery's 🔨

ROSENTHAL

# ROSENTHAL

A Rosenthal model of a dachshund, by Fritz Heidenreich, Germany, c1930, 10in (25.5cm) long.

**£450–500 Scottow Antiques** ⊞

A Rosenthal model of a fawn, Germany, c1930, 4in (10cm) wide.

**£270–300 Scottow Antiques** ⊞

A Rosenthal model of two ducks, Germany, c1937, 7in (18cm) wide.

**£360–400 Scottow Antiques** ⊞

A Rosenthal figure of a woman, by Max D. H. Fritz, entitled 'Liana', Germany, dated 1937, 6in (15cm) high.

**£300–350 Candice Horley** ⊞

A Rosenthal vase, by Tapio Wirkkala, decorated by Rosemonde Nairac, Germany, 1978, 8¼in (21cm) high, with original box.

**£35–40 retroselect** ⊞

A Rosenthal figure of a dancer, by Gustav Oppel, entitled 'Dancer in Blue Tunic', restored, Germany, dated 1937, 12in (30.5cm) high.

**£360–400 Candice Horley** ⊞

A Rosenthal coffee pot, shape by Raymond Loewy, pattern by Lucienne Day, Germany, 1950s–60s, 8in (20.5cm) high.

**£180–200 Pineapple Ice Bucket** ⊞

A Rosenthal plate, by Eduardo Paolozzi, entitled 'Homage to George Orwell', transfer-printed with an abstract design, limited edition of 3000, factory and artist's signatures, Germany, c1984, 10¼in (26cm) diam, with original box.

**£80–100 Rosebery's** ⚒
*Rosenthal has a long record of commissioning great artists to produce designs for them. The late Eduardo Paolozzi produced this limited edition in 1984. Already valuable, it is likely to rise further in the future.*

A Rosenthal cup and saucer, decorated with Flash One pattern, Germany, 1982, cup 3in (7.5cm) diam.

**£15–20 Upstairs Downstairs** ⊞
*This design epitomises the 1980s and as such will increase in value as collectors come to appreciate 'the decade that style forgot'. This first version of the Flash pattern was inspired by graffiti in New York, and a later interpretation is still made today.*

# ROYAL DOULTON

A Royal Doulton character jug, entitled 'Auld Mac', inscribed 'Auld Mac: Bang Went Saxpence', c1938, 6½in (16.5cm) high.

**£135–150 ReMemories** ⊞

*Like many British firms, Royal Doulton suffered from imports of cheap Japanese copies of their wares. They overcame this problem by exploiting a legal loophole which enabled them to register their designs in Australia.*

A Royal Doulton character jug, entitled 'Touchstone', No. D5613, 1936–60, 6in (15cm) high.

**£90–100 ReMemories** ⊞

A Royal Doulton character jug, entitled 'Long John Silver', No. D6335, 1952–78, 7¼in (18.5cm) high.

**£60–70 ReMemories** ⊞

A Royal Doulton character jug, entitled 'The Fortune Teller', No. D6497, 1959–67, 7in (18cm) high.

**£350–400 ReMemories** ⊞

A Royal Doulton character jug, entitled 'Porthos', adapted as a table lighter, No. D6625, 1958, 8in (20.5cm) high.

**£400–450 ReMemories** ⊞
*Royal Doulton frequently adapted their works for different markets. Electric lamps, ashtrays, bookends and even clocks are known to be mounted with Doulton figures.*

A Royal Doulton character Jug, entitled 'Viking', No. D6496, 1959–75, 7in (18cm) high.

**£60–70 Tenterden Antiques** ⊞

A Royal Doulton jug, from the Doultonville Collection, entitled 'Flora Fuchsia', 1986–91, 4½in (11.5cm) high.

**£75–85 Box of Porcelain** ⊞
*Doultonville was a range of novelty figures, such as jugs and candle snuffers, featuring characters that you might have found in the imaginary English village of Doultonville.*

A Royal Doulton character jug, entitled 'Granny', 1934–83, 6¼in (16cm) high.

**£55–65 Mary's Memories** ⊞

A Royal Doulton character jug, entitled 'Mark Twain', No. D6654, 1980, 7in (18cm) high.

**£90–100 ReMemories** ⊞

A Royal Doulton figure, by Leslie Harradine, entitled 'Hinged Parasol', No. HN1579, 1933–49, 6½in (16.5cm) high.

**£1,100–1,250 Pascoe** ⊞

*This is just about all you could want from a Leslie Harradine figure – with so many parts prone to damage collectors will always pay a premium for a perfect example like this.*

A Royal Doulton figural group, by Leslie Harradine, entitled 'Granny's Heritage', No. HN2031, restored, 1944–69, 6in (15cm) wide.

**£160–180 ReMemories** ⊞

*Condition is always paramount where collectors are concerned. This figure has handmade flowers, which are prone to damage. A perfect example will always be worth two- to three-times that of a restored one.*

A Royal Doulton figure, by M. Davies, entitled 'Hermione', HN2058, 1950–52, 7¾in (19.5cm) high.

**£1,100–1,250 Pascoe** ⊞

A Royal Doulton figure, entitled 'A Gentleman from Williamsburg', No. HN2227, 1960–83, 6¾in (17cm) high.

**£160–180 ReMemories** ⊞

A Royal Doulton figure, entitled 'Janine', No. HN2461, 1971–95, 8in (20.5cm) high.

**£90–100 ReMemories** ⊞

A Royal Doulton figure, entitled 'Applause', 2002, 8in (20.5cm) high.

**£135–150 Box of Porcelain** ⊞

## ESSENTIAL REFERENCE DICKENS FIGURES

A Royal Doulton Dickens figure, entitled 'Micawber', first version, c1920s, 4in (10cm) high.

**£85–95 Era Antiques** ⊞

A Royal Doulton Dickens figure, entitled 'Fagin', second version, c1940s, 4in (10cm) high.

**£65–75 Era Antiques** ⊞

A Royal Doulton Dickens figure, entitled 'Buzfuz', 1949–83, 4in (10cm) high.

**£60–70 Box of Porcelain** ⊞

• These miniature Dickens figures were first introduced in 1922 with HN numbers but then renumbered in 1933 with the prefix 'M'.

• Standing only 3½in (9cm) high, they are popular collectables.

• The so-called first versions are the miniatures. These comprise 16 figures at just 3½in (9cm) high which were introduced in 1922.

• Larger, second version, figures were produced from 1923 and reissued in 1938 with slight colour varations.

• A third batch (third version) was produced from 1952. These figues do not have the supporting foliage.

• Generally speaking, earlier versions are the most valued. They often show colour variants or other features that later examples lack.

• Almost all Doulton figures have a number on the base, usually an HN number. These numbers, which can easily be researched in a reference book, enable the figures to be dated.

# EXPERT EYE    A DOULTON FIGURE

It's the attention to detail that collectors appreciate. Look at how finely her face is painted and how the extra touches like the flowers on her hat and the line around her decolleté strengthen the design.

The cushion of the canapé is just the sort of distinguishing touch that we have come to expect from Doulton figures.

Modelled by R. Asplin in 1947 and withdrawn in 1979, 'Belle O' The Ball' is a popular figure. Seated on a canapé, she appears to be waiting for the next dance...or is she just dreaming of a handsome beau?

**A Royal Doulton figure**, entitled 'Belle O' The Ball', No. HN1997, 1947–79, 9in (23cm) wide.
**£270–300 ReMemories** ⊞

This is the HN number that identifies the figure, its designer and date.

Doulton's famous mark identifies a proud heritage.

Many figures, such as this one, are titled.

These are the registration numbers that give copyright protection to the design.

Doulton figures were first introduced in 1913 and are highly popular. Although Royal Doulton had produced some figures before this date, they created a new range in 1912 which was launched with Royal approval in 1913 after the the King and Queen had visited the Burslem factory. A figure called 'Bedtime' was seen by Queen Mary, who declared him to be 'a darling'. Doulton quickly changed its name to 'Darling' and gave it the first number in their system, HN1. The HN was for Harry Nixon, the then head decorator at the pottery. Most Doulton figures have an HN number, making them easy to identify.

ROYAL WINTON

## ROYAL WINTON

A Royal Winton Ann Hathaway's Cottage plate, with hand-painted and embossed decoration, 1930s, 8½in (21.5cm) wide.
**£60–70** Beth ⊞

A Royal Winton Ye Olde Inne plate, with hand-painted and embossed decoration, 1930s, 8½in (21.5cm) wide.
**£55–65** Beth ⊞

A Royal Winton Grimwades child's pixie plate, with embossed decoration, c1930.
**£90–100** Muir Hewitt ⊞

- Pottery of the 1930s is all about colour and these plates are a great example – but look closely as all is not what it seems.

- Mid- to late 1930s' pottery goes big on colour and hand painting.

- Freehand painting was expensive, but factories found ways around this, one of which was embossing. The raised lines acted in the same way as a transfer print, ie it acted as a guide to the decorators.

- The half-timbered cottages are typical features of this type of ware. Referred as 'cottage' wares by potters these chintzy, traditional wares were all the rage in the '30s and appealed to young married couples setting up home. Their semi-detached houses all came with a 'Delft' rack on which to display plates.

- Today these plates are generally undervalued.

- Good examples, such as these by known firms, are popular, but equally bright-and-breezy pieces from less well-known factories can still be found for £50 or less.

A Royal Winton Grimwades Ye Olde Mill jam pot, c1930, 4½in (11.5cm) high.
**£80–90** Beth ⊞

A Royal Winton Petunia pot and cover, 1950s, 4½in (11.5cm) diam.
**£35–40** Beth ⊞

A Royal Winton Grimwades Dovecote vase, 1930s, 6¼in (16cm) high.
**£100–115** Beth ⊞

A Royal Winton Petunia ceramic box and cover, 1950s, 3½in (9cm) wide.
**£45–50** Beth ⊞

A Royal Winton Petunia vase, 1950s, 5½in (14cm) high.
**£35–40** Beth ⊞

# ROYAL WORCESTER

A Royal Worcester model of a chaffinch, 1949, 3in (7.5cm) high.

**£110–125**  Worcester Antiques ⊞

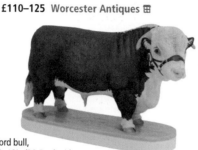

A Royal Worcester figure of John Bull, 1901, 7in (18cm) high.

**£500–550**
**Tony Horsley** ⊞

A Royal Worcester model of a Hereford bull, by Doris Lindner, edition of 500, 1959, 12in (30.5cm) wide.

**£860–950**  Worcester Antiques ⊞

*Doris Linder (1896–1979) was one of many freelance modellers used by Royal Worcester. She began working for the firm in 1930 and is mainly remembered for her animal studies, all of which were taken from life. Linder first modelled her pieces in plasticine, which she always asked to be returned so that it could be reused.*

A Royal Worcester figure, by F. G. Doughty, entitled 'August', 1960s, 5in (12.5cm) high.

**£260–290**  Worcester Antiques ⊞

*Freda G. Doughty (1895–1972) is often credited with saving Royal Worcester from extinction. Her charming figures of children were so popular that they brought an upturn in business. Designing from the early 1930s she was commissioned by Charles Dyson Perrins, the new owner whose personal fortune saved the famous factory from closure.*

# RUSKIN

A Ruskin Pottery flambé vase, impressed mark, dated 1909, 10¾in (27.5cm) high.
**£2,000–2,400 Rosebery's** 🔨

A Ruskin Pottery soufflé vase, decorated with clover leaves, impressed mark, dated 1913, 10in (25.5cm) high.
**£450–500 Fountain Antiques** ⊞

A Ruskin Pottery flambé vase, 1916, 11¾in (30cm) high.
**£2,800–3,200 Fountain Antiques** ⊞
*The flambé technique is highly valued by Ruskin collectors. These pieces were fired in secret, several times. Each firing could potentially destroy the piece, thus making it rarer and more expensive.*

A Ruskin Pottery high-fired vase, impressed mark, early 20thC, 7in (17.5cm) high.
**£880–1,000 Rosebery's** 🔨

A Ruskin Pottery lustre ginger jar, dated 1917, 5in (12.5cm) diam.
**£1,100–1,250 Fountain Antiques** ⊞

A Ruskin Pottery high-fired vase, impressed mark, early 20thC, 4¼in (11cm) high.
**£380–450 Rosebery's** 🔨

A pair of Ruskin Pottery lustre vases, dated 1922, 9in (23cm) high.
**£300–330 Ruskin Decorative Arts** ⊞

A Ruskin Pottery high-fired *sang-de-boeuf* cup and saucer, 1925, 3in (7.5cm) diam.
**£80–90 Fountain Antiques** ⊞

A Ruskin Pottery high-fired *sang-de-boeuf* bowl, 1927, 10in (25.5cm) diam.
**£720–800 Worcester Antiques** ⊞

A Ruskin Pottery jug, with crystalline glaze, 1932, 8in (20.5cm) high.
**£230–260 Worcester Antiques** ⊞

# EXPERT EYE    A RUSKIN VASE

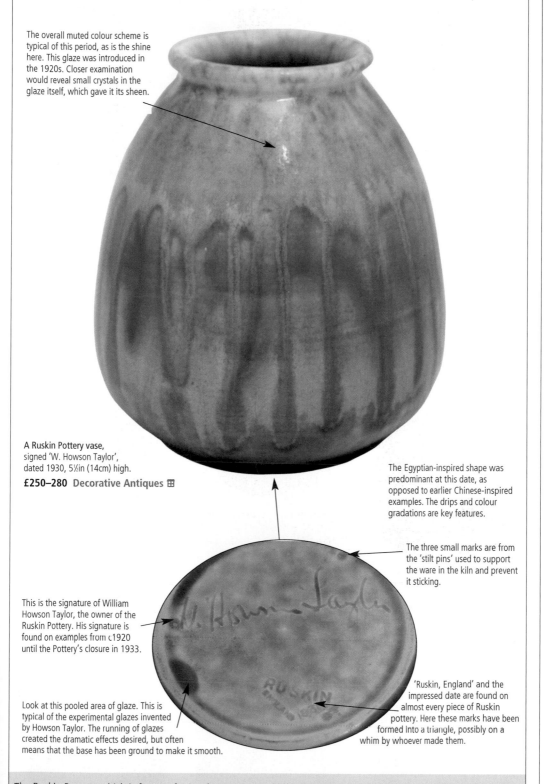

The overall muted colour scheme is typical of this period, as is the shine here. This glaze was introduced in the 1920s. Closer examination would reveal small crystals in the glaze itself, which gave it its sheen.

A Ruskin Pottery vase, signed 'W. Howson Taylor', dated 1930, 5½in (14cm) high.

**£250–280** Decorative Antiques ⊞

The Egyptian-inspired shape was predominant at this date, as opposed to earlier Chinese-inspired examples. The drips and colour gradations are key features.

The three small marks are from the 'stilt pins' used to support the ware in the kiln and prevent it sticking.

This is the signature of William Howson Taylor, the owner of the Ruskin Pottery. His signature is found on examples from c1920 until the Pottery's closure in 1933.

Look at this pooled area of glaze. This is typical of the experimental glazes invented by Howson Taylor. The running of glazes created the dramatic effects desired, but often means that the base has been ground to make it smooth.

'Ruskin, England' and the impressed date are found on almost every piece of Ruskin pottery. Here these marks have been formed into a triangle, possibly on a whim by whoever made them.

The Ruskin Pottery, which is famous for its glazes, was established in 1898 by William Howson Taylor and his father Edward, who was the principle of Birmingham School of Art, in Smethwick near Birmingham. Taylor sought inspiration from the Orient, but was well aware of the work of other potters, particularly those in Scandinavia and the firm enjoyed close links with Rörstrand in Sweden. The best public collection of Ruskin wares is on display at Wednesbury Museum and Art Gallery, not far from the site of the pottery.

# RYE

A Cinque Ports Pottery jug, marked 'The Monastery, Rye', 1950–60s, 6in (15cm) high.

**£40–45** Tenterden Antiques ⊞

A Cinque Ports jardinière, marked 'The Monastery, Rye', 1960s, 4½in (11.5cm) high.

**£5–10** New 2 You ⊞

A Cinque Ports Pottery vase, marked 'The Monastery, Rye', late 1960s, 10½in (26.5cm) high.

**£5–10** New 2 You ⊞

A Cinque Ports Pottery cruet set, 1970s, 7¾in (19.5cm) high.

**£20–25** Tenterden Antiques ⊞

A Cinque Ports Pottery vase, slight damage, 1980s, 9½in (24cm) high.

**£10–15** Tenterden Antiques ⊞

A Cinque Ports Pottery dish, commemorating the Quarter Boys clock, marked 'The Monastery, Rye', 1980s, 5in (12.5cm) diam.

**£20–25** Tenterden Antiques ⊞

A Cinque Ports Pottery advertising dish, 1980s, 5in (12.5cm) diam.

**£20–25** Tenterden Antiques ⊞

An Iden Pottery dish, 1950s, 4½in (11.5cm) diam.

**£20–25** Tenterden Antiques ⊞

An Iden Pottery dish, 1960s,
4½in (11.5cm) diam.

**£20–25 Tenterden Antiques** ⊞

An Iden Pottery mug, marked, 1970s,
3½in (9cm) high.

**£1–5 New 2 You** ⊞

An Iden Pottery souvenir dish, inscribed
'Rye' and decorated with a ship, c1990,
4½in (11.5cm) diam.

**£20–25 Tenterden Antiques** ⊞

A Rye Pottery bowl, c1950s,
9in (23cm) diam.

**£135–150 Eat My Handbag** ⊞

A Rye Pottery jardinière, 1950s,
5¼in (13.5cm) high.

**£55–65 Tenterden Antiques** ⊞

A Rye Pottery jardinière, 1950s,
7¾in (19.5cm) high.

**£50–55 Tenterden Antiques** ⊞

A Rye Pottery dish, 1950s,
7¾in (19.5cm) diam.

**£45–50 Tenterden Antiques** ⊞

A Rye Pottery dish, signed 'TC 70', 1970,
9½in (24cm) high.

**£45–50 Tenterden Antiques** ⊞

A Rye Pottery model of a robin, 1990s,
3¼in (8.5cm) high.

**£20–25 Tenterden Antiques** ⊞

## MARKET INFORMATION | RYE POTTERY

• Rye has had many potteries over the years but the majority of pieces date from the 1950s. The old Bellevue pottery which closed in 1939 was reopened after WWII by Wally and Jack Cole, who renamed it Rye Pottery.

• David Sharp (1932–93) was trained by the Coles. With George Grey he set up Rye Pottery, renamed Cinque Port Pottery in 1956. They became a limited company in the early 1960s and changed their name to Cinque Ports Pottery Ltd – note the 's' on the end of Ports – an important clue to dating.

• Sharp and Grey parted in 1964, Sharp setting up David Sharp Pottery, which is still run by his family today. They produced a wide range of goods but are famous for name plates for houses. George Grey continued with the Cinque Ports name, but moved to larger premises known as The Monastery.

• Although 1950s Rye pottery sells well, later pieces, especially those from the Cinque Ports Pottery, are undervalued.

• Look for the earlier mark, without the words 'The Monastery', which is often seen on more valuable pieces.

• The well-made pots from the 1970s are still freely available and sure to increase in value.

• Dennis Townsend was another pupil of the Coles. In 1959 he opened a pottery in the neighbouring village of Iden. He moved to larger premises in Rye in 1961 but retained the Iden name. Townsend retired in 2002.

# SCANDINAVIAN CERAMICS

**An Aluminia Marselis vase,** by Nils Thorsson, Denmark, 1950s, 5in (12.5cm) high.

**£35–40 Coltman Antiques** ⊞
*Aluminia was founded in 1862 and took over Royal Copenhagen in 1882. Particularly known for art wares produced under Nils Thorsson between 1928 and 1969, the company was renamed Royal Copenhagen in 1969.*

**A Dahl Jensen figure,** 'Sudanese Man with Cockatoo', No. 1305, Denmark, c1925, 9½in (24cm) high.

**£680–750 K & M Antiques** ⊞
*Established in 1925 by Jens Peter Dahl–Jensen in the outskirts of Copenhagen, this small pottery produced many well-modelled figures which are very collectable.*

**A Kahler Keramik earthenware vase,** by Svend Hammershoj, incised mark 'Hak' and impressed mark 'D', Denmark, 1930s–40s, 8in (20.5cm) high.

**£220–250 Freeforms** ⊞

**A Herman A. Kahler Keramik stoneware bottle,** by Nils Kahler, incised signature and mark, Denmark, 1950s, 9¼in (23.5cm) high.

**£260–290 Freeforms** ⊞

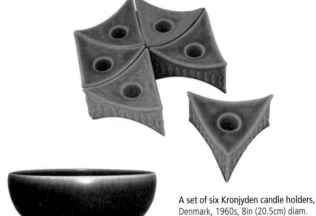

**A Palshus stoneware vase,** decorated with hare's-fur glaze, incised mark, Denmark, 1950s–60s, 3in (7.5cm) high.

**£215–240 Freeforms** ⊞
*Founded in 1948 by Per and Annelise Linneman-Schmitt, Palshus produced simple craft-inspired pieces until the early 1970s. Early examples like this one tend to have matt glazes, but later techniques included incising and rough glazes.*

**A set of six Kronjyden candle holders,** Denmark, 1960s, 8in (20.5cm) diam.

**£35–40 Coltman Antiques** ⊞
*Jens Quistgaard (b1919) is best known for his designs in cutlery and teak produced for Danish firm Dansk. He also produced works freelance including a range of pottery for Kronjyden. .*

**A Royal Copenhagen vase,** decorated with an owl, marked, Denmark, 1894–1922, 8½in (21.5cm) high.

**£65–80 Bentley's** 🪓

**A Royal Copenhagen dish,** Denmark, 1960s, 7in (18cm) diam.

**£20–25 Coltman Antiques** ⊞

**A Saxbo stoneware figural group,** by Jens Jakob Bregno, impressed mark, Denmark, 1930s, 6¾in (17cm) high.

**£380–420 Freeforms** ⊞

A Gustavsberg **Argenta jar and cover,** by Wilhelm Kåge, decorated with undersea scenes, painted and impressed marks, Sweden, 1947, 13½in (34.5cm) high.

**£1,600–1,800 Freeforms** ⊞

*The Argenta range was introduced in 1930 as a prestige line by Wilhelm Kåge and produced up to the 1950s. Other artists used this technique during the 1960s and '70s.*

A Gustavsberg **Farsta earthenware vase,** by Wilhelm Kåge, incised and impressed marks, Sweden, 1949, 9in (23cm) high.

**£990–1,100 Freeforms** ⊞

A Gustavsberg **stoneware vase,** by Berndt Friberg, with hare's-fur glaze, incised marks, Sweden, 1964, 9in (23cm) high.

**£830–930 Freeforms** ⊞

## ESSENTIAL REFERENCE

• Gunnar Nylund (1904– 97), son of a potter and a painter, was a leading figure in both the Danish and Swedish pottery and glass industries.

• He trained as an architect in Copenhagen in the 1920s but turned to ceramic design and joined local firm Bing and Grondahl, where he worked for about five years.

• On leaving Bing & Grondahl he set up his own workshop called Saxbo with colleague Nathalie Krebs. Nylund designed forms while Krebs designed glazes.

• His work brought him to the attention of leading Swedish potters Rörstrand, who offered him a position in 1930. He remained with them until 1959.

• Nylund's pieces often combine grace and utility and they are highly collectable.

A Rörstrand **stoneware vase,** by Gunnar Nylund, with incised marks, Sweden, 1940s–50s, 5¼in (13.5cm) high.

**£295–330 Freeforms** ⊞

A Rörstrand **stoneware vase,** by Gunnar Nylund, with incised marks, Sweden, 1950s, 12in (30.5cm) high.

**£155–175 Freeforms** ⊞

A Gustavsberg **stoneware bowl,** by Berndt Friberg, decorated with hare's-fur glaze, incised mark, Sweden, 1964, 3¼in (8.5cm) wide.

**£250–280 Freeforms** ⊞

An Upsala-Ekeby **vase,** with gilt backstamp, Sweden, 1950s, 8in (20cm) high.

**£25–30 retroselect** ⊞

# SHELLEY

A Shelley jug, c1930, 6½in (16.5cm) high.

**£65–75** Tenterden Antiques ⊞

A Shelley egg cup stand and four egg cups, c1930, 5in (12.5cm) square.

**£20–25** Tenterden Antiques ⊞

A Shelley breakfast cup and saucer, decorated with Rosebud pattern, c1930, cup 3in (7.5cm) high.

**£35–40** Chinasearch ⊞

A Shelley coffee cup and saucer, decorated with Chrysanthemum pattern, c1930, cup 2in (5cm) high.

**£35–40** Chinasearch ⊞

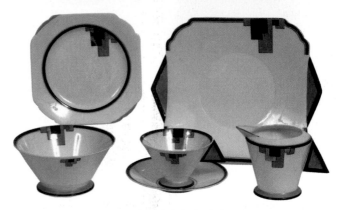

A Shelley Vogue tea service, decorated with Turkish Blue Blocks pattern, c1930, cup 3in (7.5cm) high.

**£750–900** Charterhouse 🔨

A Shelley Mode trio, decorated with Blue J pattern, 1930, 3in (7.5cm) high.

**£270–300** Beverley ⊞
*Mode and Vogue are almost identical shapes. However, Mode has a slightly taller, more conical cup shape.*

A Shelley Regent trio, decorated with Anemone Bunch pattern, 1932, cup 3in (7.5cm) high.

**£100–115** Beverley ⊞

A Shelley sandwich plate, 1930s, 10in (25.5cm) wide.

**£20–25** Old Ironmongers ⊞

A Shelley milk jug plate, decorated with Daffodil Time pattern, 1930s, 3½in (9cm) high.

**£30–35** Chinasearch ⊞

A Shelley vase, decorated with Harmony pattern, No. 923, slight damage, c1930s, 6in (15cm) high.

**£80–90** Decorative Antiques ⊞

# STUDIO POTTERY

An Ian Auld stoneware vase, impressed 'IA' seal, 1960s–70s, 8in (20cm) high.
**£80–100 Rosebery's** ⚒

A Michael Cardew Winchcombe pottery jug, c1930, 5in (12.5cm) high.
**£450–500 Offa's Dyke** ⊞

A Michael Casson stoneware bowl, 1970s–80s, 10in (25.5cm) diam.
**£200–230 Shibusa Gallery** ⊞

An Emanuel Cooper porcelain bowl, 1980s, 7in (18cm) diam.
**£120–135 Shibusa Gallery** ⊞

A Peter Lane porcelain bowl, 1990s, 8¼in (21cm) diam.
**£90–100 Shibusa Gallery** ⊞

A Bernard Leach stoneware tea caddy, BL mark and St Ives seal, 1932–74, 5½in (14cm) high.
**£580–700 Rosebery's** ⚒

A Bernard Leach stoneware vase, monogram and St Ives seal, 1932–74, 3¼in (8cm) high.
**£400–480 Rosebery's**

A Bernard Leach slipware jug, seal mark, 1930s, 3½in (9cm) high.
**£75–85 Ruskin Decorative Arts** ⊞

STUDIO POTTERY

A Shoji Hamada Tenmoku flower vase, with Nuka glaze, 1970s, 6½in (16.5cm) high, in a signed box.

**£1,600–1,800 Shibusa Gallery** ⊞

A Jane Hamlyn salt-glazed stoneware jug, c1980, 4½in (11.5cm) high.

**£40–45 Shibusa Gallery** ⊞

An Ivan Martin slipware jug, 1950s, 12in (30.5cm) high.

**£75–85 Islwyn Watkins** ⊞

An Ivan Martin slipware dish, 1950s, 14in (35.5cm) wide.

**£125–140 Islwyn Watkins** ⊞

A William Newland tin glazed earthenware vase, c1970, 4½in (11.5cm) high.

**£180–200 Shibusa Gallery** ⊞

A Katherine Pleydell-Bouverie pottery bowl, impressed mark, early 20thC, 3½in (9cm) diam.

**£60–75 Charterhouse** ⚒
*Katherine Pleydell–Bouverie was born in 1895. She was a student of Bernard Leach and worked between 1925 and 1985.*

A Dame Lucie Rie stoneware pouring vessel, 'LR' seal, post 1960s, 3¼in (8cm) high.

**£400–480 Rosebery's** ⚒

A Shimaoka Tatsuzo stoneware tea service, with *jomon zogon* inlay, c1970.

**£1,000–1,200 Shibusa Gallery** ⊞

A Winchcombe Pottery slipware jug, by Sidney Tustin, c1940, 4in (10cm) high.

**£35–40 Ruskin Decorative Arts** ⊞

A John Ward stoneware bowl, impressed seal, 1980s, 7in (18cm) high.

**£220–270 Bearnes** ⚒

## EXPERT EYE   WENFORD BRIDGE CREAM JUG

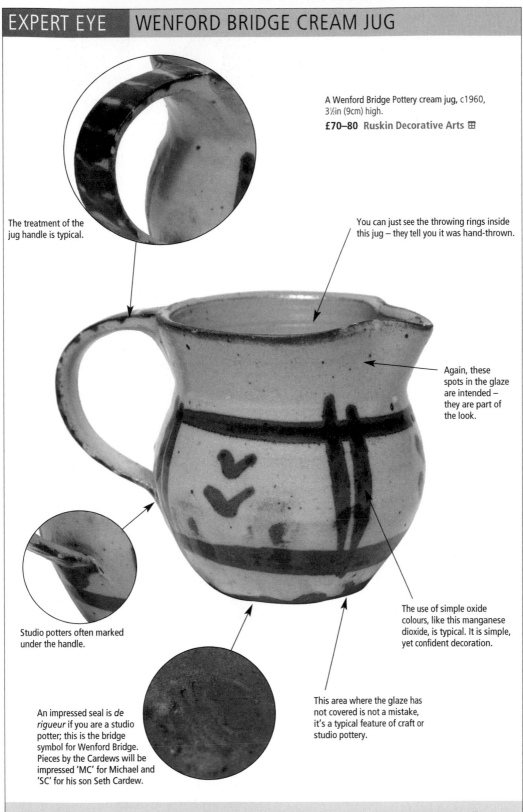

A Wenford Bridge Pottery cream jug, c1960, 3½in (9cm) high.

**£70–80  Ruskin Decorative Arts** ⊞

The treatment of the jug handle is typical.

You can just see the throwing rings inside this jug – they tell you it was hand-thrown.

Again, these spots in the glaze are intended – they are part of the look.

Studio potters often marked under the handle.

The use of simple oxide colours, like this manganese dioxide, is typical. It is simple, yet confident decoration.

An impressed seal is *de rigueur* if you are a studio potter; this is the bridge symbol for Wenford Bridge. Pieces by the Cardews will be impressed 'MC' for Michael and 'SC' for his son Seth Cardew.

This area where the glaze has not covered is not a mistake, it's a typical feature of craft or studio pottery.

Established by Michael Cardew in 1939, the Wenford Bridge pottery began life as a disused public house, the Wenford Inn, which Cardew purchased for £500. Shortly after this war was declared and Cardew retuned to Winchcombe to help Ray Finch until 1942. At this point Cardew was offered a job teaching ceramics in West Africa, where he stayed for the next six years, returning to Wenford in 1948. In 1950 Ivan McMeekin was engaged to run the pottery, which he did until 1954. Between 1954, when McMeekin left for his native Australia and 1965 when Cardew finally returned permanently form Africa, the Wenford Bridge pottery was closed. Joined by his son Seth Cardew in 1971, Michael Cardew continued to work until his death in 1983.

**SYLVAC**

# SYLVAC

A SylvaC model of a rabbit, mould No. 1067, 1930s, 4in (10cm) high.
**£25–30  Kingston Antiques** ⊞

A SylvaC model of a rabbit, 1930s, 5in (12.5cm) high.
**£30–35  Kingston Antiques** ⊞

A SylvaC model of a rabbit, with match striker, 1930s, 4in (10cm) high.
**£75–85  Tenterden Antiques** ⊞

A SylvaC model of a rabbit, 1930s, 5¼in (13.5cm) high.
**£45–50  Tenterden Antiques** ⊞

A pair of SylvaC rabbit book ends, with foil label, 1930s, 5in (12.5cm) high.
**£105–120  Tenterden Antiques** ⊞

A SylvaC model of Harry the Hare, 1930s–50s, 6in (15cm) high.
**£65–75  ReMemories** ⊞

A SylvaC rabbit and mushroom posy vase, 1930s–50s, 6¾in (17cm) high.
**£50–55  ReMemories** ⊞

A SylvaC model of a poodle, 1930s, 5½in (14cm) high.
**£45–50  Tenterden Antiques** ⊞

## MARKET INFORMATION  SYLVAC

• Sylvac green and blue bunnies and dogs have long been a collectors' favourite but values have remained steady, never quite hitting the roof.

• The emergence of fakes in the 1990s affected the market badly. These were usually made from existing figures and so tend to be slightly smaller than the genuine models, although a few were made from original moulds still held at the factory. It is almost impossible to distinguish these fakes.

• Many fakes are marked 'SylvaC Made in England Ware'.

• This mark was used between 1939 and 1950 and will not have a foil label. The presence of a foil label is a good clue to authenticity.

A SylvaC model of Dismal Desmond dog, 1930s, 5in (12.5cm) high.
**£25–30  Tenterden Antiques** ⊞

A SylvaC model of Sammy Dog, 1930s, 9½in (24cm) high.
**£75–85 Remy Fine Art ⊞**

A SylvaC model of a terrier, 1930s–50s, 5in (12.5cm) high.
**£65–75 Remy Fine Art ⊞**

A SylvaC model of a dog, 1930s–50s, 6in (15cm) high.
**£40–45 Remy Fine Art ⊞**

A SylvaC model of a sheepdog, 1930s–50s, 6in (15cm) high.
**£40–45 ReMemories ⊞**

A SylvaC model of a puppy, 1930s–50s, 2¾in (7cm) high.
**£35–40 ReMemories ⊞**

A SylvaC model of a cat, 1930s–50s, 6¾in (17cm) high.
**£35–40 ReMemories ⊞**

A SylvaC model of a horse, 1930s–50s, 6½in (16.5cm) high.
**£55–65 ReMemories ⊞**

A SylvaC Pixie posy vase, 1930s, 2¾in (7cm) high.
**£20–25 Tenterden Antiques ⊞**

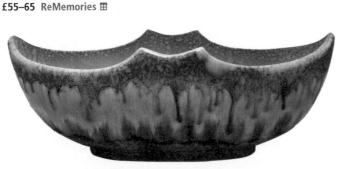

A SylvaC Modern Crescent bowl, scripted backstamp, 1939–50, 12in (30.5cm) diam.
**£35–40 Decorative Antiques ⊞**

A SylvaC beetroot face pot, 1950s, 5½in (14cm) high.
**£15–20 Tenterden Antiques ⊞**

# TROIKA

A Troika Urn vase, attributed to Benny Sirota, decorated with Aztec symbols, incised trident mark, c1963, 10in (25cm) high.

**£700–840 Special Auction Services** ⚒
*Benny Sirota was one of the three founders of the Troika pottery in St Ives, Cornwall in 1963. Sirota was the only one of the three to have had any potting experience, having worked for two years with Douglas Zadek at the Cobham Pottery.*

A Troika vase, marked, 1960s–70s, 8¾in (22.5cm) high.

**£100–120 Wellers Auctioneers** ⚒

A Troika vase, marked, 1960s–70s, 8¾in (22cm) high.

**£90–110 Wellers Auctioneers** ⚒

## ESSENTIAL REFERENCE TROIKA WHEEL VASES

A Troika wheel vase, decorated by Marilyn Pascoe, 1968–74, 7in (18cm) high.

**£150–180 Gorringes (L)** ⚒

A Troika wheel vase, c1970, 4¾in (12cm) high.

**£80–100 Charterhouse** ⚒

A Troika wheel vase, marked, 1970s, 5in (13cm) high.

**£65–75 Rosebery's** ⚒

• Associated with the rough textured wares introduced in 1968, wheel vases are a popular subject in Troika Pottery.

• Ranging in size from a few inches to over 14 in (35.5cm) high they make an impressive display.

• As with all Troika pieces, wheel vases have moulded decoration and are finished by hand.

• The more hand work and the more abstract the design, the more valuable the item will be.

• The wheel shape is also available as lamp bases. Prices for wheel vases, like all Troika, have fallen back recently.

A Troika wheel vase, by Colin Carbis, painted mark, 1976–77, 6¾in (17cm) diam.

**£190–230 Bearnes** ⚒

A Troika vase, c1970, 7in (18cm) high.
£200–250 Maxwell's

A Troika slab vase, marked, artist's monogram, 1970–83, 7in (17.5cm) high.
£160–190 Rosebery's

A Troika double base lamp, decorator's monogram, 1970–83, 13¾in (35cm) high.
£360–420 Bearnes

A Troika vase, by Marilyn Pascoe, inscribed mark, c1972, 14in (35.5cm) high.
£350–420 Sworders

A Troika Cube vase, by Alison Brigden, artist's initials, 1977–83, 15½in (39.5cm) high.
£200–240 Bearnes

A Troika Cube vase, by Alison Brigden, artist's initials, 1977–83, 15½in (39.5cm) high.
£150–180 Bearnes

A Troika ashtray, by Alison Brigden, painted mark, c1980, 7½in (19cm) square.
£130–160 Rosebery's

# US CERAMICS

**A Gabriel vase,** incised mark, America, Pasadena, 1946–62, 6in (15cm) high.

**£15–20 Heritage** ⚒
*The pottery was founded in 1929 by Winfield Leslie Sample in Pasadena, California to make art pottery. Margaret Mears Gabriel joined in 1935 and dinner wares were introduced in 1937. When Sample died in 1939 Gabriel and her husband Arthur took over the pottery and in 1946 sold the Winfield name to American China Products of Santa Monica, California, after which all the products of the Winfield Pasadena pottery were marked 'Gabriel Pasadena'. Douglas Gabriel took over in 1947 and ran the firm until 1962.*

**Four Homer Laughlin Fiesta ware jugs,** America, 1940s–70s, 7½in (19cm) high.

**£40–45 High Street Retro** ⊞
*Still popular today, the Fiesta range was designed by British designer Frederick Hurten Rhead in 1936 and was in production until 1973. It was then reintroduced in 1986, so collectors must check that their jugs are original, pre-1973 Fiesta and not modern copies. Thankfully this is a simple task – all modern jugs have a moulded handle which has a small dimple on the inside where the handle joins the body. Original jugs were hand finished and will be smooth inside.*

**An Iroquois China Co Casual stacking sugar bowl,** by Russel Wright, marked, America, 2¼in (5.5cm) high.

**£5–10 Retro2Go** ⊞
*The Iroquois China Co was founded in 1905 in Syracuse, New York State. The Casual range, designed by Russel Wright, was introduced in 1949 and in production until 1967. The indentations were highly influenced by Eva Zeisel's Museum White range of 1947. The factory closed in 1969.*

**A Roseville vase,** decorated with Clematis pattern, marked, America, c1940, 8in (20.5cm) high.
**£60–70 Heritage** ⚒

**A Roseville vase,** decorated with White Rose pattern, slight damage, marked, America, 1940, 15in (38cm) high.
**£40–45 Heritage** ⚒

A Roseville vase, decorated with Foxglove pattern, marked, America, 1942, 6in (15cm) high.

**£25–30 Heritage** 🔨

A Roseville vase, decorated with Freesia pattern, marked, America, 1945, 10½in (26.5cm) high.

**£40–45 Heritage** 🔨

A Weller jardinière, by Gerhard Liebentron, America, 1903–04, 12in (30.5cm) high.

**£200–250 GinFor's Odditiques** ⊞

A Weller vase, with applied daisies, impressed mark, America, 1930–40, 5¾in (14.5cm) high.

**£15–20 Heritage** 🔨

## ESSENTIAL REFERENCE RAYMOR SERVING WARE

A Roseville Raymor bean pot, by Ben Seibel, 1952.

**£40–45 hi+lo modern** ⊞
*The ovenproof, biomorphic Raymor line was introduced in 1952.*

A Roseville Raymor trivet, by Ben Seibel, in Terra Cotta colourway, America, 1952, 10½in (26.5cm) diam.

**£60–70 hi+lo modern** ⊞

- Venerable American Art Pottery Roseville were thrown an important lifeline in 1952 when New York retailers Richards-Morgenthau commissioned them to produce Raymor Modern Stoneware.

- Raymor was the trade name of Richards-Morgenthau who commissioned many leading US and European designers to manufacture a vast range of fashionable items for them.

- Designed by leading designer Ben Seibel it was the firm's last stand against the popularity of plastics and melamine.

- Fashioned in softer, plastic forms, it came in five colourways – Autumn Brown, Avocado Green, Beach Grey, Contempory White and Terra Cotta. Robin's Egg Blue and Chartreuse also exist but these colourways are rare.

- Sadly for Roseville the line was not popular and the factory closed in 1954.

# WADE

A Wade Heath Orcadian vase, No. 3443, 1930s, 4½in (11.5cm) high.

**£30–35 Decorative Antiques** ⊞

A Wade Heath flower vase, c1948, 6½in (16.5cm) high.

**£30–35 Jean Sears** ⊞
*This model was designed for export.*

A Wade cruet set, decorated with Capri pattern, one shaker marked, stoppers missing, 1953, 5¼in (13.5cm) high.

**£5–10 Retro2Go** ⊞

A Wade two–tier cakestand, decorated with Capri pattern, c1953, 10in (25.5cm) high.

**£25–30 Jean Sears** ⊞

A Wade vase, raised mark, Ireland, 1950s, 7½in (19cm) high.

**£15–20 Heritage** ⚒
*Wade Ireland was established in 1950 as an offshoot of the main Wade pottery to produce both industrial and novelty wares. It is famous for its grey/blue/brown glaze, which was discovered by accident in 1953 when a glaze mixer was trying to recreate the colours on a coronation tankard. The mistake lead to one of their most iconic colours.*

A Wade vase, decorated with Harvest pattern, c1957, 8½in (21.5cm) high.

**£25–30 Jean Sears** ⊞

A Wade Marmite jar, 1990s, 10½in (26.5cm) high.

**£65–80 Wellers Auctioneers** ⚒

# ESSENTIAL REFERENCE WADE & DISNEY

A set of Wade Walt Disney's Seven Dwarfs, by Jesse van Hallen, with cellulose glaze, c1938, tallest 12½in (32cm) high.

**£160–190 Charterhouse** 🔨

A Wade model of Walt Disney's Bambi, marked, 1961–65, 4½in (11.5cm) wide.

**£35–40 Bentley's** 🔨

• Wade Heath & Co was one of three companies run by members of the Wade family, the others being George Wade and Flaxman Pottery.

• From 1933 they had the right to produce designs based on characters from the famous Walt Disney Studios in the US.

• The first was The Three Little Pigs, fashioned as a jug in 1933.

• Mickey Mouse and Donald Duck were featured; the rare Donald Duck Teapot is a favourite.

• Jessie van Hallen produced Snow White and the Seven Dwarfs figures in both glazed and cellulose ranges.

• These figures pre-date the Hat Box and Blow Up ranges of the 1950s onwards.

A Wade model of Walt Disney's Trusty the Bloodhound, from *Lady and the Tramp*, 1956–65, 2¼in (5.5cm) high.

**£20–25 Tenterden Antiques** ⊞

A Wade figure of a dancer, 'Argentina', by Jessie van Hallen, with cellulose glaze, printed marks, 1930s, 9½in (24cm) high.

**£700–840 Rosebery's** 🔨
*Many of Jessie Van Hallen's figures were available in a cellulose finish as well as a normal glaze. Cellulose-glazed figures were cheaper to make as they were fired once and then painted and 'glazed' with a cold cellulose varnish, although this remained soft and prone to damage. Damaged cellulose figures are worth considerably less than perfect examples.*

A Wade model of Tom the Piper's Son, from the Nursery Favourites series, 1973, 3in (7.5cm) high.

**£10–15 Kingston Antiques** ⊞

Two Wade models of Tom and Jerry, 1980s, larger 4in (10cm) high.

**£65–75 Tenterden Antiques** ⊞

# WEDGWOOD

A Wedgwood Fairyland Imperial lustre Bowl, by Daisy Makeig-Jones, decorated with Poplar Trees pattern, the interior with Woodland Elves III Feather Hat, marked, 1915–29, 8½in (21.5cm) diam.

**£1,100–1,300  Maxwell's** 🔨

A Wedgwood Fairyland lustre bowl, decorated with Leapfrogging Elves pattern, c1930, 5in (12.5cm) diam.

**£1,450–1,600  A D Antiques** ⊞

A Wedgwood lustre vase, decorated with dragons and birds, 1920s, 5in (12.5cm) high.

**£270–300  A D Antiques** ⊞
*Wedgwood's 'ordinary' lustre wares are not to be confused with the Fairyland lustre range and are not as popular with collectors.*

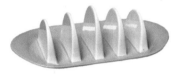

A Wedgwood Summer Sky toastrack, 1950s, 7in (18cm) long.

**£30–35  Chinasearch** ⊞

A Wedgwood black basalt Raven Stone coffee pot, by Robert Minkin, c1963, 10in (25.5cm) high.

**£80–95  Chinasearch** ⊞

A Wedgwood vase, decorated with Hathaway Rose pattern, marked, 1980s, 5¼in (13.5cm) high.

**£5–10  New 2 You** ⊞

## ESSENTIAL REFERENCE  ERIC RAVILIOUS

A Wedgwood Garden tea service, by Eric Ravilious, comprising six cups, five saucers, six side plates, a sugar bowl, milk jug and sandwich plates, printed and impressed marks, slight damage, 1950s.

**£450–540  Sworders** 🔨

• Artist, designer and illustrator Eric William Ravilious (1903–42) produced some of the most collectable Wedgwood designs of the pre- and post-WWII period.

A Wedgwood Persephone dinner service, by Eric Ravilious, 1950s, oval plate 16½in (42cm) wide.

**£240–290  Weller's Auctioneers** 🔨
*Eric Ravillious worked as a freelance artist for Wedgwood from 1935 to1940. His revolutionary designs were an unlikely success, some being produced after his death. Although 1980s' versions of his designs exist they are screen-printed rather than transfer-printed.*

• Introduced to the Wedgwood family in 1935 he was asked to submit tableware designs and a commemorative mug for Edward VIII.

• Many of his tableware designs were considered too sophisticated for the market, but his work was championed by Josiah Wedgwood V and so went into production.

• The first line to be produced was Harvest Festival, later named Persephone, in 1936, followed by Garden. These tablewares were a surprise hit with the public.

• Many of his pre-war designs were reintroduced in 1953 and continued to find a market.

• His untimely death in 1942 robbed British ceramics of one of its most promising designers.

# EXPERT EYE    FAIRYLAND LUSTRE

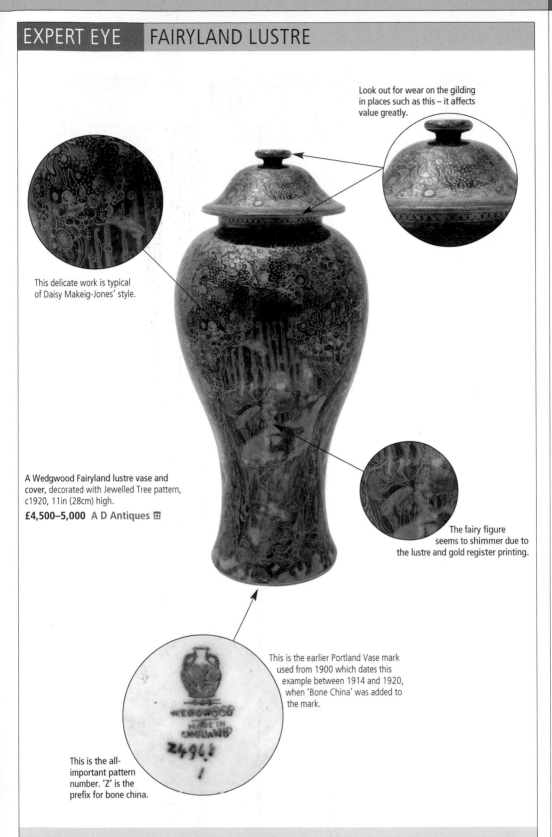

Look out for wear on the gilding in places such as this – it affects value greatly.

This delicate work is typical of Daisy Makeig-Jones' style.

A Wedgwood Fairyland lustre vase and cover, decorated with Jewelled Tree pattern, c1920, 11in (28cm) high.

**£4,500–5,000  A D Antiques** ⊞

The fairy figure seems to shimmer due to the lustre and gold register printing.

This is the earlier Portland Vase mark used from 1900 which dates this example between 1914 and 1920, when 'Bone China' was added to the mark.

This is the all-important pattern number. 'Z' is the prefix for bone china.

Born Susanna Jones in 1881 to a middle-class family, Daisy Makeig-Jones joined Wedgwood in 1909 as a humble painter. She had trained as an artist, but determined to be a designer, she wrote to Cecil Wedgwood and asked for a job. By 1914 she had been given her own studio and was beginning to develop her own designs. Fairyland lustre has always been expensive, even when new, as the complex process involved in its decoration took time. Makeig-Jones' complex designs for her fairyland range are not to be confused with her simpler 'ordinary lustre' ranges which are worth a fraction of the price of fairyland lustre.

# WEST GERMAN CERAMICS

A Bay-Keramik vase, decorated with Rimini pattern, marked, Germany, 1950s, 6¾in (17cm) high.

**£25–30  Outernational** ⊞
*This vase is decorated with one of the most sought-after patterns.*

A Bay-Keramik jardinière, marked, Germany, c1970, 6½in (16.5cm) high.

**£5–10  New 2 You** ⊞

A Bay-Keramik vase, marked, Germany, c1970, 15½in (39.5cm) high.

**£10–15  New 2 You** ⊞

A Duemler and Breiden floor vase, with copper glaze, marked, Germany, 1970s, 19¾in (50cm) high.

**£180–200  Outernational** ⊞

A Carstens Atelier vase, by Gerda Heukeroth, 1962–64, 9in (23cm) high.

**£85–95  GinFor's Odditiques** ⊞

An Ilkra vase, marked, Germany, 1950s, 6in (15cm) high.

**£35–40  Outernational** ⊞

A Jasba jug, with copper glaze, marked, Germany, 1960s, 9¾in (25cm) high.

**£40–45  Outernational** ⊞

A Kiechle plaque, Germany, 1961, 12 x 4in (30.5 x 10cm).

**£110–125  GinFor's Odditiques** ⊞
*Kiechle produced some of the best examples of this kind of work, typified by enamel on a matt black ground. Production numbers were low, so the work can be difficult to find.*

A Roth bottle vase, marked, Germany, 1970s, 9¾in (25cm) high.

**£40–45  Outernational** ⊞

# EXPERT'S EYE SCHEURICH VASE

The long neck and square section to the lip is a key Scheurich feature.

A single handle on a vase is a typical feature of these West German pieces.

The vibrant orange is another feature. The glaze is thick and opaque.

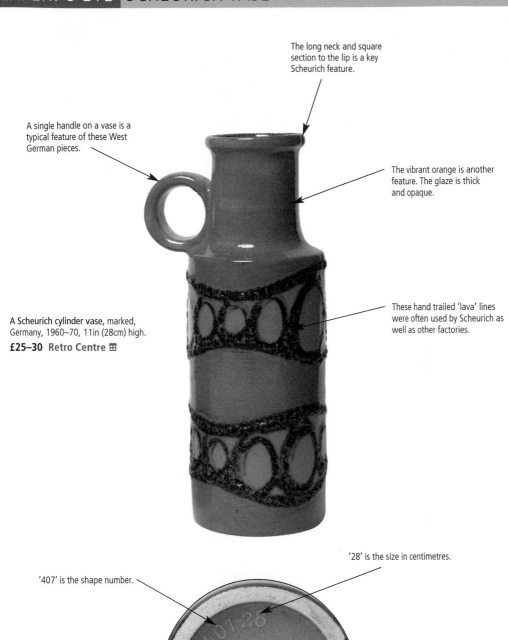

**A Scheurich cylinder vase,** marked, Germany, 1960–70, 11in (28cm) high.

**£25–30   Retro Centre** ⊞

These hand trailed 'lava' lines were often used by Scheurich as well as other factories.

'28' is the size in centimetres.

'407' is the shape number.

This 1960s–70s paper label identifies the maker – these are highly prized by collectors as wares are often unmarked.

Scheurich always used a white body.

The typical 'W. Germany' around the edge, combined with the three (or four) digit shape number, hyphen and size in centimetres is a strong clue to citing Scheurich as maker.

Scheurich began as a ceramic retailer in 1927, but moved into producing its own pottery in 1954. As one of the largest producers of this type of ware, Scheurich's pieces are often encountered by collectors. Much of the firm's output was exported across Europe and America and much is still to be discovered. It is often overlooked at flea markets where it sells for a few pounds, whereas on the stalls of savvy dealers the wares are priced at £20–30 and over – so buy now while you can afford to!

A Ruscha charger, from the Paris series, Germany, 1958, 14in (35.5cm) diam.

**£110–125 GinFor's Odditiques** ⊞

*The size of this charger makes it an uncommon example.*

A Ruscha wall plate, decorated with an Oriental scene incorporating Mount Fuji, Germany, 1958, 10in (25.5cm) diam.

**£60–70 GinFor's Odditiques** ⊞

*Ruscha was one of the largest producers of this type of work. The most common themes were birds or horses, most often on plates of 6–8in (15–20cm) diameter. Even with standard themes, the quality of the work varies widely. The size and decoration on this plate make it unusual.*

A Ruscha wall plate, decorated with Torero pattern, marked, Germany, 1950s, 7in (18cm) diam.

**£45–50 Outernational** ⊞

A Ruscha wall plate, decorated with two owls, Germany, 1960s, 11in (28cm) diam.

**£45–50 Outernational** ⊞

A Scheurich floor vase, Germany, 1960s, 20in (51cm) high.

**£220–250 GinFor's Odditiques** ⊞

A Scheurich vase, Germany, 1960s–70s, 10in (25.5cm) high.

**£250–270 GinFor's Odditiques** ⊞

A Scheurich Heinz Siery vase, marked, Germany, 1960s, 8¾in (22cm) high.

**£50–55 Outernational** ⊞

A Scheurich cylinder vase, marked, Germany, 1960–70, 11in (28cm) high.

**£25–30 Retro Centre** ⊞

A Scheurich floor vase, marked, Germany, 1970s, 20½in (52cm) high.

**£130–145 Outernational** ⊞

A Scheurich jug, marked, Germany, 1970s, 6¼in (16cm) high.

**£15–20 Outernational** ⊞

# CHRISTMAS

A bisque Santa Claus doll, with jointed limbs and moulded boots, Germany, c1900, 4¾in (12cm) high.

**£360–430 Skinner** 🔨

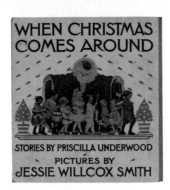

Priscilla Underwood, *When Christmas Comes Around*, illustrated by Jessie Willcox Smith, published by Duffield, New York, 1915, 11½ x 10¾in (29 x 27.5cm).

**£600–700 Sotheby's (NY)** 🔨

A Polonye porcelain group of a mother and child with a snowman, Ukraine, c1969, 8in (20.5cm) high.

**£40–45 Worcester Antiques** ⊞

A Coca-Cola motorized life-size model of Santa Claus, 1972, 66in (167.5cm) high.

**£550–650 Schmidt Museum** ⊞

A Royal Doulton figure of Santa Claus, 'Santa's List', 2005, 8in (20.5cm) high.

**£40–45 Pascoe** ⊞

A CWS Christmas biscuit tin, c1925, 6in (15cm) diam.

**£120–130 Michael Saffell** ⊞

A lithographed tinplate Christmas toy, by Strauss, spring motor not working, one reindeer missing bell, 1920s, 11in (28cm) long.

**£600–700 Skinner** 🔨

A Christmas jigsaw puzzle, by Whitman Publishing Co, No. 4424, America, 1950s–60s, 14½ x 11½in (37 x 29cm).

**£5–10 My Gigi's Treasures** ⊞

A Royal Copenhagen porcelain Christmas plate, 1884, 9¾in (25cm) diam, boxed.

**£20–25 Otford Centre** ⊞
*The diamond registration mark was used on a variety of manufactured goods from 1843 to 1883, after which the words 'Reg. No.' followed by a number were used. This mark will not date the piece, only tell you when the design was registered. This example was registered in November 1870.*

A Royal Copenhagen porcelain Christmas plate, 1976, 7in (18cm) diam.

**£10–15 Otford Antiques** ⊞

# CIGARETTE & TRADE CARDS

## CIGARETTE CARDS

**Cope Bros & Co,** Shakespeare Gallery, set of 50, 1900.
**£5–10 each** Collectors World ⊞

**J. F. Mearbeck,** At the Front for VCs, set of 30, 1915.
**£20–25** Collectors World ⊞

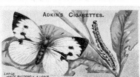

**John Player & Sons,** Curious Beaks, set of 50, 1929.
**£35–40** Soldiers of Rye ⊞

**Adkin & Sons,** Butterflies & Moths, set of 50, 1924.
**£65–75** Collectors World ⊞

**Gallaher,** Famous Film Scenes, set of 48, 1935.
**£15–20** Collectors World ⊞

**John Player & Sons,** Cats, set of 24, 1936.
**£115–130** Soldiers of Rye ⊞

Ardath Tobacco Co, Figures of Speech, set of 50, 1936.

**£30–35** London Cigarette Card Co ⊞

John Player & Sons, Famous Beauties, set of 25, 1937.

**£30–35** Soldiers of Rye ⊞

John Player & Sons, Film Stars, set of 50, 1938.

**£35–40** Soldiers of Rye ⊞

Gallaher, Racing Scenes, set of 48, 1938.

**£25–30**
London Cigarette Card Co ⊞

C.W.S. Cigarettes, Boy Scout Badges, set of 50, 1939.

**£50–60** Collectors World ⊞

W. D. & H. O. Wills, Classic Sports Cars, set of 30, 1996.

**£25–30** Murray Cards ⊞

# TRADE CARDS

Brooke Bond & Co, Out into Space, set of 50, 1958.
**£340–380 Murray Cards** ⊞

Kellogg, The Story of the Bicycle, set of 12, 1964.
**£35–40 Murray Cards** ⊞

Cadet Sweets, U.N.C.L.E., set of 50, 1966.
**£50–60 Murray Cards** ⊞

A. & B. C. Gum, Land of the Giants, set of 55, 1968.
**£75–90 Vault Auctions** ⚒

Imperial Publishing, American Golfers, set of 20, 1990.
**£5–10 Soldiers of Rye** ⊞
*Imperial Publishing are authorized to reprint the Imperial Tobacco Co series, although this series is one of their originals.*

## ESSENTIAL REFERENCE     LIEBIG CARDS

Liebig Extract of Meat Co, *Propulsione à Reazione*, set of 6, Italy, 1956.
**£5–10 Soldiers of Rye** ⊞

Liebig Extract of Meat Co, *La Musique Militaire*, set of 6, Belgium, 1922.
**£20–25 Soldiers of Rye** ⊞

Liebig Extract of Meat Co, *Chasseurs de Fourrures*, set of 6, Belgium, 1908.
**£15–20 Soldiers of Rye** ⊞

Liebig Extract of Meat Co, *Compositeurs Célèbres*, set of 6, Belgium, 1893.
**£70–80 Soldiers of Rye** ⊞

- Belgian company Leibig began producing beef extract in 1870.
- Each jar of extract came with a token which could be collected and exchanged for cards, which came in sets of six or, more unusually, 12.
- Most of Leibig's market was in Europe. As a result, cards were produced in Belgium, Holland Italy, France and Switzerland. Those produced in England are the rarest.
- Each card was printed on the back with a recipe.
- Cards ceased to be issued in 1970.
- Values range for a few pounds per set to several hundred depending on condition and rarity.
- Leibig cards are keenly collected in Belgium, where there are events that draw collectors from all over Europe.

**Chris Viner, Soldiers of Rye**

# COMICS

*Fantastic Four* comic, No.1, published by Marvel Comics, America, 1961.

**£650–750 Heritage** 🔧

*Commando* comic, No. 3, published by D. C. Thompson, 1961.

**£90–100 phil-comics** ⊞

*Sgt Fury and his Howling Commandos* comic, No. 2, published by Marvel Comics, America, 1966.

**£5–10 Comic Connections** ⊞

*Star Trek* comic, No. 17, published by Gold Key, America, 1973.

**£10–15 Comic Connections** ⊞

*The Tomb of Dracula* comic, published by Marvel Comics, America, 1973–74.

**£35–40 Comic Connections** ⊞

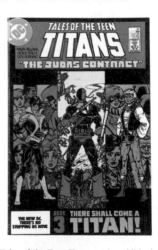

*Tales of the Teen Titans* comic, published by DC Comics, America, 1984.

**£10–20 Comic Connections** ⊞

*Mage, The Hero Discovered* comic, published by Comico, America, 1984–86.

**£1–5 Comic Connections** ⊞

*Watchmen* comic, published by DC Comics, America, 1987.

**£1–5 Comic Connections** ⊞

*V For Vendetta* comic, Vol. 1, published by DC Comics, America, 1988.

**£5–10 Comic Connections** ⊞

Sandman, Master of Dreams comic, published by DC Comics, America, 1989.
**£10–15** Comic Connections ⊞

Star Wars, Dark Empire comic, No. 3, published by Dark Horse Comics, America, 1997.
**£1–5** Comic Connections ⊞

The Ultimates comic, No. 1, published by Marvel Comics, America, 2002.
**£5–10** Comic Connections ⊞

Transmetropolitan comic, published by Vertigo Comics, America, 2002.
**£1–5**
Comic Connections ⊞

The Transformers comic, published by IDW Comics, America, 2005.
**£1–5**
Comic Connections ⊞

Batman, The Dark Night Falls comic, published by DC Comics, America, 1986.
**£5–10**
Comic Connections ⊞

Batman comic, No. 199, published by DC Comics, America, 1967.
**£5–10**
Comic Connections ⊞

## ESSENTIAL REFERENCE    IRON MAN

Tales of Suspense comic, No. 39, published by Marvel Comics, America, 1963.
**£380–450** Heritage ⚒

The Avengers comic, No. 1, published by Marvel Comics, America, 1963.
**£730–870** Heritage ⚒

Ultimate Iron Man comic, No. 1, published by Marvel Comics, America, 2005.
**£1–5** Comic Connections ⊞

• The character Iron Man first appeared in the American comic book series *Tales to Astonish* during the early 1960s.

• In 1968 he made his first apearance in his own title, *Iron Man*, and more recently as a prominent figure in the *Civil War*, which has proved to be Marvel's best-selling comic book series of recent times. A film featuring Iron Man is currently being planned.

• Many of the heros in Marvel Comics are flawed personalities struggling with personal problems as well as their duties as heros. This appeals to readers as it enables them to identify with the characters.

• The Iron Man struggles with alcohol addiction despite being a wealthy man and a hero.

The *Amazing Spider-Man* comic, No. 2, published by Marvel Comics, America, 1963.

**£600–700 Heritage** ⚒

*Daredevil* comic, No. 1, published by Marvel Comics, America, 1964.

**£600–700 Heritage** ⚒

The *Amazing Spider-Man* comic, No. 98, published by Marvel Comics, America, 1971.

**£10–15 Comic Connections** ⊞

The *Amazing Spider-Man* comic, Special 25th Anniversary Issue, published by Marvel Comics, America, 1988.

**£45–50 Comic Connections** ⊞

*Ultimate Spider-Man* comic, Vol. 1, published by Marvel Comics, America, 2002.

**£5–10 Comic Connections** ⊞

The *Amazing Spider-Man* comic, 30th Anniversary Issue, published by Marvel Comics, America, 1992.

**£5–10 Comic Connections** ⊞

# COMMEMORATIVES

## MILITARY AND NAVAL

**A Bovey Tracey Pottery two-handled mug,** commemorating the Boer War, depicting General Sir Redvere Buller, c1900, 4in (10cm) high.

**£100–110 Commemorobilia** ⊞

*General Sir Redvere Buller's family had the controlling interest in the Bovey Tracey Pottery.*

**A bone china plate,** commemorating Field-Marshall Lord Roberts VC, decorated with a photograph within a pierced border, 1915–16, 8in (20.5cm) diam.

**£70–80 Commemorobilia** ⊞

**An Alfred Meakin pottery plate,** inscribed with a message from the Prime Minister the Rt Hon D. Lloyd George, emphasizing the importance of economy in the use of food during WWI, 1917, 6in (15cm) diam.

**£35–40 Commemorobilia** ⊞

**A Caverswall bone china plate,** commemorating Earl Mountbatten, decorated with details of his distinguished career, 1979, 11in (28cm) diam.

**£65–75 Commemorobilia** ⊞

*Earl Mountbatten was killed by the IRA in 1979.*

**An Edwardian Pottery bone china plate,** commemorating HRH The Prince of Wales presenting new colours to 1st, 2nd and 3rd Battalions of the Parachute Regiment, decorated with the badge and ribbons of battle honours, 1998, 11in (28cm) diam.

**£30–35 Commemorobilia** ⊞

**A Royal Worcester porcelain bowl,** commemorating the Battle of Trafalgar, limited edition, on a turned oak base made from a wooden beam from HMS *Victory*, 2005, 9in (23cm) diam.

**£270–300 Box of Porcelain** ⚒

## EXPERT EYE | WARTIME COMMEMORATIVES

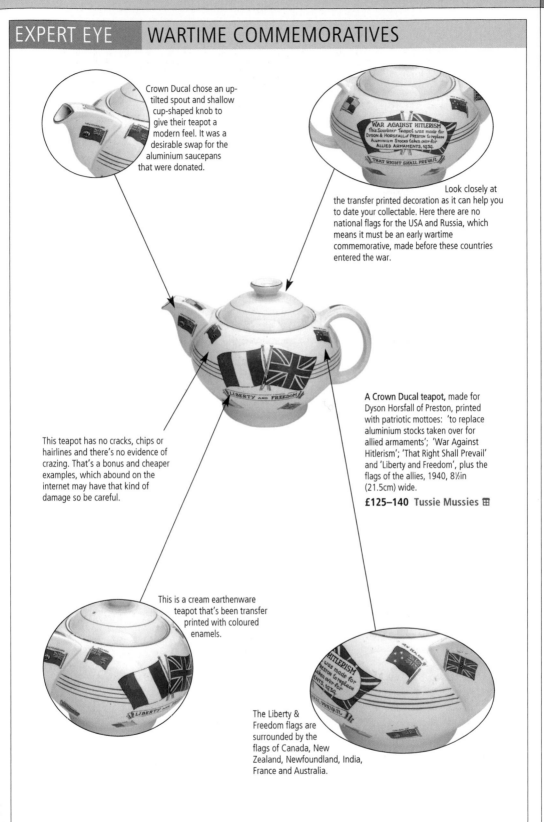

Crown Ducal chose an up-tilted spout and shallow cup-shaped knob to give their teapot a modern feel. It was a desirable swap for the aluminium saucepans that were donated.

Look closely at the transfer printed decoration as it can help you to date your collectable. Here there are no national flags for the USA and Russia, which means it must be an early wartime commemorative, made before these countries entered the war.

This teapot has no cracks, chips or hairlines and there's no evidence of crazing. That's a bonus and cheaper examples, which abound on the internet may have that kind of damage so be careful.

**A Crown Ducal teapot,** made for Dyson Horsfall of Preston, printed with patriotic mottoes: 'to replace aluminium stocks taken over for allied armaments'; 'War Against Hitlerism'; 'That Right Shall Prevail' and 'Liberty and Freedom', plus the flags of the allies, 1940, 8½in (21.5cm) wide.

**£125–140  Tussie Mussies** ⊞

This is a cream earthenware teapot that's been transfer printed with coloured enamels.

The Liberty & Freedom flags are surrounded by the flags of Canada, New Zealand, Newfoundland, India, France and Australia.

In 1940 Lord Beaverbrook, Britain's Minister of Aircraft Production called on the nation to help him build more Spitfires. The lightweight frame of the WWII fighter aircraft was made from duralumin, an aluminium alloy. All around the country, people were encouraged to donate their pots and pans for the war effort. Even kitchenalia from the Royal Household at Buckingham Palace was given to the help the cause. Teapots like these were markers of support for the scheme in the Preston area. Naturally, presentation pieces like this were kept and they are relatively common today — values vary considerably and reflect the condition.

POLITICAL

A Sherwin and Cotton photographic tile, by George Cartilage, depicting President Woodrow Wilson, c1900, 9in (23cm) high.
**£110–125**
**Brenda Kimber & John Lewis** ⊞

A Nelson ware ceramic plate, depicting the Prime Minister, Sir Winston Churchill, with ships and aircraft, possibly commemorating the Lease-Land agreement between the UK and USA, issued in the 1940s, 7in (18cm) diam.
**£50–55 Commemorobilia** ⊞

A Drostdy ware ceramic mug, commemorating Ian Douglas Smith, dated 11 November 1965, 1965, 5½in (14cm) high.
**£15–20 Godfrey Wallem** ⊞
*Ian Smith, Prime Minister of Rhodesia, declared Unilateral Independence (UDI) from the United Kingdom on 11 November 1965.*

A Wedgwood jasper ware ashtray, commemorating Sir Winston Churchill, c1969, 4½in (11.5cm) diam.
**£10–15 Tussie Mussies** ⊞

A Portmerion mug, illustrating the general election results attained by the Liberal Party, with signatures of all 14 elected liberal MPs, 1974, 4in (10cm) high.
**£30–35 Commemorobilia** ⊞

A pottery plate, by Mary Windrush, commemorating the bicentenary of American Independence, signed 'MW', 1976, 9in (23cm) diam.
**£160–180 Hope & Glory** ⊞

A teapot, inscribed 'Clintocchio, Give a Little Whistle and Always let your Conscience be your Guide', edition of 40, 2003, 9in (23cm) high.
**£175–195 Totally Teapots** ⊞

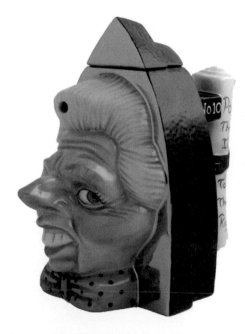

An earthenware teapot, entitled 'The Iron Lady', inscribed 'eyes to the right, nose to the left', limited edition, 2003, 9in (23cm) high.
**£200–220 Totally Teapots** ⊞

# ROYAL

## ESSENTIAL REFERENCE   EDWARD VIII COLLECTABLES

A ceramic plate, commemorating the coronation of King Edward VIII, 1937, 10in (25.5cm) diam.

**£240–270  Britannia ⊞**

A Melba ceramic globe, commemorating the coronation of Edward VIII, c1937, 3½in (9cm) high.

**£200–240  Special Auction Services ⚒**

• Edward VIII was never crowned because he abdicated on 10 December 1936 after just 325 days reign.  By this stage many of the commemorative items had already been made in preparation for the monarch's Coronation on 12 May 1937.

• It's tempting to think that all Edward VIII items must be valuable but this is not the case. For instance, the first portrait stamps showing the monarch were issued on 1 September 1936. However they were still being dispensed from stamp machines in early 1938 and had a wide circulation. A mint set is only worth about 80p today!

• The items that sell for more are those that were well made and costly at the time like the Paragon plate on the left above. Here you can see that the designer, J.A Robinson, produced a commemorative that was extremely detailed and finely finished. Equally interesting are the more quirky survivors like this ceramic globe.

• Collectors also favour Coronation ceramics that were adapted to reflect the abdication. These usually carry both dates – in many cases the abdication date was handpainted on.

A Doulton pottery mug, commemorating the Golden Jubilee of Queen Victoria, transfer-printed with images of Queen Victoria in 1837 and 1887, 1887, 3½in (9cm) high.

**£60–70**
**Commemorobilia ⊞**

A Royal Worcester ceramic plate, commemorating the coronation of King Edward VII, issued for the City of Worcester, depicting the Mayor and Mayoress, 1902, 9in (23cm) diam.

**£55–65**
**Commemorobilia ⊞**

A ceramic model of a pig, commemorating the investiture of Edward Prince of Wales at Carnarvon Castle, 1911, 3½in (9cm) long.

**£75–85  Commemorobilia ⊞**

A photograph of King George VI, signed 'Bertie', 1938, 9½ x 8½in (24 x 21.5cm).

**£1,150–1,300 Argyll Etkin** ⊞

*The personal nature of this autograph is key to its high value. Instead of signing 'George R', the king uses an abbreviation of his Christian name, Albert (Bertie).*

*The Coronation of Her Majesty Queen Elizabeth II* souvenir programme, published by King George's Jubilee Trust, 1953, 9¾ x 7in (25 x 18cm).

**£5–10 John Smart** ⊞

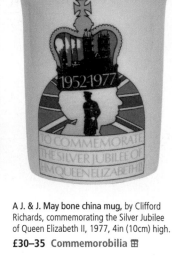

A J. & J. May bone china mug, by Clifford Richards, commemorating the Silver Jubilee of Queen Elizabeth II, 1977, 4in (10cm) high.

**£30–35 Commemorobilia** ⊞

A Wedgwood glass, decorated with a jasper ware medallion, commemorating the Silver Jubilee of Queen Elizabeth II, 1977, 5½in (14cm) high.

**£25–30 Commemorobilia** ⊞

A Richard Parrington ceramic caricature bust of Queen Elizabeth II, 'Corgi and Bess', commemorating the Silver Jubilee of Queen Elizabeth II depicting the Queen with a corgi dog draped around her neck, signed, c1977, 10¼in (26cm) high.

**£60–75 Rosebery's** 🔨

A J. & J. May bone china mug, commemorating the betrothal of Prince Charles and Lady Diana Spencer, with gilt decoration, 1981, 4½in (11.5cm) high.

**£60–70 Hope & Glory** ⊞

## TIMELINE ROYAL MUGS

A pottery mug, commemorating Queen Victoria's Diamond Jubilee, 1897, 3in (7.5cm) high.

**£65–75 Commemorobilia** ⊞

A Bishop & Stonier pottery mug, commemorating the coronation of King George V, 1911, 3in (7.5cm) high.

**£35–40 Commemorobilia** ⊞

A Royal Doulton mug, produced for the 1937 Coronation of Edward VIII, before his abdication, 1936, 4in (10cm) high.

**£60–70 Hope & Glory** ⊞

A Royal Stafford bone china mug, commemorating the coronation of King George VI and Queen Elizabeth, 1937, 4in (10cm) high.

**£50–55 Hope & Glory** ⊞

A **Waddingtons 500 piece jigsaw puzzle,** commemorating the marriage of Prince Charles and Lady Diana Spencer, 1981, 10in (25.5cm) wide.

**£15–20 Commemorobilia** ⊞

A **Coalport ceramic mug,** commemorating the marriage of Prince Charles and Lady Diana Spencer, limited edition of 2500, 1981, 3in (7.5cm) high.

**£15–20 Kingston Antiques** ⊞

A **Caverswall urn and cover,** commemorating the 21st birthday of Diana, Princess of Wales, painted with a view of Highgrove House, 1982, 10in (25.5cm) high.

**£320–360 Commemorobilia** ⊞

A **Caverswall bone china plate,** commemorating the ruby wedding of Queen Elizabeth II and Prince Philip, 1987, 8½in (21.5cm) diam.

**£25–30 Commemorobilia** ⊞

A **Royal Doulton porcelain figure of the Duchess of York,** commemorating her wedding to Prince Andrew, 1986, 8in (20.5cm) high.

**£300–330 Commemorobilia** ⊞

A **Chown bone china teapot,** commemorating the Golden Jubilee of Queen Elizabeth II, limited edition, 2002, 6in (15cm) high.

**£60–70 Hope & Glory** ⊞

A **Royal Worcester figure of Princess Margaret,** commemorating the Golden Jubilee of Queen Elizabeth II, 2002, 10in (25.5cm) high.

**£165–185 Commemorobilia** ⊞

A **pottery mug,** commemorating the coronation of Queen Elizabeth II, 1953, 3½in (9cm) high.

**£15–20 J & M Collectables** ⊞

A **Wedgwood earthenware pint mug,** designed by Richard Guyatt, commemorating the marriage of Prince Charles and Lady Diana Spencer, 1981, 4in (10cm) high.

**£55–65 Hope & Glory** ⊞
*Richard Guyatt produced his first mug for Queen Elizabeth II's coronation in 1953. His last was for the bicentennial of the Battle of Trafalgar in 2006.*

A **Lady Grace bone china mug,** commemorating the 50th birthday of Prince Charles, decorated with six pictures of Charles at various stages of his life, the handle in the shape of 50, limited edition of 100, 1998, 5in (12.5cm) high.

**£55–65 Commemorobilia** ⊞

A **Gilchrist & King Royal Mail mug,** depicting a commemorative stamp from the coronation of Queen Elizabeth II in 1953, produced at the time of her Golden Jubilee, 2003, 3in (7.5cm) high.

**£10–15 Commemorobilia** ⊞

# CORKSCREWS

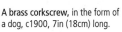

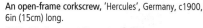

A brass corkscrew, in the form of a dog, c1900, 7in (18cm) long.
**£35–40**
**Worcester Antiques** ⊞

An open-frame corkscrew, 'Hercules', Germany, c1900, 6in (15cm) long.
**£55–65 Swan at Tetsworth** ⊞

A cast-steel lever corkscrew, 'The Signet Lever', c1900, 5in (12.5cm) long.
**£10–15**
**Christopher Sykes** ⊞

A nickel-plated corkscrew, label inscribed 'John Dewar & Sons (Distillers) Ltd, Old Highland Whisky, Perth. N.B. & London', c1900, 3in (7.5cm) high.
**£25–30 Christopher Sykes** ⊞

A steel concertina corkscrew, stamped 'H. D. Armstrong Patent', c1910, 7in (18cm) wide.
**£40–45 Christopher Sykes** ⊞

A steel Perille-style corkscrew, France, c1910, 6in (15cm) long.
**£10–15 Christopher Sykes** ⊞

A brass four-pillar corkscrew, Italy, c1920, 6in (15cm) long.
**£45–50 Christopher Sykes** ⊞

A concertina-style corkscrew, marked 'Perfect', France, c1920, 7in (18cm) wide.
**£25–30 Christopher Sykes** ⊞

A nickel-plated corkscrew, in the form of a dog, c1930, 4in (10cm) long.
**£10–15 Christopher Sykes** ⊞

A cast-brass key corkscrew, the key formed as crown cap lifter, Germany, c1950, 6in (15cm) long.
**£10–15 Christopher Sykes** ⊞

# DOLLS

## BISQUE

A Simon & Halbig Kämmer & Reinhardt bisque-headed walking doll, with sleeping eyes, pierced ears and mohair wig, jointed composition body, straight legs and head turning/walking mechanism, Germany, early 20thC, 20in (51cm) high.

**£520–580 Barbara Ann Newman** ⊞

A Heinrich Handwerck bisque-headed boy doll, No. 109, Germany, c1910, 18in (45.5cm) high.

**£580–650 Pantiles Spa Antiques** ⊞

A Limoges bisque-headed Cherie doll, France, c1910, 15in (38cm) high.

**£330–370 Pantiles Spa Antiques** ⊞

A Kestner bisque-headed boy doll, by Catterfelder Puppenfabrik, No. 263, with bent limbs and original wig, c1916, 18in (45.5cm) high.

**£360–400 Pollyanna** ⊞

A Kämmer & Reinhardt bisque doll, No. 117A, with glass eyes and closed mouth, Germany, c1920, 26in (66cm) high.

**£3,250–3,600 Bradley Gent** ⊞

A bisque-headed Jutta doll, probably by Cuno & Dressel, Germany, c1920, 22in (56cm) high.

**£450–500 Glenda Antique Dolls** ⊞

A bisque doll, with sleeping eyes and squeaker, c1920, 6in (15cm) high.

**£45–50 Pantiles Spa Antiques** ⊞

A bisque-headed baby doll, with glass sleeping eyes, composition body, original clothes, marked, Germany, 1920s, 13in (33cm) high.

**£135–160 Skinner** 🔨

# CLOTH

A primitive cloth doll, with painted features and wool wig, damaged, 1875–1925, 21in (53.5cm) high.

**£380–450** Skinner 🔨

A Norah Wellings velveteen doll, with jointed neck and limbs, cloth label, velvet overalls stitched as part of body, c1930, 17in (43cm) high.

**£60–70** Skinner 🔨

A cloth HMS *Hood* sailor doll, 1930s, 11in (28cm) high.

**£135–150** Cobwebs ⊞

A Dorothy Heizer Nefertete, Queen of Egypt cloth doll, modelled on the painted limestone head and tomb drawings, America, 1940s–50s, 10in (25.5cm) high.

**£2,500–3,000** Skinner 🔨

A cloth fisherman doll and his wife, by Ravca, with needle-sculpted and painted features, wearing traditional peasant clothing, France, mid-20thC, 17½in (44.5cm) high.

**£325–400** Skinner 🔨

A Dorothy Heizer Isabella of Castille cloth doll, America, 1940s–50s, 10in (25.5cm) high.

**£1,600–2,000** Skinner 🔨

A Dorothy Heizer Bonnie Prince Charlie cloth doll, America, 1952, 10¾in (27.5cm) high.

**£2,000–2,400** Skinner 🔨

# COMPOSITION

An Arranbee Nancy composition doll, with sleeping eyes, moulded hair, original clothes and metal trunk wardrobe, America, 1930s, 13in (33cm) high.

**£200–240  Bears of Windy Hill** ⊞

*Nancy was Arranbee's competitor to Patsy by Effanbee. The use of several moulds means that her hairstyle varies. The 16in (40.5cm) version occasionally had a wig over the moulded hair.*

A Madame Alexander composition doll, with sleeping eyes, tag and original outfit, 1937, 12½in (32cm) high.

**£135–150**
**Bears of Windy Hill** ⊞
*All original Madame Alexander dolls have tags.*

A Dean's Rag Book composition boy doll, with painted eyes and hair and cloth body, embossed mark, 1940s, 18in (45.5cm) high.

**£95–115  Skinner** ⚒

## ESSENTIAL REFERENCE    EFFANBEE

An Effanbee Suzanne composition doll, with original costume, America, 1930s, 14in (35.5cm) high.

**£115–130  Bears of Windy Hill** ⊞

An Effanbee Anne Shirley composition doll, by Dewees Cochran, with painted eyes and human hair wig, marked 'Effanbee American Children' and 'Effanbee Anne Shirley', America, 1930s, 20in (51cm) high.

**£420–500  Skinner** ⚒

An Effanbee Anne Shirley composition doll, with yarn hair, marked, America, 1940s, 20in (51cm) high.

**£115–130  Bears of Windy Hill** ⊞

• The earliest dolls are marked 'Effanbee/Anne Shirley' on the back, while later ones tend to be marked only 'Effanbee'.

• Her ground-breaking separated fingers means Anne Shirley could wear gloves.

• A few dolls included a magnet embedded in the palm so that kitchen utensils could be held. Human hair was replaced by yarn as a wartime measure.

## HARD PLASTIC

A celluloid-headed doll, with plastic body, probably Germany, 1940s, 24in (61cm) high.

**£165–185 Pollyanna** ⊞

A Pedigree Delite baby boy doll, with moulded head, c1948, 16in (40.5cm) high.

**£130–145 Pollyanna** ⊞

A Roddy hard plastic walker doll, with sleeping eyes, mohair wig and vintage dress, 1950s, 10½in (26.5cm) high.

**£10–15 Lolli Dollies** ⊞

A Rosebud baby doll, 1950, 14in (35.5cm) high.

**£130–145 Pollyanna** ⊞

A Roddy doll, with moulded head and straight legs, 1950, 10in (25.5cm) high.

**£50–55 Pollyanna** ⊞

A Roddy walker doll, with original wig, 1950s, 21in (53.5cm) high.

**£130–145 Pollyanna** ⊞

A Pedigree walker doll, with original wig, 1950s, 21in (53.5cm) high.

**£130–145 Pollyanna** ⊞

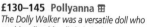

A British National Dolls Dolly Walker doll, with sleeping eyes, 'mama' voice box and original wig, marked 'BND London', 1950s, 21in (53.5cm) high.

**£130–145 Pollyanna** ⊞

*The Dolly Walker was a versatile doll who could walk with a little help from her owner. The instructions read '...hold her by her left or right hand. Balance Dolly Walker first on one foot, then the other.'*

# EXPERT EYE — A CLOSER LOOK AT A HARD PLASTIC DOLL

Although the hard plastic head is moulded it has tremendous detail. The rosebud mouth is slightly open showing her tongue and teeth. Her complexion still has plenty of original colour, as do her lips.

To make the most of the production run and broaden appeal, Pedigree issued their dolls with a variety of coloured wigs. This doll has her original brunette wig.

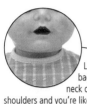

Look at the back of the neck or across the shoulders and you're likely to see the Pedigree mark. You'd expect to see 'Pedigree' in moulded script with 'Made in England' below it – the combination used from 1953 onwards. Before this 'Pedigree' appears as small capitals.

Her 'flirty' eyes have their original lashes, which so often have been trimmed or curled.

**A Lines Bros Pedigree doll,** with original dress and shoes, 1955, 14in (35.5cm) high.
**£140–155 Pollyanna** ⊞

Look closely at her hands. Here there is no cracking or discolouration. Another key feature of the 1950s improvements were smaller hands, which were better scaled to her body. The seam line that ran across the palm of earlier models disappears after 1952.

Don't be afraid to peer beneath her dress and take in the body shape. Pedigree had a big redesign in 1952 and this doll has the new slimline outline with nipped in waist. Another improvement was her voicebox, which became replaceable with a grill in the doll's back – earlier models had the grill in the front.

Having the original outfit and matching hat is a real bonus for collectors. In the late 1950s Pedigree made an array of dresses and accessories for their line of dolls, which could be purchased separately under the Mamselle Boutique label. There were also sewing patterns and knitting patterns available.

Dolls carrying the Pedigree brand name hailed from the Lines Brothers firm who also made Tri-ang toys. The name, which was officially registered in 1942 although it had been adopted before, stood for superior quality, both in the materials used, the modelling and the accessories. Hard plastic dolls were the next step on from composition and they came in a range of sizes from 6in (15cm) to 22in (56cm). Collectors are keen on examples such as this which are in 'as new' condition.

# VINYL

A Mattel Bubble-Cut Barbie doll, wearing original swimsuit, 1962, 12in (30.5cm) high, with box.

**£180–200** Magic Toy Box ⊞
*Barbie is seen here with her original swimsuit.*

A Mattel No. 6 Ponytail Barbie doll, 1962, 12in (30.5cm) high, with box.

**£160–180** Magic Toy Box⊞

A Mattel Hawaiian Ken doll, with bendable legs, surfboard and accessories, 1979, 11½in (29cm) high, with box.

**£100–120** All Dolled Up ⊞

A Mattel Skipper doll, Barbie's little sister, 1963, 10in (25.5cm) high, with box.

**£100–120** Magic Toy Box ⊞
*Although this doll is in very good condition overall, the box has been repaired with tape and this does reduce value.*

A Mattel Angel Princess Barbie doll, 1996, 11½in (29cm) high, with box.

**£10–20** Lolli Dollies ⊞

## EXPERT EYE · 1960S BARBIE

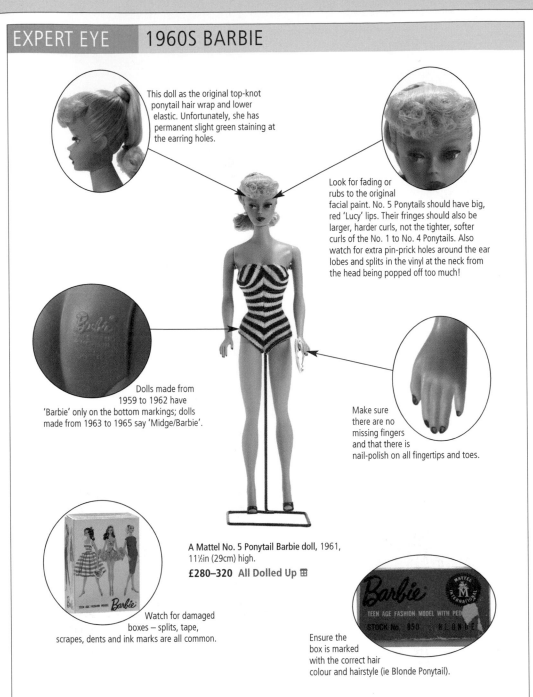

This doll as the original top-knot ponytail hair wrap and lower elastic. Unfortunately, she has permanent slight green staining at the earring holes.

Look for fading or rubs to the original facial paint. No. 5 Ponytails should have big, red 'Lucy' lips. Their fringes should also be larger, harder curls, not the tighter, softer curls of the No. 1 to No. 4 Ponytails. Also watch for extra pin-prick holes around the ear lobes and splits in the vinyl at the neck from the head being popped off too much!

Dolls made from 1959 to 1962 have 'Barbie' only on the bottom markings; dolls made from 1963 to 1965 say 'Midge/Barbie'.

Make sure there are no missing fingers and that there is nail-polish on all fingertips and toes.

A Mattel No. 5 Ponytail Barbie doll, 1961, 11½in (29cm) high.

**£280–320** All Dolled Up ⊞

Watch for damaged boxes – splits, tape, scrapes, dents and ink marks are all common.

Ensure the box is marked with the correct hair colour and hairstyle (ie Blonde Ponytail).

This is a very beautiful 1961 blonde No. 5 Ponytail Barbie. She has her original box and comes with her original black and white zebra-striped strapless swimsuit, black open-toe heels, 'pearl' earrings on posts, black wire stand and 'Barbie and Ken' booklet. A doll such as this one, with box and accessories, in this condition would be worth around £250–320. Dolls produced in 1961 such as the No. 5 Ponytail, first-edition Bubble Cuts and early Ken dolls often had shiny faces caused by the vinyl used that year, which tends to 'sweat' over time. Green staining was another problem, caused by tarnishing of the metal earring posts and can gradually spread to the doll's face. By the 1970s Mattel had switched to plastic earrings which did not react with the head vinyl. Without the tinge of green at the ears this doll would be £320–400. A 1959 No. 1 Ponytail Barbie can easily command between £2,000 and 4,500, depending on condition. The blondes are the easiest to find, followed by brunettes and then redheads (titian) are the most coveted and more elusive. Vintage Barbie collectors will usually pay the highest prices for the most rare, hard to find dolls, such as the fabulous 1966 Side-Part American Girl (bendable leg) Barbie with high-colour bright facial paint.

A Pedigree Dolls Sindy 'Country Walk' outfit 1963, in original packaging, 12½in (32cm) wide.

**£150–170** Magic Toy Box ⊞
*This set, which originally retailed for 19s 11d (£14.40 today), is particularly sought after because it still has the original bone and dog bowl. A similar set was issued by Mattel for Barbie, but the dog was a terrier rather than a poodle.*

A Pedigree Dolls Sindy 'Bowling' outfit, with Coca-Cola bottle and skittles, 1966, in original packaging, 9½in (24cm) wide.

**£145–160** Magic Toy Box ⊞

A Paul 'Ship Ahoy' outfit, 1968, in original packaging, 9½in (24cm) wide.

**£100–110** Magic Toy Box ⊞

A Pedigree Dolls New Lovely Lively Sindy doll, including charm bracelet, 1971, 13in (33cm) high, with box.

**£200–220** Magic Toy Box ⊞

A Pedigree Sindy 'Blazer Beauty' outfit, 1974, in original packaging, 6½in (16.5cm) wide.

**£50–55** Magic Toy Box ⊞

A Pedigree Sindy Party Time doll, 1981, 12in (30.5cm) high, with box.

**£150–165**
Magic Toy Box ⊞
*Party Time Sindy was only sold with blonde hair and a choice of three coloured outfits in royal blue, yellow and pink. The box included a 45rpm record entitled 'We're Havin' a Party', released by Steve Gilston.*

A Pedigree Sindy 'Free Wheeling' outfit, 1980, in original packaging, 12in (30.5cm) high.

**£20–25** Magic Toy Box ⊞

A Marx Toys Sindy doll, 1978, 13in (33cm) high, with box.

**£65–75** Magic Toy Box ⊞

A Vivid Imaginations Crazy Steps Sindy doll, with leaflet and clip bag, 2000, 11½in (29cm) high, with box.

**£100–120** Lolli Dollies ⊞

# EXPERT EYE    SINDY OUTFIT

Look at the exquisite detail of the dress and all the accessories. Pedigree was proud of the quality of Sindy's outfits and dresses are nicely labelled. Early outfits have white tags with black stitched writing. Sometimes it will say 'Made in Irish Republic', rarely 'Made in England' and most often 'Made in Hong Kong' or 'Empire made' – another way of referring to Hong Kong manufacture. Paper tags appear in the 1970s and run into the early 1980s before fabric tags are revived.

The pink dress was designed for an 'extra-special out of this world party'. Its flared hem made sure Sindy could twist away and 'make the party swing'!

A Pedigree Dolls Sindy 'Dream Date' outfit, 1963, in original packaging, 8½in (21.5cm) wide.

**£100–115  Magic Toy Box** ⊞

It's a collectors dream to see an outfit still carded, wrapped and boxed. To keep prices down, Pedigree quickly devised a production line that spanned the globe. Many of Sindy's outfits were designed in the Merton HQ, manufactured and carded in Hong Kong then shipped to the UK where they were slotted into the cardboard outer.

This inner card from Patch's 1968 'Hockey' outfit shows exactly how sets were assembled in Hong Kong. If it was complete with its outer casing it would be worth £135.

Ref 12503
DREAM DATE
12/6

Having the original selling price adds to this set's history. You can use it to get a sense of how expensive this would have been to a child at the time. The cheaper options were always the separates that appeared unboxed with hangers. The average weekly wage for a manual worker in 1963 was 35 shillings (£25 at today's values) so this set cost roughly a third of Dad's income, if you were working class. However for the daughter of a Company Director who earned £11 (£159) a week – it was a small fry purchase! The reference number just above the price links with Pedigree records and affirms the set name below. Dream Date remained in production until 1970.

Dream Date was in the first series of Sindy's outfits. It's a key collectable for any Sindy fan as it's the pink party dress that dominates the illustration on the first issue box (although inside Sindy wears 'Weekenders'). Pedigree's in-house designer, Valerie Sanders, was on board in the early days to create Sindy's highly fashionable outfits. In some cases she worked with top names like Foale & Tuffin & Hardy Amies. The big names worked up designs, which Sanders was instrumental in translating into styles that would work for a vinyl doll.

MISCELLANEOUS

A Door of Hope pearwood schoolboy doll, with carved head and hands, paper tag, China, early 20thC, 8in (20.5cm) high.

**£470–560 Skinner** 🔨

An Amanda Jane vinyl doll, with sleeping eyes, 1960, 7½in (19cm) high.

**£45–50 Pollyanna** ⊞

An Ideal Ted vinyl doll, brother of Tammy, America, 1964, 13in (33cm) high.

**£90–100 Magic Toy Box** ⊞
*Mom is one of the hardest members of the family to find. Even more so is Bud, Tammy's boyfriend, who is similar to Ted, but with very dark eyebrows.*

An Ideal Tammy doll, 1965, in rigid plastic telephone booth presentation box, 12⅛in (32cm) high.

**£170–185 Magic Toy Box** ⊞
*Tammy has a more grown-up look with her short page-boy hair. The black version is extremely rare.*

A Palitoy Dancing Marie pocket-size doll, 1970, 7in (18cm) high.

**£150–165 Magic Toy Box** ⊞
*Marie was one of Palitoy's miniature fashion dolls, like Pippa. Her novelty lies in her ability to dance – if her arms were moved her body twisted.*

A Zapff soft-bodied doll, Germany, 1970–80s, 16in (40.5cm) high.

**£25–30 Pollyanna** ⊞

A Palitoy Pippa's friend Pete doll, 1976, 7in (18cm) high.

**£80–90 Magic Toy Box** ⊞

A Bella Tressy doll, with growing hair, France, 1979, 14in (35.5cm) high.

**£55–65 Magic Toy Box** ⊞
*American Character licensed Société Bella to make this doll for the French market. It was first sold in 1965.*

# EPHEMERA

An Electrical Exhibition flyer, 1904, 6in (15cm) high.

**£1–5** Books Afloat ⊞

A souvenir programme, for the 50th performance of *Romeo and Juliet*, featuring Matheson Lang, Lyceum Theatre, London, 1908, 13in (33cm) wide.

**£10–15** J R & S J Symes ⊞

*The Illustrated London News*, 1910, 16in (40.5cm) high.

**£5–10** J R & S J Symes ⊞

A pictorial dinner menu, illustrated by André Benois, for an Italian official visit to St Petersburg, 1913, 10 x 7in (25.5 x 18cm).

**£300–330** Farahar & Dupre ⊞

A Belling Electric Fires catalogue, 1936–37, 9in (23cm) high.

**£5–10** J R & S J Symes ⊞

A Sarnia Guest House bill, for one week's stay, 1959, 8 x 4in (20.5 x 10cm).

**£1–5** Mr Moore ⊞

*Punch* magazine, 8 December 1954, 11in (28cm) high.

**£1–5** Upstairs Downstairs ⊞

## ESSENTIAL REFERENCE    COLLECTING NEWSPAPERS

*The Times*, 10 January 1705, 19 x 13in (48.5 x 33cm).

**£75–80** Mr A Harris ⊞
*Copies of The Times are particularly rare prior to 1855.*

*The News of the World*, 1870.

**£10–15** J R & S J Symes ⊞

*The Times*, 14 September 1888, 18 x 12in (45.5 x 30.5cm).

**£75–80** Mr A Harris ⊞
*This is one of a collection of five editions of The Times covering the five 'Jack the Ripper' murders.*

*Daily Sketch*, January 1915, 15 x 12in (38 x 30.5cm).

**£5–10** J R & S J Symes ⊞

• New collectors could consider a themed collection such as one copy of every paper issued, a particular period, attractive mast-heads (titles), provincial papers such as a certain town or country; types of newspaper (morning, evening, Sunday, weekly); certain dates and anniversaries, royal events, great battles or those with a particular political bias.

• Newspapers should be kept at even room temperature, away from damp and direct sunlight, in clear polythene bags and in folders.

• The values are based on historic importance of content, desirability or rarity and condition.        **Alex Harris**

# FASHION

## DRESSES & SUITS

A beaded silk georgette dress, 1920.
**£350–400 Decades** ⊞

A printed viscose tea dress, printed with stylized coffee beans, 1930s.
**£80–90 First Call** ⊞

A Fevesco linen day dress, 1940s.
**£35–40 Echoes** ⊞

A crêpe day dress, 1940s.
**£100–120 Clobber** ⊞

## ESSENTIAL REFERENCE    SEQUINS

A silk evening dress, with hand-sewn sequined decoration, 1920s.
**£500–550 Wardrobe** ⊞

A net evening dress, with sequins and beads, 1950s.
**£50–55 Echoes** ⊞

A net evening dress, with sequined decoration, 1950s.
**£200–220 First Call** ⊞

A sequined evening dress, 1930s.
**£400–450 Echoes** ⊞

• The first sequins ever used were made from paper-thin rolled gold, cut out and stitched in place.

• In the 19th century gelatine was rolled into sheets, punched and coloured with lead dyes to create a dazzling effect. Austria and Czechoslovakia were at the heart of sequin production well into the early 20th century.

• Gelatine had a nasty habit of melting in extreme heat and rain so early sequined garments were impossible to clean.

• After WWII a new base material, acetate, was used. Although it was clear, a light coating of silver made it glimmer. In the 1950s a new sandwich method using Dupont's Mylar was developed and if you look really closely you can spot it. The clear Mylar sandwiches the coloured base inside, protecting it and making it washable.

• Today's sequins are coated in aluminium rather than silver and made form vinyl .

A nylon and lace dress, 1950s.
**£70–80 Rokit (B)** ⊞
*Easy-care nylon was first unveiled by Dupont in 1938 and looked every bit as glamorous as cotton throughout this decade.*

A printed cotton day dress, with acrylic button detailing, 1950s.
**£65–75 Wardrobe** ⊞

*Simply-made summer dresses without a cotton lining, such as this one, were the high street equivalent of Dior's new look.*

An Hawaiian cotton dress, America, 1950s.
**£105–120 Dreamtime** ⊞
*During WWII Japanese fabrics were no longer available and attention turned to Hawaiian prints. By the 1950s the Hawaiian look was in full swing, helped by Hollywood actress Dorothy Lamour who popularized the Hawaiian printed sarong. Helped by Pan-Am's expanded air transportation Hawaiian-made garments flooded the US this decade.*

A floral cotton day dress, 1950.
**£25–30 Echoes** ⊞

A printed cotton day dress, 1950s.
**£75–85 Wardrobe** ⊞

A Ladyluxe woollen suit, early 1950s.
**£100–120 First Call** ⊞

A Sereford Model suit, with pencil skirt and swing coat, 1950s.
**£140–160 First Call** ⊞

A Global Inspiration printed cotton day dress, Hong Kong, early 1960s.

**£45–50 Wardrobe** ⊞

*During the late 1950s and early 1960s, British fashion manufacturers began losing ground to imports from overseas. This dress boasts Parisian style but was cheaply made in Hong Kong.*

An Allendale summer dress, 1960s.

**£30–35 First Call** ⊞

A cotton two-piece dress and coat, Switzerland, 1960s.

**£60–70 Clobber** ⊞

A Malcolm Starr lace dress, America, 1960s.

**£200–220 Circle** ⊞

*American fashion designer Malcolm Starr was known for his show-stopping outfits. He loved working with fine chiffons and crystal beads.*

A Rembrandt Miss Feraud acrylic dress, 1970s.

**£65–75 Decades** ⊞

## EXPERT EYE    1970S DRESS

Fabric care labels were a must after 1972 in the US and they had to be stitched into all garments, with only a few exceptions. A similar scheme was operated in Europe. This dress only has three symbols, as the decades progress more care symbols are introduced. The absence of the tumble drying symbol, which came later, means it's certainly a 1970s dress.

The long-line maxi style took over from the mini skirt in the 1970s. With its flowing outline, dropped waist, scooped neck and slightly flared arms this dress evokes Pre-Raphaelite fashion – a look that was spearheaded by London's famous Biba emporium.

Take a close look at the fabric. This is a synthetic wool/mix, which was popular this decade. It meant the fabric could be stretched and therefore cut to figure-hug in a really effective way.

The curving naturalistic print you can see here is another pointer to help you date. The design repeat is big and draws on early 20th-century patterns for its inspiration. Colours are natural tones – more muted than the previous decade.

A Giovannozzi printed stretch jersey maxi dress, Italy, 1970s.
**£50–55 First Call** ⊞

The 1970s was a decade that was devoted to bringing the outside in. Cutting-edge interiors took advantage of plate glass patio doors and open-plan style. So the wearer of this dress with its garden-tone colours and naturalistic pattern was echoing her surroundings quite nicely. The mixed media fabric used here cleverly avoids a debate that ran through the decade – whether synthetics or natural fabrics (championed by the likes of Laura Ashley) were the best. The price reflects the fact that this is a department store interpretation of what was coming out of London's famous Biba store. If it was the `real thing' carrying the trademark Biba label – then you'd expect to pay at least four times as much.

**Katherine Higgins**

## COATS

A Main Bocher silk and velvet evening coat, c1930.

**£530–600 Tin Tin** ⊞

A Petite Française satin jacket, with beadwork collar and buttons, 1960s.

**£50–60 Clobber** ⊞

A cotton Op Art coat, 1960s.

**£55–65 First Call** ⊞

A Charles Ingram paisley evening coat, 1960.

**£90–100 Clobber** ⊞

A silk velvet brocade evening coat, with fur trim, 1920.

**£340–380 Tin Tin** ⊞

## ESSENTIAL REFERENCE  HOUSECOATS

A Kendall's silk housecoat, 1930.

**£160–180 Clobber** ⊞

A Loguette cotton housecoat, 1950s.

**£30–35 Clobber** ⊞

A Su-Ray satin housecoat, 1950s.

**£100–120 Clobber** ⊞

• For the busy housewife housecoats were a bonus. From the 1920s to the late 1950s they were worn over clothes to provide protection while washing and cleaning the home.

• Retailers sold housecoats under a variety of headings – as 'dusters' or even 'housedresses'. The line between housecoat and negligee was also reasonably blurred as the styles were very similar. The key to telling the two apart is length – the negligee reaching down to the ankle.

• Sheer fabrics were commonplace to give a sense of lightness and enable physical work to be carried out without the wearer getting too hot and bothered.

• Styles evolved from the kimono-style wrap of the 1920s to the neatly waisted housecoat of the 1950s.

• By the 1970s the housecoat had died out as more relaxed stretch fabrics and styles of dressing became the norm.

# JACKETS, JUMPERS & BLOUSES

An Edwardian velvet jacket, printed with a paisley pattern and lined with silk.
**£100–120 Decades** ⊞

A Suzanne J. Vernaud wool jacket, with detailed pockets, France, 1930s.
**£75–85 High Street Retro** ⊞

A cotton velvet tailored jacket, with hand-sewn beaded decoration, 1940s.
**£230–260 Wardrobe** ⊞

An organza blouse, 1950s.
**£75–85 Circle** ⊞

A coral-beaded velvet top, 1950s.
**£135–150 Circle** ⊞

A sequined asymmetric top, with tie detail, 1950s.
**£90–100 Vintage Modes** ⊞

A jumper, with striped collar and detailing, 1950s.
**£40–45 First Call** ⊞

A Catherine Buckley silk blouse, 1970s.
**£100–120 Circle** ⊞

A Dorothy Perkins acrylic crocheted top, 1970s.
**£30–35 First Call** ⊞
*While the pattern on this blouse is contemporary, it draws its inspiration from a far earlier period. The flame-like design is strongly based on the paisley pattern shawls worn during the Victorian era, which were imported from the Indian Empire.*

A Maxton stretch acetate blouse, 1970s.
**£25–30 First Call** ⊞

A DKNY silk short-sleeved shirt, with integral briefs, America, 1980s.
**£75–85 First Call** ⊞

A Feminella polyester blouse, with softly padded shoulders, 1980s.
**£20–25 First Call** ⊞

## SKIRTS & TROUSERS

A cotton skirt, printed with a fruit and vegetable pattern, 1950.
**£15–20 Decades** ⊞

A printed cotton A-line skirt, with Lightning zip, 1950s.
**£30–35 First Call** ⊞

A tie-dyed cotton skirt, 1960s.
**£25–30 First Call** ⊞

A Marks & Spencer St Michael cotton skirt, 1960s.
**£25–30 Twinkled** ⊞

A printed cotton A-line mini skirt, 1970s.
**£25–30 First Call** ⊞

A pair of Bus Stop cotton flared trousers, 1970s.
**£40–45 Clobber** ⊞

A pair of Trio International striped Terylene and wool mix trousers, 1970s.
**£30–35 First Call** ⊞

A pair of PVC trousers, 1990s.
**£40–45 First Call** ⊞

# MENSWEAR – SHIRTS & JUMPERS

A Monu cotton Hawaiian shirt, c1960.
**£20–25 Repsycho** ⊞

A Marks & Spencer St Michael turtle-neck pullover, with inset ribbed neck panel, 1960s.
**£25–30 First Call** ⊞
*St Michael was registered as the Marks & Spencer trademark in 1928, just two years after the firm started selling textiles. As part of a corporate rebranding, its use was dropped in 2000.*

A Christopher New cotton shirt, with Indonesian print, 1980s.
**£10–15 First Call** ⊞

A Double 2 polyester and cotton 'That Shirt' city shirt, 1980s.
**£5–10 First Call** ⊞

An Oakland polyester shirt, 1980s.
**£10–15 First Call** ⊞

An O. C. Sportswear cotton shirt, with Tahitian print, Australia, 1980s.
**£15–20 First Call** ⊞

An Americano cotton shirt, with tropical print, 1980s.
**£15–20 First Call** ⊞

A Morley cotton shirt, 1980s.
**£15–20 First Call** ⊞
*Morley also made a line of acrylic jumpers.*

## MENSWEAR – JACKETS, TROUSERS & SUITS

A Burley Wear woollen overcoat, 1952.
**£70–80 Mr Moore** ⊞

A Honda leather jacket, 1960s.
**£65–75 Clobber** ⊞

A pair of Riviera GTX woven cotton
trousers, Canada, 1960s.
**£20–25 Clobber** ⊞
*Riviera started as trouser specialists in 1946,
opening their first manufacturing plant in
Quebec in 1952. By the 1960s, the firm was
well established and the brand was synonymous
with good quality and cutting-edge design.*

A Hardy Amies checked waistcoat, 1960s.
**£25–30 First Call** ⊞
*This was originally part of a three-piece suit.
Complete with matching jacket and
trousers, it would be worth £180.*

A Kant & Co Beatles-style two-piece suit,
India, late 1960s.
**£80–90 Clobber** ⊞
*The London tailor Douglas Millings made
many of The Beatles' early stage suits. He
took the look from friend and designer Pierre
Cardin's creations. The style was so popular
that high-street versions rapidly appeared.
This bespoke suit is an Indian tailor's take
on the Fab Four's style.*

A pair of Honorbilt wool and polyester
checked trousers, 1970s.
**£25–30 First Call** ⊞
*After decades of fashion success, Honorbilt
(formerly a division of Austin Reed) collapsed
in 1990.*

## THE EVOLUTION OF THE TIE

At the beginning of the 20th century
there were two tie styles – the long neck
tie and the short bow tie. In the post-
war decades the bow tie lost ground and
was side-lined to formal wear. This left
the long neck tie scope to change in
width, print and fabric as the decades
progressed. To help with dating, think
about what the stars were wearing in a
particular era – they set many of the
trends that the high streets mirrored.
Then look at the material – synthetics
were big from the 1960s on. Check
labels carefully and avoid anything
where the stitched lining is worn.

Bow tie - Frank Sinatra was a
fan of bow ties in the 1940s.

Polyester tie 1960s – The
slimline style is often
referred to as the `Skinny
Rockabilly' & it found
popularity in the 1950s
and 1960s.

Synthetic Tie – 1960s –
The dead straight style
was ideal for knitting so
you'll often see this
shape in wool.

A Zootz wool and polyester suit, with Opti zip, 1960s.
**£135–150 First Call** ⊞

A VDN denim-look polyester suit, 1970s.
**£145–160 First Call** ⊞

A Lord West two-piece evening suit, 1970s.
**£85–95 Rokit (B)** ⊞

A Sears suede jacket, Canada, 1970s–80s.
**£20–25 Rokit** ⊞

A Fred Perry windbreaker, 1980s.
**£45–50 Clobber** ⊞

A Schott Bros suede leather rancher's jacket, with fringe detailing, 1980s.
**£45–50 Rokit (B)** ⊞

Cotton Cravat – 1960s – The Paisley print was big around the Summer of Love. John Lennon had his Rolls Royce painted in Paisley in 1967.

Polyester pre-tied tie – 1970s. The A line shape is a marker of 70s style. Other big hints come in the form of the colour, synthetic polyester and the pre-tied elastic.

M&S 1980s – Yuppie 1980s fashion was all about power-clashing – spots went with striped shirts and geometric prints of any sort were 'in'. Note how the width reduces.

M&S 1990s – Dress down days see fewer ties sold this decade. Prints are more abstract.

# SWIMWEAR

A knitted wool swimsuit, 1930s.
**£60–70  First Call** ⊞

A knitted wool swimsuit, with boned bodice and overskirt, 1940s.
**£55–60  First Call** ⊞

A Slix swimsuit, 1950s.
**£40–45  First Call** ⊞

A stretch swimsuit, 1950s.
**£40–45  First Call** ⊞

A cotton swimsuit, France, 1950s.
**£40–45  High Street Retro** ⊞

An Aquapoise printed cotton swimsuit, with boned bodice, 1950s.
**£40–45  First Call** ⊞

A stretch swimsuit, 1960s.
**£30–35  First Call** ⊞

A Silhouette swimsuit, 1960s.
**£30–35  First Call** ⊞

This belt is largely decorative. It's a throw back to the early 1930s `Mens' Toppers', which were all-in-one two-tone bathing suits separated by a belt.

Always look carefully at buttons, poppers and studs. Quality costumes, like this, often carry a logo or maker's details — here it's the Sportsman frog.

A pair of Sportsman swimming trunks, with original plastic packaging, 1960s.

**£25–30  First Call** ⊞

1960s swimwear took advantage of stretch synthetics like Nylon and Lycra, which were often mixed for a super-stretch fit.

Having the original bag is a nice touch for a collector. It also adds a little more detail to the brand, revealing how it was sold. The makers were competitors of the hugely successful swimwear firm, Jantzen.

This decade there's a move away from 1950s boxer-style swim suits and a subtle rise in hem length. This is a trunk costume with slim thigh-hugging legs. It paves the way for the Speedo style brief, which dominated male swimwear fashion in the 1970s.

It's astonishing to think that something as familiar as men's swimming trunks didn't exist until the 1930s. Baring a chest was frowned upon and men's swimwear fashion followed women's with all-in-one bathing suits regulatory in the first few decades of the 20th century. The men's topper (from 1932), with its detachable bodice was a step forwards. This was swiftly followed by Johnny Weissmuller's promotional pictures for the BVD company (Bradley, Vohees & Day), which featured the Olympic swimming champion in trunks. Jantzen also promoted their 'streamlined' trunks around the same time. The first `topless' Olympics for men took place in 1936 and from that moment on, male swimwear never looked back. Key brands like Jantzen and BVD will always prove long-term collectables.

## BUTTONS

A set of six silver-plated buttons, France, c1900, 1in (2.5cm) diam.
**£30–35 Jessie's Button Box ⊞**

A set of six Kate Greenaway enamelled brass buttons, c1910, 1¼in (3cm) diam.
**£40–45 Jessie's Button Box ⊞**

A set of six brass buttons, each depicting a cockerel, c1920s, 1½in (4cm) wide.
**£40–45 Jessie's Button Box ⊞**

A set of six Glows celluloid buttons, 1920s.
**£25–30 Marlene Evans ⊞**

A set of six plastic buttons, 1930, ¾in (2cm) diam.
**£5–10 299 ⊞**

A pearlized celluloid flower button, c1930, 1½in (4cm) wide.
**£1–5 Clifton Hill Textiles ⊞**

A wood and chrome button, c1930, 1in (2.5cm) wide.
**£1–5 Clifton Hill Textiles ⊞**

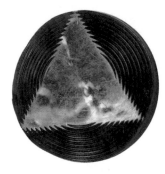

Two Bakelite buttons, c1930, larger 1½in (4cm) wide.
**£1–5 Clifton Hill Textiles ⊞**

A moulded Perspex button, c1930, 1¼in (3cm) wide.
**£1–5 Clifton Hill Textiles ⊞**

A set of four resin buttons, decorated with metal discs in the form of a flower, 1930s, 2in (5cm) diam.
**£35–40 Marlene Evans ⊞**

A set of six plastic buttons, 1930s, 1¼in (3cm) wide.
**£15–20 299 ⊞**

A set of five casein buttons, c1930, ¾in (2cm) diam.
**£1–5 Clifton Hill Textiles ⊞**

A set of six plastic buttons, 1940,
1in (2.5cm) diam.

**£10–15** 299 ⊞

A painted wooden button, c1940,
1in (2.5cm) diam.

**£1–5 Clifton Hill Textiles** ⊞

A painted wooden button, c1940,
1in (2.5cm) diam.

**£1–5 Clifton Hill Textiles** ⊞

A Famox Design glass Jumblie button,
c1950, 1½in (4cm) high.

**£10–15 Marlene Evans** ⊞

A Perspex button, with a gilt flame pattern,
1950s, 1in (2.5cm) diam.

**£1–5 Edith Cambley** ⊞

Two Perspex buttons, with gilt decoration,
1950s, 1½in (4cm) diam.

**£1–5 Edith Cambley** ⊞

## ESSENTIAL REFERENCE CASEIN

A layered casein button, c1930,
1¼in (3cm) diam.

**£1–5 Clifton Hill Textiles** ⊞

A pressed casein button, c1930,
1in (2.5cm) diam.

**£1–5 Clifton Hill Textiles** ⊞

A layered casein button, c1940,
1in (2.5cm) diam.

**£1–5 Clifton Hill Textiles** ⊞

• Casein is a milk protein. The Ancient Egyptians are known to have used it as fixative in their wall paintings. Its potential as a plastics material was explored in the late 19th century simultaneously in France and Germany. In 1900 the public saw it first hand at the Paris Universal Exhibition where it appeared under the tradename Galalith.

• Galalith was made from dry casein granules and its success bred competitors like Britain's Erinoid, widely used by Birmingham button firms when supplies of Galalith were suspended during WWI, and Aladdinite and Ameroid in the US. In 1922 BX Plastics unveiled another variant, Lactoid, which was soon joined by Dorcasine from Charles Horner, a popular material for knitting needles.

• Its heyday for use as buttons was in the late 1920s and early 1930s but by the 1960s its use was limited as other plastics took over.

• The wide variety of colours available from pastels to pearls and mottles meant casein was an ideal material for buttons. It wasn't easy to mould so most of the buttons were stamped or sliced from rods. For a two-tone effect a dyed surface was cut-back to reveal the natural colour beneath.

• Water and casein do not mix well, soaking for any length of time in water will damage your buttons so take care!

**COSTUME JEWELLERY – BRACELETS**

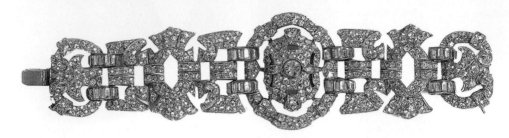

A diamond-cut paste and diamanté bracelet, France, 1920s, 2in (5cm) wide.
**£270–300  Wardrobe** ⊞

A Bakelite bangle, c1930.
**£15–20  Tony Durante** ⊞

A pressed Bakelite bangle, c1930.
**£15–20  Tony Durante** ⊞

A moulded Bakelite bangle, c1930.
**£15–20  Tony Durante** ⊞

A Bakelite bangle, with carved decoration, 1930s, 1½in (4cm) wide.
**£110–125  Wardrobe** ⊞

A Bakelite bangle, 1930s, 2in (5cm) wide.
**£90–100  Wardrobe** ⊞

A Bakelite bangle, 1930s, 1in (2.5cm) wide.
**£60–70  Wardrobe** ⊞

A gold-plated bracelet, 1940s, 7½in (19cm) long.
**£90–100  Tony Durante** ⊞

A Bakelite bangle, c1940.
**£15–20  Tony Durante** ⊞

A Gerry Fells copper bangle, late 1940s, 1½in (4cm) wide.
**£90–100  Just Jewellery** ⊞

A gold-plated bracelet, 1940s, 8in (20.5cm) long.
**£75–85 Tony Durante** ⊞

A Perspex bangle, engraved with roses, c1950.
**£25–30 Tony Durante** ⊞

A gold metal charm bangle, 1950, 7in (18cm) long.
**£40–45 Sparkle Moore** ⊞

A plastic, pearl and diamanté bangle, 1950, 1in (2.5cm) wide.
**£80–90 Sparkle Moore** ⊞

A plastic bangle, c1950.
**£10–15 Tony Durante** ⊞

A Miriam Haskell glass bead, *faux* pearl, seed pearl and paste bracelet, America, 1950.
**£290–325 Arlene De Vries** ⊞

A Trifari bracelet, America, 1950s, 1in (2.5cm) wide.
**£50–60 Just Jewellery** ⊞

A bracelet, Czechoslovakia, 1950s,
2in (5cm) wide.
**£540–600 Steinberg & Tolkien** ⊞

A Galalith bracelet, 1970s.
**£15–20 Tony Durante** ⊞

A plastic imitation jet bangle, c1980.
**£15–20 Tony Durante** ⊞

COSTUME JEWELLERY – BROOCHES

## COSTUME JEWELLERY – BROOCHES

A rhinestone hat flash/lapel brooch, 1920s–30s, 4in (10cm) wide.

**£20–25  Sue Wilde** ⊞

A Bakelite horse's head brooch, c1920, 2½in (6.5cm) wide.

**£75–85  Jessie's Button Box** ⊞

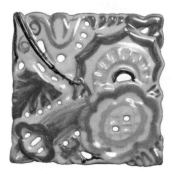

A Poole brooch, designed by Truda Carter, with perforated decoration, c1930, 2¼in (5.5cm) square.

**£220–250  Marsh-McNamara** ⊞

A metal and enamel flower brooch, 1930s, 1in (2.5cm) wide.

**£40–45  Linda Bee** ⊞

A paste swan brooch, c1940, 2in (5cm) wide.

**£45–50  Jessie's Button Box** ⊞
*The lavish use of paste and the bird motif were inspired by the glittering brooches that Cartier crafted for the Duchess of Windsor.*

A plastic Scottie dog brooch, 1930s–40s, 3in (7.5cm) diam.

**£25–30  Dreamtime** ⊞

A Galalith clock brooch, with original shop label, Austria, 1930s, 3in (7.5cm) long.

**£90–100  Wardrobe** ⊞

A silver brooch, the turban set with a stone, hallmarks for Birmingham, c1946, 1½in (4cm) high.

**£90–100  Le Boudoir** ⊞

An R. Mandle brass and enamel horse's head brooch, c1950, 2in (5cm) high.

**£75–85** Jessie's Button Box ⊞

A Jomaz paste brooch, signed, America, 1950s, 2½in (6.5cm) wide.

**£100–110** Le Boudoir ⊞

An enamelled starfish brooch, set with paste stones, 1950s, 2in (5cm) wide.

**£50–60** Jessie's Button Box ⊞

A poodle brooch, America, 1950s, 1½in (4cm) wide.

**£15–20** Dreamtime ⊞

*The poodle was a popular 1950s motif and it apeared on period fabrics and handbags as well as on countless pieces of costume jewellery. This example is particularly well detailed.*

A Weiss cut-glass costume brooch, 1950s, 3in (7.5cm) wide.

**£60–70** Le Boudoir ⊞

A Miriam Haskell brooch, set with *faux* pearls, America, c1960, 2in (5cm) diam.

**£220–250** Arlene De Vries ⊞

A Kenneth Jay Lane brooch/pendant, set with paste stones and *faux* pearls, with a paste stone in centre, America, c1960, 2in (5cm) wide.

**£150–165** Arlene De Vries ⊞

A plastic rabbit brooch, 1960s, 2½in (6.5cm) wide.

**£35–40** Dreamtime ⊞

A Joseph Warner gold metal Day and Night brooch, with open-and-shut mechanism, c1960, 2in (5cm) wide.

**£150–175** Arlene De Vries ⊞

A Lea Stein cellulose acetate owl brooch, signed, France, 1970s, 3in (7.5cm) long.

**£35–40** Wardrobe ⊞

## COSTUME JEWELLERY – NECKLACES

A Bakelite necklace, 1930s, 18in (45.5cm) long.
**£150–170  La Femme** ⊞

A straw necklace, France, 1930s,
14in (35.5cm) long.
**£65–75  Dreamtime** ⊞

A copper and enamel necklace, 1940s–50s,
15in (38cm) long.
**£100–120  Just Jewellery** ⊞

A Miriam Haskell *faux* pearl necklace,
set with paste stones in antiqued metal,
America, c1950.
**£300–350  Arlene De Vries** ⊞

A Vendome paste necklace, America, 1950s,
18in (45.5cm) long.
**£250–270  Tony Durante** ⊞
*Vendome was a top-end mark used by US-
based Coro (named after founders Cohen and
Rosenberg). The mark was used from 1944 to
attract wealthy clients to their jewellery.*

An Askel Holmsen enamelled silver
necklace, Norway, c1950.
**£70–85  Vetta Decorative Arts** ⊞

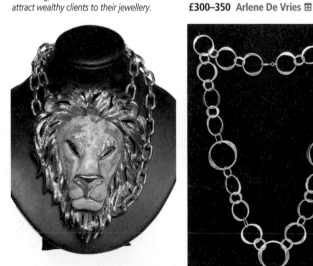

A Razza gilt-metal and plastic lion's head
necklace, made to resemble Bakelite, late
1960s, 4in (10cm) wide.
**£300–350  Arlene De Vries** ⊞

A Herman Siersbol silver necklace, Denmark,
1972, 30in (76cm) long.
**£360–400  Boom Interiors** ⊞

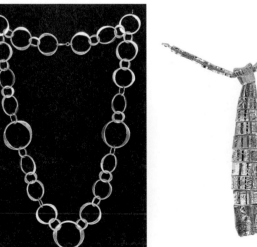

A Val Hunt kipper tie necklace, made from
recycled cans, 2003, 14in (35.5cm) long.
**£100–120  La Femme** ⊞

# EYEWEAR

A pair of plastic glasses, with diamanté decoration, France, early 1950s.
**£40–45 299** ⊞

A pair of Valentino plastic sunglasses, 1970s.
**£115–130 Rokit (B)** ⊞

A pair of Vergo plastic sunglasses, France, 1950s, 5½in (14cm) wide.
**£30–35 299** ⊞

A pair of Christian Dior plastic sunglasses, with graduated lenses, 1970s.
**£115–130 Rokit (B)** ⊞

A pair of Valentino plastic sunglasses, 1970s, 5½in (14cm) wide.
**£120–130 Rokit (B)** ⊞

Two pairs of plastic sunglasses, c1970.
**£1–5 Clifton Hill Textiles** ⊞

A pair of Christian Dior sunglasses, 1970s, with original case.
**£135–150 Rokit (B)** ⊞

A cut-steel beaded evening bag, France, 1918, 8in (20.5cm) high.
**£200–230 Tin Tin** ⊞

A knitted bag, with Bakelite clasp, c1920, 6in (15cm) wide.
**£25–30 Collectable Costume** ⊞

A beaded bag, with *faux* tortoiseshell frame, c1925, 15in (38cm) long.
**£300–340 Design Gallery** ⊞

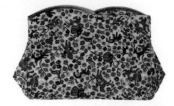

A printed fabric handbag, 1930s, 9in (23cm) wide.
**£45–50 Dreamtime** ⊞

An Art Deco-style paste evening handbag, France, 1930s, 4in (10cm) high.
**£135–150 Tony Durante** ⊞

A shagreen handbag, with silver mounts, 1930s, 8in (20.5cm) wide.
**£450–500 Sue Wilde** ⊞

A paste evening handbag, Germany, 1930s, 6in (15cm) high.
**£180–200 Tony Durante** ⊞

A printed plastic handbag, 1940s, 8in (20.5cm) wide.
**£50–55 Dreamtime** ⊞

A woven straw handbag, 1950, 14in (35.5cm) high.
**£70–80 Sparkle Moore** ⊞

A plastic clutch bag, decorated with simulated pearls, c1950, 9in (23cm) wide.
**£20–25 Jessie's Button Box** ⊞

A cord handbag, c1950, 7in (18cm) high.
**£35–40 Collectable Costume** ⊞

A cloth handbag, with a Lucite handle, 1950s, 8in (20.5cm) wide.
**£50–60 Just Jewellery** ⊞

A paste evening clutch bag, Germany, 1960, 7½in (19cm) wide.
**£180–200 Tony Durante** ⊞

A patent leather handbag, 1960,
9in (23cm) wide.
**£20–25 Decades** ⊞

A Gucci crocodile-skin handbag, 1962,
9in (23cm) wide.
**£750–850 Tin Tin Collectables** ⊞

A Lederer crocodile-skin handbag, France,
1960s, 8½in (21.5cm) wide.
**£700–800 Elizabeth Gibbons** ⊞

# HATS

A silk top hat, by R. W. Forsyth, 1900–20.

**£75–85 Mia Cartwright** ⊞

*R. W. Forsyth (known as Forsyth's) grew from humble beginnings as a gentleman's tailors and outfitters to be one of Scotland's premier outfitters in the early 20th century. They had department stores in both Edinburgh and Glasgow. The link to such a well-respected firm adds value to this hat.*

A wool hat, 1940s.

**£155–175 Tin Tin** ⊞

A cotton plate hat, 1950s.

**£45–50 Dreamtime** ⊞

**An American Union hat,** decorated with netting, with label, 1950s.

**£20–25 Just Jewellery** ⊞

An ostrich feather and silk cloche hat, by Ela Sig & Co, Barcelona, Spain, c1919.

**£270–300 Tin Tin** ⊞

A straw hat, 1920s.

**£30–35 Collectable Costume** ⊞

A felt hat, 1940s.

**£25–30 Dreamtime** ⊞

*This hat echoes the style of the stars of Twentieth Century-Fox.*

A silk velvet hat, by B. Forman & Co, America, 1950s.

**£45–50 Dreamtime** ⊞

*B. Forman & Co (est 1908) were women's apparel retailers based in Rochester, New York. In the 1960s, Forman's owner, Maurice F. Forman collaborated to open America's first shopping mall, 'Midtown Plaza', in Rochester. The firm closed in 1994.*

A silk and straw cloche hat, c1920.

**£110–125 Echoes** ⊞

A straw Panama hat, 1930s.

**£65–75 Tin Tin** ⊞

A felt hat, 1940s.

**£65–75 First Call** ⊞

A wide-brimmed hat, 1960s.

**£15–20 Decades** ⊞

## EXPERT'S EYE  1950S HAT

Seemingly simple in design this is a highly complicated piece of millinery. Each feather is stitched by hand to the hat base, which gives the hat its structure and support.

This hat was meant to be worn slightly to one side. It was a very popular style in the early 1950s and would have been a perfect match for a waisted New Look jacket and voluminous A-line skirt.

Plumage was very popular in the early 1950s for hats but later in the decade floral decoration replaced it. The feathers were curled and dyed then trimmed to fit.

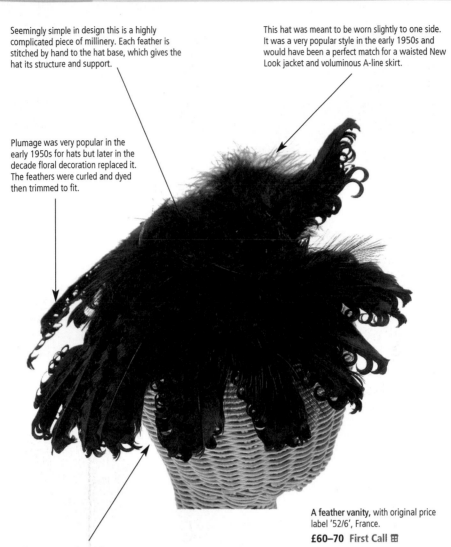

A feather vanity, with original price label '52/6', France.

**£60–70  First Call** ⊞

With a price tag of 52 shillings and 6d this was an expensive item, twice the cost of a beret-style hat, which was also popular at the time.

MADE IN FRANCE

Turn it over and take a look inside to spot the quality of construction. The lining of a hat is the last element to be added and you can see here that it hasn't been replaced and still bears its original labels. The detail and quality points to French manufacture, even without the label to prove it.

The 1950s was a crucial decade for hat design. It began with an enthusiasm to be feminine, to wear the luxurious materials and fabrics that were largely unavailable in the war years. It ended with the emergence of a teenage style that turned its back on formality and therefore hat design in favour of hairstyling and new hair cuts. This makes millinery from this period fascinating to collect. Although we're no longer a nation of hat wearers, there is still a time and a place for headwear like this. Many collectors buy to wear. If that's you – make sure your potential purchase is well-made and the applied decoration is well secured.

## SHOES

A pair of satin and kid evening shoes, c1920.
**£80–90 Echoes** ⊞

A pair of brocade and lamé evening shoes, c1930.
**£135–150 Tin Tin** ⊞

A pair of Rayne lizard and suede shoes, 1930s.
**£50–55 Tin Tin** ⊞
*The family shoe firm H. M. Rayne & Co was founded in 1889. Actress Lily Langtree promoted the firm's Langtree shoe in the 1920s and shortly afterwards Rayne's was awarded a Royal Warrant from Queen Mary. The firm was known for its high quality fashionable footwear. It was the first British firm to introduce machinery from the USA to make more flexible soles.*

A pair of suede shoes, 1940s.
**£55–65 High Street Retro** ⊞

A pair of Dal & Co leather shoes, with beaded decoration, 1950s.
**£35–40 Clobber** ⊞

A pair of Ferragamo leather shoes, Italy, 1960.
**£45–50 Rokit (B)** ⊞

A pair of Barratt's International Girl suede shoes, 1960s.
**£15–20 High Street Retro** ⊞

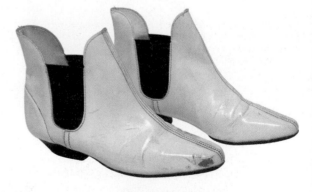

A pair of ClockHouse patent plastic boots, 1980s.
**£50–55 First Call** ⊞
*The ClockHouse brand appeared in C&A stores in the 1980s as part of young and trendy fashion. These boots are not from the 1960s, although they do have a Mary Quant feel.*

A pair of Meyer leather platform shoes, Germany, c1970.
**£270–300  Clobber** ⊞

A pair of Lugtan leather platform shoes, Spain, c1970.
**£135–150  Clobber** ⊞

A pair of Joseph Larose leather shoes,
America, Florida, 1970s.

**£35–40  Twinkled** ⊞
*Giuseppe (Joseph) Larose designed and made
shoes and matching handbags for 50 years from
1949. Marilyn Monroe, Joan Crawford and
Brooke Shields were among his celebrity clients.*

A pair of Celine leather shoes, 1970s.
**£45–50  Rokit** ⊞

A pair of Melanddi suede and leather Jam shoes, c1980s.
**£70–75  Clobber** ⊞
*Melanddi's was based in London's fashionable Carnaby Street and was
a Mecca in the late 1970s/early 1980s for 'Mod-style' fashion. These
would have looked good with a 'pork pie' hat and one of their Time
UK suits complete with trousers that had patch pockets at the knee.*

A pair of Connie Shoe Creations celluloid and leather sandals, 1980s.
**£50–55  First Call** ⊞

# FILM & ENTERTAINMENT

A celluloid Popeye brooch, c1930, 2in (5cm) high.

**£60–70 collectorsworld** ⊞

A Twentieth Century-Fox production used unit list, from *Alien*, 1978.

**£175–195 Prop Store** ⊞

A *Superman* original film script, 1978, 12in (30.5cm) high.

**£2,500–2,750 Prop Store** ⊞

A prop cat, from *Superman*, 1978, 16½in (42cm) wide.

**£900–1,000 Prop Store** ⊞

*This cat was made by legendary make-up artist Stuart Freeborn. It comes with slides showing the cat being made, with the real cat being used as a model, in the Stuart Freeborn studio. The cat, which was named 'Frisky', can be seen in a collage of scenes and Superman can be seen saving a cat from a tree. This is the stunt one that was sitting in the tree waiting to be saved.*

A set of five scripts, from *M\*A\*S\*H*, 1980–82.

**£100–125 Heritage** 🔧

An unfinished Ewok mask, by Kenny Baker, from *Star Wars – Return Of The Jedi*, 1983.

**£400–450 Prop Store** ⊞

A model taxi, from *Independence Day*, 1996, 8½in (21.5cm) long.

**£220–250 Prop Store** ⊞

An ILM model miniature mine car and barrels, from *Indiana Jones And The Temple Of Doom*, 1984, mine car 8in (20.5cm )wide.

**£1,350–1,500 Prop Store** ⊞

**S.S. TITANIC**

A plastic *S.S. Titanic* lifeboat sign, from *Titanic*, 1997, 13½ x 4in (34.5 x 10cm).

**£340–380 Prop Store** ⊞

A First Class salt shaker, from *Titanic*, 1997, 3½in (9cm) high.

**£180–200 Prop Store** ⊞

A miniature bale of straw, from *Chicken Run*, 2000, 6in (15cm) long.

**£35–40 Prop Store** ⊞

## EXPERT EYE  CHEWBACCA HAIR DISPLAY

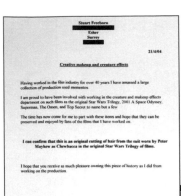

This letter is from Stuart Freeborn who also created Yoda. The paperwork that comes with an item is all-important. Some dealers offer a money-back guarantee.

**A Chewbacca hair display,** from *Star Wars – A New Hope*, 1977, together with a signed letter from the make-up artist Stuart Freeborn, 19 x 16½in (48.5 x 42cm), framed.

**£155–175  Prop Store** ⊞

This autograph was obtained 'in person'. Peter Mayhew was happy to oblige as he remembered Stuart Freeborn fondly.

One should always try to buy the most recognizable item. If it is desirable now, it should be in the future. Never buy for investment only – always buy what you love. *Star Wars* is the most sought after and requested title.

The most popular genres in film and entertainment collectables are science fiction (such as *Star Wars*) and action (such as James Bond) and, therefore, items from such movies generally command the highest prices. One of the reasons for this is that the props and costumes are generally tailored specifically for the production, usually functional gadgets such as light-up 'laser guns', space suits and other 'eye candy' pieces. Do not buy for investment only. The movie memorabilia market can be fickle and although there are sound investments to be had, blind speculation should be avoided. The golden rule is to buy what you love – try to obtain a piece from your favourite movie or a costume worn by your favourite star. If you have a choice, buy a complete costume or a hero metal weapon as opposed to the rubber vesion, or a set with missing components.

**Tim Lawes,  The Prop Store of London**

A fleece crew jacket, from *Tomb Raider*, 2001.
**£55–60 Prop Store** ⊞

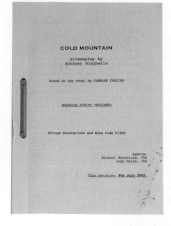

A revised production script, from *Cold Mountain*, July 2002, 11¾ x 8¼in (30 x 21cm).
**£25–30 Prop Store** ⊞

A prop copy of the *Guardian* newspaper, from *Ali G Inda House*, 2002, 24 x 15in (61 x 38cm).
**£220–250 Prop Store** ⊞

A metal and wood crossbow, from *Buffy The Vampire Slayer*, 2003, 27in (68.5cm) long.
**£2,300–2,550 Prop Store** ⊞

A production used call sheet, from *Alfie*, dated 9th September 2003, 11¾ x 8¼in (30 x 21cm).
**£10–15 Prop Store** ⊞

A David Spencer prop newspaper display, from *Love Actually*, 2003, 23½ x 14½in (59.5 x 37cm).
**£270–300 Prop Store** ⊞

A rubber helmet for Roman cavalry officer, from *King Arthur*, 2004.
**£300–350 Prop Store** ⊞

A lobby card, *Angels With Dirty Faces*, starring James Cagney and Pat O'Brien, 1938, 11 x 14in (28 x 35.5cm).
**£850–950 Cine Art Gallery** ⊞

A lobby card, *City Lights*, starring Charlie Chaplin, 1950 re-release of 1931 film, 11 x 14in (28 x 35.5cm).
**£100–115 Limelight** ⊞

A clapper board display, from *Finding Neverland*, framed with the film logo, 2004, 26in (66cm) high.
**£450–500 Prop Store** ⊞

A lobby card, *Saint Joan*, by Saul Bass Art, America, 1957, 11 x 14in (28 x 35.5cm).
**£300–330 Limelight**

A lobby card, *The Blues Brothers*, America, 1980, 11 x 14in (28 x 35.5cm).
**£110–125 Limelight** ⊞

A tin-plate clockwork musical Mickey Mouse hurdy-gurdy, by Distler & Co, Germany, 1930s, 7in (18cm) high.
**£1,350–1,500  J & S Haley** ⊞

A Mickey Mouse soft toy, possibly by Dean's Rag Book Co, c1930, 21in (53.5cm) high.
**£160–185  Pollyanna** ⊞

A Snow White celluloid brooch, c1932, 2in (5cm) wide.
**£120–135  collectorsworld** ⊞

A reprint of 1940 lobby card, *Pinocchio*, America, 1954, 11 x 14in (28 x 35.5cm).
**£220–240  Limelight** ⊞

A Disney promotional plaster figure of Donald Duck, 1950s, 17in (43cm) high.
**£180–200  Cobwebs** ⊞

A Disney *Wuzzle* Piggypine plush soft toy, 1985–87, 11in (28cm) high.
**£10–15  Kevin Ward** ⊞

A Disney *Wuzzle* Hoppopotamus plush soft toy, 1985–87, 13in (33cm) high.
**£5–10  Kevin Ward** ⊞

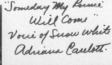

A signed photograph of Adrianna Caselotti, the voice of Snow White, from the Disney film *Snow White and the Seven Dwarfs*, 1995, 8 x 10in (20.5 x 25.5cm).
**£50–55  Autograph Collector's Gallery** ⊞

# GARDENING

A steel turfing iron, with a wooden handle, c1890, 55in (139.5cm) long.
**£25–30 Top Banana** ⊞

A metal trench digger, with a wooden handle, c1900, 38in (96.5cm) long.
**£45–50 Yew Tree** ⊞

An iron and string garden line, c1900, 19in (48.5cm) high.
**£35–40 Antique Garden** ⊞

A hand weeder, with a wooden handle, c1910, 9in (23cm) long.
**£20–25 Antique Garden** ⊞

A Brades Co steel billhook, c1910, 15in (38cm) long.
**£30–35 Antique Garden** ⊞
*A billhook is a traditional cutting tool that is halfway between a knife and an axe, sharpened on the inside of the blade's curve. It is used for cutting thick, woody plants like saplings and small branches. In the early 20th century it was such a popular tool that as many as 200 regional variants were advertised.*

An onion hoe, c1920, 15in (38cm) long.
**£5–10 Ann Lingard** ⊞

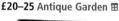

A steel hand fork, with a wooden handle, c1910, 8in (20.5cm) long.
**£20–25 Antique Garden** ⊞

A steel scythe, with a wooden handle, c1920, 65in (165cm) long.
**£25–30 Top Banana** ⊞

A steel daisy grubber, with a wooden handle and engraved detail, c1920, 19in (48.5cm) long.
**£35–40 Antique Garden** ⊞
*This ingenious tool was used for removing weeds with a strong tap root. They often had long wooden handles for greater leverage.*

A steel hand hoe, with a wooden handle, c1920, 8in (20.5cm) long.
**£25–30 Antique Garden** ⊞

A steel edging tool, with an ash handle, c1930, 35in (89cm) long.
**£25–30 Antique Garden** ⊞

A steel hand sickle, with an ash handle, c1930, 23in (58.5cm) long.
**£20–25** Antique Garden ⊞

A steel hand claw weeder and cultivator, with a wooden handle, c1930, 17in (43cm) long.
**£25–30** Antique Garden ⊞

A William Paisley brass lawn aerator, c1930, 37in (94cm) long.
**£50–60** Top Banana ⊞

A brass and steel garden sprayer, c1930, 34in (86.5cm) high.
**£80–90** Top Banana ⊞

An aluminium lawn sprinkler, c1950, 4in (10cm) long.
**£5–10** Antique Garden ⊞

A wooden Sussex trug, c1938, 21in (53.5cm) wide.
**£45–50** Antique Garden ⊞

A Dutch hoe, c1950, 54½in (138.5cm) long.
**£5–10** Ann Lingard ⊞

A Martineau & Smith brass plant sprayer, 1920–50, 24in (61cm) long.
**£30–35** Antique Garden ⊞

A Hawes copper miniature watering can, c1950, 14in (35.5cm) wide.
**£35–40** Antique Garden ⊞

## ESSENTIAL REFERENCE SHEARS & CLIPPING

A pair of steel garden shears, with wooden handles, c1930, 14in (35.5cm) long.
**£30–35** Yew Tree ⊞

A pair of steel serrated-edge shears, with wooden handles, c1930, 21in (53.5cm) long.
**£30–35** Antique Garden ⊞

A pair of Felco steel secateurs, c1940, 8in (20.5cm) long.
**£10–15** Antique Garden ⊞

• The earliest garden sheers date from the 18th century. The secateur was introduced from France in the early 19th century as an improved pruning sheer. The cutting action was like a pair of scissors and they were designed to trim woody stems.

• Old hedging sheers are popular collectors' items and buyers snap them up to both wall mount and use. Many say that you can't beat the feel and cut of vintage sheers.

• Look out for sheers with nicely patinated wooden handles. Also don't forget that vintage secateurs are not suitable for left-handed users – this is a modern improvement.

# GLASS

LONG REGARDED as the poor, unattractive relation of ceramics, glass has risen up the agenda markedly over the past few years — the ugly ducking transformed into a glorious swan. The reasons for this are subtle, but it is an undeniable fact that fresh, younger eyes find something that previous generations failed to appreciate in its sculptural, spontaneous qualities and, perhaps above all, its vibrant transparency. The result is that there have been big wins for the early-birds who picked future winners, particularly for those who bought pieces made within living memory and particularly the past 30 or 40 years. Those who picked up large, colourful and idiosyncratic pieces by Whitefriars a decade ago, for instance, have been laughing all the way to the bank, their values having soared by as much as 1000 per cent in a decade.

The plain fact is that glass needs light to live. Stuffed away in a curio cabinet it tends to look flat and boring. When lit, either by the sun or artificially, it blossoms and gains a vibrancy that leaves objects formed in other materials, such as ceramics, wood and metal, looking as unattractive as...well, unlit glass.

A Riihimaen Lasi Oy glass **Candida** vase, by Nanny Still, signed 'Nanny Still, Riihimaen Lasi Oy', Finland, 1967, 11in (28cm) high.
**£250–275 glas-design.nl** ⊞

Significant rises have also been witnessed in other areas, including certain mid-18th-century drinking glasses, especially those decorated by the Beilby family, c1760, but these have always been relatively expensive. However, with most 'serious' collectors on the lookout for areas that combine aesthetic satisfaction and potential value growth, Beilby glasses, currently starting at around £3,000 each, can hardly be recommended.

A Dartington glass sculpture, by Sarah Peterson, c2001, 12in (30.5cm) high.
**£100–110 Quay Centre** ⊞

Some of the factors that electrify prices will forever remain elusive, even after the event. However, the ability to identify the designer and maker of specific pieces has always had a catalytic effect on demand. Typically, my recent book *Miller's 20th-Century Glass*, has helped to propel the work of Helena Tynell and Nanny Still for the Finnish Riihimäki glassworks into the mainstream, and two new works on Frank Thrower's designs have caused the price of early rare pieces of Dartington to hit the roof.

The knack of combining enjoyment with profit requires the study of the available literature. Identify precisely what you like and buy the best you can afford in that category and remember, large, colourful and signed pieces by the best designers and makers invariably do better, very much better, than smaller, undistinguished ones.

**Andy McConnell**

# BRITISH

A Chance Bros glass handkerchief vase, 1970s, 7in (18cm) high.

**£20–25  Luna** ⊞

*This vase was made in three sizes and was produced into the 1990s. The pattern shown, 'Bandel', was introduced in 1962. The rarer the pattern and the larger the vase, the higher the value.*

A Jane Charles glass Urchin bowl, 1990s, 6¾in (17cm) diam.

**£35–40  Feathers Antiques** ⊞

A Jane Charles glass Ripple vase, 1990s, 15in (38cm) high.

**£145–160  Feathers Antiques** ⊞

*Contemporary makers often have little proven track record and it is therefore advisable only to buy their works if you like them. Time will tell if they will retain or improve their value.*

A Jonathan Harris cameo glass Dragon vase, the decoration carved through ten colours and silver leaf, 2003, 10¼in (26cm) high.

**£850–950  Jonathan Harris** ⊞

*The Jonathan Harris Studio has a good reputation for using a high degree of technical skill.*

A Webb glass vase, maker's mark, c1930, 7in (18cm) diam.

**£40–45  Collectable Costume** ⊞

## ESSENTIAL REFERENCE  KEITH MURRAY

A Stevens & Williams glass vase, by Keith Murray, c1935, 8½in (21.5cm) high.

**£300–350  James Strang** ⊞

A Stevens & Williams glass vase, by Keith Murray, c1935, 10in (25.5cm) high.

**£450–500  James Strang** ⊞

A Royal Brierley/Stevens & Williams engraved glass Angel Fish vase, by Keith Murray, 1930s, 10½in (26.5cm) high.

**£1,150–1,300  Gazelles** ⊞

• Keith Murray (1892–1981) was a New Zealand-born architect who turned to glass and ceramic design in 1932 when architectural work became difficult to find during the economic slump that followed the Wall Street Crash.

• After being rejected by the Whitefriars glassworks in London, he was hired in 1933 on a freelance basis by Stevens & Williams, which soon became Royal Brierley. He also worked for Wedgwood pottery and the silversmiths, Mappin & Webb.

• The full extent of Murray's designs remains uncertain, largely because many of his pieces are unsigned. Signed examples bear his acid-based signature and the name Stevens & Williams/Royal Brierley. His known work includes soft colour-tinted and colourless examples either left entirely plain or decorated with cutting, engraving or optic moulding. He looked to Modernism, Scandinavia and the English 'Regency' style of cutting for inspiration.

• It is thought that Murray provided Brierley with more than 1,000 drawings over their six-year association. Yet while Brierley promoted Murray through regular trade advertisements it often proved largely unwilling to invest in the moulds required to produce all his designs.

• The price of Murray glass has remained largely constant over recent years, ranging between the low hundreds to just over £1,000, but demand is largely restricted to Britain.

## DARTINGTON

### ESSENTIAL REFERENCE — THROWER'S TANKARDS

A Dartington glass tankard, by Frank Thrower, No. FT1, 1967, 5in (12.5cm) high.
**£100–110 Quay Centre** ⊞

A Dartington glass tankard, by Frank Thrower, No. FT1, 1977, 5in (12.5cm) high.
**£80–90 Quay Centre** ⊞

A Dartington glass tankard, by Frank Thrower, No. FT1, 1988, 5in (12.5cm) high.
**£80–90 Quay Centre** ⊞
*This tankard was made to commemorate Dartington's 21st anniversary.*

• To a great extent, Frank Thrower was the personification of Dartington Glass between its foundation in 1967 and his death in 1986. During that period he designed 500 pieces – 95 per cent of Dartington's output – several of which are remain in production today.

• Variations on Frank Thrower's commemorative tankard, given the Dartington production number FT1, were produced annually between 1967 and 1992. The shape remained the same but the large seal applied to their body changed according to the subject being commemorated.

• In the first year they were produced in colourless, Kingfisher (aquamarine) and Midnight (smoke), but only in colourless after 1969.

• In some years they were issued in limited editions of between 5 and 10,000, and were sometimes engraved by Frank's son, Kim, with an individual number.

• Like much Dartington glass, for many years these tankards languished but prices are now rising.

A Dartington smokey glass vase, by Frank Thrower, No. FT28, 1969, 6in (15cm) high.
**£35–40 Graham Cooley** ⊞

A Dartington glass pyramid, by Frank Thrower, No. FT160, c1960s, 6in (15cm) square.
**£110–125 Quay Centre** ⊞

A Dartington glass decanter, by Frank Thrower, No. FT4, c1960, 11in (28cm) high.
**£35–40 Quay Centre** ⊞

A Dartington glass vase, c1990, 16in (40.5cm) high.
**£110–125 Quay Centre** ⊞

A Dartington smokey glass vase, 1990s, 11in (28cm) high.
**£90–100 Quay Centre** ⊞

A Dartington graal glass Polar Bears vase, c1990, 8in (20.5cm) diam.
**£115–130 Quay Centre** ⊞

# DRINKS SETS

A glass lemonade set, comprising six pieces, Czechoslovakia, 1930s, 7in (18cm) high.
**£35–40** Hemswell Antiques Centre ⊞

An Art Deco set of four glasses and a decanter, with a mirrored chrome tray, Czechoslovakia, 1930s, decanter 7½in (19cm) high.
**£280–320** Roger Harris ⊞
*This set would have been expensive when first made in the 1930s and reproductions are being made today. Pre-WWII Czechoslovakian glass is difficult to identify as paperwork was lost during and after the war. This high-quality set has enamel decoration, although hard-edged black geometric enamels are more sought after.*

A frosted glass shots set, on a chrome stand, 1950s, decanter 7in (18cm) wide.
**£25–30** Hemswell Antiques Centre ⊞

A set of six glasses and a decanter, decorated with card suits, c1959, decanter 8in (20.5cm) high.
**£55–65** Worcester Antiques ⊞

A set of six high ball glasses, with transfer-printed decoration and gilding, Czechoslovakia, 1950s, 7in (18cm) high.
**£25–30** Attica ⊞

A set of five glasses and a decanter, with hand-painted and gilded decoration, Czechoslovakia, 1950s, decanter 11in (28cm) high.
**£25–30** Afonwen Centre ⊞
*This hand-made glass has a good, eye-catching design, using real gold for the gilding. This technique died out when the price of gold increased in the 1970s.*

A set of four water glasses, 1960s, 3½in (9cm) high.
**£15–20** Attica ⊞
*These glasses were designed by Alexander Hardie Williamson, who designed over 1,700 shapes and patterns between 1933 and 1974.*

A set of six Chesterfield Jungle Rhythm drinking glasses, 1950s, 5in (12.5cm) high, with original box.
**£25–30** Upstairs Downstairs ⊞

# ITALIAN

**An Alrose decanter and matching glass vase,** Italy, 1960s–70s, decanter 22½in (57cm) high.

**£90–100 Pineapple Ice Bucket** ⊞

**An Aureliano Toso glass Aventurina vase,** by Dino Martens, Italy, 1953, 11in (28cm) high.

**£2,300–2,600 Losch's** ⊞
*Signatures are unknown for Aureliano Toso from the 1950s to the 1960s. The pattern is formed by metal compounds like those from copper being melted in the glass and cooled down very slowly.*

**An Aureliano Toso glass Pittorico vase,** by Dino Martens, Italy, 1955, 27in (68.5cm) high.

**£3,900–4,300 Losch's** ⊞
*In the method of decoration used for this vase, threads of glass are laid onto the glass body.*

**An Aureliano Toso glass Oriente vase,** by Dino Martens, Italy, 1952–61, 13¾in (35cm) high.

**£5,800–6,500 Losch's** ⊞
*In vases such as this, thick colourless glass is embedded with glass chips, zanfirico canes, copper aventurine and often a star murrine.*

**A Barovier & Toso glass Calcedonio vase,** by Ercole Barovier, with label to base, Italy, 1934, 6in (15.5cm) high.

**£1,500–1,650 Losch's** ⊞

**A Barovier & Toso glass Eugeneo sculpture,** by Ercole Barovier, Italy, 1951, 8¾in (22cm) long.

**£2,700–3,000 Losch's** ⊞
*This colouration is formed when oxides are enclosed between two layers of clear glass without being fused.*

**A Barovier & Toso glass Dior bottle and stopper,** by Ercole Barovier, signed by Christian Dior, Italy, 1969, 8¼in (21cm) high.

**£2,500–2,800 Losch's** ⊞
*Horizontal and vertical canes of glass and colours are applied to colourless glass like a net.*

**A Barovier & Toso glass Intarsio bottle vase,** by Ercole Barovier, Italy, 1961, 14¾in (37.5cm) high.

**£2,950–3,250 Losch's** ⊞
*To make this vase two or more different coloured glass triangles are applied to a colourless glass body in regular formation.*

**A Cenedese *sommerso* glass decanter,** Italy, 1960s–70s, 23in (58.5cm) high.

**£230–260 Pineapple Ice Bucket** ⊞

Two Murano glass birds, Italy, 1950s, largest 8½in (21.5cm) high.

**£50–55  Retro Art Glass** ⊞

Two Murano glass dancing figures, Italy, 1950s, 11in (28cm) high.

**£220–250  Frank Dux Antiques** ⊞

A Murano glass bowl, by Dino Martens, in the form of a bird, Italy, 1950s, 8in (20.5cm) high.

**£120–135  Coltman Antiques** ⊞

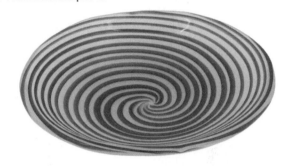

A Murano glass dish, Italy, 1950s, 9in (23cm) wide.

**£45–50  Coltman Antiques** ⊞

A Murano glass dish, Italy, 1960s, 6¼in (16cm) wide.

**£15–20  Tenterden Antiques** ⊞

A Murano glass vase, Italy, 1960s, 3½in (9cm) high.

**£20–25  Tenterden Antiques** ⊞

A Murano glass paperweight, in the form of a stylized dolphin, Italy, 1960s, 5in (12.5cm) high.

**£15–20  Tenterden Antiques** ⊞

A Murano glass vase, by Archimede Seguso, with engraved signature to underside, Italy, 1980s, 5in (12.5cm) high.

**£65–75  Rosebery's** 🔨

ITALIAN

**A Venini Pezzato glass Americano vase,**
by Fulvio Bianconi, acid-etched signature to
base, Italy, 1951, 6in (15cm) high.

**£3,800–4,300** Losch's ⊞
*The name of the piece depends on the
colours used. In this case rectangular and/or
square pieces of glass are fused together to
form a vessel of patches.*

**A Venini *zanfirico* glass figure,** by Fulvio
Bianconi, Italy, 1952, 10¾in (27.5cm) high.

**£1,650–1,850** Losch's ⊞
*In the process for this figure, thin glass
threads are fused together and processed
into vases and figurines.*

**A Venini glass Forato vase,** by Fulvio
Bianconi, with acid-etched signature to base,
Italy, 1952, 10¾in (27cm) high.

**£1,500–1,650** Losch's ⊞
*This vase uses a technique where the vessel
is pierced to create one or more openings.*

**A Venini glass *fasce verticali* vase,** by Fulvio
Bianconi, Italy, 1953, 9in (23cm) high.

**£4,300–4,800** Losch's ⊞
*This vase was made using a technique where
wide canes of glass are fused together.*

**A Venini glass jug,** with cane decoration,
stamped mark, Italy, 1950s, 10in (25.5cm) high.

**£450–550** Rago Arts 🗡

**A Venini Mosaico *zanfirico* vase,** by Paolo
Venini, with acid-etched signature, Italy,
1955, 13¾in (35cm) high.

**£5,500–6,100** Losch's ⊞
*To make this vase several glass canes were
placed together into a pattern and then fused
into one cane. The resulting cane is then sliced
into discs which are placed in the desired
pattern and then fused and blown into shape.*

**A Venini glass *bolle* bottle,** by Tapio
Wirkkala, with incised signature and mark to
base, Italy, 1965, 11in (28cm) high.

**£1,100–1,250** Losch's ⊞
*This vessel was made from two or more
individual glass bubbles blown to the
same diameter; the opened bubbles are
then fused together.*

**A Venini glass Pioggia vase,** by Ginette
Venini, with incised signature, Italy, 1965,
9½in (24cm) high.

**£1,750–1,950** Losch's ⊞
*This vase was made using a technique where
bands of glass are pulled and stretched to
create a pattern on a blank of glass.*

**A Venini Troncho vase,** by Toni Zuccheri,
with incised signature, Italy, 1966,
11¾in (30cm) high.

**£2,700–3,000** Losch's ⊞

# LALIQUE

## ESSENTIAL REFERENCE  RENE LALIQUE

A Lalique opalescent glass box and cover, 'Libellules', the cover moulded with three dragonflies, moulded mark, France, designed c1921, 6¾in (17cm) diam.

**£600–700  Rosebery's**

A Lalique Feuilles opalescent glass pin tray, 'Feuilles', signed, France, 1930s, 6¾in (17cm) wide.

**£230–260  Mike Weedon**

A Lalique glass tumbler, 'Bamboo, France, 1930s, 5in (12.5cm) high.

**£75–85  Mike Weedon**

- René Lalique was arguably the world's greatest glass designer.

- The combination of his extraordinary aesthetic sense and understanding of glass moulding techniques have resulted in some of the most engaging and collectable glass ever produced.

- The rarest and therefore most sought-after designs are those that had a short production span. Some pieces have remained in production since the 1920s or '30s.

- The degree of opalescence affects value – the richer the colour, the higher the price.

- Pieces bearing René Lalique's name tend to be more desirable than those designed his son Marc or granddaughter Marie-Claude.

A Lalique glass vase, 'Ceylon', France, 1930s, 9½in (24cm) high.

**£4,000–4,500**
**Mike Weedon**

A Lalique opalescent plate, 'Actiniy', signed, France, 1930s, 11in (28cm) diam.

**£400–460  Mike Weedon**

A Lalique clear and opalescent glass bowl, 'Poissons No. 1', stencil mark, France, c1945, 8½in (21cm) diam.

**£190–220  Rosebery's**

A Lalique glass bowl, France, c1945, 13in (33cm) diam.

**£590–650  Muir Hewitt**

A Lalique glass dish, with a bird, France, 1970s, 4in (10cm) diam.

**£75–85  Vetta Decorative Arts**

A Lalique glass and chrome table lamp, France, c1960, 9in (23cm) high.

**£200–250  Quay Centre**

## MDINA

A Mdina glass paperweight, in the form of a seahorse, Malta, 1960s, 6in (15cm) high.

**£15–20 Hemswell Antiques Centre** ⊞

A Mdina glass vase, signed, Malta, c1970, 8in (20.5cm) high.

**£20–25 Retro Centre** ⊞

A set of three Mdina glass Ocean paperweights, Malta, c1970, largest 13in (33cm) high.

**£130–145 Retro Centre** ⊞

• Michael Harris quit his job as a lecturer at the Royal College of Art, London, to found Mdina Glass on Malta in 1968. Virtually without practical glassmaking experience himself, he hired local apprentices on the strict condition that they too knew nothing of the craft. The pieces he designed and produced, predominantly for the tourist market, echoed the colours of the island and the Mediterranean that surround it: deep and sky-blue, aquamarine and amber.

• Harris left Malta in 1972 after selling his interest to Eric Dobson, his former business partner. In 1985, the works passed into the hands of Joseph Said, the first apprentice hired by Harris, and who still owns it today.

• Dobson and Said reversed Harris' general policy to sign his work, with the distinctive scrolling 'Mdina' scripted signature exclusively post-dating Harris' signature. Pieces attributable to Harris are the most sought-after elements of Mdina's production, with pieces bearing his signature, 'Michael Harris Mdina Glass Malta', the most valued of all.

A Mdina glass bottle, Malta, 1970s, 13in (33cm) high.

**£50–55 Luna** ⊞

A Mdina glass bottle, with trailed decoration, Malta, c1970s, 14in (35.5cm) high.

**£75–85 Retro Centre** ⊞

A Mdina glass bottle, with trailed decoration, signed, Malta, 1970s.

**£35–40 Retro Centre** ⊞

# MONART

## ESSENTIAL REFERENCE  MONART

A Monart glass bowl, 1920s, 5in (12.5cm) diam.
**£70–80  Ruskin Decorative Arts** ⊞

A Monart glass vase, with coloured inclusions, 1930, 6½in (16.5cm) high.
**£300–340
Decorative Antiques** ⊞

A Monart glass vase, 1930, 5½in (14cm) high.
**£90–100
Steven Bishop** ⊞

• Monart glass was produced at Moncrieff's glassworks at Perth, Scotland, between 1922 and 1961. A variety of glass ware, from bottles to fine crystal, has been produced in Scotland for centuries, but Monart is probably the most distinctive.

• Aside from its characteristic vivid colours and swirling effects, Monart glass is unique in that it has a raised and polished pontil mark at the centre of the base of the vast majority of pieces. No other glassworks in the world used the same method.

• The works were managed by John Moncreiff, its designs were created by his wife, Elizabeth, and produced by members of the Spanish-born Ysart dynasty: Salvador Ysart and his sons: Paul, Augustine, Vincent and Antoine.

• The price of Monart glass has remained static, or risen only slightly, in recent years, partially because the sale of a major private collection in 2003 flooded the market. Nevertheless, large pieces in attractive colours still fetch premiums, most especially their table-lamps, often formed in the Art Nouveau style.

A Monart glass vase, with mottled and swirled inclusions, c1950, 7in (18cm) high.
**£55–65  Locke & England** ⚒

A Monart glass bowl, 1950, 8¾in (22cm) diam.
**£120–135  Steven Bishop** ⊞

# PAPERWEIGHTS

A **Caithness Glass Reflections paperweight**, Collectors Club No. 92, 1970s, 2¼in (5.5cm) high.

**£30–35** Feathers Antiques ⊞

A **Caithness Glass Ribbons paperweight**, 1980s, 3in (7.5cm) high.

**£20–25** Feathers Antiques ⊞

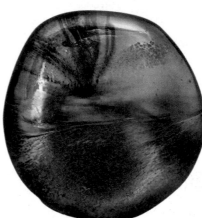

An **Okra Studio Glass paperweight**, by Richard P. Golding, 2005, 9in (23cm) high.

**£230–260** Collectors Bits ⊞

A **Caithness Glass Sand Dancers paperweight**, 1980s–90s, 4¼in (11cm) high.

**£35–40** Feathers Antiques ⊞

A **Glasform Landscape paperweight**, by John Ditchfield, signed, 1990s, 4½in (11.5cm) high.

**£95–110** Feathers Antiques ⊞

A **Perthshire F crown paperweight**, limited edition of 250, 1981, 3in (7.5cm) diam.

**£380–420** Sweetbriar Gallery ⊞

A **Phoenix Hot Glass Studio Magma paperweight**, 1980s–90s, 4in (10cm) high.

**£35–40** Feathers Antiques ⊞

A **Sanders & Wallace feather paperweight**, 1980s–90s, 3in (7.5cm) high.

**£35–40** Feathers Antiques ⊞

A **Whitefriars glass paperweight**, by William Wilson, c1953, 4in (10cm) diam.

**£45–50** Country Seat ⊞

A Baccarat Bouquet paperweight, limited edition, France, 1986, 3in (7.5cm) diam.
**£400–440**
Sweetbriar Gallery ⊞

A Baccarat close-pack paperweight, limited edition, France, 1986, 3in (7.5cm) diam.
**£380–420**
Sweetbriar Gallery ⊞

A Ken Rosenfeld paperweight, America, 2005, 2¼in (5.5cm) diam.
**£200–220**
Sweetbriar Gallery ⊞

A Paul Stankard Bouquet paperweight, America, 1981, 3in (7.5cm) diam.
**£2,250–2,500** Sweetbriar Gallery ⊞

A Paul Ysart Magnum paperweight, decorated with a millefiori butterfly within a garland of alternate canes, Scotland, 1930s, 3¼in (8.5cm) diam.
**£680–750** Sweetbriar Gallery ⊞

A Paul Ysart Magnum paperweight, with PY cane, decorated with a butterfly over a flower, Scotlkand, 1930s, 3¼in (8.5cm) diam.
**£1,050–1,200** Sweetbriar Gallery ⊞

PRESSED GLASS

# PRESSED GLASS

A Davidson pressed-glass Pearline dish, with handle, 1886, 6in (15cm) wide.

**£70–80** Just Glass ⊞

A Davidson pressed-glass fruit bowl, c1888, 10in (25.5cm) diam.

**£65–75** Just Glass ⊞

A Davidson pressed-glass Pearline dish, 1889, 9in (23cm) diam.

**£75–85** Just Glass ⊞

A Davidson pressed-glass Pearline basket, c1890, 5in (12.5cm) wide.

**£35–40** Just Glass ⊞

A pressed-glass double inkwell, with brass covers, c1920, 4in (10cm) wide.

**£35–40** Just Glass ⊞

A pressed-glass egg basket, in the form of a cockerel, c1900, 9in (23cm) high.

**£35–40** Just Glass ⊞

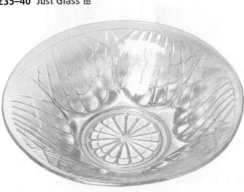

A Jobling opalescent pressed-glass bowl, c1930, 11in (28cm) wide.

**£100–120** Muir Hewitt ⊞

A pressed-glass Jacobean pattern bowl, early 1950s, 10in (25.5cm) diam.

**£5–10** Brackley Antiques ⊞

SCANDINAVIAN

# SCANDINAVIAN

An Alsterfors glass vase, by P. O. Ström, signed, Sweden, 1970, 5in (12.5cm) high.

**£85–95 glas-design.nl** ⊞

*Ström's opaque designs for Alsterfors remain uncovered by available literature, but increasing demand, especially for large, monumental pieces, particularly when signed and in good colours, has doubled prices in recent years.*

An Alsterfors cased glass vase, by P. O. Ström, Sweden, c1960, 7in (18cm) high.

**£125–140 Ruskin Decorative Arts** ⊞

## ESSENTIAL REFERENCE | IITTALA

An Iittala glass Orkidea vase, by Timo Sarpaneva, with large air inclusion bubble and aperture, engraved 'Timo Sarpaneva 3568', c1987, 6½in (16.5cm) high.

**£80–95 Rosebery's** 🔨

*Designed in 1953 and named 'Orkidea', Finnish for orchid, this vase was produced until 1973. It was reissued in 1985 and is still in production today, making the later vases quite common and of lower value than the originals, which were only produced for seven years and may now cost many thousands of pounds.*

An Iittala I-glass bottle vase, by Timo Sarpaneva, engraved 'T. Sarpaneva 2518', Finland, 1960s, 9½in (24cm) high.

**£180–200 Freeforms** ⊞

*This vase was designed in 1961 and produced until 1966.*

An unfinished Iittala glass Savoy vase, by Alvar Aalto, Finland, 1960s, 12½in (32cm) high.

**£430–475 glas-design.nl** ⊞

*This is a very unusual and possibly unique piece. However, the fact that it is really unusual limits its appeal to the academic collector.*

• Founded in 1881, Iittala took Finnish glass design upmarket from 1936 with Alvar Aalto's iconic Modernist Savoy vase. Drawing on the talents of Gunnel Nyman, Kaj Franck, Tapio Wirkkala and Timo Sarpaneva, Iittala made a conscious effort to target the international design-conscious and giftware market.

• The award of Grand Prix to Wirkkala and Sarpeneva at the 1951 and 1953 Milan Triennale exhibitions helped to confirm Iittala alongside Sweden's Orrefors at the highest echelon of sophisticated glass design.

• However, Iittala continued to produce its 'greatest hit' designs over several decades, a fact that complicates their value among collectors. For instance, Aalto's Savoy vase has remained in constant production since 1937, and second-hand pieces are invariably cheaper than new ones.

• Likewise, Sarpaneva's Orkidea (Orchid) vase, 1953, has been reproduced over several decades whereas his Lancetti, 1952, was made for only five years. The result is that the value of the former is relatively low compared to the latter. Similarly Wirkkala's Kanterelli, 1946–47, has also been reproduced several times.

A Johansfors glass bowl, by Bengt Orup, signed, Sweden, 1970s, 21in (53.5cm) diam.

**£95–105 Coltman Antiques** ⊞

*Bengt Orup was a leading designer for Johansfors between 1952 and 1973, contributing thousands of designs, most of them unsigned. This bowl is signed, but is an uncommercial shape, and its value is dented by the similarly-shaped pieces made in their thousands in China for Ikea.*

An Iittala glass Finlandia vase, by Timo Sarpaneva, moulded to represent ice, engraved mark' Timo Sarpaneva' to underside, 1960s, 9in (23cm) high.

**£170–200 Rosebery's** 🔧

*Timo Sarpaneva's Finlandia vases, 1964–70, were blown into carved pinewood moulds, which were gradually, and intentionally, destroyed through repeated contact with hot glass.*

A glass vase, possibly by Riihimäki, Finland, 1970–72, 10in (25.5cm) high.

**£35–40 Graham Cooley** ⊞

*It has not been established precisely who designed and made this piece. It might be Riihimäki, but it does not appear in the catalogues.*

A glass sculpture, in the style of Paul Kedelv for Flygsfors, Sweden, c1970, 10in (25.5cm) high.

**£30–35 Glass etc** ⊞

*Paul Kedelv's most important contribution to Flygsfors during his time as its leading designer (1949–56) was the exuberant Coquilles range of vases and objects. These are easily identified as every piece was applied with an engraved signature that stated 'Kedelv', 'Coquilles' and/or 'Flygsfors' plus the last two digits of the date, such as '52'. These proved very influential and approximations of the range were produced by glassworks spread across the globe, from the United States to Czechoslovakia and Venice. However, none are by Kedelv/Flygsfors unless signed to that effect.*

## MARKET INFORMATION  SCANDINAVIAN GLASS

• Post-WWII Scandinavian glass has proved the strongest performer in glass over the past year and continues to surge. Its dynamic shapes and colours are perfectly attuned to today's well-lit homes, and improving literature on the subject is enabling many more pieces to be dated and attributed to their designers and makers.

• The extraordinary post-war success of Sweden's Orrefors, which emerged from nowhere to lead international glass design within a decade or two, encouraged others, both at home and in neighbouring Finland and Denmark, to follow suit.

• The appeal of designs by architect Jacob Bang, his son Michael and Per Lütken for the Danish firm Holmegaard are enjoying a resurgence, most notably for large sculptural pieces and the vividly coloured Carnaby and Palet ranges of 1968 and 1970.

• The rise of Finnish design after 1945, in ceramics, furniture and stainless steel as well as glass, was perhaps more notable. Kaj Franck, Tapio Wirkkala and Timo Sarpeneva's cool pieces for Iittala and Nuutajärvi won the leading post-war prizes but were later rivalled by the post-Modernist sculptural shapes of Nanny Still, Helena Tynell and Tamara Aladin for Riihimäki.

• Norway was the lesser of the Nordic glassmaking quartet. Willy Johansson contributed a huge number of designs to Hadeland over his 46-year career between 1942 and 1988, ranging from colourless stemware to complex studio pieces. Like his compatriot, Benny Motzfeldt, demand for his work has been limited by an absence of available English-language literature.

Two Holmegaard glass Rondo vases, by Per Lütken, Denmark, 1960s, largest 4in (10cm) high.

**£35–40 Coltman Antiques** ⊞
*These vases were designed in 1950 and made in three sizes.*

A Holmegaard glass dish, by Per Lütken, signed and dated, 'Holmegaard 19PL69', Denmark, c1969, 7½in (19cm) diam.

**£30–35 Special Auction Services** 🔨

A Kastrup-Holmegaard cased-glass Gul vase, Denmark, 1960s, 17in (43cm) high.

**£260–290 Ruskin Decorative Arts** ⊞
*This is attributed to Otto Brauer, 1962, but is derived from a 1958 Lütken design. Made in several sizes and colours, the biggest and the brightest now command the highest prices.*

A Holmegaard glass Napoli vase, by Michael Bang, Denmark, 1969–71, 10in (25.5cm) high.

**£115–130 Coltman Antiques** ⊞

A Holmgaard glass Carnaby vase, by Per Lütken, Denmark, 1970s, 12in (30.5cm) high.

**£165–185 Richard Wallis Antiks** ⊞

## ESSENTIAL REFERENCE PER LUTKEN

A Holmegaard glass Unamak vase, by Per Lütken, designed in 1952, Denmark, 1959, 9in (23cm) high.

**£35–40
Coltman Antiques** ⊞

A Holmegaard glass Heart sculpture, by Per Lütken, engraved 'Holmgaard 19PL59', Denmark, 1952, 18½in (47cm) high.

**£130–145 Glass etc** ⊞
*Lütken's Heart was produced by Holmegaard 1956–75, in several sizes, this being the largest. It appeared in two colours: aqua and smoke.*

A Holmegaard cased-glass Carnaby vase, by Per Lütken, Denmark, c1960, 9in (23cm) high.

**£200–240
Ruskin Decorative Arts** ⊞

- Per Lütken ventured across most forms and decorative styles, from geometric cutting to organic, amorphous forms, from wine glasses to sculptures and every form of table glass, and from colourless through streaky to bold, solid colour statements.

- Demand for Lütken's work has recovered from a low during the 1990s, particularly for large, organic sculptural pieces, such as his Heart vases (1952–76), his vivid Carnaby range (1968–76), and the limited edition Four Seasons series of giant suncatchers designed in 1976 to celebrate Holmegaard's 150th anniversary.

## EXPERT EYE  PALLET SERIES

All Carnaby and Palet pieces were double skinned, with the colours being laid over the white core, so they are invariably heavier than equivalent single-skin pieces. The available colours were white over cased in sky-blue, yellow, tangerine, green and smoke-amber.

Pieces sealed with cartouches embossed with lettering for OLIE, KAFFE and TEE tend to be less popular than unmarked pieces in non-Danish markets.

A pair of Holmegaard glass Palet tea and coffee jars, designed by Michael Bang, Denmark, 1970s, largest 6in (15cm) high.

**£50–55** Coltman Antiques ⊞

Being of high quality, the finish is always smooth to the touch. Some inferior copies have rough mould seams.

Palet was formed exclusively in yellow, red, smoke-amber and green, all over white. Similar pieces in any colour other than these are not Palet, and indeed were not made by Holmegaard.

Holmegaard, the Royal Danish glassworks founded in 1825, produced two ranges of bright opaque colour-cased glassware within two years: Per Lütken's Carnaby, 1968, and Michael Bang's Palet, 1970. Carnaby, produced in sky-blue, red and yellow, over a white core, was a decorative series of vases and candlesticks. Palet was intended to be a utilitarian kitchen range. It comprised bottles labelled for OLIE, KAFFE, TEE, MARGARINE and SUKKER; herring dishes; egg cups; salt and pepper cruets; two sizes of tankards and bowls of various sizes. Carnaby and Palet proved very influential and derivatives were produced by numerous Swedish glassworks, most notably the Modernist shapes designed by P. O. Ström for Alsterfors from c1968. Optimistic misattributions to Holmegaard of these abound, most notably on the internet, with virtually any vaguely similar items being routinely assigned to either Lütken or Bang. Pattern drawings of the entire Palet series are illustrated in the Holmegaard section of my recent book *Miller's 20th Century Glass*.

**Andy McConnell, Glass Etc**

**A Kosta glass Unika,** by Vicke Lindstrand, signed 'LU 2026', Kosta etched mark, Sweden, 1950–51, 7in (18cm) high.

**£1,500–1,650 Losch's** ⊞

*This item uses a technique in which several layers of glass are cased and removed leaving a design specific to the series between the layers of clear glass.*

**Three Kosta glass vases,** by Vicke Lindstrand, Sweden, 1955–56, 11in (28cm) high.

**£180–200 each Coltman Antiques** ⊞

## ESSENTIAL REFERENCE VICKE LINDSTRAND

**A Kosta glass Rune vase,** by Vicke Lindstrand, marked 'S 104', Sweden, 1950–51, 8¼in (21cm) high.

**£1,750–1,950 Losch's** ⊞

**A Kosta glass model of a group of penguins,** by Vicke Lindstrand, Sweden, 1955–56, 11in (28cm) high.

**£1,000–1,200 Losch's** ⊞

*This group uses black and white glass with a clear overlay, the technique making each penguin unique.*

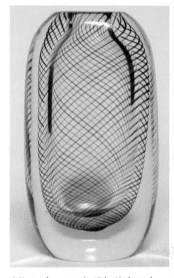

**A Kosta glass vase,** by Vicke Lindstrand, with woven trail decoration, signed and numbered, Sweden, 1958, 6in (15cm) high.

**£240–260 Afford Decorative Arts** ⊞

• Kosta, the Royal Swedish Glassworks founded in 1742, found itself entirely eclipsed by the meteoric rise of its upstart neighbour Orrefors during the 1920s and '30s. The designs of Edward Hald, Simon Gate and Victor (Vicke) Lindstrand from 1928, proved so radical and technically compelling that most of Kosta's output appeared mundane in comparison.

• Kosta hoped to redress the balance in 1951 by hiring Lindstrand, who remained at its works until 1974. Aside from rare artistic studio pieces, Lindstand's contribution at Orrefors had largely been in engraved pieces, whereas at Kosta he ruled the roost and was allowed virtually unlimited artistic freedom.

• Lindstand's output for Kosta covered wide-ranging territory, from utilitarian services, such as the best-selling bubble-based Mambo, 1955, through crystal and furnace-worked animal figures to labour-intensive unique studio pieces. Unlike the Orrefors design team, which benefited from extensive publicity, Lindstand's Kosta period has been largely ignored by accessible, English-language literature. This fact leaves his 23-year career due largely ripe for a wider reappraisal.

A Kosta glass ashtray, by Vicke Lindstrand, Sweden, c1960, 7in (18cm) diam.
**£45–50 Coltman Antiques** ⊞

A Kosta glass Colora vase, by Vicke Lindstrand, signed 'LH1672', Sweden, 1962, 8in (20cm) high.
**£2,500–2,750 glas-design.nl** ⊞

A Kosta glass Ventana vase, by Mona Morales, signed 'Kosta SS 166', Sweden, 1960s, 4½in (11.5cm) high.
**£240–270 glas-design.nl** ⊞

A Kosta glass Boda Bird bowl, by Kjell Engman, painted with birds, with engraved marks, Sweden, c1970, 5¾in (14.5cm) high.
**£80–100 Special Auction Services** 🔨

A Kosta glass vase, by Anna Ehrner, signed 'Kosta 47753 A. Ehrner', Sweden, 1977, 8in (20cm) high.
**£195–220 glas-design.nl** ⊞

A Kosta glass bowl, by Paul Hoff, decorated with a fish, Sweden, 1970s, 10in (25.5cm) diam.
**£350–400 Coltman Antiques** ⊞

**A Nuutajärvi Notsjö glass Rosenbladet bowl,** by Gunnel Nyman, Finland, 1948, 8¾in (22.5cm) diam.

**£2,250–2,500  Losch's** ⊞

**A Nuutajärvi Notsjö glass Rengasilautanen bowl,** by Kaj Franck, signed 'Nuutajärvi Notsjö Kaj Franck', Finland, 1960s, 10¼in (26cm) diam.

**£3,000–3,500  Losch's** ⊞
*To make this bowl, several glass rings of different sizes were melted together. Every Lautanen is unique.*

**A Nuutajärvi Notsjö glass Rökfiligranglas vase,** by Gunnel Nyman, signed 'Nuutajärvi Notsjö Gunnel Nyman - 53', Finland, 1947, 14¼in (36cm) high.

**£950–1,100  Losch's** ⊞

**A Nuutajärvi Notsjö glass vase,** by Kaj Franck, Finland, 1955, 4¾in (12cm) high.

**£290–320  glas-design.nl** ⊞

**A Nuutajärvi Notsjö glass model of a kiwi,** by Kaj Franck, signed 'Kaj Franck Nuutajärvi Notsjö', Finland, 1976, 2¾in (7cm) high.

**£270–300  glas-design.nl** ⊞

## ESSENTIAL REFERENCE  NUUTAJARVI

**A Nuutajärvi Notsjö glass vase,** by Gunnel Nyman, with etched mark to base, Finland, c1947, 9¾in (25cm) high.

**£370–420  glas-design.nl** ⊞

**A Nuutajärvi Notsjö glass Shifonki vase,** by Gunnel Nyman, etched mark to base, Finland, 1947, 7in (18cm) high.

**£500–550  glas-design.nl** ⊞
*This is a classic piece by a rare designer.*

**A Nuutajärvi Notsjö glass Prisma vase,** by Kaj Franck, engraved 'K. Franck Nuutajärvi Notsjö-62', Finland, 1962, 12¾in (32.5cm) high.

**£120–135  Freeforms** ⊞

• Three significant designers contributed to Nuutajarvi (pronounced Noot-eye-arvi) post-WWII: Gunnel Nyman (1946–48), Kaj Franck (1950–89) and Oiva Toikka (from 1959). Though often overshadowed by Sarpaneva and Wirkkala's brilliance for neighbouring Iittala, all three continue to enjoy widespread admiration.

• Nyman, whose career was terminated by her untimely death aged 39 in 1948, blazed a trail for a series of respected Finnish female post-war glass designers. She is best known for her vases containing tightly-controlled bubbles but her oeuvre also encompassed a wide range of furnace-worked sensual forms, either left plain or cased, cut or engraved.

• Franck ranks among the most influential glass designers of his age. A Lunning Prize winner in 1955, many of the pieces can appear unremarkable from today's perspective. However, the original inspiration behind many of the objects found in modern design shops can be traced to Franck's drawing board. For instance, the trend away from matching services towards mix-and-match glass and crockery was advocated by Franck as early as 1952.

# ESSENTIAL REFERENCE ORREFORS

An Orrefors glass vase, by Edvin Ohrström, signed 'Orrefors Edvin 86 Edvin Ohrström', Sweden, 1947, 4in (10cm) high.
**£2,900–3,200 Losch's** ⊞

An Orrefors experimental glass Ariel bowl, by Edvin Ohrström, signed 'Ariel glas of Ohrström', Sweden, 1948–50, 7½in (19cm) diam.
**£2,000–2,250 Losch's** ⊞

An Orrefors glass Ariel vase, by Edvin Ohrström, engraved 'Orrefors Ariel 531 F Ohrström', Sweden, 1957, 14in (35.5cm) high.
**£900–1,000 Freeforms** ⊞
*The base of most Orrefors glassware made before the 1990s, with the exception of individual wine glasses, was engraved in diamond-point with a code that indicated the name of the designer, its date-related production number and other details.*

• Orrefors Glasbruk (founded 1898) was an obscure Swedish glassworks until it was taken over in 1913 by Johan Ekman, a Gothenburg papermaker, whose interest centred on its large tracts of softwood forests. Fortunately for glassmaking history, Ekman's manager Albert Ahlin promptly fell in love with the spontaneity of the process, and by hiring two remarkable young designers, Simon Gate and Edward Hald, set the Orrefors legend in motion.

• Most of the 20th century's leading glassworks employed at least one great designer. Orrefors became the greatest by hiring a succession of them: Sven Palmqvist and Nils Landberg, both 1927, Vicke Lindstrand in 1928, Edvin Ohrström in 1930, Ingeborg Lundin, in 1947 and Evan Englund in 1974.

• Orrefors' designers did not simply direct their efforts towards traditional form and conventional decoration. Gate, Lindstrand and Ohrström pioneered the demanding Graal and Ariel techniques, while Palmqvist not only developed the similar Raka, from 1944, and Ravenna, 1948, but also invented centrifuge glass casting in 1954. The use of this technique became widespread across the glassmaking world and was used by Frank Thrower for forming Dartington's avocado and sweetcorn dishes and the Daisy range, 1971 and 1977.

An Orrefors glass vase, by Simon Gate, engraved with a mermaid, signed 'Orrefors G 1133.32AD', Sweden, 1932, 8¾in (22cm) high.
**£900–1,000 Losch's** ⊞
*Simon Gate and Edward Hald's fondness for engraving, and the commercial success of their designs, encouraged Orrefors to establish a school of engraving in 1922. Two of its leading designers, Nils Landberg and Sven Palmqvist first arrived at Orrefors as engraving students.*

An Orrefors glass 1000 Windows bowl, by Simon Gate, Sweden, c1940, 8½in (21.5cm) wide.
**£300–350 James Strang** ⊞
*Inspired by the English Regency style of cutting patterns into lead crystal, Simon Gate designed his Portal series of vases and bowls in 1934. Exploiting the refractive properties of crystal, the polished cuts acted as lenses, creating kaleidoscopic effects. Later renamed 1000 Windows, the series enjoyed a prolonged production span, with this bowl continuing in production until at least 2005.*

An Orrefors glass Graal vase, by Edward Hald, engraved 'Orrefors Sweden Graal No. 557 Edward Hald', Sweden, 1941, 8in (20.5cm) high.
**£450–500 Freeforms** ⊞

An Orrefors glass Kraka vase, designed by Sven Palmqvist, signed with serial numbers to the base, Sweden, c1958, 7in (18cm) high.

**£650–720**
**Afford Decorative Arts** ⊞

An Orrefors glass Kraka vase, by Sven Palmqvist, signed 'Orrefors Kraka PU427 Sven Palmqvist', Sweden, 1960, 3½in (9cm) high.

**£270–300  glas-design.nl** ⊞

An Orrefors glass Kraka vase, by Sven Palmqvist, marked with engraved signatures 'Orrefors Kraka 1=322 Sven Plamqvist', and 'S.G.A. 1956 1 Pris', Sweden, c1956, 14in (35.5cm) high.

**£550–650**
**Special Auction Services** ⚒

- Kraka was one of several techniques developed by Palmqvist. It was built up through layers of coloured glass, the decorative effect being devised around a fine mesh rather than an engraved or blasted central core.

- Early versions relied on glue-soaked tulle, the material used to make bridal veils, then copper mesh and, later, plastic packaging nets. The area of glass around the net was sandblasted and the resulting blank cased within a layer of colourless glass.

- Kraka was produced until 1988. Early examples are identifiable by their low production numbers and the inclusion of only one colour; two- and three-colour examples are generally later.

An Orrefors Tulpanglas, by Nils Landberg, signed 'Orrefors Expo N 312–57', Sweden, 1957, 15¾in (40cm) high.

**£840–930  Losch's** ⊞
*Tulpan was an especially fine art glass series.*

An Orrefors glass Ravenna bowl, by Sven Palmqvist, signed 'Orrefors Ravenna No. 15502 Sven Palmqvist', Sweden, 1959, 10¾in (27.5cm) wide.

**£1,650–1,850  Losch's** ⊞
*This piece was formed by using a blank with an overlay casting which was sandblasted, the cavities then filled with colour and the object reheated. Finally the piece was coated with clear glass.*

**An Orrefors glass Expo vase,** by Sven Palmqvist, engraved 'Orrefors Expo PU 240-62 Sven Palmqvist', 1962, 9½in (24cm) diam.

**£700–800 Freeforms** ⊞

**An Orrefors smoked glass vase,** Sweden, c1960, 9½in (24cm) high.

**£180–195 Ruskin Decorative Arts** ⊞

**An Orrefors glass candle holder,** marked '3964–311', 1967, 4¾in (12cm) high.

**£20–25 20th Century Marks** ⊞

**An Orrefors glass vase,** by Olle Alberius, Sweden, 1980s, 14in (35.5cm) high.

**£160–180 Coltman Antiques** ⊞

## ESSENTIAL REFERENCE    GRAAL & ARIEL GLASS

**An Orrefors glass Ariel vase,** by Edvin Ohrström, signed 'Orrefors Ariel No. 261 Edvin Ohrström', Sweden, 1930s, 7in (18cm) high.

**£1,150–1,300 Losch's** ⊞

**An Orrefors glass Ariel vase,** by Ingeborg Lundin, engraved 'Orrefors Ariel D. U. 233H Ingeborg Lundin', Sweden, 1959, 5in (12.5cm) high.

**£800–900 Freeforms** ⊞

**An Orrefors glass Graal vase,** by Eva Englund, signed 'Orrefors Eva Englund Expo 2318–78', Sweden, 1978, 7in (17.5cm) high.

**£1,750–1,950 Losch's** ⊞
*Eva Englund designed a large range of Graal pieces for Orrefors.*

• The historic forms of glass decoration, which include enamelling, cutting, engraving and gilding, are applied to the outer surface of the glass. Graal and Ariel are entirely different in that they are formed within the body of the glass.

• Both were created in a similar fashion. With Graal, developed at Orrefors in 1917 by master blower Knut Bergqvist and designer Simon Gate, a small colourless blank is gradually coated with one or more layers of coloured glass, in a process similar to cameo. The resulting multi-layered core is cooled, then etched, cut or engraved with the desired motifs. It is then reheated to around 450°C, fixed to a blowing iron, coated with an outer layer of clear glass and finally blown and shaped.

• Ariel, first created in 1937 by Vicke Lindstand, Gustav Berqvist and Edvin Ohrström, also at Orrefors, differs from Graal in that it contains air pockets, as well as differing colours, within the colourless outer casing. The effect is achieved by sandblasting the multi-coloured blank to create a series of cavities that retain air pockets within the finished piece.

• Ariel is most closely associated with Edvin Ohrström who spent years developing its possibilities before leaving Orrefors in 1957. His vase Ariel No. 125 achieved the highest price ever paid for a piece of glass in Sweden when it sold in 1988 for almost £100,000. In contrast to this exceptional price for an exceptional piece, fine examples by leading designers and makers start around £750.

**Andy McConnell, Glass Etc**

A Riihimäki glass vase, by Helena Tynell, signed, Finland, 1960, 10¾in (27cm) high.
**£300–330 glas-design.nl** ⊞

A Riihimäki glass Rex decanter, by Nanny Still, with label, Finland, 1964–65, 9¾in (25cm) high.
**£100–110 glas-design.nl** ⊞

A Riihimäki glass Pompadour vase, by Nanny Still, with label, Finland, 1966, 7½in (19cm) high.
**£80–90 glas-design.nl** ⊞
*This vase was part of a large series of about 12 different shapes, all known as Pompadour vases.*

A Riihimäki glass Fantasma vase, by Nanny Still, signed 'Nanny Still Riihimaen Lasi Oy', Finland, 1967, 7¾in (19.5cm) high.
**£130–150 glas-design.nl** ⊞

A Riihimäki glass Stellaria vase, by Nanny Still, with label, Finland, 1967, 7in (18cm) high.
**£155–175 glas-design.nl** ⊞

A Riihimäki glass vase, Finland, 1970s, 11in (28cm) high.
**£65–75 Luna** ⊞
*Known among collectors as the 'Cog' vase, this design was attributed to Tamara Aladin and was made in several vivid colours.*

A Riihimäki glass Metsä vase, by Helena Tynell, signed 'Riihimaen Lasi Oy', Finland, 1968, 5in (12.5cm) high.
**£270–300 glas-design.nl** ⊞

A Riihimäki glass Ahkeraliisa vase, by Helena Tynell, 1969, 8¾in (22cm) high.
**£270–300 glas-design.nl** ⊞
*An unsigned piece would only be worth £80–100.*

## MARKET INFORMATION RIIHIMAKI

• Riihimäki Lasi Oy (Riihimäki Glass Works), founded in the rural town of the same name in 1910, was Finland's largest glassmaker, with 1,200 employees melting 30,000 tons of glass annually at its peak in 1968.

• The cool and sophisticated products of its neighbour, Iittala, have long taken precedence over Riihimäki's post-war decorative wares. However, it is the latter that has shown the greatest price increase across all categories of glass in the past year. This marks an acceleration of a general trend.

• The price increases have been across the board, but particularly for Tynell's idiosyncratic Pikku Matti decanter series, 1969, redolent of Japanese tinplate robots, and Still's monumental planetary vases, including Nebulosa, Kometti, Stelleria, Fenomena and Fantasma, in colourless, tangerine and green.

• The greatest part of Riihimäki's decorative production was in dozens of differently shaped tube vases that were cheap when originally retailed and remain widely available for about £20. However, demand for rarer pieces, such as elements of Still's Harekiini series, 1958, and signed studio pieces, is outstripping supply with inevitable consequences.

A Riihimäki glass Maaherra decanter, by Helena Tynell, with label, Finland, 1970, 10¼in (26cm) high.

**£195–220** glas-design.nl ⊞

A Riihimäki glass Pikku Matti decanter, by Helena Tynell, with label, Finland, 1970, 7½in (19cm) high.

**£195–220** glas-design.nl ⊞

A Riihimäki glass Pajazzo vase, by Nanny Still, signed ' Nanny Still Riihimaen Lasi Oy', Finland, 1970, 7in (18cm) high.

**£220–245** glas-design.nl ⊞

A Riihimäki glass Paivankukka vase, by Helena Tynell, with label, Finland, 1972, 9½in (24cm) high.

**£125–140** glas-design.nl ⊞

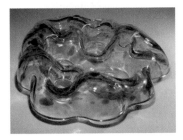

A Riihimäki glass Kuukävely sculpture, by Helena Tynell, signed 'Helena Tynell Riihimaen Lasi Oy', Finland, 1973, 9¾in (25cm) diam.

**£430–475** glas-design.nl ⊞

A Riihimäki glass vase, Finland, 1970s, 7in (18cm) high.

**£15–20** Luna ⊞

A Riihimäki glass Kuikka carafe, by Helena Tynell, Finland, 1970s, 5½in (14cm) high.

**£120–145** glas-design.nl ⊞

A Riihimäki glass Aitanlukko vase, by Helena Tynell, Finland, 1974, 8¼in (21cm) high.

**£70–85** glas-design.nl ⊞

A Riihimäki glass Piironki bottle/vase, by Helena Tynell, with label, Finland, 1974, 8¼in (21cm) high.

**£70–85** glas-design.nl ⊞

A Riihimäki glass Egg Head sculpture, by Nanny Still, signed 'Nanny Still Riihimaen Lasi Oy', Finland, 1973, 9½in (24cm) high.

**£430–500** glas-design.nl ⊞

# WHITEFRIARS

A Whitefriars glass amber ribbon trail trumpet vase, by Harry Powell, c1890, 10½in (26.5cm) high.

**£260–290  Country Seat** ⊞

A Whitefriars glass emerald wave Skittle lamp base, c1930, 11in (28cm) high.

**£270–300  Country Seat** ⊞

A Whitefriars glass optic vase, by W. Wilson, No. 9087, c1935, 9½in (24cm) high.

**£240–270  Country Seat** ⊞

A Whitefriars glass tywilight vase, by James Hogan, No. 9376, 1940s, 6in (15cm) high.

**£90–100  Decorative Antiques** ⊞

A Whitefriars sapphire glass bowl, by James Hogan, 1940s, 11in (28cm) wide.

**£90–100  Ruskin Decorative Arts** ⊞

A pair of Whitefriars glass table candlesticks, by W. Wilson, No. 9371, c1954, 4in (10cm) high.

**£180–195  Country Seat** ⊞

A Whitefriars cased-glass baluster vase, by W. Wilson and Geoffrey Baxter, No. 9415, c1954, 10in (25.5cm) high.

**£240–270  Country Seat** ⊞

A Whitefriars glass twilight fork vase, by W. Wilson, No. 9468, c1955, 10in (25.5cm) high.

**£115–130  Country Seat** ⊞

*The inspiration for this vase was drawn from Per Lütken's designs for Holmegaard, Denmark.*

A Whitefriars midnight soda glass vase, by Geoffrey Baxter, c1960, 7in (18cm) high.

**£75–85 Ruskin Decorative Arts** ⊞

A Whitefriars smoke glass vase, by Geoffrey Baxter, 1961, 6in (15cm) high.

**£50–55 Graham Cooley** ⊞

A James Powell Whitefriars soda glass Barrel vase, by Geoffrey Baxter, c1962, 7in (18cm) high.

**£60–70 Ruskin Decorative Arts** ⊞

A Whitefriars glass Knobbly vase, by W. Wilson and Harry Dyer, c1964, 7½in (19cm) high.

**£90–100 Country Seat** ⊞

A Whitefriars glass Nuts and Bolts vase, by Geoffrey Baxter, c1967, 10in (25.5cm) high.

**£420–470 Country Seat** ⊞
*Very few Whitefriars designs were given pet names – they were all referred to by their production numbers, in this case 9669. The names were coinded by the women who worked in the packing shop.*

A Whitefriars willow glass Drunken Bricklayer vase, by Geoffrey Baxter, c1967, 13in (33cm) high.

**£780–880 Country Seat** ⊞

A Whitefriars willow glass Bark vase, by Geoffrey Baxter, c1967, 7½in (19cm) high.

**£65–75 Country Seat** ⊞

A Whitefriars kingfisher blue glass Drunken Bricklayer vase, by Geoffrey Baxter, c1969, 13in (33cm) high.

**£480–580 Wellers Auctioneers** 🔨

A pair of Whitefriars tangerine glass Drunken Bricklayer vases, by Geoffrey Baxter, No. 9673, 1969–74, 8¼in (21cm) high.

**£200–250 Rosebery's** 🔨

A pair of Whitefriars pewter textured glass candlesticks, by Geoffrey Baxter, c1970, 3½in (9cm) diam.
**£40–45** Country Seat ⊞

A Whitefriars tangerine glass Banjo vase, by Geoffrey Baxter, No. 9681, c1970, 12½in (32cm) high.
**£520–630** Bearnes 🔨

A Whitefriars tangerine textured glass vase, by Geoffrey Baxter, c1970, 12¾in (32.5cm) high.
**£560–680** Bearnes 🔨

A Whitefriars glass Hook vase, by Geoffrey Baxter, c1970, 7in (18cm) high.
**£115–130** Country Seat ⊞

A Whitefriars tangerine glass Pineapple vase, by Geoffrey Baxter, c1970, 7in (18cm) high.
**£115–130** Country Seat ⊞

A Whitefriars tangerine glass Cello vase, by Geoffrey Baxter, 1972, 7in (18cm) high.
**£160–180** Fragile Design ⊞

A Whitefriars sage glass Gherkin vase, by Geoffrey Baxter, c1972, 12in (30.5cm) high.
**£800–900** Country Seat ⊞

# EXPERT EYE  ONION VASE

Geoffrey Baxter's textured ranges, distinguished by their rough surfaces, were inspired by slightly earlier Scandinavian designs, most specifically by Timo Sarpaneva's Finlandia vases for littala, 1964. These were formed in wooden moulds which gradually and intentionally disintegrated through usage, leaving a charred impression on the surface of the pieces formed within them.

Geoffrey Baxter's later designs marked a return to organic shapes, similar in theme to some of his early contributions dating from the early- to-mid 1950s, shortly after he had joined the works from the Royal College of Art.

A Whitefriars lilac glass Onion vase, by Geoffrey Baxter, c1974, 10½in (26.5cm) high.
**£1,350–1,500 Country Seat ⊞**

The value of collectable Whitefrairs pieces is often driven by rarity of colour, with lilac being among the least common.

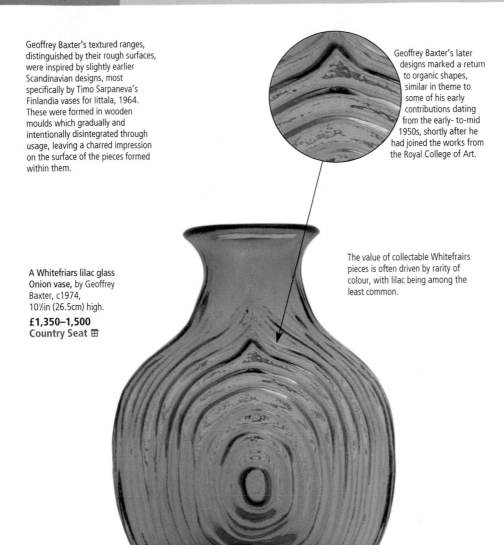

All these vases have circular polished pontil marks in the centre of their bases.

All Whitefriars textured pieces were formed in two layers of glass, with the initial thin layer of colour being 'cased' within a thicker outer layer of colourless. The colourless section is generally only visible at the base.

The Onion vase, factory pattern No. 9828, was among the last of Geoffrey Baxter's Scandinavian-inspired textured series. Following the introduction in 1967 of the Banjo and Drunken Bricklayer vases (pattern Nos. 9672 and 9681), the Onion first appeared in the 1974 sales catalogue, just six years before the works closed. It was produced in a limited number of colours: Kingfisher, Sage and the rarest, Lilac. The idiosyncratic textured ranges were not cheap, at around £10 each, but have proved to be a good investment as values have gained about 1,000 per cent over the decades.

**Andy McConnell, Glass Etc**

## UNITED STATES

A Blenko glass Crackle vase, with label, America, 2001, 13in (33cm) high.

**£35–40** RetroArtGlass.com ⊞

A Blenko glass Crackle pitcher, by Wayne Husted, with an applied Jonquil handle, soft pontil mark, America, 1954–64, 10¾in (27.5cm) high.

**£50–55** RetroArtGlass.com ⊞

A Blenko glass Crackle jug, America, 1950–60, 8in (20.5cm) high.

**£50–55** RetroArtGlass.com ⊞

A pair of Imperial pressed glass candlesticks, marked, America, late 1960s, 3in (7.5cm) high.

**£30–35** RetroArtGlass.com ⊞

A pair of Fenton glass goblets, America, 1930s, largest 5¾in (14.5cm) high.

**£25–30** RetroArtGlass.com ⊞

A Sam Herman iridescent glass vase, applied with raised trails and shoulders, engraved mark, America, dated 1971, 9½in (24cm) high.

**£420–520** Rosebery's 🔨

A Fenton pressed glass Amberina goblet, by Frank Fenton, with label, America, 1969–1973, 5in (12.5cm) high.

**£15–20** RetroArtGlass.com ⊞
*The inspirated for this vase was drawn from the central European repertoire.*

A Viking crackle glass patio light, with label, America, 1970s, 4⅛in (11.5cm) high.

**£25–30** RetroArtGlass.com ⊞

A Louis Comfort Tiffany cased-glass Favrile vase, engraved 'L. C. Tiffany Favrille 901k', America, c1910, 5¾in (14.5cm) high.

**£1,900–2,300** Rosebery's 🔨

A glass sculpture, by Tom Patti, etched mark 'Patti 78', America, 1978, 5¾in (14.5cm) wide.

**£5,500–6,500**
Rago Arts & Auction Centre 🔨

# GRAMOPHONES

An HMV Loud Tone gramophone needles tin, by The Gramophone Co, containing approximately 200 needles, 1920s, 6½ x 4¾in (16.5 x 12cm).

**£10–15** Tin Shop ⊞

A Songster gramophone needles tin, 1920s, 4½ x 3in (11.5 x 7.5cm).

**£10–15** Tin Shop ⊞

A Verona gramophone needles tin, containing original needles, 1940s, 1½ x ½in (4 x 1cm).

**£15–20** Tin Shop ⊞

A Columbia Grafonola Viva-tonal gramophone, model No. 117, in an oak case, c1926, 19in (48.5cm) wide.

**£90–100** On The Air ⊞

An HMV gramophone, model No. 194, with patented re-entrant tone chamber, 1928, 44½in (113cm) high.

**£2,250–2,500**
**Early Technology** ⊞

An HMV portable gramophone, model No. 102, 1931, 16in (40.5cm) wide.

**£220–250** Decographics ⊞
*Original advertisements bill this model as 'the world's finest portable'. Unusually, the 102 came in several colours and they were more expensive to buy than the traditional black. When new, this would have retailed at £6 (more than two weeks' wages for most). Coloured portables like this and the similar blue examples are sought after by collectors.*

An HMV 145 gramophone, with 5b sound box, in an oak case, restored, c1932, 34½in (87.5cm) high.

**£270–300** Decographics ⊞
*The 145 is admired by collectors for its sound quality. It has the advantage of not being too bulky and has record storage space beneath.*

An RCA Victor Special Model K portable phonograph, by John Vassos, with clockwork motor and imitation tortoiseshell carrying handle, 1930s, 16½in (42cm) wide.

**£900–1,100** Skinner ⚒
*This is very much a cutting-edge designer piece that is of museum quality. John Vassos was an American industrial designer who applied his talent to everyday objects. In 1939, RCA's first consumer television set, designed by him, was unveiled at the New York World's Fair.*

# KITCHENWARE

sk me what kitchen utensils I adore using and I'll tell you about a Nutbrown rolling pin, a Melaware butter dish and my Tala vegetable strainer. These 1950s gems are just as serviceable now as the day they were made – that's a key reason more and more collectors are snapping up vintage kitchenalia. Today's retro-styled kitchens, which pay homage to the teak-effect Hygenia flat-packs of the 1960s are perfectly accessorised with original utensils and gadgets. The same is true of those cosy farmhouse kitchens complete with an Aga and pine table. With that setting as a backdrop, 1930s storage jars, mottled handmincers and nicely patinated wooden utensils fit like a dream. Adventurous collectors who choose to cook with vintage kitchenware swear by the feel of the handles, the solidity of the build and the streamlined style. Those who value display over use are a little pickier about what they select. With a growing number of vintage outlets opening up this year, there's certainly no shortage of kitchenalia to choose from. The issue is

the condition of what's on offer. It's easy to forget that kitchenware was designed to work for its living and times were hard in days gone by. This explains the cracks and chips that many have suffered over the years. In the early 20th century bread was the staple diet of the household and slicing a loaf on a carved wooden board was a task that ran on and on. Needless to say, for every good condition pre-war bread board there are 20 split or worn examples. Boxes are a real bonus for pre-war gadgets but they're increasingly hard to find. Generally it means that what's inside has been well looked after and it hasn't suffered drawer damage. In the pages that follow you'll notice how good condition items, which have somehow avoided the strains and stresses of kitchen life, fetch the highest prices. However, compared with other collecting areas those tags are still relatively low. Added to this, there's a stream of new areas like Tupperware and Pyrex that are sizzling away offering so much scope for a beginner.

**Katherine Higgins**

A fruitwood oat crusher, with wooden handle, 1930s, 9in (23cm) long.

**£30–35 Jean Sears** ⊞

An ACME tin nut grater, 1888, 7in (18cm) long.

**£40–45 Below Stairs** ⊞

A wooden pan scourer, c1900, 5in (12.5cm) high.

**£20–25**
**Cottage Collectables** ⊞

*Woman's Own Cook Book*, published by George Newnes, London, 1964, 10in (25.5cm) high.

**£10–15 Jane Wicks** ⊞

A ceramic rolling pin, decorated with a paisley pattern, with wooden handles, c1960s, 12in (30.5cm) long.
**£5–10 Quay Centre** ⊞

# BREADBOARDS & KNIVES

A carved sycamore breadboard, c1900, 15in (38cm) diam.

**£135–150  Bread & Roses** ⊞

A carved sycamore breadboard, 1910, 12in (30.5cm) diam.

**£35–40  Jane Wicks** ⊞

A child's carved sycamore breadboard, c1920, 6in (15cm) diam.

**£65–75  Skip & Janie Smithson** ⊞

A carved sycamore breadboard, 1920s, 12in (30.5cm) diam.

**£40–45  Jean Sears** ⊞

A carved breadboard, with knife, c1950, 13 x 8in (33 x 20.5cm).

**£25–30  Ann Lingard** ⊞

## ESSENTIAL REFERENCE   BREAD KNIVES

A J. Nowill & Sons bread knife, with carved wood handle, c1880, 12in (30.5cm) long.

**£40–45  Below Stairs** ⊞

An Artes bread knife, with carved handle, c1900, 13in (33cm) long.

**£30–35  Below Stairs** ⊞

- Although bakeries existed in towns at the turn of the 20th century, in the rural setting bread was still very much home-made. In both cases, the ingredients used resulted in loaves with noticeably harder crusts than today.

- A bread knife was an essential domestic item and a steel blade made slicing easy. The best quality knives hailed from Sheffield where there were skilled cutlery makers and wood turners. Look closely at the blade to see if you can spot a maker's mark.

- Knives with turned and carved wooden handles are the most sought-after. The more intricate the carving, the more valuable the bread knife. If it matches a board and you have a set then this is a bonus.

- In 1928, the first machine that both sliced and wrapped loaves was invented – the result was 'Kleen Maid Sliced Bread', which changed the course of breadmaking for good.

**ENAMEL WARE**

A Judge Ware enamel cooking pot, with cast-iron lid, c1890, 16in (40.5cm) diam.

**£90–100** Martin's Antiques ⊞

A Prince Wares enamel candle holder, 1920, 10in (25.5cm) wide.

**£15–20** Jane Wicks ⊞

An enamel lidded canister, France, c1930, 13in (33cm) high.

**£40–45** Quay Centre ⊞

A Judge enamel double saucepan, 1930s, 8in (20.5cm) high.

**£15–20** Jane Wicks ⊞

A Kockums enamel measuring jug, 1930, 4in (10cm) high.

**£10–15** Jane Wicks ⊞

An enamel flour bin, probably Holland, 1940, 9in (23cm) high.

**£25–30** Jane Wicks ⊞

An enamel colander, France, c1940, 16in (40.5cm) wide.

**£25–30** Quay Centre ⊞

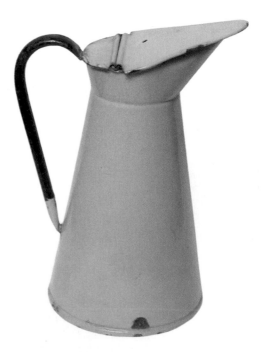

An enamel jug, with hinged cover, 1940s, 13in (33cm) high.

**£30–35** Quay Centre ⊞

## EXPERT EYE  KOCKUMS COFFEE POT

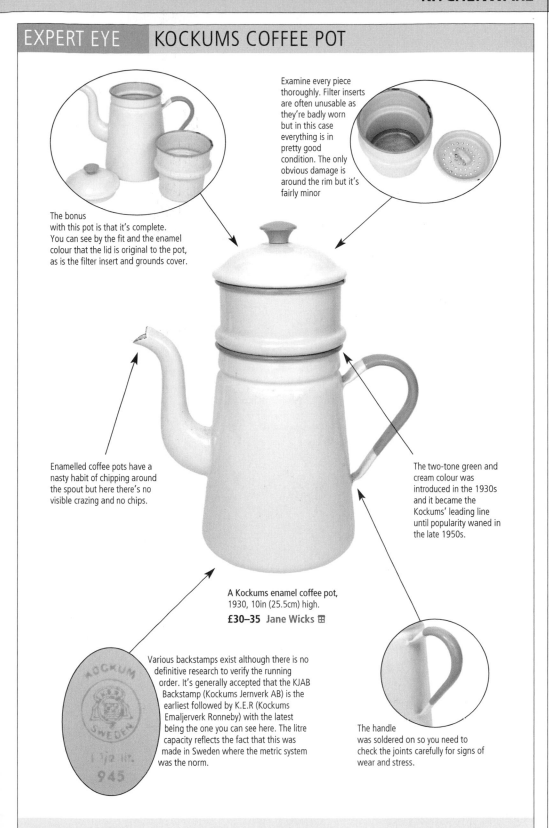

The bonus with this pot is that it's complete. You can see by the fit and the enamel colour that the lid is original to the pot, as is the filter insert and grounds cover.

Examine every piece thoroughly. Filter inserts are often unusable as they're badly worn but in this case everything is in pretty good condition. The only obvious damage is around the rim but it's fairly minor

Enamelled coffee pots have a nasty habit of chipping around the spout but here there's no visible crazing and no chips.

The two-tone green and cream colour was introduced in the 1930s and it became the Kockums' leading line until popularity waned in the late 1950s.

A Kockums enamel coffee pot, 1930, 10in (25.5cm) high.
**£30–35 Jane Wicks** ⊞

Various backstamps exist although there is no definitive research to verify the running order. It's generally accepted that the KJAB Backstamp (Kockums Jernverk AB) is the earliest followed by K.E.R (Kockums Emaljerverk Ronneby) with the latest being the one you can see here. The litre capacity reflects the fact that this was made in Sweden where the metric system was the norm.

The handle was soldered on so you need to check the joints carefully for signs of wear and stress.

Enamelled ware was part and parcel of the pre-war kitchen, only giving way to stainless steel in the 1960s. Bread bins, storage canisters, saucepans and colanders were all treated to a protective coating of enamel and in the hospital setting clean white enamel wares were widely used for their sanitary qualities. Collectors like collecting brands and this has helped to fuel interest in Kockums. The first colours they made were white and granite. Around 1920 they unveiled 'karlblatt', which had a cobalt exterior and white interior. This was soon followed by the hugely popular two-tone green and cream you can see here. Condition is everything when it comes to collecting enamel wares so check very thoroughly for small chips and crazing.

GADGETS & MOTHERS' HELPS

A Beatrice cast-iron coffee grinder, 1908, 5in (12.5cm) wide.
**£80–90 Below Stairs** ⊞

A cast-iron table-mounted mincer, with original beechwood pushing block, 1900–20s, 9in (23cm) high.
**£35–40 Below Stairs** ⊞

A Bakelite knife sharpener, with wooden handle, 1920s, 6in (15cm) long.
**£5–10 Quay Centre** ⊞

A Landers, Frary & Clark electric toaster, America, 1914, 7¼in (18.5cm) high.
**£25–30 Silversnow Antiques** ⊞
*Based in Connecticut, USA, Landers, Frary & Clark adopted their name in 1862. Their first product for the American housewife was the 'Household scale'. In the 1890s they introduced a Bread Maker and Food Chopper followed by a Coffee Percolator in 1905. This model E3342 toaster was patented on 28 July 1914. Shortly after appliance production stopped as the entire firm's resources were switched to making bayonets to supply WWI soldiers.*

A Buss cast-iron vegetable slicer, 1920s, 9in (23cm) high.
**£50–55 Jean Sears** ⊞

A metal bean slicer, 1930, 6in (15cm) high.
**£10–15 Jane Wicks** ⊞

A Manning Bowman chrome and porcelain electric egg cooker, model No. 1077, with Bakelite feet, America, 1930s, 5½in (14cm) high.
**£50–55 Vintage Swank** ⊞

A Harper enamelled metal food mincer, 1940, 11in (28cm) high.
**£10–15 Jane Wicks** ⊞

A J. J. Blow glass and metal butter churn, 1940, 14½in (37cm) high.
**£35–40 Jane Wicks** ⊞

A Tala metal and brass Food Decorator Set, with four nozzles, 1940.

**£15–20** Ashmans Vintage Clothing ⊞

A wire mesh strainer, mesh damaged, paint worn, 1940s, 9in (23cm) long.

**£1–5** My Gigi's Treasures ⊞

An Ice-O-Mat chrome ice crusher, 1950s, 9in (23cm) high.

**£30–35** Luna ⊞

A set of Harper metal scales, model No. 3178, with weights, 1950, 12½in (32cm) wide, boxed.

**£20–25** Jane Wicks ⊞

*The British firm of John Harper & Co had a history that went back to 1790. In the 19th century they made a name for their cast lock cases, patented padlocks and door bolts. In the 20th century the firm sidelined into bicycles and oil stoves. These scales mirror Harper's commitment to a top quality finish.*

A Gentry metal Ejecta-fork, with insulated rosewood handle, 1960s, box 7½in (19cm) wide.

**£1–5** New 2 You ⊞

*The rosewood handle not only insulated but fitted very nicely with 1960s' interiors.*

A Brinkman Popall Popper, by Emery L. Brinkman, America, Kansas, 1960s–70s, 16in (40.5cm) long.

**£5–10** My Gigi's Treasures ⊞

*This popcorn-making device was invented and hand made by Emery L. Brinkman of Topeka, Kansas, and sold by mail order. It fitted over a pot and when the handle was turned, the blade stirred the kernels. The lid is hinged to allow steam to escape.*

A Teflon BOC Sparklets Cream Maid, with original cream whipper bulbs, box and booklet, 1970s, 11in (28cm) high.

**£10–15** New 2 You ⊞

*This is another use for Sparklets beyond conventional soda syphons, and was the precursor to the spray cream available today.*

## MOULDS

A copper and tin jelly mould, c1900, 6in (15cm) diam.

**£100–115** Below Stairs ⊞

A tin-lined copper mould, in the form of a cockerel, c1910, 11in (28cm) high.

**£30–35** Lewis Antiques ⊞

A two-piece pewter ice mould, c1900, 10½in (26.5cm) high.

**£80–90** Below Stairs ⊞

A tin jelly mould, c1910, 6in (15cm) diam.

**£10–15** Quay Centre ⊞

A galvanized metal chocolate mould, with wooden handle, 1930, 7in (18cm) diam.

**£15–20** Lewis Antiques ⊞

A tin mould, in the form of a rabbit, 1920s, 7in (18cm) high.

**£20–25** Quay Centre ⊞

Six fluted candy moulds, Sweden, 1940s, 2¼in (5.5cm) wide.

**£1–5** Knick Knack Nook ⊞

A ceramic jelly mould, impressed with emblems including a Tudor rose and a Union flag, registered 1900, 8in (20.5cm) wide.

**£100–115** Below Stairs ⊞

A Wedgwood ceramic jelly mould, depicting children playing in a band, c1910, 8in (20.5cm) wide.

**£115–130 Skip & Janie Smithson** ⊞

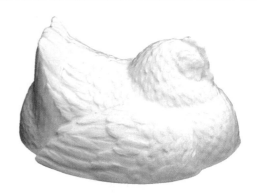

A Shelley ceramic jelly mould, in the form of a hen on a nest, c1920, 8in (20.5cm) wide.

**£220–250 Skip & Janie Smithson** ⊞

A ceramic jelly mould, in the form of a cat on a cushion, 1929, 6in (15cm) wide.

**£80–90 Below Stairs** ⊞

A Shelley ceramic jelly mould, 1940s, 7in (18cm) diam.

**£10–15 Quay Centre** ⊞

A glass jelly mould, 1940s, 7in (18cm) wide.

**£5–10 Jane Wicks** ⊞

A glass jelly mould, 1940s , 9in (23cm) wide.

**£5–10 Jane Wicks** ⊞

A Swan aluminium jelly mould, c1950, 13in (33cm) diam.

**£5–10 Quay Centre** ⊞

A Diamond aluminium jelly mould, c1950, 5in (12.5cm) diam.

**£1–5 Quay Centre** ⊞

## PLASTIC

A Nally plastic five-piece kitchen storage set, America, c1950, largest 8in (20.5cm) high.

**£45–50** Twinkled ⊞

A set of four Bakelite egg cups and stand, 1930s, 5in (12.5cm) wide.

**£15–20** Upstairs Downstairs ⊞

A set of Melaware melamine salt and pepper pots, 1950, 3in (7.5cm) high.

**£5–10** Jane Wicks ⊞

A Paramount plastic egg cup set, with salt pot, 1950s, tray 8in (20.5cm) diam.

**£15–20** Twinkled ⊞

A set of six plastic napkin rings, 1950s, 2in (5cm) diam.

**£20–25** Jane Wicks ⊞

An Albertini lemon squeezer, Italy, 1960s, 7in (18cm) high.

**£5–10** Twinkled ⊞

A plastic and stainless-steel butter dish, Denmark, 1970s, 7in (18cm) wide.

**£5–10** Twinkled ⊞

A set of three Melaware plastic beakers, c1970, 5in (12.5cm) high.

**£5–10** Quay Centre ⊞

A set of five Melaware plastic cereal bowls, 1970s, 5in (12.5cm) diam.

**£5–10** Quay Centre ⊞

A transparent plastic strawberry fruit salad dish, 1980s, 13in (33cm) wide.

**£10–15** Twinkled ⊞

A Tupperware bowl and cover, marked, 1970s, 7½in (19cm) diam.
**£1–5** New 2 You ⊞

A Tupperware bowl, marked, 1970s, 6in (15cm) diam.
**£1–5** New 2 You ⊞

A Tupperware lemon squeezer, marked, 1970s, 4½in (11.5cm) diam.
**£1–5** New 2 You ⊞

A set of six Tupperware sundae pots, marked, 1970s, 5½in (14cm) high.
**£5–10** New 2 You ⊞

A set of four Tupperware pots, marked, 1970s, 3½in (9cm) high.
**£5–10** New 2 You ⊞

A Tupperware container and cover, marked, 1970s, 13½in (34.5cm) wide.
**£1–5** New 2 You ⊞

A set of two Tupperware containers, marked, 1980s, largest 7in (18cm) high.
**£1–5** New 2 You ⊞

## MARKET INFORMATION      TUPPERWARE

- Vintage Tupperware collecting is big in the USA and European collectors are beginning to catch on to this trend.
- The 'Golden Era' for collecting are the years from the late 1940s to the mid 1960s with great interest surrounding the first Tupperware Party products sold in 1951.
- Coloured Tupperware tends to fetch the highest prices but interesting designs like pitchers and cheese keepers also attract interest.
- It's a market place that's set to go far but full of affordable buys right now. Typically the highest prices for the best and rarest pieces don't go much beyond £15.

## PYREX

A Pyrex glass mixing bowl, 1960, 13in (33cm) wide.
**£15–20 Jane Wicks** ⊞

A Pyrex and plastic ice bucket, in the form of a pear, 1960s, 10½in (26.5cm) high.
**£45–50 Pineappple Ice Bucket** ⊞

A Pyrex glass and plastic hand mixer, 1960, 9½in (24cm) high.
**£10–15 Jane Wicks** ⊞

A Pyrex casserole dish, marked, 1970s, 9in (23cm) diam.
**£5–10 New 2 You** ⊞

A Pyrex bowl, marked, 1970s, 9in (23cm) diam.
**£1–5 New 2 You** ⊞

A Pyrex gravy boat, marked, 1970s, 8in (20.5cm) wide.
**£1–5 New 2 You** ⊞

A Pyrex glass teapot, American, c1980s, 5in (12.5cm) high.
**£30–35 Luna** ⊞

## OVEN-TO-TABLE WARE

A Fire King glass platter, 1950, 12in (30.5cm) wide.
**£5–10 Jane Wicks** ⊞

A Fire-King Candleglow dish, marked, America, 1967–72, 8in (20.5cm) square.
**£5–10 Retro2Go** ⊞

A Phoenix glass sauce boat and stand, 1950, 8in (20.5cm) wide.
**£10–15 Jane Wicks** ⊞

A Phoenix glass tureen and cover, 1950s, 6in (15cm) diam.
**£15–20 Jane Wicks** ⊞

A Phoenix glass oven to table set, comprising seven dishes, 1950, largest 10in (25.5cm) diam.
**£25–30 Jane Wicks** ⊞

Two Phoenix glass bowls, 1950s, largest 6in (15cm) diam.
**£5–10 Jane Wicks** ⊞

A Phoenix glass bowl, 1950s, 6in (15cm) diam.
**£5–10 Jane Wicks** ⊞

## STORAGE

A set of three C. H. Brannam glazed pottery spice jars, c1950, 3in (7.5cm) high.
**£60–65  Lewis Antiques** ⊞

A Crown Devon ceramic coffee storage jar, with a plastic cover, marked, 1950s, 6in (15cm) high.
**£5–10  New 2 You** ⊞

A Crown Devon ceramic suger storage jar, with a plastic cover, marked, 1950s, 6in (15cm) high.
**£5–10  New 2 You** ⊞

A ceramic salt pot, with a wooden cover, Denmark, 1960s, 7in (18cm) high.
**£35–40  Jean Sears** ⊞

## ESSENTIAL REFERENCE  TONI RAYMOND

A Toni Raymond Pottery ceramic coffee storage jar, with a wooden cover, c1960, 7in (18cm) high.
**£5–10  Quay Centre** ⊞

A Toni Raymond Pottery ceramic salt pot, with a wooden cover, 1960s, 6in (15cm) high.
**£10–15  Quay Centre** ⊞

A Toni Raymond Pottery ceramic storage jar, with a wooden cover, 1960s, 7in (18cm) high.
**£15–20  Quay Centre** ⊞

• The Toni Raymond Pottery began making wares in Torquay, Devon in 1951. In 1967 they expanded by buying the Babbacombe pottery and pieces marked with this backstamp offer collectors another complimentary avenue.

• In the 1960s and '70s kitchens across the nation were treated to their range of distinctive hand-painted floral pottery. The most commonly seen pieces are storage jars, clearly marked in black script lettering with their contents.

• The floral designs inspired imitators so do look for the stamped 'Toni Raymond' mark on the base. Cheaper copies were screen-printed rather than handpainted.

# LIGHTING

## CEILING & FLOOR LIGHTS

A holophane glass and metal ceiling lamp, America, c1930, 13in (33cm) high.

**£450–500  Chameleon** ⊞

A plastic ceiling light, in the style of Verner Panton, 1960s, 14in (35.5cm) diam.

**£240–270  Vintage Swank** ⊞

A fibreglass Ghost floor lamp, on a marble base, Germany, c1965, 64in (162.5cm) high.

**£700–800  Boom Interiors** ⊞

A Luna floor lamp, Italy, 1968, 66in (167.5cm) high.

**£1,400–1,550  Eat My Handbag** ⊞

## ESSENTIAL REFERENCE  SPACE AGE STYLE

A rocket spun fibre and teak floor lamp, 1960s, 38in (96.5cm) high.

**£75–85
Pineapple Ice Bucket** ⊞

A chrome Sputnik-style ceiling light, with 11 bulbs, Germany, 1960s, 18in (45.5cm) diam.

**£180–200  Retro Centre** ⊞

A Vistosi metal and plastic Saturn Sputnik ceiling light, Italy, 1960s, 25in (63.5cm) long.

**£300–330
High Street Retro** ⊞

• The race to the moon, which began with the launch of Sputnik 1 in 1957 and culminated with the first moon landing in 1969, had a powerful effect on design.

• Furniture makers, ceramics designers and textile makers worked hard to incorporate 'Space Age' motifs into their pieces. Planetary-styled spheres and circles were key to the look.

• The Vistosi lamp on the right shows just how realistic designs became. Suspended chromed balls are surrounded by rings of metal as a means of stylizing what was known about Saturn at the time. Saturn was not only the name of the launch rocket for the Apollo mission but also the subject of an avidly read book, *The Planet Saturn*, published in 1962.

# DESK & TABLE LIGHTS

A cast-brass and ceramic table lamp, the hand-painted shade decorated with abstract floral motifs, 1910, 16in (40.5cm) high.
**£580–650 Turn On Lighting** ⊞

A brass library lamp, with a glass shade, France, c1910, 20in (51cm) high.
**£280–310 Quay Centre** ⊞

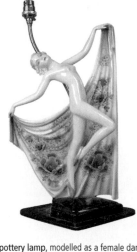

A pottery lamp, modelled as a female dancer, slight damage, 1920s, 18½in (47cm) high.
**£160–190 Rosebery's** 🔨

A cold-painted spelter table lamp, modelled as an exotic male dancer, on an alabaster base, c1930, 13¾in (35cm) high.
**£180–210 Rosebery's** 🔨

An Art Deco bronzed-metal desk lamp, with moulded Egyptian-style decoration, c1930, 14¼in (36cm) high.
**£70–80 Rosebery's** 🔨

An Art Deco aluminum and frosted glass planetary-style table lamp, pierced with an arrow, 1930s, 11in (28cm) high.
**£170–190 Vintage Swank** ⊞

A Pifco Bakelite and metal Night Watch light and watch stand, battery operated, 1950s, 4½in (11.5cm) high.
**£20–25 collectorsworld** ⊞

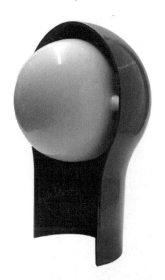

A Vico Magistretti plastic table lamp, with a swivel globe, Italy, 1966, 16in (40.5cm) high.
**£220–250 Vintage Swank** ⊞
*A true innovator in modern design, Magistretti was the first Italian to use moulded plastics in the 1960s. Many of his items were sold through outlets such as Artemide.*

A pair of Stilnovo Angel metal table lamps, Italy, 1968, 27½in (70cm) high.
**£1,600–1,800 Boom Interiors** ⊞

A Softlite plastic mushroom table lamp,
1960s, 16in (40.5cm) high.

**£70–80 Vintage Swank** ⊞

A chrome and plastic mushroom table lamp,
1960s, 21in (53.5cm) high.

**£45–50 Attica** ⊞

A plastic table lamp, 1960s,
13¾in (35cm) high.

**£45–50 Wellers** ⚒

A pair of Philips metal table lamps, 1960s, 17in (43cm) high.

**£160–180 High Street Retro** ⊞

A plastic-coated tubular-metal desk lamp, c1965, 31in (78.5cm) wide.

**£85–95 Twinkled** ⊞

A Living Jewel aluminium glitter lamp,
with sliver glitter flakes, 1960s,
15½in (39.5cm) high.

**£55–65 Pineapple Ice Bucket** ⊞

A studio pottery lamp base, decorated with
applied and impressed patterns, c1970,
18in (46cm) high overall.

**£30–35 Rosebery's** ⚒

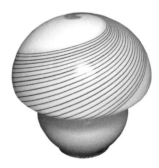

A pair of Canadezi hand-blown glass table
lamps, Italy, 1972, 13in (33cm) high.

**£770–850 Boom Interiors** ⊞

An Artemide Sintesi metal light, by Ernesto
Gismondi, Italy, 1975, 17in (43cm) high.

**£145–160 High Street Retro** ⊞

# MILITARY & NAVAL

## BADGES

A Worcestershire Regiment brass star valise, with King's crown and regimental motto 'Firm', 1901–52, 4in (10cm) high.

**£100–115 Worcester Antiques** ⊞
*This badge was first issued in 1890 and was then withdrawn.*

A Black Watch brass badge, economy issue, 1914–18, 3in (7.5cm) high.

**£55–65 A B Coins & Medals** ⊞

A Tank Corps brass cap badge, 1917–21, 1½in (4cm) diam.

**£25–30 Worcester Antiques** ⊞

A zinc army tank battle badge, marking 50 tank engagements, Germany, 1939–45, 2½in (6.5cm) high.

**£630–700 Chelsea Military** ⊞

A 20th Hussars badge, 1940, 1½in (4cm) high.

**£1–5 Quay Centre** ⊞

A King's Own Regiment brass cap badge, c1943, 2in (5cm) wide.

**£15–20 Worcester Antiques** ⊞

A Fife and Forfar Regiment badge, 1960, 2in (5cm) wide.

**£5–10 Quay Centre** ⊞

A King's Royal Rifle Corps badge, 1970, 2in (5cm) high.

**£1–5 Quay Centre** ⊞

A Royal Fusiliers QC badge, 1980, 2in (5cm) high.

**£1–5 Quay Centre** ⊞

## CAPS & HELMETS

A Prussian officer's leather and brass *Pickelhaube*, Prussia, c1900.
**£850–950 Chelsea Military** ⊞

A Prussian officer's leather and brass *Pickelhaube*, with parade plume, Prussia, c1900, 12in (30.5cm) high.
**£2,250–2,500 Chelsea Military** ⊞

An Army Medical Corps officer's cloth helmet, with King's crown, 1902–10.
**£580–650 Q & C Militaria** ⊞

A Model 16 helmet, with armoured sniper protection front plate, Germany, 1914–18.
**£880–980 Michael D Long** ⊞

A National Socialist German Workers Party officer's cloth and leather cap, 1940s.
**£630–700 Q & C Militaria** ⊞

A steel helmet, possibly Medical Corps, painted with a red cross, Japan, 1939–45.
**£120–140 Godfrey Wallem** ⊞

A Royal Horse Guards officer's helmet, after 1953.
**£1,550–1,750 Michael D Long** ⊞

# MEDALS

A group of 11 Royal Medical Corps medals, including Member of the British Empire, Distinguished Conduct Medal, Military Service Medal, 1914–45.
**£3,000–3,500 Chelsea Military** ⊞

A group of four medals, awarded to Sergeant Lancaster of Royal Field Artillery, Distinguished Conduct Medal George V, 1914–15 Star, British War Medal and Victory Medal, 1914–18.
**£1,000–1,200 Jim Bullock Militaria** ⊞

A group of three medals, Iron Cross 2nd Class, Prinzen war Luftshultze Honor cross, 1914–18 Cross with swords, 1914–45.
**£380–430 Tussie Mussies** ⊞

A group of six medals, awarded to a Royal Navy petty officer, 1939–45 Star, Atlantic Star with bar, Africa Star, Burma Star, War Medal, Naval General Service Medal with bar, 1945–48.
**£220–250 Jim Bullock Militaria** ⊞

A group of seven medals, awarded to South African pilot Johannes Louw, including Distinguished Flying Cross 1945 Italy, Africa Star, Italy Star, 1939–45 War Medal, South Africa Overseas Medal and 1953 Coronation Medal awarded to members of the armed forces killed in action.
**£2,600–2,900 Q & C Militaria** ⊞

An Africa General Service Medal, awarded to a rifleman in the Rifle Brigade, with bar Kenya, 1952–56.
**£115–130 Jim Bullock Militaria** ⊞

A Royal Signals medal, awarded to Staff Sergeant A. McIvor, with bar Northern Ireland, 1960–95.
**£55–65 Tussie Mussies** ⊞

A Campaign Service Medal, bars Malay Peninsula and Borneo, 1962–66.
**£100–115 A B Coins & Medals** ⊞

A group of two medals, awarded to a Sergeant/Warrant Officer in the Royal Artillery, Campaign Service Medal with bars Northern Ireland and South Arabia and Long Service and Good Conduct Medal bar Regular Army, 1960s–70s.

**£250–280**
Jim Bullock Militaria ⊞

A NATO medal, bar Former Yugoslavia, 1994.

**£15–20** Q & C Militaria ⊞

A group of five medals and neck badge, awarded to Arthur Robert Adams, Penang Volunteers, Knight Commander of the British Empire neck badge and breast star, 1902 Coronation Medal, 1911 Coronation Medal, Long Service Medal, Colonial Auxiliary Forces Decoration, c1911, in a fitted case, 9in (23cm) long.

**£1,450–1,650** Q & C Militaria ⊞

## MILITARY

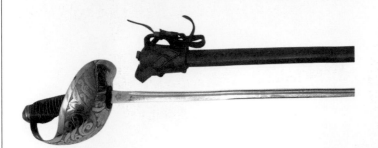

A Household Cavalry 1912 pattern sword, 1912, 43in (109cm) long.

**£760–850 Chelsea Military** ⊞

A tin, with a paper label depicting Princess Alexandra, 1914, 4½in (11.5cm) high.

**£50–60 Tussie Mussies** ⊞

An MK 1X trench periscope, by R. & J. Beck, 1918, 23in (58.5cm) high.

**£100–120 Rosebery's** ⊞

A Macintyre Pottery Royal Army Medical Corps match holder and striker, 1914–18, 3½in (9cm) diam.

**£40–45 Tussie Mussies** ⊞

A naval sword, Japan, 1914–18, 38in (96.5cm) long.

**£200–230 Grimes Militaria** ⊞

A tin gas mask container, Germany, 1930–45, 12in (30.5cm) long.

**£30–35 Tussie Mussies** ⊞

A Mk II anti-gas eyeshield, 1939–45, 10in (25.5cm) long.

**£1–5 Tussie Mussies** ⊞

A wood and steel WWI trench fighting knife, America, 1917, 13¾in (35cm) long.

**£250–280 Tussie Mussies** ⊞

A steel-bladed commando third pattern fighting knife, in leather holder, 1939–45, 13in (33cm) long.

**£75–85 Tussie Mussies** ⊞

A Bakelite No. 69 pattern hand grenade, 1940, 3½in (9cm) high.
**£20–25  Godfrey Wallem** ⊞

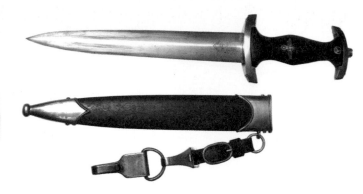

An SA dagger, by Purna, with original hanger and coat hook, Germany, c1940, 12in (30.5cm) long.
**£350–400  A B Coins & Medals** ⊞

A stoneware rum bottle and canvas carrier, 1937 patent, 1945, 15in (38cm) high.
**£55–65  Tussie Mussies** ⊞

A Nazi Non-Commissioned Officer's sword, 1940s, 30in (76cm) long blade.
**£110–130  Q & C Militaria** ⊞

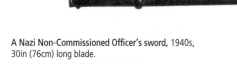

A base metal flint striking lighter, No. 63, inscribed 'Sgt. RIF Stock, Korea 51–52, 55–56, TK Co, 34th Inf. Regt.', 1950s, 2½in (6.5cm) high.
**£20–25  Tussie Mussies** ⊞

A hand-beaten brass MGM21 shell case, America, 1920s, 15in (38cm) high.
**£45–50  Tussie Mussies** ⊞

A brass and copper shell case photograph frame, 1918, 13in (33cm) high.
**£45–50  Tussie Mussies** ⊞

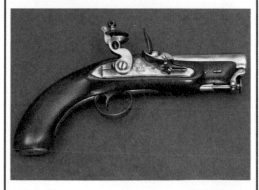

## NAVAL

A Royal Navy Air Service enamel and gilt filigree sweetheart brooch, 1914–18, with box, 3in (7.5cm) wide.

**£30–35 Godfrey Wallem** ⊞

A Bakelite US Navy ship's clock, by Seth Thomas, America, c1935, 8in (20.5cm) diam.

**£200–230 Oldnautibits** ⊞

A US Navy ship's clock, by Seth Thomas, America, 1942, 7in (18cm) diam.

**£90–110 James D Julia** 🔨

A Kriegesmarine U-boat gyro sextant, by C. Plath, Hamburg, Germany, c1942, with fitted deck box, 16in (40.5cm) wide.

**£400–450 Oldnautibits** ⊞

A Spode ceramic plate, commemorating the formation of the Royal Navy Submarine Service in the Royal Navy, limited edition of 750, 1976, 10in (25.5cm) diam.

**£75–85 Tussie Mussies** ⊞

A Royal Navy Far East fleet blazer badge, 1960s, 6in (15cm) square.

**£5–10 Cobwebs** ⊞

# PUBLICATIONS & EPHEMERA

A York and Lancaster Regiment silk postcard, c1914.

**£35–40**
**Memories Collectors Shop** ⊞

*The Navy List containing Officers on the Active List of The Royal Navy,* published by His Majesty's Stationery Office, 1933, 8½in (21.5cm) high.

**£25–30  Books Afloat** ⊞

*The Protection of Your Home Against Air Raids,* published by the Home Office, 1939, 9in (23cm) high.

**£1–5  Tussie Mussies** ⊞

*The Australian Army at War 1939–1944,* Australia, 8 x 6in (20.5 x 15cm).

**£5–10  J R & S J Symes** ⊞

A Prisoners of War information sheet and a Red Cross Safe Conduct pass, America, 1944.

**£10–15  Tussie Mussies** ⊞

A copy of the *News Chronicle,* 31 March 1945, 16in (40.5cm) wide.

**£5–10  Cobwebs** ⊞

*Ground Observers' Guide,* a Ground Observer Corp Air Force manual, with brochures and citizen reporting form, 1950s, 8in (20.5cm) wide.

**£10–15**
**Antique Mystique** ⊞

A Field Post Office postcard, 1918, 5½ x 3½in (14 x 9cm).

**£1–5  Quay Centre** ⊞

A standard army postcard, with fixed replies for censorship, 1917, 5½ x 3½in (14 x 9cm).

**£1–5  Quay Centre** ⊞

A letter, from an Italian Prisoner of War Camp for British soldiers, 1942, 5½in (14cm) wide.

**£1–5  Quay Centre** ⊞

# MODERN TECHNOLOGY

## CALCULATORS

An Otis King nickel-plated pocket calculator, in original card box with advertisement, c1922.
**£90–100** Charles Tomlinson ⊞

A Fowler & Co nickel-plated long scale calculator, in original metal case, c1924.
**£75–80** Charles Tomlinson ⊞
*Fowler & Co was a firm of calculator makers based in Manchester. By 1912, the firm had three patents for circular calculators. The most popular was their double-sided long scale calculator. It was a well-engineered device that was assembled by hand. It cost four times the price of a straight slide rule. The case shown is missing the circular metal tag which would show Fowler & Co's details.*

A Curta Type II Liechtenstein calculator, in original container, 1968.
**£270–300** Charles Tomlinson ⊞
*The Curta was the predecessor to the electronic calculators we know today. It first appeared in 1948 and ran through to the 1970s. This is the Type II version, which was introduced in 1954. Having the original case is a real bonus for collectors.*

A Commodore 989r calculator, 1975.
**£90–100** Pepe Tozzo ⊞

A Sinclair Cambridge calculator, 1973.
**£50–60** Pepe Tozzo ⊞

A Sinclair Oxford 300 calculator, 1975.
**£115–130** Pepe Tozzo ⊞

A Sinclair Oxford 200 fluorescent calculator, 1975.
**£45–50** Pepe Tozzo ⊞

CALCULATORS

A Dixons Prinztronic M calculator, 1975.
**£10–15** Pepe Tozzo ⊞

A Dixons Prinztronic Mini calculator, 1975.
**£120–130** Pepe Tozzo ⊞

A Dixons Prinztronic Mini Scientific calculator, 1975.
**£15–20** Pepe Tozzo ⊞

A Casio VX-2000 calculator, 1977.
**£115–130** Pepe Tozzo ⊞

A Calcu-Pen ballpoint pen, with integral calculator, slight damage and some dead LED segments, Japan, 1976.
**£40–45** Vintage Pens ⊞

A Hewlett Packard 16c calculator, 1982.
**£125–140** Pepe Tozzo ⊞

## COMPUTER GAMES

An Atari Touch Me hand-held game, 1978.

**£15–20 Pepe Tozzo** ⊞

*Popular theory is that it was the Atari Touch Me that gave Milton and Bradley the idea for their phenomenally successful Simon electronic game. The Touch Me was based on Atari's own arcade game of the same name from 1974. The calculator-like case and use of LED display shows its calculator derivation.*

A Tronica Fightez hand-held game, c1980, 4½in (11.5cm) wide.

**£1–5 John Smart** ⊞

A 3 Dimensions Fightez hand-held game, c1980, 4¾in (12cm) long.

**£1–5 John Smart** ⊞

A KitKat hand-held game, c1980, 4in (10cm) long.

**£1–5 John Smart** ⊞

A Tom Knight's Mission clockwork pocket arcade game, c1980, 5¾in (14.5cm) wide.

**£1–5 John Smart** ⊞

A Video Technology Space Blasters computer game, 1988.

**£5–10 John Smart** ⊞

Two Nintendo Game Boys, original and pocket versions, 1989.

**£15–20 Pepe Tozzo** ⊞

*The Game Boy was released in 1989. The original console was superseded by the pocket version in 1996 which was replaced soon after by the colour version. The Game Boy was destined to rule the portable console world until the arrival of Sony's PSP machine.*

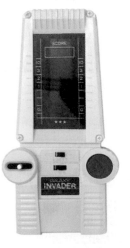

A Computer Games Galaxy Invader, 1980s.

**£15–20 John Smart** ⊞

A Systema Pirate game, 1980s–90s.

**£1–5 John Smart** ⊞

An M&M battery-powered electronic game, 1997.

**£1–5 Gloucester Antiques** ⊞

# RADIOS

A BTH C2 radio, in a walnut case, 1923,
19in (48.5cm) wide.
**£1,450–1,600** On The Air ⊞

A Revophone crystal radio set, 1924,
11in (28cm) wide.
**£135–150** On The Air ⊞

An Efescaphone crystal radio set, c1924,
9in (23cm) long.
**£200–230** Early Technology ⊞

An AJS Type F6 radio, in a veneered
mahogany case, 1924, 19in (48.5cm) wide.
**£700–800** On The Air ⊞

A Phillips radio player, in a Bakelite case,
c1931, 19in (48.5cm) high.
**£540–600** On The Air ⊞

A Portadyne model S radio, in a walnut-
veneered case, 1933, 18in (45.5cm) high.
**£90–100** On The Air ⊞

An Ekco AC 76 radio, in a Bakelite
case, 1936, 16in (40.5cm) diam.
**£630–700** On The Air ⊞

A Beethoven model AD 303 radio,
in a leather case with chrome trim,
1936, 11in (28cm) high.
**£60–70** Philip Knighton ⊞

A Pilot Blue Peter radio, in a walnut case, restored, 1940s,
20in (51cm) wide.
**£120–135** Decographics ⊞

An FADA model 1000 Bullet radio, in a catalin case with pull-up handle, label to underside, America, 1945, 10in (25.5cm) long.

**£350–450 Skinner** 🔨

A Delco radio, 1947, 11½in (29cm) long.

**£270–320 Mastro Auctions** 🔨

A Bush DAC 90A radio, in a Bakelite case, restored, 1948, 12in (30.5cm) wide.

**£35–40 Decographics** ⊞

A Zenith Trans-Oceanic radio, in a Rexine case, c1952, 17in (43cm) wide.

**£90–100 On The Air** ⊞

A Philips radio, 1965, 12in (30.5cm) wide.

**£30–35 Junktion** ⊞

A Bush pocket transistor radio, c1966, 6in (15cm) high.

**£5–10 Pepe Tozzo** ⊞

*Bush was one of many manufacturers releasing compact and pocket radios during the 1960s, taking advantage of the Pop era. The interiors of these radios were simple but robust and most examples will still work today, despite not being treated very well during their lifetime.*

A Vesta V36 mini transistor adio, c1967, 5in (12.5cm) wide.

**£5–10 Pepe Tozzo** ⊞

A Parsons plastic novelty tube radio, 1997, 6in (15cm) wide.

**£5–10 Collectables** ⊞

A Sony SRF-SX906 radio, c2000, 4in (10cm) high.

**£10–15 Pepe Tozzo** ⊞

TELEPHONES & MOBILES

A metal No. 16 skeleton telephone, c1900, 12in (30.5cm) high.
**£530–580** Telephone Lines ⊞

A Bakelite 200 series
telephone, 1940–50,
8in (20.5cm) high.
**£300–330** Luna ⊞

A Strowger automatic candlestick telephone, with glass
mouthpiece, c1920s, 9in (23cm) high.
**£220–250** Telephone Lines ⊞

An Ericsson Ericofon moulded plastic telephone, Sweden, 1950s, 8in (20.5cm) high.

**£95–110 Kingston Antiques** ⊞

A GPO 746 Series plastic telephone, with restyled casings, 1960–70, 10in (25.5cm) wide.

**£80–90 Telephone Lines** ⊞

A GPO 700 Series plastic telephone, c1970s, 8½in (21.5cm) wide.

**£35–40 Telephone Lines** ⊞
*This was the first all-plastic telephone made by GPO, and was available in a range of colours*

A Nokia 101 analogue mobile telephone, 1988, 6½in (16.5cm) high, with box.

**£35–40 retrobrick** ⊞

A Motorola 6800x anologue mobile telephone, c1992, 9½in (24cm) high, with box.

**£70–75 retrobrick** ⊞

A Nokia 2110 GSM digital mobile telephone, 1994, 6in (15cm) high, with box.

**£55–60 retrobrick** ⊞

A Motorola MR501 Star TAC mobile telephone, 1996, 4in (10cm) high, with box.

**£45–50 retrobrick** ⊞

An Ericsson GH198 GSM digital mobile telephone, c1996, 6in (15cm) high, with box.

**£35–40 retrobrick** ⊞

# TELEVISIONS

A Silvertone Medalist television, with built-in phonogram, c1963, 23in (58.5cm) wide.
**£85–95  Harry Poster** ⊞

A Zenith Chromacolor II television, in a wooden cabinet, mid-1970s, 25in (63.5cm) wide.
**£75–85  Harry Poster** ⊞

An RCA Model 21S television, in a wooden case, c1954, 21in (53.5cm) wide.
**£50–55  Harry Poster** ⊞

An Orion TVR-7120 portable television, late 1970s, screen 2¼in (5.5cm) high.
**£35–40  Pepe Tozzo** ⊞
*The Orion was based on the Normende TR-101 multi-standard TV. Many other manufacturers used the same unit for their versions. It used six AA batteries and was a much more reliable and usable unit than the earlier, but more collectable, Sinclair Microvision MTV1.*

A Philco Model B370 plastic portable television, on a revolving base, mid-1970s, 9in (23cm) wide.
**£85–95  Harry Poster** ⊞

## MARKET INFORMATION  TELEVISIONS

• Within the last few years television collecting has become quite popular. Sets produced during the late 1930s are sought after, but since most are priced at £2,500 and over they are beyond the pocket of most collectors.

• As a general rule, most collectable black and white televisions from the 1940s and early 1950s are priced at around £100–500. The more common sets from this period often turn up for between £15 and £50.

• Colour sets from 1954 to 1956 with 15–21in (38–53.5cm) round colour cathode ray tubes are priced from £75 to several thousand pounds.

• Later sets including common floor model consoles and combination TVs (TV, radio and phonograph), and larger table-top models that have a very square look can be found for £15 or less.

• Some of the very trendy TVs from the late 1960s and 1970s, such as the space ship-shaped Panasonic and the spherical set from JVC are popular, but still quite common. These often sell for £50–175.

**Harry Poster, harryposter.com**

# MONEY

## BANKNOTES

A Treasury £1 note, first issue, signed by John Bradbury, 1914.
**£450–500 Collectors World** ⊞

A Treasury £1 note, 1919.
**£50–60 Collectors World** ⊞

A Bank of England £10 note, signed by B. G. Catterns, 1929.
**£220–250 British Notes** ⊞

A British Linen Bank £1 note, 1932.
**£35–40 Colin Narbeth** ⊞

A Bank of England £1 note, emergency war issue, signed by K. O. Peppiatt, 1940.
**£15–20 Collectors World** ⊞

A Bank of England £1 note, Guernsey overprint, signed by K. O. Peppiatt, 1941.
**£180–200 Collectors World** ⊞

A Martin's Bank £1 note, 1957.
**£145–165 British Notes** ⊞

A Bank of England £10 note, signed by J. Q. Hollom, 1964.
**£20–25 Collectors World** ⊞

A Currency Commission £1 note, with Irish Free State fractional prefix, 1928.

**£190–220 British Notes** ⊞

A Provincial Bank of Ireland £5 note, 1951.

**£45–55 British Notes** ⊞

A Central Bank of Ireland £50 note, 1977.

**£160–180 Colin Narbeth** ⊞

*The portrait is that of Lady Lavery, used on Irish notes from 1928 to 1977. It was engraved by John Harrison, who was regarded as one of the finest portrait engravers in the world. Some collectors who like miniature art specialize in his portrait work. Although a freelancer the printer Waterlow & Sons regarded him as their chief portrait engraver. His animated portrait of Sun Yat Sen for Chinese notes caused a stir when, on changing their printer, the Chinese insisted on using the same vignette. This meant the new printers had to go cap-in-hand to Waterlows and ask if they could borrow it!*

A Commercial Bank of Scotland £1 note, 1919.

**£270–300 Colin Narbeth** ⊞

A Clydesdale Bank £1 note, 1925.

**£180–200 British Notes** ⊞

A Bank of Scotland £1 note, 1951.

**£5–10 Colin Narbeth** ⊞

*This £1 note of the Bank of Scotland, dated 12 October 1951, is part of a long series bearing a central medallion of the Goddess of Fortune. Following representations made by the Lord Lyon King of Arms, the Scottish Royal Arms were replaced in 1935 by the Bank's Arms, and were dispensed with altogether in 1945.*

A Bank of Scotland £10 note, 1963.

**£200–225 British Notes** ⊞

A Reichsbank 100 mark note, Germany, 1908.
**£1–5** Colin Narbeth ⊞

A Government of the Straits Settlements $1 note, depicting George V, 1935.
**£25–30** Collectors World ⊞

A Bank Lsiersnia 100 zloty note, issued during the German occupation of Poland, 1941.
**£1–5** Colin Narbeth ⊞
*This 100 Zlotych Polish note of 1939 has the distinction of being the first banknote for WWII collectors. It has a long rectangular overprint indicating the German Occupation and setting up the 'General Gouvernement'. It was a provisional issue – it was only in use for two months but has been heavily forged.*

A States of Guernsey sixpenny note, WWII emergency issue, 1942.
**£220–250** Colin Narbeth ⊞

A British North Borneo Company $1 note, 1930.
**£90–100** Collectors World ⊞

A Reichsbank 20 mark note, Germany, 1939.
**£5–10** Colin Narbeth ⊞
*This note has the girl with edelweiss design and is one of the first to show the eagle and swastika symbol of the Third Reich. Together with the Hitler Youth 5 Reichsmark it remained in circulation throughout the war. Hitler's portrait never appeared on banknotes because he hated them – indeed he threw the President of the Reichsbank into a concentration camp.*

A Hrvatska Dravna Banka 5000 kuna note, Croatia, 1940s.
**£1–5** Colin Narbeth ⊞

A WWII Allied Liberation currency 100 franc note, France, 1944.
**£15–20** Colin Narbeth ⊞

A Japanese Government 1 shilling note, issued during the Japanese occupation of Oceania, 1940s.
**£1–5** Colin Narbeth ⊞

A Hong Kong & Shanghai Banking Corporation $5 note, 1954.
**£35–40 Colin Narbeth** ⊞

A Government of British Honduras $2 note, 1958.
**£135–150 Colin Narbeth** ⊞
*Notes printed with this date are particularly sought after.*

A Bahamas Government 10 shilling note, 1960s.
**£90–100 Colin Narbeth** ⊞

A Reserve Bank of New Zealand £1 note, 1960.
**£20–25 Colin Narbeth** ⊞
*The famous explorer Captain J. Cook is featured on the front of the note and a sailing ship is shown on the reverse. These notes were issued from 1940 to 1967 with three changes of signature. The 1960 note is signed by R. N. Fleming (1956–67).*

A 20 baht note, Thailand, 1970s.
**£1–5 Colin Narbeth** ⊞

A Government of Belize $10 note, 1975.
**£135–150 Colin Narbeth** ⊞

## ESSENTIAL REFERENCE FAMOUS & INFAMOUS LEADERS

A Bank of Uganda 100 shilling note, depicting Idi Amin, 1970.
**£1–5 Colin Narbeth** ⊞

A 25 dinar note, depicting Saddam Hussein, Iraq, 1986.
**£1–5 Colin Narbeth** ⊞

A 10 yuan note, depicting Mao Tse Tung, China, 1999.
**£1–5 Colin Narbeth** ⊞

- An interesting and informative collection can be made of world leaders past and present, such as Ghengis Khan, who features on Mongolian notes.

- Although Hitler never allowed his portrait to appear on banknotes, two other leaders compete with him for the world's worst leader: Stalin of Russia who wiped out millions of peasant farmers and three-quarters of the officers of his army, and Mao Tse Tung of China whose 'cultural revolution' wrought havoc throughout China.

- Colonel Gadaffi is featured at prayer on Libya's notes from 1988 and appears to be rehabiliated with the USA. His unfortunate predecessor Omar El Mukhtar, who also still features on notes, was hanged from a street lamp aged 72.

- Saddam Hussein of Iraq, who was also hanged, is portrayed on many notes. These notes circulated for some time during the Allied occupation because the Allies had not prepared any notes to replace them.

**COINS**

A copper Edward VII one penny coin, showing low horizon, 1902.

**£5–10 Coincraft** ⊞

*The low and high horizons refer to the levels of the sea, visible on the right-hand side by Britannia's gown. The low tide only appeared on the 1902 penny, and the halfpenny of that year.*

A George V wreath crown, 1928.

**£220–250 Coincraft** ⊞

*The wreath crown was so-called because of the wreath surrounding the crown on the reverse of the coin. It was issued between 1927 and 1936, with the exception of 1935 when the commemorative rocking horse crown was minted. The second commonest year of issue was 1928.*

A proof £5 coin, 1937.

**£780–930 Dix Noonan Webb** ⚒

A George VI one penny coin, 1950.

**£15–20 Coincraft** ⊞

An Elizabeth II error sovereign, 1963.

**£730–870 Heritage** ⚒

A silver Churchill crown, 1965.

**£1–5 Coincraft** ⊞

*This piece was issued to commemorate Sir Winston Churchill, who died in 1965 and was the first commoner to appear on a British coin. Although the coins appear silver, they are in fact a mixture of copper and nickel.*

A copper Elizabeth II one penny coin, not issued for circulation, 1970.

**£5–10 Coincraft** ⊞

A gold Elizabeth II £5 coin, commemorating the 90th birthday of Queen Elizabeth the Queen Mother, in original British Royal Mint box with certificate, 1990.

**£360–430 Heritage** ⚒

## EXPERT EYE    SPOT THE DIFFERENCE

By 1949, 'IND IMP', which denoted the title Emperor of India, no longer appeared on the reverse of the coin.

'FD' is the abbreviation of *Fidei Defensor*, Latin for 'Defender of the Faith'.

This issue continued until the King's death in 1952.

A George VI threepenny coin, 1937.
**£135–150  Coincraft** ⊞

The 1949 issue is the rarest of this type of 3d piece featuring George VI

This design appeared between 1937 and 1949.

By the end of George V's reign the silver threepenny coin had become unpopular owing to its small size, so a more substantial brass coin was introduced. Between 1937 and 1944 three types of threepenny coin were minted, one in brass and two in silver, one of the latter being Maundy money which was not in general circulation. The 'brass' coins were actually composed largely of copper, 20 per cent zinc and one per cent nickel, which was added for durability, and the new dodecagonal shape distinguished it from the previous version. A threepenny coin was issued for Edward VII and, although never officially released, some coins did escape into circulation. Depending on condition and the vagaries of the market, these coins could now be worth £15,000–20,000. During WWII the shape of the threepenny coin changed slightly in that the corners became rounded. This is because steel, which was needed to make new dies, was in short supply.

**Coincraft**

A Liberty Double Eagle $20 coin, America, 1903.
**£600–720** Heritage ⚒

A silver Morgan $1 coin, America, 1921.
**£100–120 James D Julia** ⚒

A $20 coin, America, 1927.
**£300–360 Dix Noonan Webb** ⚒

A Peace $1 coin, America, 1928.
**£640–770** Heritage ⚒

A Kennedy half-dollar coin, type two reverse, 1964.
**£300–360** Heritage ⚒
*This coin was discovered in a roll of 1964–D halves received by a Whitman employee on the first day of issue in 1964. Ken Bressett, editor of the Guide Book, was present when the piece was discovered. He commented, 'This exceptional piece was unlike other coins in that roll, and was apparently a first strike from newly polished dies.'*

A Library of Congress $10 coin, America, 2000.
**£1,900–2,300** Heritage ⚒
*This piece was issued on the eve of the new millennium and was one of only 12 assigned the ultimate grade by the Professional Coin Grading Service.*

A Lincoln red one cent coin, America, 1925.
**£170–200 Heritage** ⚒

A Lincoln one cent coin, America, 2000.
**£580–700 Heritage** ⚒

An Elizabeth II gold $100 coin, Australia, 2000.
**£400–500 Heritage** ⚒

An Empire Tientsin dragon $1 coin, year 3, with value in English and Chinese, China, 1911.
**£150–180 Heritage** ⚒

A proof half-crown, Eire, 1939.
**£580–680 Dix Noonan Webb** ⚒

A 10 korona coin, Hungary, 1912.
**£30–35 Sworders** ⚒

A 20 franc coin, France, 1913.
**£40–50 Heritage** ⚒

An ECU coinage set, 1992.
**£15–20 Coincraft** ⊞
*The ECU, or European Currency Unit, was initially proposed as the common EU coinage. This final set was never issued after the decision was taken to adopt the Euro. In 2002 member countries wishing to do so were invited to adopt the common currency. The Euro has a common reverse, with an obverse particular to each country.*

# MONEY BOXES

A cast-iron mechanical money box, by Hubley, in the form of a dog jumping through a hoop, America, 1920s, 9in (23cm) wide.

**£270–300 John & Simon Haley** ⊞

A pottery money box, in the form of a girl's head, 1920s, 4in (10cm) high.

**£35–40 John & Simon Haley** ⊞

A Pascalls mini chocolate dispensing machine money box, 1920s, 6in (15cm) high.

**£120–135 Below Stairs** ⊞

A tin Post Office air mail post box money box, 1930, 4in (10cm) high.

**£50–60 M&C Cards** ⊞

A tinplate mechanical money box, Germany, 1930s, 7in (18cm) high.

**£250–280 Cabinet of Curiosities** ⊞

A Halifax Building Society metal money box, 1930, 2½in (6.5cm) high.

**£20–25 David Huxtable** ⊞

A Martin's Bank metal money box, 1930, 2½in (6.5cm) high.

**£20–25 David Huxtable** ⊞

A Lloyds Savings Bank money box, 1937, 4½in (11.5cm) high.
**£15–20** David Huxtable ⊞

A Midland Bank metal money box, 1930s, 5in (12.5cm) high.
**£15–20** David Huxtable ⊞

A tinplate Jumbo Savings Bank mechanical money box, 1940s–50s, 5in (12.5cm) high.
**£40–45** John & Simon Haley ⊞

A tinplate mechanical clown money box, by Chein, America, 1950s, 5in (12.5cm) high.
**£25–30** John & Simon Haley ⊞

A plastic Robot Machine Bank clockwork money box, 1978, 5in (12.5cm) high.
**£45–50** Mimi Fifi ⊞

A plastic post box money box, with a combination lock, 1970s, 5in (12.5cm) high.
**£5–10** M&C Cards ⊞

Five Dresden Bank plastic money boxes, by Luigi Colani, 1970s, 3½in (9cm) long.
**£10–15 each** High Street Retro ⊞

A ceramic money box, in the form of a Volkswagen camper van, 1990s, 8½in (21.5cm) long.
**£10–15** Feathers Antiques ⊞

# PENS

A Mabie Todd Swan eyedropper fountain pen, the gold-filled chased filigree overlay with an engraved cartouche, c1910, 5¼in (13.5cm) long.

**£340–380** Hans's Vintage Fountain Pens ⊞

A Mabie Todd eyedropper fountain pen, with gold-filled overlay and a safety screw cap, America, c1920, 5¼in (13.5cm) long.

**£430–480** Hans's Vintage Fountain Pens ⊞

A Parker Vacumatic Maxima pen, the 9ct gold nib with 'London 1939 PPCo' hallmark, Canada, 1939, 5¼in (13.5cm) long.

**£270–300** Hans's Vintage Fountain Pens ⊞

A Mabie Todd Swan leverless pen, c1940, 5in (12.5cm) long.

**£90–100** Hans's Vintage Fountain Pens ⊞

A Watermans W515 fountain pen, c1946, 5in (12.5cm) long.

**£65–75** Hans's Vintage Fountain Pens ⊞

A Mont Blanc Monte Rosa pen, No. 042G, with an EF 14ct gold Monte Rosa nib, made for export only, in a Monte Rosa box with papers, Germany, 1952, 5in (12.5cm) long.

**£85–95** Hans's Vintage Fountain Pens ⊞

A Parker 51 Navy Grey fountain pen, 1950, 5½in (14cm) long.
**£50–55  Hans's Vintage Fountain Pens** ⊞

A Conway Stewart 67 fountain pen, 1950s, 5¼in (13.5cm) long.
**£30–35  Hans's Vintage Fountain Pens** ⊞

A Pelikan fountain pen, No. 400NN, with a 14ct gold Pelikan nib, Germany, 1950s, 5in (12.5cm) long.
**£95–105  Hans's Vintage Fountain Pens** ⊞

A Sheaffer Imperial White Dot silver cartridge pen, with gold-plated trim and 14ct gold nib, 1975, 5¼in (13cm) long.
**£170–190 Vintage Pens** ⊞

A Parker 180 cartridge pen, with a lacquer finish and gold-plated trim, with a 14ct gold nib, France, 1980, 5½in (14cm) long.
**£135–150 Vintage Pens** ⊞

A Parker Classic TX cartridge/converter pen, with a gold-plated trim and nib, 1986, 5¼in (13.5cm) long.
**£20–25  Vintage Pens** ⊞

A Parker 180 Guirland silver-plated cartridge/converter pen, with a gold nib, France, 1990, 6in (15cm) long.
**£170–190 Vintage Pens** ⊞

# PERFUME BOTTLES

A frosted glass perfume bottle, with floral decoration, France, c1930, 2in (5cm) high.

**£170–190 Bourbon-Hanby Arcade** ⊞

A glass perfume bottle, with gilded decoration, c1930, 3in (7.5cm) high.

**£60–70 Bourbon-Hanby Arcade** ⊞

A crystal perfume bottle, with gilded decoration, Germany, 1930s, 4in (10cm) high.

**£75–85 Tony Durante** ⊞

A cut-glass perfume bottle, Czechoslovakia, 1930s, 4in (10cm) high.

**£65–75 Vanessa Turner** ⊞

A frosted glass perfume atomiser, with raised decoration, 1930s, 5in (12.5cm) high.

**£130–145 Bourbon-Hanby** ⊞

A silver perfume bottle, with engine-turned decoration and an ivory stopper, 1930s, 2in (5cm) high.

**£75–85 Tony Durante** ⊞

A bottle of Saturday Night Lotion, 1950s, 5½in (14cm) high.

**£10–15 Rin Tin Tin** ⊞

A Lanvin A Veil of My Sin frosted glass lotion bottle, with contents, 1981, 4in (10cm) high.

**£15–20 Silversnow Antiques** ⊞

*Jeanne Lanvin worked with Russian emigrée Madame Zed to create the Mon Péché (My Sin) fragrance in 1925. It was a breakthrough scent for Lanvin that remained popular until it was discontinued in 1988. This fragranced lotion bottle is worth a little less than the more prized eau de toilette or parfum.*

A Jean Paul Gaultier atomiser perfume bottle, 1990s, 11½in (29cm) high.

**£200–220 Silversnow Antiques** ⊞

*This bottle is a modern version of Schiaparelli's 1930s' 'Shocking' made for Mae West. This perfume is said to be inspired by Madonna.*

# PEZ DISPENSERS

A PEZ plastic Easter chick dispenser, Austria, 1990s, 4½in (11.5cm) high.

**£10–15** Mimi Fifi ⊞

A PEZ plastic hockey player dispenser, Spain, 1990s, 4½in (11.5cm) high.

**£15–20** Mimi Fifi ⊞

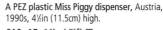

A PEZ plastic Miss Piggy dispenser, Austria, 1990s, 4½in (11.5cm) high.

**£10–15** Mimi Fifi ⊞

A PEZ plastic dispenser, Spain, 1990s, 4½in (11.5cm) high.

**£15–20** Mimi Fifi ⊞

A PEZ plastic Droopey dispenser, America, 1990s, 4½in (11.5cm) high.

**£5–10** Mimi Fifi ⊞

A PEZ plastic Pebbles Flintstones dispenser, America, 1990s, 4½in (11.5cm) high.

**£5–10** Mimi Fifi ⊞

A PEZ plastic Astérix dispenser, France, 1997, 8½in (21.5cm) high.

**£1–5  V Sprigg** ⊞

A PEZ plastic Speedy Gonzales dispenser, America, 1990s, 4½in (11.5cm) high.

**£5–10  Mimi Fifi** ⊞

A PEZ plastic Super Mario dispenser, America, 1990s, 4½in (11.5cm) high.

**£10–15  Mimi Fifi** ⊞

A PEZ plastic Power Trucks dispenser, Japan, c2000, 4½in (11.5cm) high.

**£5–10  Mimi Fifi** ⊞

A PEZ plastic Marge Simpson dispenser, America, 2002, 8½in (21.5cm) high.

**£1–5  John Smart** ⊞

A PEZ plastic Cars dispenser, 2006, 4½in (11.5cm) high.

**£1–5  Mimi Fifi** ⊞

## EXPERT EYE   PEZ DISPENSER

A PEZ plastic dispenser,
Japan, 2006, 4½in
(11.5cm) high.
**£10–15** Mimi Fifi ▦

The earliest dispsensers
resembled lighters as they did
not have character heads.

Different colour bodies were
occasionally issued, with the
result that some colours are
rarer than others.

Feet did not appear until
the mid-1980s but are
not important as colletors
are looking for the
character head.

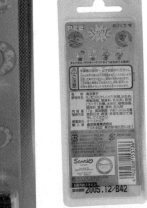

Collectors look for Pez in
original packaging and classify
them as MOC - mint on card,
or MIB – mint in bag/box.

Pez models differ according to the country in which they were made, although some models were repackaged and reissued in another country at a later date. For example, the Japanese 'Hello Kitty' was issued in Japan on cards with all Japanese text; it was later reissued in the US in English, in cellophane bags – collectors seek both issues. Accessories ('clothing', T-shirts and toy cars) were only issued in Europe and these are highly prized in America, while the advertising pieces that came out in the US from the 1950s is now sought after in Europe. It is very difficult to date Pez dispensers unless they have been documented in books and price guides. The vintage models are easily recongnizable as they date from the 1940s – the first advertised Pez was made in Germany but they did not appear in the US until 1952. The patent number printed along the side of the packet also helps as it indicates the series: from 1952 for first series, 1968 for the second series, 1974 for the third series, 1976 for the fourth series and then Patent No. 4,966,305 for the fifth series.

**Rita Delaforge, Mimi Fifi**

# POSTCARDS

## GREETINGS

A birthday greetings postcard, embossed with silver, c1900.
**£1–5 Postcard Club** ⊞

A New Year's greetings postcard, c1900.
**£1–5 Postcard Club** ⊞

An embossed Valentine Greeting postcard, c1900.
**£1–5 Postcard Club** ⊞

A 'jewelled' birthday greetings postcard, c1900.
**£1–5 Postcard Club** ⊞

A Good Luck postcard, by Josephine M. Duddle, from the Regent series, c1917.
**£1–5 J & M Collectables** ⊞

A birthday greetings postcard, by Donald McGill, from the XL Series, c1936.
**£1–5 J & M Collectables** ⊞

A birthday greetings postcard, depicting an original painting by Madeleine Renaud, 1943.
**£1–5 J & M Collectables** ⊞

# VIEWS

A souvenir postcard, depicting New York, by Raphael Tuck & Sons, painted by Florence Robinson, 1900–05.
**£5–10 J & M Collectables** ⊞

A hand-coloured photographic postcard, depicting Rye High Street, 1908.
**£1–5 Soldiers of Rye** ⊞

A postcard, depicting St Peter-Port, Guernsey, by Raphael Tuck & Sons, 1909.
**£1–5 Soldiers of Rye** ⊞

A hand-coloured photographic postcard, depicting Parkstone, Isle of Wight, 1908.
**£1–5 Soldiers of Rye** ⊞

A hand-coloured photographic postcard, depicting Trafalgar Square, London, 1908.
**£1–5 Soldiers of Rye** ⊞

A photographic postcard, depicting the Cairngorm Mountains, from The Best of All Series, published by J. B. White, Dundee, 1938.
**£1–5 Soldiers of Rye** ⊞

# POSTERS

## ADVERTISING

A Michelin poster, by Fr. Aikin, printed by Ch. Verneau, France, 1908, framed 42 x 33in (106.5 x 84cm).

**£270–320 Mastro Auctions** 🔨

A poster, by Delval, 'Fap'Anis', printed by Wall Publicity, Paris, 1920s, 46¾ x 62½in (119 x 159cm).

**£145–170 Mastro Auctions** 🔨

A Hungarian wines poster, by György Konecsni, printed by Klösz Coloroffset, c1935, 24¾ x 18½in (63 x 47cm).

**£200–250 Van Sabben** 🔨

A Mossant Hats poster, by Leonetto Cappiello, France, 1930s, 62½ x 46in (159 x 117cm).

**£140–170 Mastro Auctions** 🔨

A Roxy American Cigarettes poster, America, c1950, 45¾ x 32½in (116 x 82.5cm).

**£720–850 Van Sabben** 🔨

A *Regards* magazine poster, by C. Guion, France, 1945, 15¾ x 11¾in (40 x 30cm).

**£720–850 Van Sabben** 🔨

A circus poster, 1950, 30 x 20in (76 x 51cm).

**£45–50 Dodo** ⊞

A savings advertising poster, 1953, 19 x 14in (48.5 x 35.5cm).

**£75–85 Cobwebs** ⊞

A Matzner Bathing Salts poster, by Professor
Walter Hofmann, Germany, 1957,
67 x 47in (170 x 119.5cm).

**£150–180 Mastro Auctions** 🔨

A Springbok advertising poster, by Chas Shiers, South Africa, late 1960s, 30 x 20in (76 x 51cm).

**£20–25 GWR Auctions** 🔨

A Philips Infraphil poster, c1960,
23½ x 15½in (60 x 39.5cm).

**£720–850 Van Sabben** 🔨

A poster, by Koen van Os, 'Bata op stap?
Stap Op', Holland, c1960, 45¾ x 32¾in
(116 x 83cm).

**£190–220 Van Sabben** 🔨

A poster, by Dick Bruna, printed by De Jong &
Co, 1961, 25¼ x 17½in (64 x 44.5cm).

**£250–300 Van Sabben** 🔨

An IBM poster, by Clarence Lee, advertising
Palm Beach, printed by M. P. Lavore,
America, 1964, 37¾ x 26¼in (96 x 66.5cm).

**£240–280 Van Sabben** 🔨

An IBM poster, printed by M. P. Lavore,
America, 1965, 39¼ x 24¾in (99.5 x 63cm)

**£280–330 Van Sabben** 🔨

A Bergasol poster, by Bernard Villemot,
printed by Bedos & Cie, France, c1975,
69 x 47¼in (175.5 x 120cm).

**£400–480 Van Sabben** 🔨

A Paris 1937 International Exhibition poster, by Jean Carlu, printed by Bedos & Cie, France, 1937, 47¼ x 31½in (120 x 80cm).

**£150–180  Onslow Auctions** 🔨

A poster, by Andries D. Copier, 'Het Glas 1940', printed by De Jong & Co, Holland, 1940, 40½ x 28¾in (103 x 73cm).

**£175–200  Van Sabben** 🔨

A poster, by Pieter Brattinga, 'th. hofstede - crull ceramiek', printed by De Jong & Co, Holland, c1950, 30 x 20¼in (76 x 51.5cm).

**£120–140  Van Sabben** 🔨

A poster, by Benno Wissing, 'G. Braque', Holland, 1956, 31¾ x 22in (80.5 x 56cm).

**£65–75  Van Sabben** 🔨

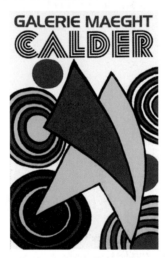

A poster, by Alexander Calder, printed by Arte, France, c1960, 31½ x 19in (80 x 48.5cm).

**£80–95  Van Sabben** 🔨

A poster, by Willem Sandberg, 'Agi Design', printed by De Jong & Co, Holland, 1961, 39½ x 27½in (100.5 x 70.5cm).

**£95–110  Van Sabben** 🔨

A poster, by Ben Shahn, 'Ben Shahn Graphik', Germany, 1962, 34 x 24in (86.5 x 61cm).

**£145–170  Van Sabben** 🔨

A poster, by Henry Heerup, 'Cobra', Holland, 1966, 27¼ x 19¾in (69 x 50cm).

**£80–95  Van Sabben** 🔨

A poster, by Francis Bacon, printed by Arte, France, c1975, 28 x 17¾in (71 x 45cm).

**£240–280  Van Sabben** 🔨

# FILM

A film poster, by Dolly Rüdeman, *Moulin Rouge*, starring Olga Tschechowa, printed by Strang & Co, Holland, 1928, 36¾ x 23¾in (93.5 x 60.5cm).

**£950–1,150 Van Sabben** 🔨

A film poster, *Paris Mes Amours*, starring Josephine Baker, France, 1950, 30 x 23in (76 x 58.5cm).

**£400–450 Limelight** ⊞

A film poster, *The Dam Busters*, starring Richard Todd and Michael Redgrave, America, 1955, 40 x 26in (101.5 x 66cm).

**£400–450 Cine Art Gallery** ⊞

A film poster, *Professor Beware*, starring Harold Lloyd, 1938, 41 x 27in (104 x 68.5cm).

**£1,100–1,250 Limelight** ⊞
*This poster has everything going for it – rarity, condition, desirability and number of survivals. Harold Lloyd was popular when this poster was originally issued and has since become a legendary comic actor.*

A film poster, *The African Queen*, starring Humphrey Bogart and Katharine Hepburn, America, c1951, 40¼ x 27¼in (102 x 69cm).

**£95–115 Onslow Auctions** 🔨

A film poster, *Lady and the Tramp*, America, 1955, 22 x 28in (56 x 71cm).

**£500–550 Limelight** ⊞

A film poster, *Road to Morocco*, starring Bing Crosby, Bob Hope and Dorothy Lamour, America, 1942, 36 x 14in (91.5 x 35.5cm).

**£850–950 Limelight** ⊞

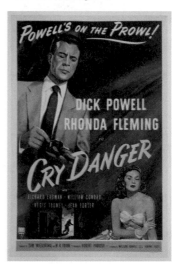

A film poster, *Cry Danger*, starring Dick Powell and Rhonda Fleming, America, 1951, 41 x 27in (104 x 68.5cm).

**£750–850 Limelight** ⊞

A film poster, *The Gold Rush*, starring Charles Chaplin, America, 1956 re-release, 30 x 40in (76 x 101.5cm).

**£450–500 Limelight** ⊞

A film poster, *The Little Hut*, starring Ava Gardner, America, 1957, 41 x 27in (104 x 68.5cm).

**£580–650 Limelight** ⊞

A film poster, *Some Came Running*, starring Frank Sinatra, Dean Martin and Shirley MacLaine, America, 1959, 41 x 27in (104 x 68.5cm).

**£500–550 Limelight** ⊞

A film poster, *Peeping Tom*, 1960, 30 x 40in (76 x 101.5cm).

**£2,700–3,000 Cine Art Gallery** ⊞
*This is a rare and desirable poster. The film had a cult following due to its nature, and consequently cult collectability. Moreover, the poster has a strong and enduring design.*

A film poster, *The Seven Year Itch*, starring Marilyn Monroe, Germany, c1960, 41 x 27in (104 x 68.5cm).

**£300–350 Limelight** ⊞

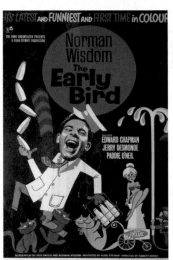

A film poster, *The Early Bird*, starring Norman Wisdom, 1966, 41 x 27in (104 x 68.5cm).

**£90–100 Limelight** ⊞

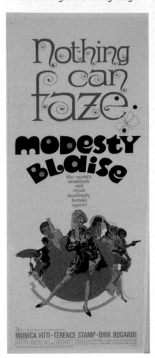

A film poster, *Modesty Blaise*, starring Dirk Bogarde and Terence Stamp, America, 1966, 36 x 14in (91.5 x 35.5cm).

**£200–250 Limelight** ⊞

## MARKET INFORMATION POSTERS

• Original film posters and lobby cards continue to be highly collectable, with prices generally on the up as more people begin to collect vintage cinema materials, or select them as alternatives to art or other home and office design options.

• Collectors concentrate on different artistes and genres. Hepburn, Bond, Monroe, Hitchcock, Disney and Chaplin remain very sought after, as do iconic titles such as *The Godfather*, *Jaws*, *The Thomas Crown Affair* and *Downhill Racer*. Anything illustrated by Saul Bass is hot, including *Vertigo*, *Anatomy of Murder* and *The Man with the Golden Arm*.

• Re-releases usually have an 'R' before the re-release date. For example, 'R1969' would denote a poster for the cinematic re-release of the film in 1969.

• A Six sheet of *The Outlaw* featuring Jane Russells sold at Christie's for £45,000 in 2003; *The Mummy* sold at Sotheby's for £227,000 in 1997 and a record £300,000 was paid in 2005 for an original poster for Fritz Lang's 1927 classic, *Metropolis*.

• The most popular format continues to be either the US One Sheet or the UK Quad, but more and more people are collecting Lobby Cards.

• Linen-backing or paper-backing (depending on format) is the best way to preserve posters, and when framing it is vital to ensure that acid-free mount and barrier boards are used.                     **Sue Wilson, Limelight**

A film poster, *The Mikado*, 1967, 30 x 40in (76 x 101.5cm).

**£270–300** Limelight ⊞

A film poster, *Wonderwall*, 1968, 30 x 40in (76 x 101.5cm).

**£580–650** Limelight ⊞

A film poster, *Downhill Racer*, starring Robert Redford, America, 1969, 41 x 27in (104 x 68.5cm).

**£680–750** Limelight ⊞

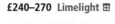

A film poster, *The Illustrated Man*, America, 1969, 41 x 27in (104 x 68.5cm).

**£240–270** Limelight ⊞

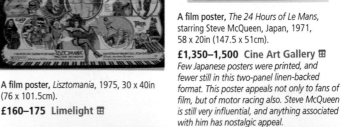

A film poster, *The 24 Hours of Le Mans*, starring Steve McQueen, Japan, 1971, 58 x 20in (147.5 x 51cm).

**£1,350–1,500** Cine Art Gallery ⊞
*Few Japanese posters were printed, and fewer still in this two-panel linen-backed format. This poster appeals not only to fans of film, but of motor racing also. Steve McQueen is still very influential, and anything associated with him has nostalgic appeal.*

A film poster, *The Night Porter*, starring Dirk Bogarde and Charlotte Rampling, America, 1974, 28 x 22in (71 x 56cm).

**£175–195** Limelight ⊞

A film poster, *Lisztomania*, 1975, 30 x 40in (76 x 101.5cm).

**£160–175** Limelight ⊞

A film poster, *For Your Eyes Only*, America, 1981, 22 x 28in (56 x 71cm).

**£160–175** Limelight ⊞

A film poster, *Requiem for a Dream*, 2000, 11¾ x 15¾in (30 x 40cm).

**£45–50** J Costello ⊞

A film poster, *Big Fish*, 2004, 11¾ x 15¾in (30 x 40cm).

**£10–15** J Costello ⊞

# HEALTH

A poster, by Leonetto Cappiello, advertising La Croix-Soleil bandages, printed by Devambez, Paris, France, 1919, 47¼ x 31½in (120 x 80cm).

**£480–570** Van Sabben 🔨

A Red Cross poster, by Alfred G. Pelikan, 'Give', 1932, 16½ x 11½in (42 x 29cm).

**£160–190** Van Sabben 🔨

A Red Cross poster, by Newell C. Wyeth, 'Answer the Call!', America, 1953, 18¾ x 15in (47.5 x 38cm).

**£160–190** Van Sabben 🔨

A United Nations poster, by Hans Erni, 'World Health Organisation', printed by Georges Lang, France, 1950, 30¼ x 23¼in (77 x 59cm).

**£65–75** Van Sabben 🔨

A first aid poster, 1950, 30 x 20in (76 x 51cm).

**£240–270** Dodo ⊞

A Red Cross and St John poster, 'Give an Extra Penny a Week to the Penny-A-Week Fund', printed by Charles & Read, London, c1950, 30 x 19¾in (75 x 50cm).

**£240–280** Van Sabben 🔨

A Ligue Nationale Française Contre Le Cancer poster, by Guy Georget, 'Dépister et Vaincre Le Cancer', printed by Bedos & Cie, France, c1965, 22¾ x 15in (58 x 38cm).

**£65–75** Van Sabben 🔨

An Air Force poster, by Raymond J. Prohaska, 'Air Force Nurse, Respect, Responsibility, Reward', c1970, 13½ x 10¼in (34.5 x 26cm).

**£55–65** Van Sabben 🔨

# ROCK & POP

A concert poster, by Hapshash & the Coloured Coat, for The Jimi Hendrix Experience, the Crazy World of Arthur Brown and Tomorrow, at the Saville Theatre, 1967, 29¾ x 19½in (75.5 x 49.5cm) high.

**£450–500 BeatBooks** ⊞

A concert poster, by Mike McInnerney, for the 14-Hour Technicolor Dream benefit concert at Alexandra Palace, London, 1967, 29¾ x 19½in (75.5 x 49.5cm).

**£720–800 BeatBooks** ⊞

A promotional poster, by Hapshash & The Coloured Coat, for concerts by Arthur Brown and Soft Machine, 1967, 29¼ x 19in (74.5 x 48.5cm).

**£300–350 BeatBooks** ⊞

A promotional poster, by Tom Wilkes, for the Monterey Pop Festival, America, 1967, 21¼ x 12¼in (54 x 31cm).

**£630–700 BeatBooks** ⊞

A promotional poster, 'Simon & Garfunkel', America, 1968, 33 x 22in (84 x 56cm).

**£200–250 Limelight** ⊞

A promotional poster, for the Woodstock Music & Art Fair, America, 1969, 24 x 17½in (61 x 44.5cm).

**£160–190 Mastro Auctions** ⚲

A promotional poster, for Bob Marley & The Wailers, printed by I.P.A., America, c1970, 31½ x 46¼in (80 x 117.5cm).

**£280–320 Van Sabben** ⚲

A promotional poster, 'Stone The Crows', c1970, 30 x 40in (76 x 101.5cm).

**£160–180 Limelight** ⊞

A promotional poster, for Captain Beefheart and the Magic Band, Armadillo World Headquarters Concert, America, 1974, 17 x 11in (43 x 28cm).

**£55–65 Heritage** ⚒

A promotional poster, for Led Zeppelin, 'The Song Remains The Same', America, 1976, 41 x 27in (104 x 68.5cm).

**£200–250 Limelight** ⊞

A lobby card, for U2 'Rattle and Hum', America, 1988, 11 x 14in (28 x 35.5cm).

**£40–45 Limelight** ⊞

A promotional poster, by David Singer, advertising a Paul McCartney concert at the University of California, Berkeley, America, 1990, 20½ x 29in (52 x 73.5cm).

**£65–80 Heritage** ⚒

SPORTING

An LNER Railway poster, after Thomson, 'Then and Now', 1920s, 40 x 24in (101.5 x 61cm).

**£3,000–3,400 Manfred Schotten** ⊞

A Greyhound Racing poster, c1930, 88½ x 40¼in (225 x 102cm).

**£600–720 Van Sabben** 🔨

A Bilbao 1934 Regatas de Outboards 3er Tourist Trophy poster, by D. Morales, published by Jesus Alverez, Spain, 1934, 39 x 27½in (99 x 70cm).

**£100–120 Onslow Auctions** 🔨

A Power-Bilt Golf Clubs poster, America, c1935, 17 x 21in (43 x 53.5cm).

**£110–130 Hunt Auctions** 🔨

A Championnat du Monde poster, by Percival Pernet, printed by Affiches Atar, Switzerland, 1946, 39½ x 25½in (100.5 x 65.5cm).

**£880–1,000 Van Sabben** 🔨

A D. H. Neumann Co poster, featuring Joe DiMaggio, 1940s, 22 x 17in (56 x 43cm).

**£270–320 Hunt Auctions** 🔨

A poster, 'Houlgate', France, 1950, 38¾ x 24½in (98.5 x 62cm).

**£440–520 Van Sabben** 🔨

An Olympic Games poster, by Jean Brian, 'Xmes Jeux Olympiques d'Hiver Grenoble', printed by Generale Grenoble, France, 1967, 37¾ x 24¾in (96 x 63cm).

**£130–150 Van Sabben** 🔨

# TRAVEL

A poster, by Adolph Willette, 'Côte d'Azur', c1905, 42½ x 31in (108 x 78.5cm).

**£150–180  Van Sabben** 🪓

A Northern Pacific Railway, by Edward Vincent Brewer, 'Rodeo Parade', c1920, 39¾ x 30¼in (101 x 77cm).

**£170–200  Mastro Auctions** 🪓

A Modena-Express poster, Italy, 1925, 39 x 28in (99 x 71cm).

**£300–350  Dodo** ⊞

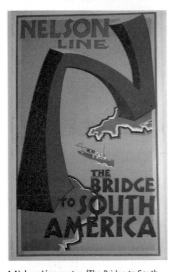

A Nelson Line poster, 'The Bridge to South Africa', 1930, 40 x 25in (101.5 x 63.5cm).

**£340–380  Dodo** ⊞

A Belgium/Luxembourg Tourist Office poster, by Poleff, printed by Protin et Vuidar, Belgium, 1932, 39¼ x 24½in (100 x 62cm).

**£60–75  Onslow Auctions** 🪓

A Swiss Federal Railways poster, by Fretz Bros, Switzerland, 1935, 40¼ x 25¼in (102 x 64cm).

**£130–160  Onslow Auctions** 🪓

A poster, by Otto Altenkird, 'In a German Forest', printed for German railway, Germany, c1935, 39¾ x 25in (101 x 63.5cm).

**£100–120  Onslow Auctions** 🪓

A PLM poster, by E. A. Schefer, 'Paris-Lyon 4h.50', France, 1935, 37½ x 22in (95 x 56cm).

**£450–540  Onslow Auctions** 🪓

A poster, by Werner von Axster-Heudtlass, 'Winter in Germany', printed for German railways, Germany, c1935, 39¾ x 25in (101 x 63.5cm).

**£100–120  Onslow Auctions** 🪓

TRAVEL

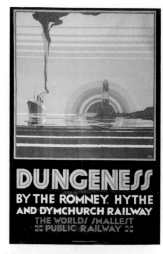

A Romney, Hythe and Dymchurch Railway poster, by N. Cramer Roberts, 'Dungeness', printed by Vincent Brooks Day & Sons, 1936, 102 x 63in (259 x 160cm).

**£400–480 Onslow Auctions** 🔨

An LNER poster, by J. Bateman, 'London', 1937, 40¼ x 25¼in (102 x 64cm).

**£450–550 Onslow Auctions** 🔨

An LNER poster, by J. C. Moody, 'County Durham', printed by Jordison & Co, 1937, 40¼ x 25¼in (102 x 64cm).

**£220–270 Onslow Auctions** 🔨

A poster, by Arthur Zelger, 'Serfaus Tyrol Austria', printed by WUB-Druck, Austria, c1950, 23¾ x 16¾in (60.5 x 42.5cm).

**£130–155 Van Sabben** 🔨

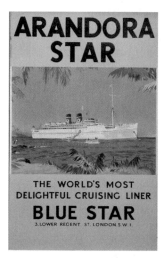

A Blue Star Line poster, 'Arandora Star', 1950, 40¼ x 25¼in (102 x 64cm).

**£150–180 Onslow Auctions** 🔨

An LNER poster, by Frank Mason, 'London via Harwich', printed by Waterlow & Sons, early 1940s, 40 x 25in (101.5 x 63.5cm).

**£920–1,100 GWR Auctions** 🔨

A British Railways poster, by Jack Merriott, 'Penzance for The Lizard and Land's End Peninsulas', printed by Charles Read, 1950s, 40 x 25in (101.5 x 63.5cm).

**£350–420 GWR Auctions** 🔨

A British Railways poster, by Wooten, 'Bristol', printed by Waterlow & Sons, 1950s, 40 x 25in (101.5 x 63.5cm).

**£580–700 GWR Auctions** 🔨

A British Railways poster, 'Sawbridgeworth, Hertfordshire', 1950s, 40 x 25in (101.5 x 63.5cm).

**£190–230 GWR Auctions** 🔨

An SNCF poster, 'Côte d'Azur', printed by Draeger, France, 1951, 39¾ x 24½in (101 x 62cm).

**£150–180** Onslow Auctions

An SNCF poster, by Maurice Utrillo, 'Paris, Montmartre', printed by De Plas, France, 1953, 101 x 62in (256.5 x 157.5cm).

**£100–120** Onslow Auctions

A BOAC silkscreen poster, by Aldo Cosomati, 'Fly B.O.A.C. U.S.A.', 1953, 30 x 20in (76 x 51cm).

**£100–120**
Onslow Auctions

A British Railways Southern Railways poster, 'The Brussels Night Ferry Through Sleeping Car Train', printed by Leonard Ripley, 1957, 40¼ x 24¾in (102 x 63cm).

**£100–120**
Onslow Auctions

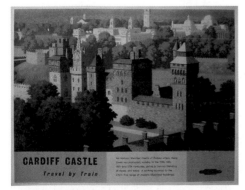

A British Railways Western Region poster, by Ronald Lampitt, 'Cardiff Castle', printed by Jordison & Co, 1960, 50 x 40¼in (127 x 102cm).

**£260–320** Onslow Auctions

A London Transport poster, by Pat Keely, advertising a twenty-mile sightseeing bus tour, printed by Waterlow & Sons, c1960, 40 x 25in (101.5 x 63.5cm).

**£240–280 Van Sabben** 🔨

A poster, by Pablo Picasso, 'Côte d'Azur', printed by Mourlot, France, c1960, 39½ x 26in (100.5 x 66cm).

**£270–310 Van Sabben** 🔨

A poster, 'Nice', printed by Mourlot, France, c1965, 39 x 24½in (99 x 62cm).

**£95–110 Van Sabben** 🔨

A David MacBrayne poster, 'Scotland's Western Highlands and Islands', printed by John Horn, 1960s, 40¼ x 24⅞in (102 x 63cm).

**£120–145 Onslow Auctions** 🔨

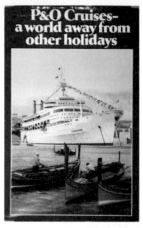

A P&O poster, by Withams, 'P&O Cruises – a World Away from Other Holidays', advertising the Canberra and Oriana cruise ships, 1970s, 40¼ x 24⅞in (102 x 63cm).

**£45–55 Onslow Auctions** 🔨

A poster, by Pierre Fix-Masseau, 'Collection Venice Simplon Orient-Express', printed by I.P.A., France, 1982, 39¾ x 24⅛in (101 x 62cm).

**£240–280 Van Sabben** 🔨

## ESSENTIAL REFERENCE SHELL POSTERS

A Shell poster, by W. J. Steggles, 'The Tattingstone Wonder, Suffolk', Landmark series, No. 497, printed by Waterlow & Sons, c1937, 30 x 45¼in (76 x 115cm).

**£150–180 Onslow Auctions** 🔨

A Shell poster, by Clifford and Rosemary Ellis, 'Chanter's Folly and Dry Dock, Appledore', Landmark series, No. 491, printed by Waterlow & Sons , c1937, 30 x 45¼in (76 x 115cm).

**£350–420 Onslow Auctions** 🔨

A Shell poster, by Denis Constanduros, 'Llanthony Abbey, Monmouthshire', Landmark series, No. 498, printed by Waterlow & Sons, c1937, 30 x 45¼in (76 x 115cm).

**£220–270 Onslow Auctions** 🔨

• Shell advertising posters were mounted on the sides of their petrol tankers and are rarer than railway posters.

• Jack Bebbington commissioned the finest commercial artists of the 1920s and '30s.

• The reputations of many now famous modern British artists were made as a result of their designs for Shell. In some cases the posters command higher prices than the original paintings, a situation brought about by competition between buyers.

• Shell Posters are often collected by theme, such as those from the Landmark series shown here.

**Patrick Brogue, Onslow Auctions**

# WARTIME

A poster, by W. H. Caffyn, 'Come Along, Boys! Enlist To-Day',
printed by Haycock Cable Co, c1914, 30 x 20in (76 x 51cm).

**£70–85 Onslow Auctions** ⚒

A copy of a public warning poster, for airships and aeroplanes, 1917,
30in (76cm) high.

**£5–10 Tussie Mussies** ⊞

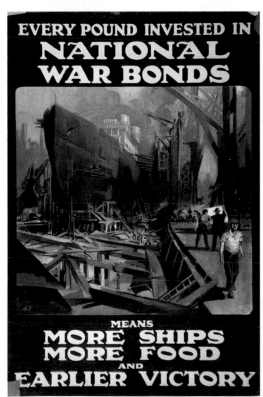

A poster, by A. J., 'Every Pound Invested in National War Bonds Means
More Ships, More Food and Earlier Victory', 1939–45,
30 x 19¾in (76 x 50cm).

**£40–50 Onslow Auctions** ⚒

A poster, by Jean Carlu, 'Give 'em Both Barrels', 1941, 15 x 20in (38 x 51cm).

**£200–240 Van Sabben** ⚒

A poster, by Claudius, 'Tegen
Zwarten Handel', Holland, 1943,
29¼ x 20in (74.5 x 51cm).

**£140–165 Van Sabben** ⚒

A poster, by Peter Beekman,
'Landelijke Frontzorgcollecte',
Holland, 1944, 31½ x 21¾in
(80 x 55.5cm).

**£80–95 Van Sabben** ⚒

# POWDER COMPACTS

A chrome-plated and celluloid powder and rouge compact, decorated with a Victorian scene, c1920, 2¼in (5.5cm) wide.

**£45–50 Sue Wilde** ⊞

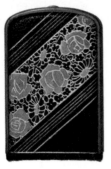

A Mondaine embossed leather powder and rouge compact, 1920–30, 2in (5cm) wide.

**£60–70 Sue Wilde** ⊞

A Tango enamelled and chrome-plated powder compact, with lipstick, America, 1920–30, 2¼in (5.5cm) high.

**£135–145 Sue Wilde** ⊞

A brass and celluloid powder and rouge compact, decorated with sailing boats, c1925, 2in (5cm) diam.

**£40–45 Sue Wilde** ⊞

A Milrone nickel and enamel miniature vanity compact, decorated with a geometric design, America, c1925, 1½in (4cm) wide.

**£80–90 Sue Wilde** ⊞

A Fisher cold-painted powder compact, America, 1925–35, 2½in (6.5cm) high.

**£200–250 Sue Wilde** ⊞

A Tango chrome and enamel compact, America, 1925–30, 2¼in (5.5cm) high.

**£120–130 Sue Wilde** ⊞

A DuBarry powder compact, decorated with a ballerina, c1930, 2in (5cm) diam.

**£90–100 Sue Wilde** ⊞

A guilloche enamel powder and rouge compact, 1925–30, 2½in (6.5cm) wide.

**£80–90 Sue Wilde** ⊞

A Volupté brass compact, decorated with a butterfly's wing and dog, America, c1930, 2in (5cm) square.

**£60–70 Sue Wilde** ⊞

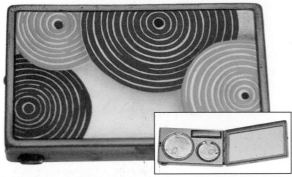

A Houbigant brass and celluloid powder compact, France, 1930–40, 3in (5.5cm) wide.

**£70–80  Sue Wilde** ⊞

An enamel compact, decorated with an owl, 1930–40, 3in (7.5cm) high.

**£45–50  Sue Wilde** ⊞

A Coty brass and enamel Houppes powder compact, stamped 'Coty, Paris', France, c1930, 2¼in (5.5cm) diam, together with a similar cardboard powder box.

**£20–25  Rosebery's** 🔨

A powder compact, decorated with flowers, France, c1930, 3½in (9cm) square.

**£45–50  Le Boudoir** ⊞

An Adi Brothers silver and guilloche enamel compact, 1934, 3in (7.5cm) high.

**£250–280  Sue Wilde** ⊞

An enamel and chrome compact, with a comb, Continental, 1935–40, 8in (20.5cm) long.

**£180–200  Sue Wilde** ⊞

A sterling silver powder compact, decorated with a 14ct gold band, America, c1935, 2½in (6.5cm) wide.

**£150–165  Sue Wilde** ⊞

A Rex celluloid powder compact, decorated with a horse and rider, America, 1935–40, 5in (12.5cm) wide.

**£70–80  Sue Wilde** ⊞

A Rex celluloid compact, decorated with a gazelle, America, 1935–40, 5in (12.5cm) wide.

**£60–70  Sue Wilde** ⊞

A silver and guilloche enamel powder compact, with pierced silver decoration, Austria, 1930s, 2¼in (5.5cm) diam.

**£150–165  Sue Wilde** ⊞

An enamel powder compact, in the form of a suitcase, France, 1930s–40s, 3in (7.5cm) wide.
**£70–80 Sue Wilde** ⊞

A silver powder compact, decorated with a Military Police badge, 1940, 2½in (6.5cm) square.
**£60–75 Tussie Mussies** ⊞

A Bakelite roll-top powder compact, with a sprung hinge, Germany, 1940–50, 4in (10cm) wide.
**£90–100 Sue Wilde** ⊞

A Clover brass musical powder compact, with enamelled decoration, 1940–50, 3¼in (8.5cm) wide.
**£80–90 Sue Wilde** ⊞

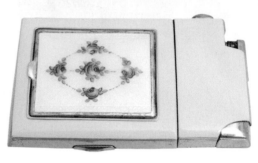

A Marathon guilloche enamelled combination cigarette lighter and rouge compact, America, 1940s–50s, 4in (10cm) wide.
**£110–130 Sue Wilde** ⊞

A chrome, enamel and carved jade combination cigarette case and powder and rouge compact, 1940s–50s, 3in (7.5cm) wide.
**£160–180 Sue Wilde** ⊞

An Elgin brass and silver-plated compact, the cover with a Victorian boot design decorated with garnets, America, c1950, 4½in (11.5cm) wide.
**£125–140 Sue Wilde** ⊞

An Elizabeth Arden brass powder compact, America, c1950, 3in (7.5cm) wide.
**£90–100 Sue Wilde** ⊞
*The Harlequin mask compact was manufactured in the 1940s, a period when novelty compacts were growing in popularity and included such designs as a hand, roulette wheel and globe. Elizabeth Arden was acclaimed worldwide for her attitude to 'total skin care'. In 1931 she produced a booklet 'In Quest of the Beautiful', and had locations in London, New York, Berlin, Paris, Madrid and Rome.*

A Kigu enamelled brass compact, in the form of a flying saucer, 1950s, 2¾in (7cm) diam.
**£45–55 Special Auction Services** ⚒

# EXPERT EYE | ANNETTE COMPACT

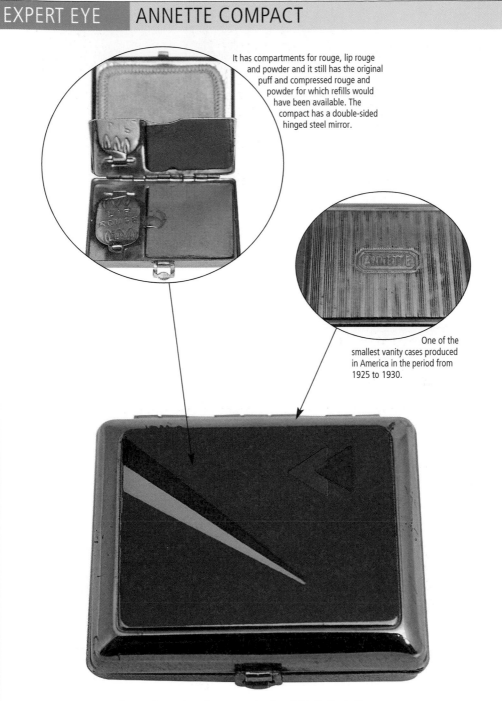

It has compartments for rouge, lip rouge and powder and it still has the original puff and compressed rouge and powder for which refills would have been available. The compact has a double-sided hinged steel mirror.

One of the smallest vanity cases produced in America in the period from 1925 to 1930.

An Annette brass and enamel powder compact, America, c1930, 2in (5cm) wide.
**£60–70  Sue Wilde** ⊞

Very little is known about the history of the Annette compact as they are quite rare. Finding one in un-used condition is a bonus, and the value of the compact is increased if it has its original pouch and presentation box. It is advisable to remove loose powder as it can cause damage, but solid powder and rouge should be left in the compact. This example of an Annette compact reflects the spirit of the Art Deco period with it's strong geometric pattern and bright colouring. It would have been an affordable fashion accessory, enabling less wealthy ladies to acquire a very stylish object equal to the beauty of the more expensive couterparts. Collecting compacts can be very rewarding, whether made from gold, silver, brass, Bakelite or other material.The beauty of design, combined with great technical skill on the inside, provide a fascinating and winning combination.

# RAILWAYANA

A Natal Government Railways silver-plated sugar bowl and cream jug, South Africa, 1905, 3in (7.5cm) high.

**£75–85  Castlegate ⊞**

A South African Railways silver-plated sugar bowl, South Africa, 1905, 4in (10cm) high.

**£50–55  Castlegate ⊞**

A Southern Railway glazed ceramic jug, by John Maddock & Sons, with hinged pewter cover, Southern Railway garter crest, 1940s, 4in (10cm) high.

**£25–30  GWR Auctions ⚒**

A Great Western Railway brush, with wooden handle, early 20thC, 3in (7.5cm) high.

**£40–45  Gloucester Antiques ⊞**

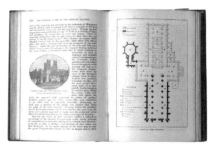

*The Official Guide to the Midland Railway*, published by Cassell & Co, London, 21st edition, 1915, 6¾ x 5in (17 x 13cm).

**£80–90  Barter Books ⊞**

A London & North Western Railway wooden whistle, pre-1923, 3½in (9cm) long.

**£55–65  Gloucester Antiques ⊞**

A London & North Eastern Railway enamelled lifeboat badge, 1923–47, 1¼in (3cm) diam.

**£50–55  Gloucester Antiques ⊞**

A London & North Eastern Railway St John Ambulance Association badge, 1923–47, 1in (2.5cm) diam.

**£25–30  Gloucester Antiques ⊞**

A Great Central Railway brass and white metal button, pre-1927, 1in (2.5cm) diam.

**£15–20  Gloucester Antiques ⊞**

## EXPERT EYE — LTPB WHISTLE

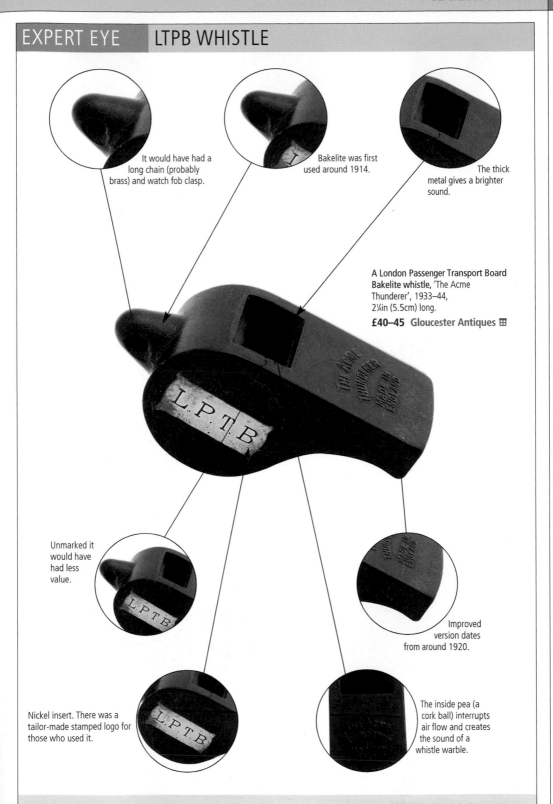

It would have had a long chain (probably brass) and watch fob clasp.

Bakelite was first used around 1914.

The thick metal gives a brighter sound.

A London Passenger Transport Board Bakelite whistle, 'The Acme Thunderer', 1933–44, 2¼in (5.5cm) long.

**£40–45 Gloucester Antiques** ⊞

Unmarked it would have had less value.

Improved version dates from around 1920.

Nickel insert. There was a tailor-made stamped logo for those who used it.

The inside pea (a cork ball) interrupts air flow and creates the sound of a whistle warble.

Public transport across London was unified in 1933 and became known as the London Passenger Transport Board (LPTB) – commonly known as LT or London Transport. It took charge of all London's transport networks – bus, tram and Underground – but not the overground services of the mainline companies. The previously independent Metropolitan and Waterloo and City Lines were finally absorbed the LPTB. Frank Pick took the helm as Managing Director and unified the look of the LPTB group. The distinctive Underground roundel was adapted for the first bus stop signs, posters were commissioned to celebrate the various forms of transport and the diagrammatic Underground Map we still use today was first trialled in 1933. Everything associated with the birth of the LPTB is a desirable collectable today. Obviously some categories are more valuable than others – for instance an original Underground Poster from the Pick era can command high prices.

A Great Western Railway lamp repeater, in a mahogany case, 1920s, 10in (25.5cm) high.
**£130–145** Collectables ⊞

A Chester General Station Railway Servants Refreshment Society cup, by Dunn Bennet & Co, damaged, c1937, 3in (7.5cm) high.
**£40–45** Gloucester Antiques ⊞

A London Transport enamelled cap badge, from 1939, 2in (5cm) diam.
**£10–15** Gloucester Antiques ⊞

A Great Western Railway block bell, on a mahogany base, c1930s, 10in (25.5cm) wide.
**£130–145** Collectables ⊞

A London & North West Railway Absolute block instrument, 1930s, 25in (63.5cm) high.
**£200–250** Collectables ⊞

A British Railways Eastern Region enamelled cap badge, late 1940s, 3in (7.5cm) wide.
**£40–45** Gloucester Antiques ⊞

A British Rail Western Region National desk time recorder, in an oak case, 1950s, 12in (30.5cm) high.
**£140–155** Collectables ⊞

A British Railways enamelled armband badge, c1950s, 4in (10cm) wide.
**£20–25** Jean Sears ⊞

A Denver Zephyr train head-rest cover, America, 1950s–60s, 18½ x 15½in (47 x 39.5cm).
**£10–15** Silversnow Antiques ⊞

# LAMPS

A Great Western Railway Coppertop 3 aspect guard's handlamp, with glasses, copper, non-standard reservoir and burner, and plain front lens, c1900, 14in (35.5cm) high.

**£120–145 GWR Auctions** 🪓

A Great Western Railway paraffin head lamp, with original burner, 1940s, 12in (30.5cm) high.

**£115–130 Collectables** ⊞

A Southern Railway tin paraffin side lamp, 1940s, 18in (45.5cm) high.

**£55–65 Collectables** ⊞

A British Railways steel red stop oil lamp, 20thC, 21in (53.5cm) high.

**£45–50 Jean Sears** ⊞

A British Railways Southern general purpose oil hand lamp, c1950, 13in (33cm) high.

**£50–55 Collectables** ⊞

A British Railways Midlands gauge lamp, 1950s, 10in (25.5cm) high.

**£40–45 Collectables** ⊞

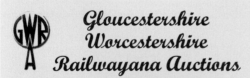
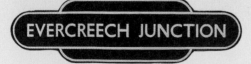

## PLATES & SIGNS

A brass engine number plate, from a dock tank engine, 1907, 13in (33cm) wide.

**£65–75** Grimes Militaria ⊞

A Great Western Railway cast-iron notice, pre-1923, 35in (89cm) wide.

**£160–185** Collectables ⊞

A Great Western Railway cast-iron registration plate, 1928, 9in (23cm) wide.

**£50–60** Collectables ⊞

A London Midland & Scottish Railway cast-iron wagon registration plate, 1936, 9in (23cm) wide.

**£30–35** Gloucester Antiques ⊞
*This plate was fixed to private owners' wagons to denote that they had been passed to run on LMS tracks.*

A Cravens cast-iron wagon plate, from a coal hopper wagon, 1950, 11in (28cm) wide.

**£40–45** Gloucester Antiques ⊞

A diesel locomotive engine nameplate, c1959, 48in (122cm) wide.

**£800–960** GWR Auctions 🔨
*The Alnwick Castle was built by Hudswell Clarke and worked on the Manchester ship canal. These nameplates are not as highly prized as those of mainline locomotives – a less atractive name would be worth around £300.*

A Birmingham Railway Carriage & Wagon Co brass plaque, 1962, 4in (10cm) wide.

**£250–280** Gloucester Antiques ⊞

A Chas. Roberts & Co wagon builder's plate, 1965, 11½in (29cm) wide.

**£35–40** Gloucester Antiques ⊞

A British Railways steel and enamel totem, 1950s, 36in (91.5cm) wide.

**£270–330** GWR Auctions 🔨

A British Railways Western Region cast-iron registration plate, 1967, 10in (25.5cm) wide.

**£10–15** Collectables ⊞

# ROCK & POP

The Rolling Stones, a set of three signed album pages mounted with a photograph, 1960s, album page 3½ x 3in (9 x 7.5cm), framed.

**£1,500–1,750** Fraser's ⊞

A Jimi Hendrix Experience concert programme, with artwork by Marijke Koger, 1967, 8in (20.5cm) high.

**£270–300** BeatBooks ⊞

A tour programme, for the Jimi Hendrix Experience package tour including Pink Floyd, The Move, Amen Corner and The Nice, 1967, 10½in (26.5cm) high.

**£200–250** BeatBooks ⊞

A Count Basie concert programme, c1970, 10 x 8in (25.5 x 20.5cm).

**£15–20** Collectors Corner ⊞

A pair of drumsticks, signed by Pink Floyd's Nick Mason, with a copy of *Inside Out* and a photograph, c2005.

**£50–60** Heritage ⚒

A cotton Whitesnake T-shirt, c1980.
**£35–40 Clobber** ⊞

A cotton Iron Maiden T-shirt, c1980.
**£35–40 Clobber** ⊞

A cotton Black Sabbath T-shirt, 1981.
**£35–40 Clobber** ⊞

A Rolling Stones lobby card, No. 7, 'Let's Spend The Night Together', 1983, 11 x 14in (28 x 35.5cm).
**£115–130 Limelight** ⊞

A cardboard jigsaw puzzle of Queen's 'The Miracle', by Jigstars Queen Productions, 1989, with box, 12in (30.5cm) square.
**£20–25 Sweet Memories** ⊞

John Denver, a signed photograph, 1994, 10 x 8in (25.5 x 20.5cm).
**£95–105**
**Autograph Collector's Gallery** ⊞

A Michael Jackson roadie's leather and fabric jacket, from the 'Dangerous' tour, 1990s.
**£360–400 Cobwebs** ⊞

Sheena Easton, a signed photograph, 2001, 10 x 8in (25.5 x 20.5cm).
**£25–30**
**Autograph Collector's Gallery** ⊞

Jerry Lee Lewis, a signed photograph, 2003, 10 x 8in (25.5 x 20.5cm).
**£70–80**
**Autograph Collector's Gallery** ⊞

Mariah Carey, a signed photograph, 2004, 10 x 8in (25.5 x 20.5cm).
**£50–55**
**Autograph Collector's Gallery** ⊞

WOODSTOCK FESTIVAL PROGRAMME

Programmes were printed on good-quality paper. Many surviving programmes have mud and water stains and, although stains may indicate that a programme is authentic, they do not add value. Collectors look for programmes that are in mint condition

A Woodstock Festival programme book, designed by Bertram Cohen, 1969, 11in (28cm) high.

**£360–400** BeatBooks ⊞

The 1988 boxed set of recordings from Woodstock was issued with a replica programme. To differentiate between an original and replica programme look at the *I-Ching* quotation on the back – the original has a round full stop whereas on the replica version it is square.

The naturalistic imagery used for the cover design reflects the hippie movement's growing longing for a life of rural harmony in the countryside.

The Woodstock festival was the apogee of the hippie movement and a response to the widespread political unease and discontent regarding the war in Vietnam. The biggest ever event of its kind, an estimated 450,000 fans attended at its height, temporarily making it the third-largest city in New York State. Just one month before the festival took place the venue was moved to Bethel from its original site at Woodstock, as a result of misgivings felt by local authorities. The headlining act was Jimi Hendrix, who played the last set at 8.30 on the Monday morning. His rendition of 'The Star Spangled Banner' with feedback was his personal protest against the Vietnam war, although there were only about 30,000–40,000 fans left to hear the now famous performance.

**Andrew Sclanders, BeatBooks**

## THE BEATLES

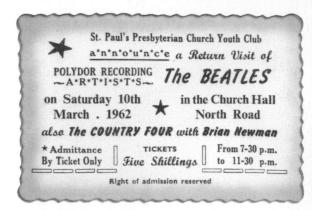

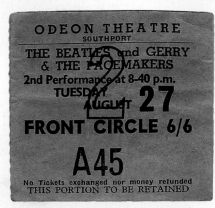

A ticket, for a Beatles concert at St Paul's Presbyterian Church Youth Club, dated 10 March 1962, 4½ x 3½in (11.5 x 9cm).

**£340–400 Heritage** 🔨

A ticket, for a Beatles concert at the Odeon Theatre, Southport, with Gerry & The Pacemakers, 27 August 1963.

**£200–240 Heritage** 🔨

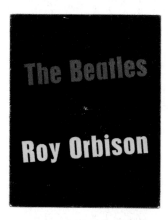

A tour programme, signed by The Beatles, 1963, 8 x 10¼in (20.5 x 26cm).

**£1,600–2,000 Mastro Auctions** 🔨

Paul McCartney and Paul Harrison, a photographic postcard, c1963, 3 x 5in (7.5 x 12.5cm).

**£5–10 Collectors Corner** ⊞

The Beatles, 'Please Please Me', stereo LP record, second issue, by EMI, 1963.

**£145–160 Sweet Memories** ⊞

The Beatles, 'A Hard Day's Night', mono LP record, first issue, by EMI, 1964.

**£50–60 Sweet Memories** ⊞

A stage pass, for the Beatles' Christmas Shows at the Hammersmith Odeon, 1964–65.

**£135–165 Heritage** 🔨

A lobby card, No. 5, for Help!, America, 1965, 11 x 14in (28 x 35.5cm).

**£340–380 Limelight** ⊞

The Beatles, 'Rubber Soul', mono LP record, first issue, by EMI, 1965.

**£70–80 Sweet Memories** ⊞

The Beatles, a signed photograph, 1965, framed and glazed, 10 x 8in (25.5 x 20.5cm).

**£9,000–10,000 Fraser's** ⊞
*This photograph features the Beatles wearing casual dress on a beach in the Bahamas. It was taken during the filming of Help!*

An RIAA gold album award, for the Beatles' 'Revolver', commemorating the sale of 500,000 albums, 1966–67, in a frame 21 x 17in (53.5 x 43cm).

**£3,700–4,500 Heritage** ⚒

The Beatles, 'Singles Collection', comprising 26 single records, 1982.

**£145–175 Heritage** ⚒
*This set marked the first time that all of the UK 45rpm singles had been released with picture sleeves. Previously only 'Strawberry Fields' and 'Let It Be' had been released with picture sleeves.*

A Kuwait Airways luggage sticker, signed by the Beatles, 1966, 4in (10cm) diam.

**£2,600–3,200 Heritage** ⚒
*This sticker came from the group's final tour in 1966, on the way from Japan to the Philippines. Security was so tight at this point that autographs were becoming increasingly scarce.*

An animation cel, from the Beatles' *Yellow Submarine*, 1968, in a frame 16 x 12in (40.5 x 30.5cm).

**£400–500 Mastro Auctions** ⚒

A Coalport porcelain letter rack, from the Beatles Collection, 2006, 8in (20.5cm) high.

**£30–35 Box of Porcelain** ⊞

A Beatles *Yellow Submarine* poster, signed by Heinz Edelmann, limited edition of 500, 1968, 39 x 25¾in (99 x 65.5cm).

**£180–220 Heritage** ⚒

The Beatles, 'Sergent Pepper's Lonely Hearts Club Band', stereo LP record, by EMI, repressing, 1969.

**£50–60 Sweet Memories** ⊞

A Coalport porcelain group of Sergent Pepper's Lonely Hearts Club Band, limited edition, 2006, 7in (18cm) high.

**£90–100 Box of Porcelain** ⊞

## EXPERT EYE     THE BEATLES v THE FOUR SEASONS

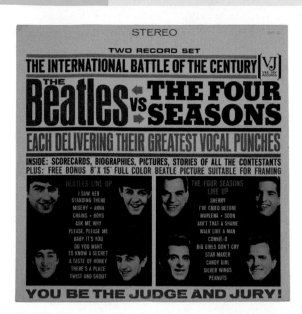

**The Beatles**, 'The Beatles vs The Four Seasons', stereo LP record, by Vee-Jay, with original poster, 1964.

**£2,300–2,750 Heritage** ⚒

The stereo recording is the rarest pressing available.

The front cover featured drawings of all four members of both bands together with a listing of all the tracks included on the album.

The poster included with the record should be in mint or near mint condition.

The back cover was designed as a scorecard — collectors look for unmarked copies.

This album is in fact repackaged tracks from 'Introducing the Beatles' and 'The Golden Hits of the Four Seasons', both previously issued by Vee-Jay. The album was released in August 1964 in both mono and stereo and eventually reached No. 142 in the charts, having sold only 18,700 mono and 725 stereo versions out of a total pressing of 30,500. Vee-Jay had for some time been anxious to release new Beatles material but were unable to obtain the rights from EMI/Capitol, who would only allow them to reissue previous recordings with different covers. With 'The Beatles vs The Four Seasons' Vee-Jay's hoped that they would be able to convince the record-buying public that they were purchasing something new.

**Garry Shrum, Heritage**

# GUITARS

A Martin 0-17 acoustic guitar, 1937, 38in (96.5cm) high.

**£2,350–2,600**
**Vintage & Rare Guitars** ⊞

A Gibson L4 Sunburst accoustic guitar, with Nick Lucas inlays, 1946, 41in (104cm) high.

**£2,450–2,700**
**Vintage & Rare Guitars** ⊞

A Martin rosewood 000-21 acoustic guitar, 1953, 39in (99cm) high.

**£5,900-6,500**
**Vintage & Rare Guitars** ⊞

A Martin 0-18 guitar, 1968, 39in (99cm) high.

**£3,500–3,900**
**Vintage & Rare Guitars** ⊞

A Gibson Dove acoustic guitar, 1969.

**£2,450–2,700**
**Vintage & Rare Guitars** ⊞

A Gibson L Series acoustic guitar, c1940s, 41in (104cm) high.

**£1,450–1,600**
**Vintage & Rare Guitars** ⊞

An Epiphone Broadway electric
guitar, 1958, 42in (106.5cm) high.
**£1,700–1,900**
**Vintage & Rare Guitars** ⊞

A Fender Jazzmaster electric
guitar, 1959, 41in (104cm) high.
**£2,800–3,250**
**Vintage & Rare Guitars** ⊞

A Gibson ES 350 electric guitar,
1959, 42in (106.5cm) high.
**£5,800–6,500**
**Vintage & Rare Guitars** ⊞

A Burns Vista Sonic electric bass
guitar, 1963, 47in (119.5cm) high.
**£1,100–1,300**
**Vintage & Rare Guitars** ⊞

An Epiphone Riviera XII electric
guitar, 1967, 44in (112cm) high.
**£2,500–2,900**
**Vintage & Rare Guitars** ⊞

A Gretsch 6120 Nashville electric
guitar, with Paul Bigsby tailpiece,
1967, 42in (106.5cm) high.
**£2,700–3,000**
**Vintage & Rare Guitars** ⊞

GUITARS

A Gibson ES 335 TDC guitar, early 1970s.
**£3,500–3,900**
**Vintage & Rare Guitars** ⊞

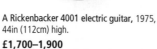

A Rickenbacker 4001 electric guitar, 1975, 44in (112cm) high.
**£1,700–1,900**
**Vintage & Rare Guitars** ⊞

A Fender Telecaster left-handed electric guitar, 1975, 39in (99cm) high.
**£3,500–3,900**
**Vintage & Rare Guitars** ⊞

A Music Man Sting Ray electric bass guitar, with string-through body, 1976, 44in (112cm) high.
**£1,800–2,100**
**Vintage & Rare Guitars** ⊞

A Gibson Les Paul Delux electric guitar, 1977, 45in (114.5cm) high.
**£1,700–1,900**
**Vintage & Rare Guitars** ⊞

A Copley six-string electirc guitar, with Beach Boys logo, pick guard signed by Brian Wilson and Mike Love, 1970s.
**£150–180** **Heritage** 🔨

An Eleca six-string electric guitar, with Alice Cooper logo and signature, 1970s.
**£165–200 Heritage** 🔨

A Copley six-string electric guitar, signed by Keith Richards, 1980s.
**£300–360 Heritage** 🔨

A six-string electric guitar, with mother-of-pearl pick guard and Guns N' Roses logo, signatures include Axl Rose, Slash and Duff McKagan, 1980s–90s.
**£200–240 Heritage** 🔨

## EXPERT EYE  FENDER PRECISION BASS

A Fender Precision electric bass
guitar, 1966, 45in (114.5cm) high.
**£5,200–5,800**
**Vintage & Rare Guitars** ⊞

The neck plate is where the serial
number is generally to be found.
This can help ascertain the age of
the guitar.

The headstock carries the brand name and
model name of the instrument. On some
versions the serial number will be found
here also.

This colourway is known as
sunburst. It is the classic
colourway for this type of guitar.
Colour variations were rare in the
1950s and so add to value.

Fender Precision bass guitars first appeared in the early 1950s. Guitars made prior to 1965 are more desirable because Fender was taken over by CBS in that year, although owing to increasing scarcity guitars made up to 1970 are now sought after, depending on condition. During the 1960s it was quite common for guitars to be customized, and while this may be interesting, it does not increase value. An approximate date can be worked out from the serial number, but these were not used sequentially by the makers. Another indicator is the transfer logo – before 1965 the 'spaghetti logo' was used, which had a thinner font. From 1964 to 1967 a larger gold typeface with a black outline was used so that it would be more visible in publicity shots or when seen in films or on TV. A better indicator of date is the potentiometer inside the guitar. These have a seven-digit code of which the fourth and fifth give the year, the sixth and seventh the week. However, in 1966 CBS bought so many potentiometers that stocks lasted until 1970. Any potentiometers dated 1968 or 1969 are probably replacements. Another place to look for a date is at the end of the neck but this is hidden by the body, so can only be seen if the neck is removed. Although not from the sought-after 1950s production, this is a classic Fender bass, an essential purchase for any serious collector. This guitar has never lost its popularity and almost every bass player will have used one. A classic guitar in excellent conditon is a good investment – unlike some other investments, their prices have never dropped.

**Vintage & Rare Guitars**

## ELVIS PRESLEY

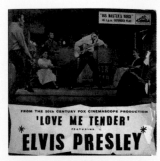

An Elvis Presley concert ticket, for Cleveland Arena, Ohio, unused, America, 1956, 2 x 4¾in (5 x 12cm).

**£1,200–1,450 Mastro Auctions** 🔨

Elvis Presley, 'Love Me Tender', EP record, with replaceable centre, by HMV, 1957.

**£70–75 Beanos** ⊞

A quantity of Elvis Presley's hair, in a plastic container, 1950s, 3¼in (8.5cm) high.

**£1,600–2,000 Mastro Auctions** 🔨

Elvis Presley, a photographic postcard for King Creole, 1958, 3 x 5in (7.5 x 12.5cm).

**£5–10 Collectors Corner** ⊞

Elvis Presley, 'Love Letters', 7in single record, by HMV, Japan, c1960.

**£35–40 Spinna Disc Records** ⊞

Elvis Presley, 'Long Tall Sally', EP record, by HMV, Japanese, c1960.

**£70–80 Spinna Disc Records** ⊞

Elvis Presley, a photographic postcard, Germany, c1960, 8 x 6in (20.5 x 15cm).

**£5–10 Collectors Corner** ⊞

Elvis Presley, a photographic postcard for Follow That Dream, 1962, 6 x 3in (15 x 7.5cm).

**£5–10 Collectors Corner** ⊞

Elvis Presley, a press photograph, 1964, 5 x 10in (12.5 x 25.5cm).

**£5–10 Collectors Corner** ⊞

A plasic Elvis Presley lamp, with a cardboard shade, 1970s, 17in (43cm) high.

**£45–50 Pineapple Ice Bucket** ⊞

## EXPERT EYE    PRESLEY'S PENDANT

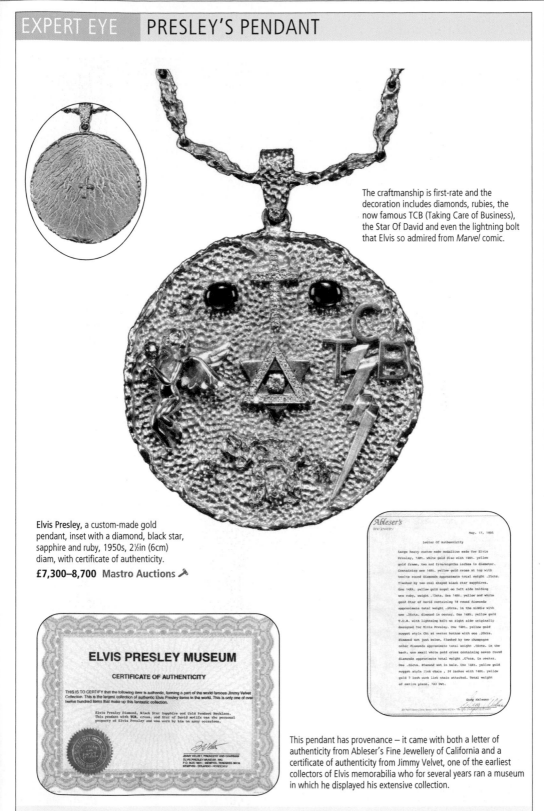

The craftmanship is first-rate and the decoration includes diamonds, rubies, the now famous TCB (Taking Care of Business), the Star Of David and even the lightning bolt that Elvis so admired from *Marvel* comic.

**Elvis Presley,** a custom-made gold pendant, inset with a diamond, black star, sapphire and ruby, 1950s, 2½in (6cm) diam, with certificate of authenticity.

**£7,300–8,700 Mastro Auctions** 🔨

This pendant has provenance — it came with both a letter of authenticity from Ableser's Fine Jewellery of California and a certificate of authenticity from Jimmy Velvet, one of the earliest collectors of Elvis memorabilia who for several years ran a museum in which he displayed his extensive collection.

Elvis Presley's influence on popular culture can't be overstated. In the 1950s he almost single-handedly turned the guitar into a billion-dollar industry and his influence on future rock stars such as the Beatles is best summed up by the now famous John Lennon quote: 'Before Elvis there was nothing'. Any memorabilia personally owned by Presley is highly coveted by serious collectors. Key to collecting Elvis memorabilia is that the item should come from a very reputable source, as does this pendant. Elvis liked to bestow jewellery on his many family and friends. Several of these pieces have come up for sale and where the provenance linking back to Presley is strong very high prices are achieved.

**Brian Marran, Mastro Auctions**

## RECORDS & CDS

Cliff Richard and the Drifters, 'Serious Charge', mono EP record, by Columbia, 1959.

**£15–20 Spinna Disc Records** ⊞

Dave "Baby" Cortez, 'The Happy Organ', 'Love Me as I Love You', 'The Whistling Organ', 'I'm Happy', EP record, by London Records, 1959.

**£20–25 Spinna Disc Records** ⊞

Don Gibson, 'That Gibson Boy', mono LP record, by RCA, 1959.

**£50–60 Spinna Disc Records** ⊞

Chubby Checker, 'Twist with Chubby Checker', mono LP record, Columbia records, 1960.

**£20–25 Spinna Disc Records** ⊞

Duane Eddy, '$1,000,000.00 Worth of Twang', mono LP record, by London, 1960.

**£25–30 Spinna Disc Records** ⊞

Chet Atkins, 'Chet Atkins' Teensville', mono LP record, by RCA, US import, 1960.

**£15–20 Spinna Disc Records** ⊞

Fats Domino, 'The Fabulous "Mr D"', LP record, by London, 1961.

**£25–30 Spinna Disc Records** ⊞

Billy Preston, 'The Most Exciting Organ Ever', mono LP record, by Sue Records, 1962.

**£25–30 Spinna Disc Records** ⊞

Jim Reeves, 'Bimbo', mono LP record, by London, 1962.

**£15–20 Spinna Disc Records** ⊞

The Cascades, 'Rhythm Of The Rain', stereo LP record, by Warner Brothers, 1963.

**£35–40 Spinna Disc Records** ⊞

Gerry and the Pacemakers, 'How Do You Like It?', stereo LP record, by Columbia, 1963.

**£35–40 Spinna Disc Records** ⊞

Ruth Brown, 'Gospel Time', mono LP record, by Philips, 1963.

**£70–80** Sweet Memories ⊞

Little Stevie Wonder, 'The 12 Year Old Genius', mono LP record, by Oriole Records, 1963.

**£180–200** Sweet Memories ⊞

Ben E. King, 'What Now My Love', 'mono EP records, by Atlantic, 1964.

**£25–30** Spinna Disc Records ⊞

Marvin Gaye, 'Originals from Marvin Gaye', mono EP record, by Tamla Motown, 1964.

**£35–40** Spinna Disc Records ⊞

Little Stevie Wonder, 'I Call it Pretty Music But...The Old People Call it Blues', mono EP record, by Stateside, 1964.

**£135–150** Sweet Memories ⊞
*This was Stevie Wonder's first single.*

The Dudley Moore Trio, 'Genuine Dud', stereo LP record, by Decca, 1966.

**£25–30** Spinna Disc Records ⊞

The Temptations, 'The Temptations in a Mellow Mood', mono LP record, by Tamla Motown, 1967.

**£20–25** Spinna Disc Records ⊞

Cream, 'Disraeli Gears', stereo LP record, by Reaction, 1967.

**£50–60** Sweet Memories ⊞

The Kinks, 'The Village Preservation Society', mono LP record, by PYE, 1968.

**£180–200** Sweet Memories ⊞

Various Artists, 'The Unfolding of the Book of Life', Vol 1, LP record, by Island, 1969.

**£135–150** Sweet Memories ⊞
*This is a first issue on a pink label with the orange eye logo.*

Juicy Lucy, 'Lie Back and Enjoy It', stereo LP record, by Vertigo, with gatefold sleeve, 1970.

**£65–75** Sweet Memories ⊞

Marvyn Gaye, 'What's Going On', by Tamla Motown, 1st issue embossed sleeve and lyric insert sheet, 1971.

**£15–20** Collectors Corner ⊞

Budgie, 'Budgie', stereo LP record,
by MCA, 1971.
**£10–15 Spinna Disc Records** ⊞

Nancy Wilson, 'Nancy – Naturally', stereo LP
record, by Capitol, c1972.
**£10–15 Spinna Disc Records** ⊞

James Brown, 'Slaughter's Big Rip off',
original soundtrack, by Polydor, 1973.
**£15–20 Collectors World** ⊞

Giles Farnaby's Dream Band, 'Giles Farnaby's
Dream Band', steroe LP record, by Decca, 1973.
**£90–100 Sweet Memories** ⊞

Pink Floyd, 'The Best of Pink Floyd', stereo LP
record, by Colombia, 1974.
**£90–100 Sweet Memories** ⊞

Gil Scott-Heron, 'The Revolution Will Not be
Televised', by RCS, 1975.
**£10–15 Collectors World** ⊞

## ESSENTIAL REFERENCE | PICTURE DISCS

Saturnalia, 'Magical Love', 3-D 12in single
record picture disc, by Matrix, 1973, 12in.
**£45–50 Sweet Memories** ⊞
*This was the world's first 3-D picture disc.*

Marillion, 'Lavender', 12in picture disc single
record, by EMI records, 1985.
**£20–25 Sweet Memories** ⊞

Madonna, 'Cause a Commotion', 12in
picture disc single record, by Sire, 1987.
**£25–30 Sweet Memories** ⊞

• The first picture disc was Saturnalia's 'Magical Love', issued in 1971. It did not succeed because Saturnalia were an obscure band on an obscure label and, owing to the small numbers pressed, it is now a rare novelty record. The disc was reissued in 1973, but picture discs did not become popular until the 1980s.

• Picture discs were made by pressing a picture into vinyl, with a 3-D middle glued to the centre.

• Value depends on the recording artist – picture discs per se are not valuable.

• You should collect bands and music that you like – an affordable collection can easily be built this way. If you wish to collect for value, look for discs by famous artists and bands such as Madonna, Queen and Iron Maiden. During the 1980s records were issued in various formats, with picture discs being relatively scarce.

**Sweet Memories**

# ESSENTIAL REFERENCE PUNK & NEW WAVE

'The Roxy London WC2', compilation LP record, by EMI, 1977.
**£20–25** Sweet Memories ⊞

Radio Stars, 'Holiday Album', stereo LP record, by Chiswick, 1978.
**£25–30** Sweet Memories ⊞

Xray Spex, 'Germfree Adolescents', stereo LP record, by EMI, 1978.
**£25–30** Sweet Memories ⊞

- Punk and New Wave were a reaction to insipid Glam Rock.
- Punk arrived with the Sex Pistols, who caused a sensation when they appeared on the front pages of the Sunday newspapers.
- Initially people bought Punk records out of curiosity.
- Punk records are not widely collected at the moment, so it is possible to build a good collection for a modest investment.
- Most collectable is the Sex Pistols' 'God Save The Queen' on A & M records. Released in 1977 and withdrawn on the day of issue, a copy can fetch up to £6,000. In contrast, the same record on the Virgin label would be worth about £6.00.

**Sweet Memories**

'Catch a Wave', compilation double LP record, by Nice, 1978.
**£20–25** Sweet Memories ⊞

Iron Maiden, 'Stranger in a Strange Land', 12in single, by EMI, Japan, 1986, 12in.
**£45– 50** Sweet Memories ⊞

Pet Shop Boys, 'Introspective', cassette tape, by Parlophone, 1988.
**£65–75** Sweet Memories ⊞

Napalm Death, 'Harmony Corruption', stereo double LP record, 1990.
**£15–20** Spinna Disc Records ⊞

The Cross, 'New Dark Ages, 12in single record, by Electrola, Germany, 1991.
**£180–200** Sweet Memories ⊞
*The Cross featured Queen's Roger Taylor. This single was only issued in Germany.*

Jethro Tull, 25th anniversary four-CD boxed set, limited edition, by Chrysalis, 1993, 11½in (29cm) wide.
**£90–100** Sweet Memories ⊞

# ROCKS & FOSSILS

A carcharodon megalodon fossil tooth, c3 million years old, Florida, America.

**£140–160 Bloomsbury** 🔨

A mosasaur jaw, with 24 teeth, on natural matrix, Kouribdga Formation, Morocco, Cretaceous period, 100 million years old.

**£5,800–7,000 Sotheby's (S)** 🔨

A chrysocolla nodule freeform, on a metal stand, Congo, 18in (45.5cm) wide.

**£1,800–2,200 Sotheby's (S)** 🔨

A diplomystus dentatus, in sandstone matrix, Wyoming, America, Lower Eocene period, 55 million years old, 7 x 17½in (18 x 44.5cm).

**£300–360 Bloomsbury** 🔨

An ammonite, on a bronze base, Morocco, Jurassic period, 135 million years old, 30in (76cm) high.

**£2,000–2,400 Sotheby's (S)** 🔨

An audoliceras ammonite, Volga River, Russia, Jurassic period, 135 million years old, 18in (45.5cm) high.

**£5,500–6,500 Sotheby's (S)** 🔨

Two ammonites, on Devonian marble bases, Morocco, Jurassic Period, 135 million years old, 16in (40.5cm) high.

**£1,800–2,200 Sotheby's (S)** 🔨

A baby psittacosaurus, in a stone matrix, China, 130 million years old, 15in (38cm) long.

**£440–520 Mastro Auctions** 🔨

A keichousaurus, in a stone matrix, 240 million years old, 11 x 4in (28 x 10cm).

**£270–320 Mastro Auctions** 🔨

# SCIENTIFIC & MEDICAL

## SCIENTIFIC INSTRUMENTS

A torsion balance, model 0, 1930s, 14in (35.5cm) high.

**£15–20  Grimes Militaria** ⊞
*The torsion balance was invented in the 18th century to measure very weak forces. In the 20th century, the instrument's ability to measure the earth's natural gravity field was explained, and in the 1920s and '30s it was key in the early stages of petroleum exploration.*

A leather-covered pocket barograph, 0–2000ft, with original ink bottle charts, retailed by Negretti & Zambra, London, in a boxwood case with provenance, France, c1912, 7in (18cm) wide.

**£1,000–1,200  Richard Twort** ⊞

A desk barometer, by Zeiss Ikon, the glass case with chromed-steel border, on a chromed-steel base, maker's mark to glass, paper instructions to underside, Germany, c1930, 6¼in (16cm) high.

**£200–240  Rosebery's** 🔨

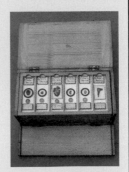

MEDICAL

# MEDICAL

A price list of chemical preparations, published by The British Drug Houses, London, 1917, 9in (23cm) high.

**£10–15** **J R & S J Symes** ⊞
*British Drug Houses was founded in 1908 as a wholesaler to private chemists. In the 1920s, they jointly manufactured newly discovered insulin with Allen & Hanburys (the A. B. Partnership).*

*Year Book and Medical Guide*, published by Ucal, 1934, 7in (18cm) high.

**£5–10** **J R & S J Symes** ⊞
*The string loop attached to the book indicates that it was hung up for reference.*

A Soda-Mint bottle, by Burroughs Wellcome & Co, post-1924, 2in (5cm) high.

**£1–5** **David Huxtable** ⊞
*Always read the small print. The Wellcome Foundation was established in 1924, which means that this bottle must post-date that year.*

A plastic life-size anatomical model of a woman, by Denoyer Geppert Co, with glass eyes, cut-away right side and torso, and numbered organs, damaged, missing pieces, marked, America, 1920s, on an ebonized base, 38in (96.5cm) high.

**£260–320** **Skinner** 🔨

A Heartometer, 1930s, 9½in (24cm) high.

**£260–320** **Mastro Auctions** 🔨
*This instrument was used to measure and record blood pressure, pulse rate, heart rate and vascular circulation.*

An anatomical head, on a metal stand, 1950, 23in (58.5cm) high.

**£175–195** **Curious Science** ⊞

A set of nickel-plated mobile operating tools, Germany, 1920, in a wooden case, 20in (51cm) wide.

**£2,000–2,250** **Curious Science** ⊞

A first aid booklet, 1930s, 5in (12.5cm) high.

**£1–5** **Tussie Mussies** ⊞

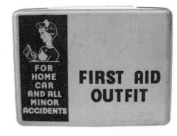

A First Aid Outfit, in a tin box, 1957, 8in (20.5cm) wide.

**£30–35** **Steptoes Dog** ⊞

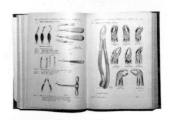

A medical catalogue, featuring surgical instruments, appliances and hospital equipment, published by Down Bros and Mayer & Phelps, London and Toronto, 1955, 10in (25.5cm) high.

**£45–50** **Early Technology** ⊞

# SHIPPING

A painted brass boat badge, from HMS *Frobisher*, c1925, 7in (18cm) high.

**£270–300 Books Afloat ⊞**

*Always turn things over – here the reverse is stamped with the ship's name, but you could easily miss it. Royal Naval Boat badges were actual ships' fittings and not to be confused with ships' presentation plaques. Usually cast from brass and painted, they would have been mounted on the port and starboard bows of the ships' boats. Badges command a strong following from collectors and are very sought-after items. If the associated ship had an interesting career or battle honours, this further increases value. Fakes do exist, so take care.*

A brass ship's oil lantern, by Bulpitt, c1900, 17in (43cm) high.

**£200–230 Oldnautibits ⊞**

A brass ship's bell, from the herring drifter *City of Perth*, Peterhead, 1907, 8in (20.5cm) diam.

**£360–400 Books Afloat ⊞**

## ESSENTIAL REFERENCE     REFIT RELICS

A wooden money box, made from the teak timbers of HMS *Snapdragon*, 1940s, 3in (7.5cm) high.

**£20–25 Oldnautibits ⊞**

*HMS* Snapdragon *was launched on 3 September 1940 and served in the Mediterranean during WWII. On 19 December 1942, she was attacked and sank.*

A wooden letter rack, made from the timbers of HMS *Iron Duke*, c1930, 5in (12.5cm) wide.

**£20–25 Oldnautibits ⊞**

*Admiral Jellicoe's flagship* Iron Duke *saw combat service at the Battle of Jutland in 1916. On 30 May 1928, she went through a refit.*

A wooden barrel, made from the bowsprit of HMS *Victory*, c1937, 2in (5cm) high.

**£15–20 Oldnautibits ⊞**

• Ships' fittings were built for a long and hard life at sea. Check build quality, materials used and signs of wear. If it is lightly made or looks very fresh, beware. There are many replica items on offer masquerading as original fittings.

• Where possible try to establish the vessel the item came from. In many cases this information has been lost, but if the ship's name can be confirmed this adds greatly to the interest and the value.

• Most nautical treen souvenirs date from the late Victorian era to WWII. They were produced commercially using timber salvaged from ships, either when broken up or taken when undergoing restoration or repair. They are almost always made from hardwood such as oak or teak.

• There is a wide variety of treen souvenirs available including napkin rings, candle holders and even a model lighthouse. They always have a brass or silver plaque with details of the vessel the wood came from, and if relevant any famous events during her career and a date.

• Treen souvenirs are still modestly priced and can form a unique and interesting collection, especially where funds or space are limited.

**Geoffrey Pringle  Oldnautibits**

A felt pennant, from HMS *Striker*, c1950, 17in (43cm) wide.
**£10–15 Oldnautibits ⊞**

A mahogany and brass ship's wheel, c1950, 36in (91.5cm) diam.
**£370–420 Oldnautibits ⊞**

A wooden working model of the battleship HMS *Warspite*, c1950s, 59in (150cm) long.
**£680–750 Q & C Militaria ⊞**
*The Queen Elizabeth class battleship HMS* Warspite *was built in 1913 and served at Jutland during WWI. In WWII she served in the Norway Campaign, Crete, the Mediterranean and the Battle of Calabria, where she achieved the longest range hit ever recorded from a moving warship to a moving target. She was nicknamed 'The Old Lady' by Admiral Sir Andrew Cunningham. In 1947, she was sold for scrap and finally broken up in 1950.*

A brass shipbuilder's plaque, from the bulk carrier *Nordic Chieftain*, 1974, 13in (33cm) wide.
**£270–300 Books Afloat ⊞**

A wooden working model of a paddle steamer, c1950, 39in (99cm) long.
**£270–300 Q & C Militaria ⊞**

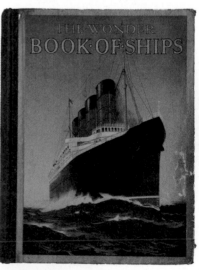

A Midland Railway Co photographic postcard, advertising the steamer route between England and Ireland, depicting the turbine steamer *Londonderry*, c1910.
**£35–40 Memories ⊞**

*The Wonder Book of Ships*, published by Ward Lock & Co, London, 1916, 10in (25.5cm) high, illustrated.
**£10–15 Cobwebs ⊞**

## ESSENTIAL REFERENCE — BAGGAGE LABELS

A Royal Mail Steam Packet Co adhesive baggage label, 1920s,
7in (18cm) wide.

**£5–10 Cobwebs** ⊞

A Royal Mail Steam Packet Co
celluloid baggage tag, with
leather strap, c1920s,
2in (5cm) diam.

**£25–30 Cobwebs** ⊞

A P&O baggage label,
1960s–70s, 5in (12.5cm) high.

**£1–5 Books Afloat** ⊞

• Baggage labels are issued by passenger shipping lines to help identify passengers' luggage for delivery to the cabin or if not wanted on voyage, to the luggage hold.

• Most labels found today tend to date from the 19th and 20th centuries.

• Some collectors specialize in a single line, while others built their collection across a vaiety, such as the White Star Line, the Royal mail Steam Packet Co, Cunard Line and others.

• Labels relating to specific ships such as the Blue Riband Holder Lusitania or famour ships such as RMS *Titanic*, will command a heavy premium.

• Labels can be very decorative, particularly those dating from the golden years of ocean travel, the 1930s.

• Try to find examples in mint condition. Some collectors expand their interest to include labels still tied or pasted to vintage luggage, which can be a great way of displaying the collection, if space allows.

**Geoffrey Pringle  Oldnautibits**

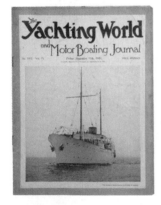

*The Yachting World and Motor Boating Journal*, 11 September 1931,
11 x 9in (28 x 23cm).

**£10–15 Home & Colonial** ⊞

A British Hovercraft Corporation publicity brochure, 1960s, 12 x 8in (30.5 x 20.5cm).

**£15–20 Cobwebs** ⊞

Six ABC booklets, 1950s–60s,
6 x 4in (15 x 10cm).

**£5–10 each Cobwebs** ⊞

A Union-Castle Safmarine leaflet, 1970s,
8in (20.5cm) high.

**£5–10 Cobwebs** ⊞

A Hoverspeed Hales Trophy Challenge brochure, 1990, 11in (28cm) high.

**£10–15 Cobwebs** ⊞

## LINERS

A Cunard Line passenger list, for the New York to Trieste voyage commanded by Captain A. H. Rostron, 1912, 9 x 6in (23 x 15cm).

**£220–270** Henry Aldridge ⚒

A White Star Line RMS *Britannic* launch brochure, 1914, 8 x 9in (20.5 x 23cm).

**£1,000–1,200** Henry Aldridge ⚒

A powder compact, from RMS *Pretoria Castle*, c1950, 3in (7.5cm) diam.

**£45–50** Cobwebs ⊞

A Victory jig-saw puzzle, decpicting the Cunard White Star Line *Queen Elizabeth*, 1950s, 7 x 9in (18 x 23cm).

**£20–25** Cobwebs ⊞

A pair of P&O silver-plated salt and pepper pots, from the SS *Iberia*, c1960, 2in (5cm) high.

**£25–30** Books Afloat ⊞

A Delft Holland-America Line souvenir platter, decorated with the SS *Rotterdam*, 1961, 12in (30.5cm) diam.

**£50–60** Books Afloat ⊞

A Cunard commemorative plate, by Eschenbach, made for the *Caronia* Millennium cruise, Germany, 1999, 12in (30.5cm) diam.

**£30–35** Cobwebs ⊞

A *Queen Mary II* maiden voyage commemorative spoon, limited edition of 100, 2004, 5in (12.5cm) long.

**£25–30** Cobwebs ⊞

A Red Star Line chocolate cup and saucer, by Stonier & Co, Liverpool, c1905, cup 3in (7.5cm) diam.

**£250–280** Books Afloat ⊞

A photographic postcard, by Charles and Russell, depicting the launch of RMS *Titanic*, 1911, 4 x 6in (10 x 15cm).
**£1,900–2,300 Henry Aldridge**
*The ship was launched from Belfast where she was built by Harland & Wolff.*

A Western Union telegraph, sent from the White Star Line to Senator J. A. Hughes, 1912, 5 x 9in (12.5 x 23cm).
**£10,000–12,000 Henry Aldridge**
*A letter of provenance accompanies this infamous telegram, which predicted the safe arrival of the Titanic at Halifax. It was sent on the same day that the ship sank, and a rumour subsequently circulated that the White Star Line was aware of the loss but withheld the information while the ship was reinsured.*

A Fosbery & Co life jacket, from RMS *Titanic*, cork blocks missing, 1912.
**£43,000–52,000 Henry Aldridge**
*This jacket was recovered by Robert Edwards, quartermaster of the cable ship* Mackay Bennett, *sent to recover victims of the* Titanic.

A hymn sheet, from a memorial service for the victims of RMS *Titanic*, 1912, 5in (12.5cm) wide.
**£15–20 M&C Cards**

Mrs Alma White, *The Titanic Tragedy, God Speaking to Nations*, published by The Pentecostal Union, New Jersey, America, 1912, 7½in (19cm) high.
**£135–150 Books Afloat**

## MARKET INFORMATION — TITANIC

- RMS *Titanic* has become the most famous ship in history, commanding huge interest worldwide. She sank on 10 April 1912 with 1635 passengers and crew.

- Following the discovery of the wreck by Dr Bob Ballard on 1 September 1985, media interest has increased significantly and the Hollywood movie further added to the ship's allure.

- Prior to the discovery of the wreck, collectors had a limited choice of material, mainy ephemera and items that were recovered from survivors or taken from the sea by rescuers. In recent years relics from the ship have been salvaged. Although the ethics of these actions are debatable, there is little doubt that these titems will, in the course of time, be offered on the collectors' market – at a price.

- When buying any *Titanic*-related items, be sure to check the provenance very thoroughly, as many film props are now being offered for sale which further complicates the picture. Buy from known and reliable sources and if it looks too good to be true, it probably is.

- RMS *Titanic* was owned and operated by the White Star Line. This association means that original White Star items are keenly collected and, while not cheap, are more affordable than *Titanic* memorabilia, which is fetching significant prices.

**Geoffrey Pringle  Oldnautibits**

# SMOKING

## CIGARETTE PACKETS

A W. D. & H. O. Wills Pirate Cigarettes packet, with contents, c1910.

**£280–330 Hunt Auctions** 🔨

A Sweet Caporal Cigarettes packet, with contents, America, 1910.

**£320–380 Hunt Auctions** 🔨

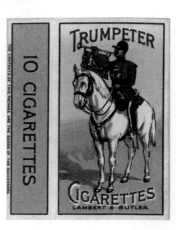

A Lambert & Butler Trumpeter Cigarettes packet, c1930.

**£15–20**
**Cigarette Packet Collectors** ⊞

A B. Morris & Sons Virginia Blend Fez Cigarettes packet, c1930.

**£20–25**
**Cigarette Packet Collectors** ⊞

A W. D. & H. O. Wills Gold Flake Cigarettes packet, c1930, 3in (7.5cm) high.

**£1–5 Collectables** ⊞

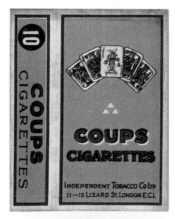

An Independent Tobacco Co Coups Cigarettes packet, c1930.

**£10–15**
**Cigarette Packet Collectors** ⊞

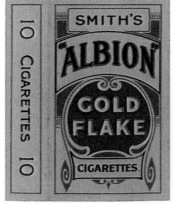

An F. & J. Smith's Albion Gold Flake Cigarettes packet, c1930.

**£10–15**
**Cigarette Packet Collectors** ⊞

A Hignett Bros & Co Memnon Cigarettes packet, c1935.

**£15–20**
**Cigarette Packet Collectors** ⊞

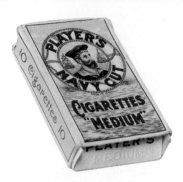

A Player's Navy Cut cigarette packet, 1930s–40s, 3in (7.5cm) high.
**£1–5  Collectables** ⊞

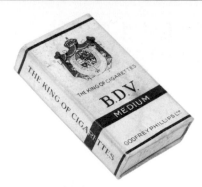

A Godfrey Phillips B.D.V. cigarette packet, 1930s, 3in (7.5cm) high.
**£1–5  Collectables** ⊞

A Player's Weights cigarette packet, pre-1939, 3in (7.5cm) high.
**£1–5  Soldiers of Rye** ⊞

A W. D. & H. O. Wills Pirate Cigarettes packet, c1950.
**£5–10**
**Cigarette Packet Collectors** ⊞

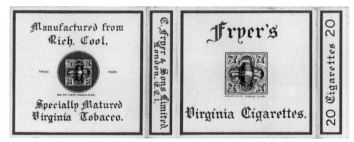

A C. Fryer & Sons Virginia Cigarettes packet, c1950.
**£5–10  Cigarette Packet Collectors** ⊞

A Woodbine Virginia Cigarettes packet, 1960s, 3in (7.5cm) high.
**£1–5  Collectables** ⊞

A Player's Cigarettes packet, 1970s, 3½in (9cm) wide.
**£1–5  Collectables** ⊞

## MARKET INFORMATION        CIGARETTE PACKETS

• Early cigarette packets, that is pre-1920, are sought after. Flip-top boxes from 1965 and after are considered less desirable.

• It is quite possible to build and affordable collection dating from 1920 to 1965, for prices ranging from as little as 10p to £10.00.

• Prices depend on age and scarcity. A Victorian item, in mint condition, was recently sold for £350.00.

• Generally speaking cigarette packets are currently collected by enthusiasts with established collections, but an amateur can build up a comprehensive collection quite quickly. Most UK collectors prefer British brands and those exported to English-speaking countries, so there is huge collecting potential for cigarette packets from the rest of the world.

• As always, buy from a reputable source and do not buy poor-quality items. If buying via the internet do look for a detailed description.
**Cigarette Packet Collectors**

# LIGHTERS

A composite Scottie dog petrol cigarette lighter, c1930,

**£145–160** Gazelles ⊞

A Lorenzl gilt-metal table cigarette lighter, in he form of a girl wearing a trouser suit, marked, Austria, 1930s, 8¼in (21cm) high.

**£320–390** Wellers Auctioneers ⚒

A Ronson Mastercase chrome lighter and cigarette case, with spark wheel brush, extra flint container and instruction booklet, 1930s, 4½in (11.5cm) high, boxed.

**£95–110** Vintage Swank ⊞

A Ronson Futura chrome table lighter, in the form of a speedboat, 1930s, 5½in (14cm) wide.

**£125–135** Vintage Swank ⊞

A Parker of London Silent Flame table lighter, the Bakelite base surmounted by a chrome figure of a woman, 1930s, 5in (12.5cm) high.

**£160–180** Vintage Swank ⊞
*The flame is produced when the wand touches the metal figure, which is charged by two batteries in the base.*

A cut-glass and chrome touch-tip table lighter, 1950s, 5in (12.5cm) high.

**£80–90** Vintage Swank ⊞

A glass table lighter, with dimpled sides, 1950s, 4½in (11.5cm) high.

**£45–50** Vintage Swank ⊞

A Barclay white metal and plastic petrol lighter, with on/off buttons, 1950s, 4in (10cm) wide.

**£50–55** Tony Durante ⊞

An American Safety Razor Co gilt-metal and plastic lighter, America, c1950, 3in (7.5cm) high.

**£20–25  Tony Durante** ⊞

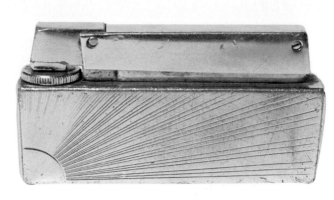

A Rowenta white metal petrol lighter, Germany, 1950s, 3in (7.5cm) long.

**£15–20  Tony Durante** ⊞

A Cygnus anodized metal table lighter, Japan, 1950s, 4½in (11.5cm) high.

**£75–85  Vintage Swank** ⊞

A Dorset Light Industries plastic and shagreen table lighter, 1950s, 4in (10cm) high.

**£135–150  Humbleyard** ⊞

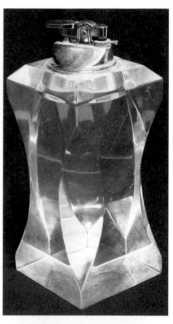

A Perspex lighter, 1960s, 7in (18cm) high.

**£30–35  Geoffrey Robinson** ⊞

A white metal lighter, modelled as the bust of a knight with visor, Japan, 1960s, 5in (12.5cm) high.

**£60–70  Tony Durante** ⊞

A plastic cigarette lighter, modelled as a postbox, 1970, 5in (12.5cm) high.

**£20–25  M&C Cards** ⊞

A Partner metal and *faux* tortoiseshell musical lighter, 1970s, 3½in (9cm) high.

**£15–20  Tussie Mussies** ⊞

## MATCH BOOKS & BOXES

A Norddeutscher Lloyd Bremen book of matches, Germany, 1930s, 2in (5cm) wide.

**£5–10 Cobwebs** ⊞

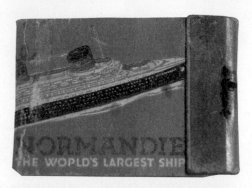

A Normandie Line book of matches, France, c1934, 2in (5cm) wide.

**£15–20 Cobwebs** ⊞

A Bibby Line matchbox, 1950, 2in (5cm) wide.

**£1–5 Books Afloat** ⊞

A New Zealand Shipping Co matchbox, c1950, 2in (5cm) wide.

**£1–5 Books Afloat** ⊞

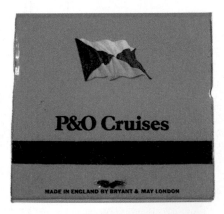

A Bryant & May Blue Star Line matchbox, c1950s, 2in (5cm) wide.

**£1–5 Books Afloat** ⊞

A Cunard Line matchbox, 1950s, 2in (5cm) wide.

**£1–5 Books Afloat** ⊞

A Bryant & May P&O Cruises matchbook, from the SS *Canberra*, c1970, 2in (5cm) wide.

**£1–5 Books Afloat** ⊞

A Ben Line Containers matchbook, 1970s, 2in (5cm) wide.

**£1–5 Books Afloat** ⊞

A Sealink ferry *St Edmund* matchbox, 1970s, 2in (5cm) wide.

**£1–5 Books Afloat** ⊞

# MISCELLANEOUS

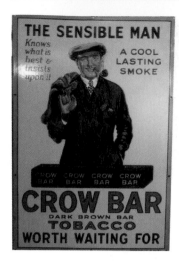

A cold-painted bronze novelty cigarette box, surmounted with a sphinx enclosing a maiden, over an Egyptian figural frieze, Austria, early 20thC, 6¼in (16cm) wide.

**£1,800–2,200  Gorringes (L)** ⚒

A Crow Bar Tobacco enamel advertising sign, early 20thC, 36 x 24in (91.5 x 61cm).

**£1,400–1,700  Gorringes (L)** ⚒

A W. D. & H. O. Wills Westward Ho! Smoking Mixture enamel advertising sign, 1920, 36in (91.5cm) high.

**£330–370  Junktion** ⊞

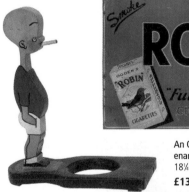

An Ogden's Robin Cigarettes tin and enamel advertising sign, 1920s, 18¼in (46.5cm) wide.

**£135–145  Dantinman** ⊞

A Salvador Rodriguez Charles the Great Cigars box, inside papers intact, NRA seal and tobacco stamp, America, 1920s–40s, 8½ x 5¼in (21.5 x 13.5cm).

**£15–20  Silversnow Antiques** ⊞

A wooden figure of Henry smoking a cigarette, ashtray missing, America, c1930, 9½in (24cm) high.

**£80–85 collectorsworld** ⊞
*The American comic strip character, Henry, was created by Carl Anderson and featured in an animated film and a book.*

An Ogden's Redbreast Flake enamel advertising sign, c1930, 38 x 130in (96.5 x 330cm).

**£120–145  Charterhouse** ⚒

A Gallaher's No. 8 Brown Shag tobacco tin, with embossed lid, small dent, 1930s, 6½ x 4¾in (16.5 x 12cm).

**£10–15  Tin Shop** ⊞

A Marcovitch Black & White Cigarettes tin, c1950, 4in (10cm) wide.

**£1–5  M&C Cards** ⊞

# SPORT

## BASEBALL – BALLS

A Pepper Martin & More baseball, signed, America, 1934, 9in (23cm) diam.

**£70–80** Heritage 🔨

A New York Giants baseball, signed, America, 1938, 9in (23cm) diam.

**£220–260** Heritage 🔨

A Cincinnati Reds National League Champions baseball, signed by the team, America, 1939.

**£300–360** Mastro Auctions 🔨

A baseball, signed by Harry Truman, America, 1946–59.

**£2,300–2,800** Heritage 🔨

A Minneapolis Lakers basketball, signed by the 56 players, America, 1956.

**£980–1,200** Heritage 🔨

A New York Yankees World Champions ball, inscribed 'World Champs 1958 N. Y. Yankees', signed by 27 players including Casey Stengal, Enos Slaughter, Whitey Ford and Mickey Mantle, America, 1958.

**£1,250–1,500** Mastro Auctions 🔨

A Cincinnati Reds baseball, signed by the team, America, 1970, 9in (23cm) diam.

**£60–70** Heritage 🔨

A New York Yankees baseball, signed by the team, America, 1976, 9in (23cm) diam.

**£300–360** Heritage 🔨

A National League All-Star team baseball, signed by 31 players including Bonds, Sandberg, Lasorda, Daulton, Glavine and Gwynn, America, 1993.

**£230–280** Hunt Auctions 🔨

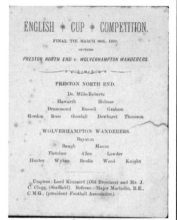

# BASEBALL – BATS, GLOVES, HATS & JERSEYS

A Houston Astros 'Shooting Star' home jersey, worn by Cesar Cendeno, America, 1972.

**£520–620 Mastro Auctions** 🔨

An Atlanta Braves game work road jersey, worn by Phil Neikro, America, 1980.

**£840–1,000 Mastro Auctions** 🔨

A Cardinals game jersey, worn, signed and dated by Ozzie Smith, America, 1995.

**£80–100 Heritage** 🔨

A Rawlings Texas Rangers Washington jersey, worn by Kevin Mench, America, 2002.

**£35–40 Heritage** 🔨

*As part of the Turn Back the Clock promotions that took place that year, the Texas Rangers sported these grey tops with navy-blue identifiers of 'Washington' on the front and number '28' on the reverse.*

A Clearwater Phillies Minor League jersey, worn by Ryan Howard, America, 2003.

**£1,450–1,800 Hunt Auctions** 🔨

A Boston Red Sox game cap, worn by Carl Yastrzemski, America, c1975.

**£980–1,200 Heritage** 🔨

A Ty Cobb Georgia Patch sample decal bat, America, 1910–28, 22in (56cm) long.

**£1,200–1,450 Mastro Auctions** 🔨

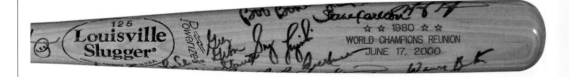

A Philadelphia Phillies team baseball bat, signed by the team, America, 1980.

**£380–450 Hunt Auctions** 🔨

A baseball bat, used by Larry Walker, decorated with transfers, slight damage, America, 2004–05, 42in (106.5cm) long.

**£60–70 Heritage** 🔨

A baseball bat, used and signed by David Eckstein, restored, America, 2005–06, 42in (106.5cm) long.

**£160–200 Heritage** 🔨

## EXPERT EYE    BOSTON BRAVES SILK UNIFORM

The number 29 stitched in black lined red twill points to this uniform being worn by pitcher Ernie White (nicknamed 'Cabbage Head'). Numbers first appeared on jerseys in 1916 (then discretely on the sleeve) but the trend didn't really take off until the New York Yankees took to field in 1929 with big numbers emblazoned on their backs.

The red trim on the shoulders and sleeve ends is the only detail that sets this jersey apart from the Club's standard flannel jerseys – they have their trim running along the side, the neck and the button panel.

A Boston Braves silk uniform, America, 1948.

**£3,400–4,000**
Mastro Auctions

The Braves' famous tomahawk logo was introduced in 1946 and was used until 1952.

This uniform was worn during the Braves 1948 night games. Playing at night beneath arc lighting was something that didn't happen before 1935. Shiny reflective fabrics like satin and silk were used for night games to add to the spectators' viewing pleasure. Script logos also began to appear on jerseys in the style of neon lighting. The collarless jersey style dates back to 1906 when it largely replaced fold down collars. On the inside of this neckline there's the label showing the manufacturer 'Horace Partridge' and a flap tag with the size 42 .

The handwritten note on the trouser's waistband suggests they link to Ray Sanders who played in the 1948 season.

The Boston Braves started life as the Boston Red Stockings in 1871. After various changes the team acquired the nickname 'Braves' in 1912, which they adopted and used, in the main, from then on. 1948 was a key year for the Boston Braves who secured their first National League pennant win since their victory in 1914. Game worn uniforms are always of interest to collectors, especially if they're in good original condition like this set. Knowing their history is vital. Here, the jersey number points to it being worn by Ernie White who played for the Braves from 1940 to 1948. The 1948 season was his last, and a historic one for the Braves, which adds to its cachet.

# BASEBALL – PRINTED MATERIAL

A photograph of Fred Tenney, America, 1900–20, 7 x 5in (18 x 12.5cm).

**£500–600**
Mastro Auctions 🔨

A photograph of Boss Schmidt, by Carl Horner Studios, America, 1910–20, 7 x 5in (18 x 12.5cm).

**£1,700–2,000**
Mastro Auctions 🔨

A photograph of the Crescents baseball team, America, 1907, 10 x 13in (25.5 x 33cm).

**£275–325** Hunt Auctions 🔨

A World Series ticket stub, America, 1913, 6½in (16.5cm) long.

**£450–550** Hunt Auctions 🔨

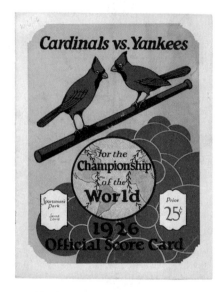

A World Series programme, America, 1926, 8in (20.5cm) high.

**£380–450** Mastro Auctions 🔨

A World Series ticket stub, America, 1927, 6½in (16.5cm) long.

**£400–500** Hunt Auctions 🔨

A New York Giants vs Brooklyn Dodgers Opening Day ticket, America, 1955, 7½in (19cm) wide.

**£345–525** Hunt Auctions 🔨

A New York Yankees team panorama photograph, America, 1972, 7¼ x 35in (18.5 x 89cm).

**£1,750–2,000** Mastro Auctions 🔨
*This photograph was once owned by Micky Mantle.*

A United States passport, for Joe DiMaggio, America, 1979, together with a letter of authentication from the family.

**£1,600–1,900** Hunt Auctions 🔨

# BASEBALL – MISCELLANEOUS

A Boston Braves pennant, America,
1914–15, 29in (74cm) long.

**£920–1,100** Hunt Auctions

A Boston Braves leather pillow top,
decorated with a photograph of the World
Champion 'Miracle Braves' of 1914, America,
22in (56cm) square.

**£1,550–1,850** Hunt Auctions

A silver-plated baseball trophy, presented
to Carl Noden, inscribed 'For Making the
Highest Pitching Average in the Factory
League E. Moline, Ill', slight damage,
America, 1916.

**£160–190** Hunt Auctions

A Reach baseball trophy, America, 1930,
19in (48.5cm) high.

**£280–330** Hunt Auctions

A New York Yankees canvas and leather
equipment bag, attributed to Joe DiMaggio,
America, 1940s–50s.

**£400–480** Hunt Auctions

A New York Mets World Series trophy,
inscribed 'Darryl Strawberry', America, 1986,
7¼in (18.5cm) diam.

**£5,400–6,500** Mastro Auctions

A Salvino figure of Mickey Mantle, No. 1480 of 1732
with an autographed plaque, America, 1991,
7½in (19cm) high.

**£260–300** Hunt Auctions

A Washington Nationals RFK Stadium 2005 Inaugural Season baseball,
with a Washington Nationals tin money box, 2005, 3in (7.5cm) diam.

**£5–10** collectorsworld

# BASKETBALL

**An Acme Thunderer celluloid whistle,** used by James Naismith, America, c1900.

**£6,600–8,000 Heritage** ⚒

*This whistle was used by Dr Naismith when he coached and refereed basketball at the University of Kansas. It bears the seal of the retailer Lowe & Campbell Sorting Goods, Lawrence, Kansas. For more information on the Acme Thunderer celluloid whistle see page 309.*

**Five Reach Basketball Guides,** owned by James Naismith, America, 1905–10, 18 x 26in (45.5 x 66cm).

**£4,800–5,800 Heritage** ⚒

**A photograph of James Naismith and his family,** America, 1930, 7 x 4½in (18 x 11.5cm).

**£2,100–2,500 Heritage** ⚒

**A Spalding basketball,** signed by Bill Russell and Wilt Chamberlain, America, 1950s.

**£700–850 Hunt Auctions** ⚒

**A New York Knicks home jersey,** worn by Bill Bradley, America, early 1970s.

**£2,300–2,750 Mastro Auctions** ⚒

**A Spalding New York Knicks Championship basketball,** signed by B. Bradley, W. Reed, E. Monroe, W. Frazier, R. Holtzman and D. Debusschere, America, 1970s.

**£275–325 Hunt Auctions** ⚒

**An Air Jordan poster,** signed by 43 basketball coaches including Jim Valvano, America, early 1990s, 24½ x 22¼in (62 x 56.5cm).

**£380–450 Mastro Auctions** ⚒

# BOXING

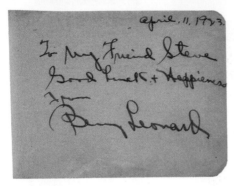

An autograph album page, inscribed and signed by Benny Leonard, April 11, 1923, 4 x 5in (10 x 12.5cm).

**£25–30 Heritage** 🔨

*Widely regarded as one of the finest lightweight pugilists who ever entered the ring, Benny Leonard fought over 210 bouts, only being knocked out four times. The Hall of Fame dubbed him the 'Ghetto Wizard' for his scuffling through the streets of the East Side of New York City.*

A Joe Louis v Max Schmeling souvenir matchbook, 1936, 3½ x 5½in (9 x 14cm).

**£30–35 Heritage** 🔨

A leather boxing head guard, 1930s–40s.

**£100–115 Alan Pezaro** ⊞

A pair of leather boxing gloves, 1930–40.

**£80–90 Alan Pezaro** ⊞

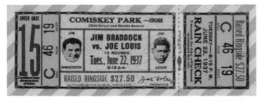

A Joe Louis v Jim Braddock World Heavyweight Championship ticket, America, 1937, 7in (18cm) wide.

**£450–550 Heritage** 🔨

A Rocky Marciano v Jersey Joe Walcott Heavyweight Championship ticket, America, 1953, 5½in (14cm) wide.

**£10–15 Heritage** 🔨

A pair of leather boxing gloves, 1950s, 9in (23cm) long.
**£25–30** Sporting Antiques ⊞

A Muhammad Ali and Sir Henry Cooper presentation, containing two Everlast boxing gloves signed by both fighters, with a photograph of the famous knock down signed by Sir Henry Cooper, mounted, 1960s, framed and glazed, 33¾ x 47¼in (86 x 120cm).
**£950–1,150** Graham Budd 🔨

A Golden Gloves Trophy, won by Cassius Clay, inscribed 'City of Louisville, Golden Gloves, Novice Division, Winner 1957', 13¼in (33.5cm) high, together with a letter of authenticity.
**£4,200–5,000** Heritage 🔨

An unused World's Heavyweight Championship Clay v Liston ticket, together with an envelope from the promoter, Chris Dundee, America, 1964, 7in (18cm) long.
**£4,500–5,500** Heritage 🔨

A Muhammad Ali and Joe Frazier 'Thrilla in Manila' poster, by LeRoy Nieman, 1975, 22 x 14in (56 x 35.5cm).
**£80–90** Heritage 🔨

## ESSENTIAL REFERENCE | COLLECTING ALI

A Denys Fisher plastic action figure of Muhammad Ali, 1976, 10in (25.5cm) high.
**£170–185** Magic Toy Box ⊞

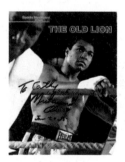

A Sports Illustrated magazine cover, signed and inscribed by Muhammad Ali, 1985, 11¾in (29.5cm) high.
**£65–75** Heritage 🔨

An Everlast boxing glove, signed by Muhammad Ali, 1990.
**£260–310** Heritage 🔨

• Muhammad Ali was arguably the greatest heavyweight boxer of all time. The combination of his talent, intelligence and personality brought him worldwide fame.

• Early material is usually the most expensive, following the general rule that the earlier the item, the more sought after it is.

• Fight-worn robes, trunks, shoes, etc are among the most collectable items, followed by tickets from key fights, programmes and posters. The most valuable posters are those that were used at the venue on the night of the fight. More common and therefore less expensive are the closed circuit television posters that were used all over the United States.

• The most popular signed items from the last 20 years include boxing gloves, photographs, programmes, posters and even baseballs. Ali's doodlings with signature, although common, make for very interesting display pieces and remain popular. The value of his autograph continues to climb even though they are plentiful there is little, if any, downside to buying at current prices.

• Authenticity is very important and it is recommended that high-end memorabilia be purchased from well-known auction houses. Autographs should have a letter of authenticity from a reputable company.

**Brian Marren, Mastro Auctions**

# CRICKET

A set of six Victorian waistcoat buttons, decorated with images of batsmen, ½in (1.5cm) diam.

**£175–200  Alan Pezaro ⊞**

A Victorian walnut inkwell in the form of a cricket ball, the well supported on crossed cricket bats, the pen rests carved as bales, 7in (18cm) wide.

**£240–270  Alan Pezaro ⊞**

A ceramic plate, commemorating the six for 24 score made by Sydney F. Barnes in Australia in 1908, c1910, 6in (15cm) diam.

**£150–165  Alan Pezaro ⊞**

*Sydney F. Barnes (1873–1967) was a famous international bowler.*

A photograph of the South African cricket team, signed by Deane, Catterall, Nupen, Carter, Taylor, Nourse, Commaille, Blackenberg, Ward, Bissett, Hands and Meintjes, 1924, 10 x 13½in (25.5 x 34cm).

**£300–360  Graham Budd ⚒**

A W. D. & H. O. Wills Woodbine Cigarettes tinplate advertising cricket game scorer, 1930s–40s, 6in (15cm) wide.

**£80–90  Alan Pezaro ⊞**

A cricket bat, signed by the England and Australia Test teams, 1934, 34¼in (87cm) high.

**£650–780  Graham Budd ⚒**

A Burleigh ware jug, 'The Cricketer', 1930s, 8in (20.5cm) high.

**£2,000–2,200  Gazelles ⊞**

A cricket ball, signed by Ian Botham and inscribed 'Oval', on a wooden plinth with an engraved plaque, 1986, 2¾in (7cm) diam.

**£650–780  Graham Budd ⚒**

*This ball was hit by Ian Botham for 24 runs in an over off Derek Stirling during the England v New Zealand Test at The Oval, London.*

FISHING

## FISHING

A Hardy No. 7 The Pope two-piece split fly rod, with original canvas sleeve, c1950, 120in (305cm) long.

**£20–25 Rosbery's** 🔨

A Salter brass fishing scale, c1920, 10in (25.5cm) long.

**£60–70 Manfred Schotten** ⊞

A fishing rod tube, c1930, 8in (20.5cm) long.

**£30–35 Sporting Antiques** ⊞

An Allcock packet of hooks, in the form of a trout fisher's creel, the creel lid opening to reveal contents, 1930s, 3½ins (9cm) wide.

**£35–40 Old Tackle Box** ⊞

A box of fishing fly tying materials, 1930s, 4in (10cm) square.

**£60–70 Manfred Schotten** ⊞

A Hardy wooden trout releaser, early 1940s, 4½in (11.5cm) diam.

**£40–45 Old Tackle Box** ⊞
*This item was used for retrieving snagged trout or salmon flies. The Hardy name has been stamped, but it was not catalogued. The style and crude construction indicate that it was made during WWII.*

A J. W. Young Gildex alloy and steel multiplier, with angled end plates and a hinged fold-away foot, in original case, c1950, 2½ins (6.5cm) diam.

**£25–30 Old Tackle Box** ⊞

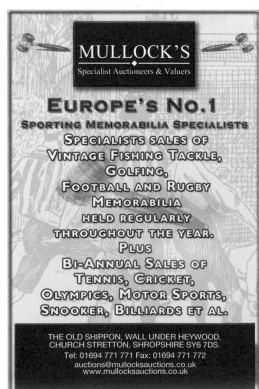

# AMERICAN FOOTBALL

A photograph of the Boston Yanks football team, America, 1945, 8 x 16in (20.5 x 40.5cm).

**£145–175 Hunt Auctions** ⚒

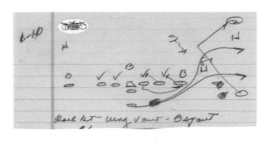

A hand-drawn football manoeuvre, by Vince Lombardi, America, 1958, 3½in (9cm) high.

**£50–60 Heritage** ⚒

A cheque paid to the McDonald Florist, signed by Vince Lombardi, America, 1960, 8in (20.5cm) long.

**£145–175 Heritage** ⚒

*Vince Lombardi (1913–70) was one of American football's most successful head coaches. He led the Green Bay Packers to three consecutive NFL Championship wins in 1965, 1966 and 1967 – a record that is still unbroken today.*

A signed photograph of the Green Bay Packers, entitled 'Kings in Court' and signed by Hofers Bart Starr, Paul Hornung, Forrest Gregg, Jim Taylor, and Jim Ringo, as well as Fuzzy Thurston, Bob Skroronski, Ron Kamer, Boyd Dowler, Max McGee and Jerry Kramer, together with a letter of authenticity, America, 1962, 20 x 16in (51 x 40.5cm).

**£160–200 Heritage** ⚒

A New York Jets Super Bowl III salesman's sample trophy, America, 1969, 18in (45.5cm) high.

**£1,500–1,800 Mastro Auctions** ⚒

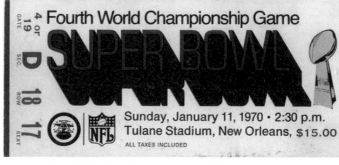

A Super Bowl IV football ticket stub, America, 1970, 4½in (11.5cm) long.

**£100–120 Heritage** ⚒

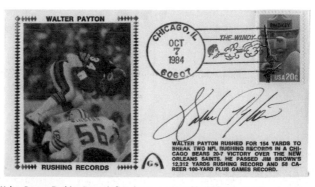

A Walter Payton Rushing Records first day cover, signed by Walter Payton, America, 1984, 5in (12.5cm) wide.

**£60–70 Heritage** ⚒

A leather football, used in the University of Chicago v University of Illinois game, 3 November 1917, America, 16in (40.5cm) long.

**£480–570 Mastro Auctions** 🔨

A Philadelphia Eagles jersey, worn by Bill Bradley, America, 1974–75.

**£250–300 Hunt Auctions** 🔨

An Oakland Raiders jersey, worn by Jim Otto, signed and inscribed 'H.O.F. 1980', America.

**£30–35 Heritage** 🔨

A San Francisco 49'ers helmet, signed by the team, America, 1987.

**£100–120 Heritage** 🔨

A San Francisco 49'ers Super Bowl World Championships football, signed by the team, America, 1989, 16in (40.5cm) long.

**£230–270 Heritage** 🔨

An official World League football, America, 1990, 16in (40.5cm) wide.

**£25–30 Heritage** 🔨

A Riddell NFL 75th Anniversary helmet, signed by 32 players including Unitas, Greene, Van Buren, J. Brown, Olsen, Burkas, Rice and Graham, America, 1994.

**£245–300 Hunt Auctions** 🔨

A New York Rangers home jersey, worn by Mark Messier, signed, America, 1995–96.

**£1,300–1,600 Mastro Auctions** 🔨

# ASSOCIATION FOOTBALL

A leather football, c1930.

**£40–45 Sporting Antiques** ⊞

A pair of leather football boots, with leather studs, 1950s.

**£145–160 Alan Pezaro** ⊞

A No. 8 international jersey, worn by Bryn Allen in the Wales v Scotland season, 1950–51.

**£600–720 Budd Auctions** 🔨

A World Cup Winners shirt, signed by nine England finalists, 1966.

**£180–220 Budd Auctions** 🔨

A leather football, signed by Pelé and the Santos team, 1975, 11in (28cm) diam.

**£350–420 Budd Auctions** 🔨

A Welsh International cap, worn by Terry Yorath, inscribed '1976–1977'.

**£650–780 Budd Auctions** 🔨

A Leeds United Premier League football shirt, worn by Gary McAllister, 1990–96.
**£30–35 Rosebery's** ⊞
*Gary McAllister played for Leeds United between 1990 and 1996.*

An England No. 8 jersey, worn by Paul Ince, 1993–94.
**£300–360 Budd Auctions** 🔨

A football boot, worn by Sir Stanley Matthews, together with a certificate of authenticity signed by Sir Stanley's daughter, Mrs Jean Gough for the Sir Stanley Matthews Auction, 17th October 2000.
**£1,000–1,200 Budd Auctions** 🔨

An Everton No 18 jersey, worn by Wayne Rooney, 2003–04.
**£200–240 Budd Auctions** 🔨

An Arsenal No. 28 Community Shield jersey, worn by Kolo Toure, 2004.
**£150–180 Budd Auctions** 🔨

An England v Croatia Euro 2004 No. 9 jersey, worn by Wayne Rooney and inscribed 'Croatia v England 21.06.2004'.
**£500–600 Budd Auctions** 🔨

An England v Croatia Euro 2004 No. 7 jersey, worn by David Beckham, inscribed 'Croatia v England 21.6.2004'.
**£500–600 Budd Auctions** 🔨

## MARKET INFORMATION          FOOTBALL COLLECTABLES

• Do buy from a reputable source, such as a good auction house or dealer. When making internet purchases be cautious, ask as many questions as possible and ask for provenance. The older the item the better.

• Pre-1960s football programmes are currently sought after, particularly England International Matches and FA Cup Final programmes.

• Modern players' jerseys are currently unpopular, owing to the number of replica jerseys available. These tend to be confused with player-issued items.

• Fans are keen collectors, particularly of memorabilia relating to their particular club, although some do collect items with a broader appeal.

• A world record price of £19,000 was recently paid for a mint copy of the 1889 FA Cup Final programme.

**Graham Budd, Budd Auctions**

A photograph of the first Chelsea team, 1905–06, 28 x 36in (71 x 91.5cm).

**£4,200–5,000 Budd Auctions** 🔨
*Chelsea Football Club was started by businessman and sporting enthusiast Henry Augustus Mears, who had built Stamford Bridge Stadium but failed to persuade Fulham Football Club to move from their Craven Cottage ground. He managed to get Football League status for Chelsea and they started in the Second Division in 1905–06. This is the first team group photograph and features Chelsea's famous first goalkeeper, Fatty Foulke.*

A photograph of the crowd at the Chelsea v Stockport County match, at Stamford Bridge, London, 2nd September 1911, 10 x 12in (25.5 x 30.5cm).

**£150–180 Budd Auctions** 🔨

A Burnley Football Club League Champions winning team photograph, 1920–21, 18 x 24in (45.5 x 61cm), in original frame.

**£1,800–2,200 Budd Auctions** 🔨

An official photograph of the Burnley and Celtic Select teams, at the Patrick Gallacher Benefit Match at Celtic Park, 5 May 1921, 14 x 16in (35.5 x 40.5cm).

**£360–430 Budd Auctions** 🔨

An international programme for England v Scotland, at Wembley Stadium, London, 31 March 1928, 20½in (52cm) high.

**£700–840 Budd Auctions** 🔨

An international programme for Switzerland v England, played at the Stadium Neufield, Bern, 21 July 1945, 20½in (52cm) high.

**£1,600–1,900 Budd Auctions** 🔨

An international programme for Italy v England, played at the Studio Comunale di Torino, Italy, 14 June 1973, 20½in (52cm) high.

**£300–360 Budd Auctions** 🔨

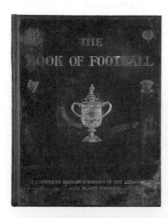

*The Book of Football: A Complete History and Record of the Association and Rugby Games*, published by The Amalgamated Press, 1906, original gilt- and silver-tooled pictorial cloth, rebound.

**£150–180 Budd Auctions** ⚒

An illustration of public school football colours, 1925, framed.

**£55–65 Sporting Antiques** ⊞

A metal and enamel Football Association Steward Final Tie pin badge, 1929, 1½in (4cm) high.

**£230–250 Toys & Hobbies** ⊞

A Coppa Del Mondo official report for the 1934 World Cup, published by the F.I.G.C., Italy, 1934.

**£240–290 Budd Auctions** ⚒

A metal and enamel Football Association Steward Final tie pin badge, 1935, 1½in (4cm) high.

**£200–220 Toys & Hobbies** ⊞

W. A. & A. C. Churchman, Association Footballers, set of 50, 1938.

**£35–40 Soldiers of Rye** ⊞

W. D. & H. O. Wills, Association Footballers, set of 50, 1939.

**£60–70 Soldiers of Rye** ⊞

A metal and enamel Football Association Steward badge, 1951, 1½in (4cm) high.

**£90–100** Toys & Hobbies ⊞

A metal and enamel Football Association Steward badge, 1953, 1in (2.5cm) high.

**£70–80** Toys & Hobbies ⊞

A commemorative World Cup Willie medal, 1965, 2½in (6.5cm) diam.

**£25–30** Toys & Hobbies ⊞

A Washington Pottery World Cup Willie dish, 1965, 4¾in (12cm) diam.

**£60–70** Toys & Hobbies ⊞

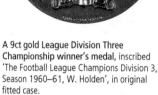

A 9ct gold League Division Three Championship winner's medal, inscribed 'The Football League Champions Division 3, Season 1960–61, W. Holden', in original fitted case.

**£850–1,000** Budd Auctions 🔨

A Shredded Wheat World Cup Willie jigsaw, 1965–66, puzzle 9¼in (23.5cm) wide, with original envelope.

**£25–30** Toys & Hobbies ⊞

*The Sun* 3D Gallery of Football Stars, George Best, set of 50, 1973, 5¾in (14.5cm) high.

**£1–5** M&C Cards ⊞

An England v Cameroon sponsor's commemorative gilt medal, inscribed 'The Guinness International, England V Cameroon, Wembley Stadium, 6 February 1991', with ribbon suspension, 1991, in original fitted case.

**£40–50** Budd Auctions 🔨

A FIFA Congress medal, presented to Paulo Cesar at Munich, June 2006, 3in (7.5cm) diam.

**£100–120** Budd Auctions 🔨

## EXPERT EYE    WORLD CUP WILLIE – 1966

This item is rare and in good condition – the mascot on the top detaches easily and is often lost. This is a popular cross-over collectable appealing to a number of interest groups – fans of football, tin collectors and advertising enthusiasts.

Look closely at this tin – it is in pristine original condition with no scratches or damage to the lithography.

**MADE IN GREAT BRITAIN**

With an increasing number of products coming from the Far East, Lovell's proudly displayed the 'Made in Great Britain' stamp as an indicator of good quality.

A Lovell's Toffees World Cup Willie tin, 1966, 7in (18cm) high.
**£500–600  Toys & Hobbies** ⊞

Lovell's had a long association with football, producing their own amateur team from sweet workers in their Newport toffe factory in the pre-WWII years. The club played with great success, winning the Welsh Football league six times (including 1966) before closing in 1969.

All items carry the FA logo and copyright.

World Cup Willie was designed to promote the 1966 World Cup and was the first character ever developed for a live sporting event. Although hundreds of items were made, they were all only available for just one year. World Cup Willie appeared on a huge range of items from T-shirts to balloons and, somewhat bizarrely, adorning packets of ladies stockings. In 1966, when England won the World Cup for the first, and so far only time, Willie was the mascot for the whole event. He reappeared briefly for the Mexican World Cup of 1970 but, unlike his previous appearance, was mascot for the English team only.

# GOLF

An 18thC-style square-toe iron, with a hickory shaft, c1880, 39in (99cm) long.
**£320–360 Grimes Militaria** ⊞

A golf iron with a silver head, Birmingham 1914.
**£500–600 Budd Auctions** ⚒

A G. Patterson of Eyemouth T-shaped putter, 1914.
**£440–530 Budd Auctions** ⚒

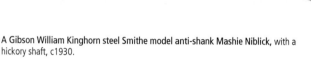

A Gibson William Kinghorn steel Smithe model anti-shank Mashie Niblick, with a hickory shaft, c1930.
**£55–65 Sherwood Golf Antiques** ⊞

A pair of adjustable Euro clubs, 1960.
**£120–145 Budd Auctions** ⚒
*The club at the bottom is a prototype, the other is the final product. It is believed that this type of club never went into commercial production.*

A 24ct gold-plated presentational golf club, inscribed 'Joe DiMaggio 14th Italian Invitational 1972' and 'Canadian Club 24ct gold plt' to the reverse, America, with original box and letter of authentication from the DiMaggio family.
**£260–300 Hunt Auctions** ⚒
*This is a cross-over collectable that appeals collectors of both golf and baseball, as well as fans of Marilyn Monroe, who was married to DiMaggio briefly in 1954.*

A golf bag, owned by Joe DiMaggio, together with 13 irons and putters, 4 woods, various golf balls, tees and Joe DiMaggio identification tournament tags, together with a letter of authentication, America, c1970.
**£320–380 Hunt Auctions** ⚒

A bronzed spelter figure of a golfer, on a wooden base, America, c1925, 8in (20.5cm) high.
£200–240 Alan Pezaro ⊞

A silver golfing trophy, America, c1928, 7in (18cm) high.
£300–350 Alan Pezaro ⊞

A Hagenauer nickel figure of a lady golfer, Austria, c1930, 9in (23cm) high.
£720–800 James Strang ⊞

A silver-plated cruet set, modelled as three golf balls, with crossed golf clubs handle, c1930, 5in (12.5cm) high.
£250–280 Alan Pezaro ⊞

A chrome-plated cast-brass car mascot, in the form of a golfer, 1930s, 5in (13cm) high.
£90–100 Charterhouse ⚒

A chrome-plated cast-brass car mascot, in the form of a golfer standing on a Dunlop 31 golf ball, 1930s, 3½in (9cm) high.
£45–50 Charterhouse ⚒

A porcelain jug and bowl, decorated with golfers, c1910, bowl 4in (10cm) diam.

**£130–145** Bac to Basic ⊞

A Royal Doulton Kingsware jug and two beakers, by Charles Crombie, decorated in relief with a golfing scene, 1920s, mug 6in (15cm) high.

**£800–900** Manfred Schotten ⊞

A Goldscheider porcelain figure of a golfer, Austria, c1930, 10½in (26.5cm) high.

**£1,150–1,300** Banana Dance ⊞

A Royal Doulton Series Ware fruit bowl, by Charles Noke, decorated with a golfing scene, inscribed 'All Fools are not Knaves but all Knaves are Fools, He that Complains is Never Pitied', 1930, 8in (20.5cm) diam.

**£180–200** Budd Auctions ⚒

A photograph of Sandy Herd, signed, 1936, 10 x 8in (25.5 x 20.5cm).

**£120–145** Budd Auctions ⚒
*Sandy Herd was the 1902 Open Champion.*

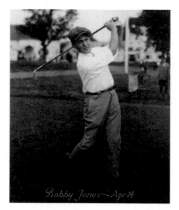

A photograph of Bobby Jones, America, 1920s, 9½ x 7½in (24 x 19cm).

**£260–300** Mastro Auctions ⚒

A photographof Bobby Jones, aged 14, by G. Pietzcher, 1930s, with a letter of provenance, 20 x 16in (51 x 40.5cm).

**£1,800–2,000** Hunt Auctions ⚒

A photograph of Max R. Marston, by G. Pietzcher, 1930s, with a letter of provenance, 20 x 16in (51 x 40.5cm).

**£860–1,000** Hunt Auctions ⚒
*This is one of a series of photographs of golf champions.*

John Player & Sons, Golf, set of 25, 1939.

**£135–150** Collectors World ⊞

A Ryder Cup flag, signed by the European team, 2006, framed, 34 x 39in (86.5 x 99cm).

**£2,100–2,500** Budd Auctions ⚒

# HOCKEY

A Toronto Maple Leafs hockey goalkeeper's mask, worn by Bernie Parent, America, 1971.

**£6,400–7,600 Hunt Auctions** ⚖

A Philadelphia Blazers hockey jersey, America, 1972–73.

**£1,250–1,500 Hunt Auctions** ⚖

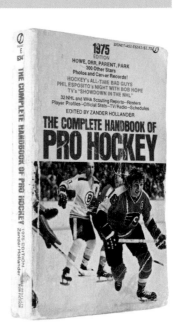

Zander Hollander, *The Complete Handbook of Hockey*, signed by several hockey stars including Denis Potvin, Billy Smith, Bob Nystrom, Guy LaFleur, Tony Esposito, Stan Mikita, Phil Esposito and Bibby Hull, America, 1975.

**£55–65 Heritage** ⚖

A Philadelphia Firebirds hockey jersey, said to have been worn by Mike Penasse, America, 1976–77.

**£580–700 Hunt Auctions** ⚖

Topps Bubblegum, 36 unopened wax packs of Hockey cards, 1980–81, 6in (15cm) high.

**£190–230 Hunt Auctions** ⚖

A Dallas Stars outdoor playoffs banner, inscribed 'Aim to Reclaim', making reference to their 1998–99 National Hockey League title, America, 2001, 99 x 31in (251.5 x 78.5cm).

**£25–30 Heritage** ⚖

A Hockey Hall of Fame First Day Cover, signed by Gordie Howe, Maurice Richard, Jean Beliveau, Bobby Hull and Bobby Orr, America, 1984, 7½in (19cm) wide.

**£50–60 Heritage** ⚖

# HORSE RACING

Two brass and enamel Newbury horse racing badges, 1915, 1in (2.5cm) square.

**£35–40 Malcolm Welch** ⊞

Gallagher, Famous Jockeys, set of 48, 1936, 2½in (6.5cm) high.

**£45–50 Soldiers of Rye** ⊞

## ESSENTIAL REFERENCE    KENTUCKY DERBY

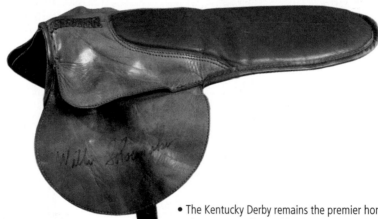

A leather racing saddle, worn by the 1986 Kentucky Derby winner, Ferdinand, ridden by Willie Shoemaker, displayed in a clear plastic case, America, 1986, 16¼in (41.5cm) square case.

**£5,200–6,200 Mastro Auctions** 🔨

• The Kentucky Derby remains the premier horse race in North America and, possibly, the world. The race attracts the best three-year-olds in the world and is bet on by millions of fans each year. It is the first leg in horse racing's Triple Crown – this fact alone conspires to make it the most collected race in the sport. Even casual sports fans are impressed by the grandeur of the day.

• There is a wide range of memorabilia available to everyone from the occasional race fan to the serious horse racing collector. Some of the most popular Kentucky Derby collectables are items that were at the race, including the commemorative glasses that go back several decades. Race-day programmes are popular to collect and date to when the race started in the late 19th century, as are uncashed Derby tickets for the winning horse. Programmes and tickets are subject to wear and tear and those in good condition command a premium.

• Some of the most expensive memorabilia associated with the Kentucky Derby are items worn by jockeys or even saddles. Items worn by a jockey whose horse went on to win the Triple Crown command huge premiums. For instance, the saddle used by Willie Shoemaker in 1986 to win the Kentucky Derby on Ferdinand was recently sold at auction for over £5,000. Provenance of these items is the key to value.

• The last Triple Crown winner was Affirmed in 1978, making any Triple Crown memorabilia scarce and expensive. Jen Cruget's Kentucky Derby jockey's trophy was sold for £37,500 after he rode Seattle Slew to a Derby and then Triple Crown win in 1977.

• The most expensive Kentucky Derby collectable would be an owner's trophy. These have changed hands in private sales for over £50,000. A Triple Crown winner's trophy would also command a large premium.

**Brian Marren, Mastro Auctions**

# OLYMPICS

A Pathe Baby 9mm film of the Olympic Association Football competition, the reel inscribed 'VIIIth Olympiad, Paris, 1924, Association Football', France, 1924.

**£420–500** Budd Auctions ⚒

A Berlin Olympics participation medal, designed by Otto Placzek, decorated with five athletes, inscribed 'XL Olympiade Berlin 1936', the reverse with a bell and the 3rd Reich eagle holding the five Olympic rings, Germany, 1936.

**£140–165** Wellers Auctioneers ⚒

An Olympic Games commemorative *Puukko* knife, by Iiasakki Jarvenpaa, the handle engraved with Olympic rings and the 1940 mark, the leather scabbard decorated with the Finnish flag, Finland, Helsinki, 1940, 10½in (27cm) long.

**£155–185** Bloomsbury ⚒
*The planned Tokyo Olympics of 1940 were cancelled after Japan invaded China. They were rescheduled for Helsinki but cancelled after Russia's invasion. They were the only Olympic Games to be cancelled twice.*

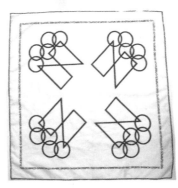

A nylon Olympic scarf, by Lila Howard, New York, America, 1980, 29in (73.5cm) square.

**£20–25** Twinkled ⊞

An Olympic Games official souvenir programme, for the London Olympic Games, 1948, 11¼ x 8½in (28.5 x 21.5cm).

**£30–35** John Smart ⊞

The Atlanta Olympics opening ceremony torch, used by Mohammad Ali, America, 1996, 22in (56cm) long.

**£1,800–2,200** Hunt Auctions ⚒

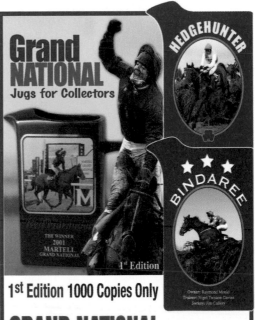

# TENNIS

A wooden tennis racket, by Howier & Sons of St Andrews, with an inlaid handle, Scotland, c1900, 27in (68.5cm) long.

**£110–125  Manfred Schotten** ⊞

A Locke & Co bone china match holder, in the form of a tennis ball, the handle in the form of a tennis racket, c1900, 2½in (6.5cm) high.

**£100–120  Alan Pezaro** ⊞

A Fix gilt brooch, in the form of two tennis rackets, each with a faux pearl tennis ball, France, c1910, 1½in (4cm) wide.

**£35–40  Cufflink Shop** ⊞

A Jubilee Lawn Tennis Championships bronze medal, depicting the Gentleman's Singles trophy, the reverse inscribed 'Wimbledon 1877–1926' and 'M. A. Thomas', 1926, 2½in (6.5cm) diam.

**£90–110  Budd Auctions** ⚒

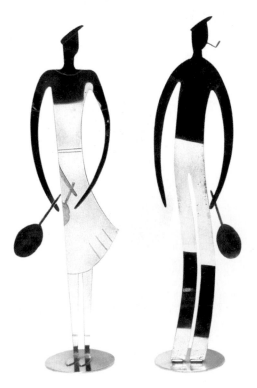

A pair of Hagenauer chrome-plated figures of tennis players, Austria, c1930, 14in (35.5cm) high.

**£1,450–1,600  James Strang** ⊞

A Burleigh Ware handpainted jug, 'The Tennis Player', with hand-painted decoration, 1930s, 8in (20.5cm) high.

**£2,000–2,200  Gazelles Ltd** ⊞

# EXPERT EYE · BRADWELL TANKARD

The handle is probably the most distinctive feature of the Sports Series tankards. Here you can see that the potters have cleverly incorporated a tennis racket. For the golf series the handle is made from a golf bag while the rugby tankards in the series feature a player clutching a rugby ball.

Interestingly, this British-made tankard actually celebrates two US tennis players. The reason is that in 1947 they were both Wimbledon winners. Margaret Osborne DuPont (as she became after her marriage that year) took home the women's trophy and serve-volley star, Jack Kramer won the men's championship.

**A Royal Bradwell Sporting series tankard,** decorated with tennis players Jack Kramer and Margaret Osborne, c1947, 5½in (14cm) high.

**£45–50** **Alan Pezaro** ⊞

This side is decorated with an image of Margaret Osborne.

Royal Bradwell was the tradename of the Arthur Wood pottery, based at the Bradwell Works, Stafffordshire. Their Sports Series encompassed rugby, golf and other popular games.

This is the only tennis-themed tankard ever produced by Royal Bradwell, although other sporting mugs and tankards items were made. The one-pint tankard and came in two colourways – coloured and brown. After WWII coloured wares were much more expensive to produce and therefore considered luxury items. The mug pictured here is the relatively common brown version.

**Bredan Casey**

# STAINLESS STEEL

An Old Hall stainless steel Campden coffee set, designed by Robert Welch, 1957, 7in (18cm) high.

**£60–75 Fieldings** 🔨

A stainless steel bowl, with rattan handles, Denmark, 1959, 8¾in (22cm) wide.

**£40–45 Modern Warehouse** ⊞

A Leonard stainless steel and teak cruet set, Denmark, 1950s–70s, 4¾in (12cm) high.

**£10–15 ModCats.com** ⊞

A Dansk Designs polished stainless steel candleholder, designed by Bertil Vallian, France, 1970s–80s, 5in (13cm) wide.

**£20–25 Fragile Design** ⊞

A Stelton satin-polished stainless steel Cylinda Line ice bucket, designed by Arne Jacobsen, Denmark, 1967, 7in (18cm) high.

**£135–150 Modern Warehouse** ⊞

A Stelton stainless steel Cylinda Line teapot, designed by Arne Jacobsen, Denmark, 1967, 4½in (11.5cm) high.

**£150–180 Fieldings** 🔨

A stainless steel sardine and cheese set, 1960s, 7in (18cm) wide, in original box.

**£5–10 Steptoes Dog** ⊞

An Old Hall teak and stainless steel hors d'oeuvres tray, designed by Robert Welch, 1960s, 17 x 9in (43 x 23cm).

**£60–70 Fragile Design** ⊞

An AS Rostfrei stainless steel and teak cruet set, on a Lazy Susan, Sweden, 1960s, 20 x 12in (51 x 30.5cm).

**£45–50 Fragile Design** ⊞

# EXPERT EYE ALVESTON TEAPOT

The simple, fluid body resembles the flying saucer form made so famous by American 'B' movies of the period and must have been radical. However, the cleanliness of the design proved extremely popular. Welch's designs using stainless steel fitted with the modern movement in interior design: simple, elegant and clean.

Take a look at the spout, which is very fluid and organic, echoing Scandinavian design of the period. Welch visited Sweden in 1954 and was heavily inspired by the work and designs he saw there.

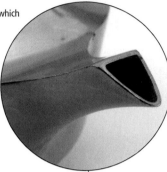

An Old Hall stainless steel Alveston teapot, designed by Robert Welch, 1962, 5in (12.5cm) high.

**£80–100 Fieldings** ⚒

Teapots are household objects that were once used – so check for condition as scratches and dents will reduce value.

The handle is made as a single unit and echoes the designs of American furniture designers such as Charles Eames and Harry Bertoia.

DESIGNED BY R.WELCH
*Old Hall*
ENGLAND
18/8 STAINLESS STEEL

Old Hall produced a large amount of wares that were not designed by Welch. Look out for 'Designed by R. Welch' above the usual oval stamped mark.

Robert Welch was born in 1929 and studied art and design at Birmingham and the Royal College of Art, London, where his final project was the development and design of household wares in stainless steel. He established his first design studio in Chipping Campden, Gloucestershire, in 1955 and in the same year was appointed consultant for Old Hall tableware – a relationship that was to prove highly influential for both parties. Welch's stainless steel designs are now highly collectable – these include the Alveston range of table wares and the Campden Range which, launched in 1956, was the first mass-produced product range. His designs have won many awards, and items once seen as household objects are being elevated to the status of design classics. **Will Farmer**

A stainless steel toast rack, with integral crumb plate, 1960s, 7in (18cm) long.
**£10–15 Steptoes Dog** ⊞

An Old Hall stainless steel Campden coffee set, by Robert Welch, 1957, 7in (18cm) high.
**£70–80 Fragile Design** ⊞

A pair of stainless steel and plastic cruets, inscribed 'S' and 'P', Sweden, 1960s, 4¼in (11cm) high.
**£15–20**
**Special Auction Services** 🔨

Fifteen Nagel stainless steel modular candlesticks, designed by Caesar Stoffi, 1960s, 9½in (24cm) high.
**£110–130 Special Auction Services** 🔨

A Gense stainless steel fruit bowl, with stamped mark and original paper label, Sweden, 1960s–70s, 14in (35.5cm) diam.
**£50–55 ModCats.com** ⊞

A Lundtofte stainless steel and rosewood sugar bowl and creamer, Denmark, 1960s–70s, bowl 3¾in (9.5cm) diam.
**£20–25 ModCats.com** ⊞

A stainless steel toast rack, with integral crumb tray, 1972, 7in (18cm) long.
**£5–10 Steptoes Dog** ⊞

A Polaris stainless steel vase, designed by Olay, No. 4585, Norway, 1960s–70s, 8¼in (21cm) high.
**£85–95 ModCats.com** ⊞

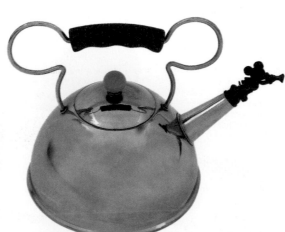

An Alessi stainless steel Mickey Mouse teapot, designed by Michael Graves, limited edition, 1986, 9in (23cm) high.
**£80–100 Fieldings** 🔨

An Alessi stainless steel Juicy Salif lemon squeezer, designed by Philippe Starck, 1989, 11½in (29cm) high.
**£35–40**
**Fieldings** 🔨

# CUTLERY

A Georg Jensen stainless steel and silver Pyramid pattern carving set, Denmark, c1945, knife 12¼in (31cm) long.

**£190–220 Heritage** ⚒

A Georg Jensen stainless steel and silver Pyramid pattern serving set, comprising a cheese slice and a bottle opener, Denmark, c1945, cheese slice 7in (18cm) long.

**£65–75 Heritage** ⚒

Four International Silver Co stainless steel and silver knives, America, c1957, 9in (23cm) long.

**£20–25 Heritage** ⚒

A set of A. Michelsen stainless steel flatware, by Arne Jacobsen, comprising 47 pieces, impressed marks, Denmark, c1957.

**£410–460 Rosebery's** ⚒
*This design was first produced for the SAS Hotel, Copenhagen.*

A set of Taylor's Eye Witness stainless steel Alveston cutlery, designed by Robert Welch, 1961.

**£150–180 Fieldings** ⚒

A set of Glosswood stainless steel cutlery, comprising 12 pieces with rosewood handles, 1960s, 12¼in (31cm) long, with box.

**£40–45 Fragile Design** ⊞

A set of stainless steel fondue forks, with teak handles, 1960s, 11in (28cm) long, with box.

**£10–15 Fragile Design** ⊞

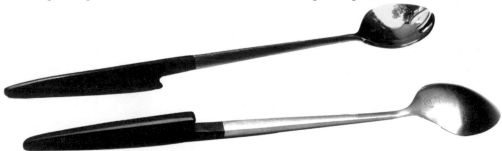

An Epic stainless steel salad spoon and fork, with resin handles, Japan, 1960s–70s, 12½in (32cm) long.

**£15–20 ModCats.com** ⊞

# TEDDY BEARS & SOFT TOYS

A Chad Valley mohair teddy bear, with growler, 1940s–50s, 24in (61cm) high.

**£300–350 Pollyanna** ⊞

A Chad Valley mohair teddy bear, 1950s, 22in (56cm) high.

**£180–200 Bourton Bears** ⊞

A Chad Valley teddy bear, wearing a later knitted suit, 1955–60, 8¼in (21cm) high.

**£90–100 Teddy Bears of Witney** ⊞

A Chiltern mohair Hugmee teddy bear, with plastic eyes and Rexine pads, c1940, 16in (40.5cm) high.

**£150–165 Long Street Antiques** ⊞

A Chiltern mohair Ting-a-Ling musical teddy bear, 1940s–50s, 11in (28cm) high.

**£270–290 Dolls, Bears & Bygones** ⊞

A Chiltern teddy bear, with glass eyes, plastic nose and Rexine pads, 1950–55, 10¾in (27cm) high.

**£90–100 Teddy Bears of Witney** ⊞

A Chiltern Hugmee teddy bear, 1950s, 28in (71cm) high.

**£450–500 Bourton Bears** ⊞

A teddy bear, possibly by Farnell, replacement pads, 1930s–40s, 30in (76cm) high.

**£410–450 Pollyanna** ⊞

A Farnell teddy bear, with growler, hump on back, pads restored, 1930s, 42in (106.5cm) high.

**£1,800–2,000 Pollyanna** ⊞

*This was the largest teddy bear made by Farnell.*

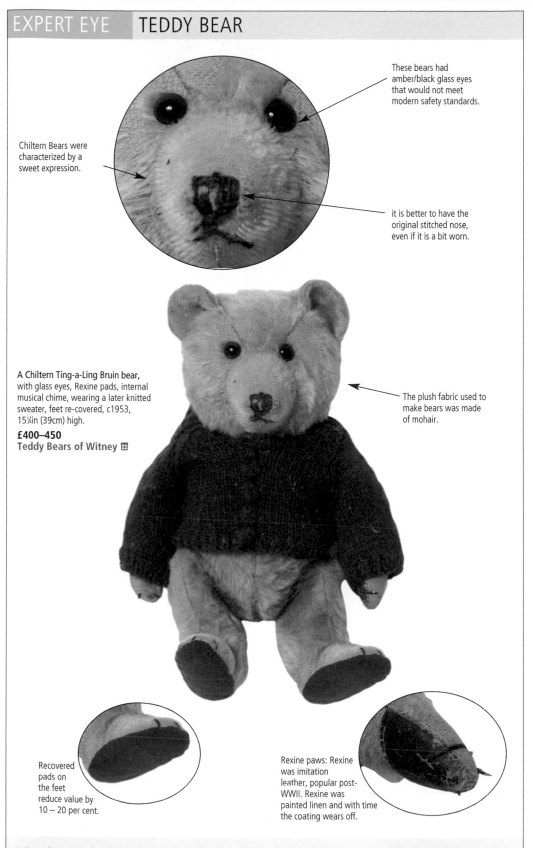

These bears had amber/black glass eyes that would not meet modern safety standards.

Chiltern Bears were characterized by a sweet expression.

it is better to have the original stitched nose, even if it is a bit worn.

**A Chiltern Ting-a-Ling Bruin bear,** with glass eyes, Rexine pads, internal musical chime, wearing a later knitted sweater, feet re-covered, c1953, 15¼in (39cm) high.

**£400–450**
**Teddy Bears of Witney** ⊞

The plush fabric used to make bears was made of mohair.

Recovered pads on the feet reduce value by 10 – 20 per cent.

Rexine paws: Rexine was imitation leather, popular post-WWII. Rexine was painted linen and with time the coating wears off.

Chiltern bears are becoming more difficult for the collector to find – they are a very English style of bear which is popular. Buyers should look for examples that are in good condition, with an expression that appeals to them. If the bear has its original label it is a plus. Some early labels were stuck to the feet with water-based glue and have since gone missing. Chiltern bears were made until 1967, when the company was taken over by Chad Valley, who in turn was taken over by Woolworths in 1988.

A Steiff mohair teddy bear, with shoe-button eyes, moth damage, two replacement pads, Germany, c1905, 16½in (42cm) high.

**£1,600–2,000 Skinner** ⚒

A Steiff teddy bear, with ear button, Germany, c1907, 14in (35.5cm) high.

**£1,100–1,300 Worcester Antiques** ⊞

A Steiff mohair teddy bear, with ear button, restored, Germany, c1915, 12in (30.5cm) high.

**£1,000–1,100 Bourton Bears** ⊞

A Steiff mohair teddy bear, with ear button, Germany, c1950, 9in (23cm) high.

**£200–220 Church Hill Antiques** ⊞

A Steiff teddy bear, with bead eyes and ear button, later ribbon and bells, Germany, 1910–15, 3¾in (9.5cm) high.

**£400–450 Teddy Bears of Witney** ⊞
*This bear has unusually large ears.*

A Steiff mohair teddy bear, with ear button, Germany, c1950s, 3½in (9cm) high.

**£155–175 Teddy Bears of Witney** ⊞

A Steiff mohair teddy bear, with glass eyes, ear button and original pads, Germany, 1950s, 6in (15cm) high.

**£200–230 Bourton Bears** ⊞

A Steiff Scottish teddy bear, limited edition, Germany, 2000, 12in (30.5cm) high.

**£180–200 Pollyanna** ⊞
*This bear is highly sought after*

A Chad Valley rabbit, with glass eyes, c1920, 9½in (24cm) high.
**£150–170 Sue Killinger** ⊞

A Farnell velvet and felt Mumfie elephant, 1930s, 8in (20.5cm) high.
**£250–280 Dolls, Bears & Bygones** ⊞

A Steiff mohair rabbit, with glass eyes, Germany, 1950s, 11in (28cm) high.
**£95–115 Skinner** ⚒

A Chad Valley Lenny the Lion glove puppet, with rubber face, 1950s, 9in (23cm) high.
**£55–65 Magic Toy Box** ⊞

A Steiff lion, Germany, 1950s, 9in (23cm) high.
**£85–95 Newark Antiques** ⊞

A pair of Merrythought hippos, 1960s, 9in (23cm) long.
**£60–70 Tin Tin** ⊞

A Steiff mohair Brosus dinosaur, button and tags missing, tail kink, Germany, 1960s, 29½in (75cm) long.

**£300–360 Skinner** ⚒

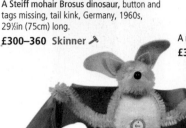

A mohair poodle, c1960, 18in (45.5cm) high.

**£35–40 Pollyanna** ⊞

A Steiff Halloween cat, with button, ear tag and chest tag, Germany, 1959–67, 4in (10cm) high.

**£100–110 Teddy Bears of Witney** ⊞

A Steiff mohair Eric bat, with stitched-on tag, button missing, Germany, 1960s, 14½in (37cm) wide.

**£210–250 Skinner** ⚒

A Steiff mohair cat, with glass eyes, Germany, 1960s, 9in (23cm) long.

**£60–70 Bears of Windy Hill** ⊞

A Tonka Keeper tortoise, 1985, 15in (38cm) high.

**£5–10 Kevin Ward** ⊞

A Hornby Hobbies Pound Purry, 1986, 12in (30.5cm) long.

**£5–10 Vintage Toybox** ⊞

## ESSENTIAL REFERENCE SCHUCO

A Schuco mohair rabbit, Germany, 1935, 3½in (9cm) high.

**£55–65 Cabinet of Curiosities** ⊞

A Schuco mohair bell-hop chimp perfume bottle, with glass eyes and detachable head, Germany, 1920s, 5in (12.5cm) high.

**£135–150 Bears of Windy Hill** ⊞

A Schuco Yes/No chimpanzee, wearing a chef's outfit, tail operates head mechanism, apron missing, Germany, 1950–53, 10¼in (26cm) high.

**£180–200 Teddy Bears of Witney** ⊞

• Schuco specialized in tiny 'piccolo' bears up to 20–30cm high. Produced during the 1920s and '30s in a wide range of colours they are very collectable. They were made of mohair covering a metal body.

• These little bears were often in the form of powder compacts and scent bottles.

• Schuco perfected the 'Yes/No' bear. The engineering involved was so goodthat many are still in working order.

• Collectors should look for bears in good condition and unusual colours as these are the more desirable examples.

**Teddy Bears of Witney.**

# TELEPHONE CARDS

A BT telephone card, advertising Nescafé, 1980–90, 3½in (9cm) wide.

**£1–5 Collectables** ⊞

A BT telephone card, c1990, 3½in (9cm) wide.

**£1–5 Collectables** ⊞

A British Virgin Islands telephone card, Cultural Heritage issue No. 2, c1990, 3½in (9cm) wide.

**£1–5 Collectables** ⊞

A Sun Shine telephone card, Japan, 1990, 3½in (9cm) wide.

**£1–5 Collectables** ⊞

A telephone card, depicting a Bullit train, Japan, 1990, 3½in (9cm) wide.

**£1–5 Collectables** ⊞

A telephone card, depicting 'Santa Claus's House', Japan, 1992, 3½in (9cm) wide.

**£1–5 Collectables** ⊞

A LifeSavers 85th Anniversary telephone card, America, 1997, 3⅜in (8.5cm) wide.

**£5–10 KARS Unlimited** ⊞

A BT telephone card, advertising an exclusive offer from the Radio Times, 1994, 3½in (9cm) wide.

**£1–5 Collectables** ⊞

A telephone card, commemorating the 50th anniversary of D-Day, France, 1994, 3½in (9cm) wide.

**£1–5 Collectables** ⊞

An Amerivox telephone card, advertising the TeleCard World Conference and Exposition, America, 1994, 2½in (6.5cm) wide.

**£5–10 KARS Unlimited** ⊞

An Amerivox phone card, advertising the International Phone Card Conference and Exposition, America, 1995, 3¼in (8cm) wide.

**£1–5 KARS Unlimited** ⊞

A ScoreBoard Coca-Cola phone card, America, 1995, 2½in (6.5cm) wide.
**£60–65 KARS Unlimited ⊞**

A telephone card, Germany, 1997, 3½in (9cm) wide.
**£1–5 Collectables ⊞**
*This telephone card was produced as part of a campaign to reduce vandalism of public telephone boxes.*

A BT telephone card, depicting Bo-Peep from *Toy Story*, No. 5 of a set of six, 1996, 3½in (9cm) wide.
**£1–5 Collectables ⊞**

A telephone card, advertising ISDN lines, Germany, 1997, 3½in (9cm) wide.
**£1–5 Collectables ⊞**

A Nabisco Oreo Cookie telephone card, America, 1997, 3¼in (8.5cm) wide.
**£1–5 KARS Unlimited ⊞**

A Pink Panther Happy Easter telephone card, America, 1997, 3¼in (8.5cm) high.
**£20–25 KARS Unlimited ⊞**

A BT Tom and Jerry Special Edition telephone card, 1998, 3½in (9cm) wide.
**£1–5 Collectables ⊞**

A telephone card, depicting a snake, Cyprus, 2002, 3½in (9cm) wide.
**£1–5 Collectables ⊞**

A telephone card, advertising the Wonderbra, Cyprus, 2001, 3½in (9cm) wide.
**£1–5 Collectables ⊞**

## MARKET INFORMATION TELEPHONE CARDS

• Telephone cards were produced in large quantities from the late 1980s to the mid-1990s. Owing to increased use of mobile phones and the internet they are less popular in the UK than elsewhere in the world.

• Collectors seek attractive pictorial cards – many have themed collections.

• The basic Telecom card is not very desirable – made in large numbers they sell for about 50p. Mercury phone cards are more sought after as fewer were produced.

• Most telephone cards on offer are used, and sell from 50p to £2.50. An unused, sealed card in good condition could fetch as much as £5.00. Cards depicting popular TV characters can sell for about £2.00

• Ordinary green telephone cards are not hot, but cards issued by H.M. Prisons are currently sought after.

• Phone cards are very affordable, durable and easy to display.

• Recent phone cards have chips embedded in them.

# TOOLS

## GAUGES & MEASURING

A wooden spirit level, c1900, 18in (45.5cm) long.
**£55–65  Quay Centre** ⊞

An ebony and brass mortice gauge, c1900, 7in (18cm) long.
**£55–65  Quay Centre** ⊞
*This special type of marking gauge is used to mark wood so that a mortice can be cut into it. The brass glider is adjusted to the gap between the fixed and adjustable spurs, matching the width of the mortice chisel.*

A polished steel gauge, by B. W. Gerrish, 1930s, 5½in (14cm) wide.
**£20–25  Jean Sears** ⊞

An aluminium beam compass, 1930s, 11in (28cm) long, with case.
**£25–30  Frank Scott-Tomlin** ⊞
*Collectors appreciate the fact that this is complete and in its original case.*

A combination square, by Brown & Sharpe, with scriber, America, c1940, 6in (15cm) long.
**£75–85  Quay Centre** ⊞

A combination square, protractor and centrefinder, by Starrett, Scotland, c1950, 12in (30.5cm) long, witth original case.
**£90–100  Quay Centre** ⊞

A chain conveyor designer installer's rule, with incline gauge, 1950s, 24in (61cm) long, with original canvas case.
**£25–30  Jean Sears** ⊞

An architect's set of mahogany curves, 1950s, 16in (40.5cm) wide, in original mahogany box.
**£45–50  Jean Sears** ⊞

## DRILLS, BRACES & PLANES

A corner brace, by Millers Falls, America, c1910, 18in (45.5cm) long.
**£85–95  Quay Centre** ⊞

A mini drill, c1900, 8in (20.5cm) long.
**£45–50  Quay Centre** ⊞

A jeweller's steel and brass pump drill, with a wooden handle, early 20thC,
12in (30.5cm) high.
**£25–30  Frank Scott-Tomlin** ⊞

A bullnose plane, with a rosewood wedge, c1900, 3½in (9cm) long.
**£90–100  Quay Centre** ⊞

A mahogany and steel jack plane, by Brooksbank, c1900,
12in (30.5cm) long.
**£270–300  Quay Centre** ⊞

A rosewood and iron bullnose rebate plane, by Ed Preston, No.1366,
c1910, 4in (10cm) long.
**£90–100  Quay Centre** ⊞

A beech and brass fillister/rabbet plane, by Varvell of York,
c1900–50, 9½in (24cm) long.
**£70–80  Jean Sears** ⊞

# OTHER TOOLS

A wood and metal scraper, by Stanley, c1920, 8in (20.5cm) long.

**£25–30 each  Top Banana** ⊞

Two wood bossing mallets, for dressing lead, 1920–30, 12in (30.5cm) long.

**£10–15 each  Antique Garden** ⊞

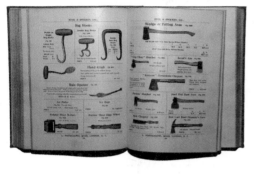

A Buck & Hickman tool and supplies catalogue, hardback, 1928, 9in (23cm) wide.

**£75–85  Early Technology** ⊞

A pair of reed cutting knives, for musical instruments, 20thC, 8in (20.5cm) long.

**£50–60  Woodville Antiques** ⊞

*These knives were always used as a pair – one for cutting and the other for scraping the reed.*

A set of copper and steel soldering irons, with wooden handles, c1900–50, 16in (40.5cm) long.

**£10–15  Antique Garden** ⊞

A pair of steel chisels, by Ward, with boxwood handles, c1930, longest 1½in (4cm) long.

**£65–75  Quay Centre** ⊞

A polished steel floorboard nail puller, by Newey Champion, Birmingham, 20thC, 17in (43cm) long.

**£30–35  Jean Sears** ⊞

A set of six hacksaw blades, 1950s, 10¼in (26cm) long, in original packaging.

**£1–5  Dantinman** ⊞

# TOYS

## BATTERY-OPERATED

A battery-operated musical Jolly Chimp, with teeth that chatter, with original box, c1960, 10in (25.5cm) high.

**£40–45  Mr & Mrs Hill** ⊞

A Tayo tinplate battery-operated Mercury Cougar Fire Chief car, Japan, c1966, 10½in (26.5cm) long, with original box.

**£80–90  Dave's Classic Toys** ⊞

An ASC tinplate battery-operated musical Monkeemobile, Japan, 1960s, 12in (30.5cm) long.

**£180–200  J & S Haley** ⊞

A battery-operated remote-control Cute Poodle, Japan, 1960s, with original box, 9in (23cm) square.

**£5–10  Rin Tin Tin** ⊞

A tin and plastic battery-operated aeroplane, Japan, 1960s, 16in (40.5cm) long.

**£50–60  Junktion** ⊞

A tinplate battery-operated harbour patrol boat, Japan, 1960s, 12in (30.5cm) long.

**£45–50  J & S Haley** ⊞

A tinplate battery-operated Chevrolet Highway Patrol car, Japan, 1960s, 14in (35.5cm) long.

**£115–130  Dave's Classic Toys** ⊞

# BRITAINS

A Britains lead figure of a Rangers football player, dated 1904, 2in (5cm) high.

**£30–35  Scottish Antique & Arts** ⊞

A Britains lead Royal Army Medical Corps ambulance wagon, No145, c1916, 11in (28cm) long, with original box.

**£680–750  Decographics** ⊞

A Britains diecast 155mm Breech Loading Gun, with automatic shell case ejection, 1960, 14in (35.5cm) long, with original packaging.

**£135–150  Militaryman** ⊞

A Britains lead diecast car, 1930s, 2½in (6.5cm) long.

**£55–65  collectorsworld** ⊞

A Britains Military Vehicles half-track motorcycle Kettenkrad, No 9780, 1974, 6in (15cm) long, with original box.

**£50–55  Colin Baddiel** ⊞

A Britain's plastic figure of a knight on a horse, on a metal base, China, c1990s, 4in (10cm) high.

**£1–5  Collectables** ⊞

A Britain's plastic figure of a cowboy on horse, on a metal base, China, 1990s, 3½in (9cm) high.

**£1–5  Collectables** ⊞

## CLOCKWORK

A Marx clockwork Moon Mullins and Kayo hand-car, Germany, c1930, 5¾in (14.5cm) long.
**£135–160 Skinners** 🔨

A Lehmann tinplate climbing monkey, Germany, early 20thC, 8½in (21.5cm) high.
**£45–55 Locke & England** 🔨

A tinplate clockwork ship, Japan, early 20thC, 8in (20.5cm) long.
**£320–360 J & S Haley** ⊞

A Technofix tinplate clockwork GE 255 Zundapp-style racing bike, slight damage, c1946, 8in (20.5cm) long.
**£95–110 Wallis & Wallis** 🔨

A clockwork figure of a boy with a suitcase, Japan, c1950, 6in (15cm) high.
**£40–45 Upstairs Downstairs** ⊞

A Well's tinplate clockwork trolley bus, 1950, 8in (20.5cm) long.
**£160–180 Roy Laycock** ⊞

A Sutcliffe Toys Bluebird II Speedboat, 1958, 12in (30.5cm) long, with original box.
**£500–550 Militaryman** ⊞

A Brimtoy plastic and tinplate Lyons Tea lorry, 1950s, 6in (15cm) long.
**£45–50 Scottish Antique & Arts** ⊞

A Sutcliffe tinplate clockwork boat, late 1950s, 7½in (19cm) long, with original box.
**£200–240 Militaryman** ⊞

A Tucher & Walter tinplate clockwork model of RMS *Queen Mary*, Germany, 1990s, 25in (63.5cm) long, with box.
**£150–180 Wallis & Wallis** ⚒

A Marx Toys clockwork Mr Smash figure, 1975, 6in (15cm) high, with original box.
**£135–150 Metropolis Toys** ⊞

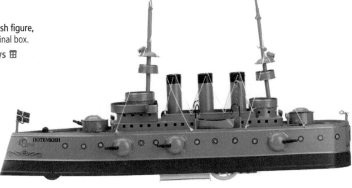

A Tucher & Walter tinplate clockwork model of the battleship *Potemkin*, Germany, 1990s, 21½in (54.5cm) long, with box.
**£150–180 Wallis & Wallis** ⚒

# CONSTRUCTION

An Airfix 007 James Bond & Odd Job models kit, 1966, with box, 9¼in (23.5cm) wide.

**£160–180** Metropolis Toys ⊞

An Airfix Bullfinches model kit, 1976, 4¾ x 9in (12 x 23cm).

**£5–10** John Smart ⊞

An Airfix Henry VIII model kit, 1970s, with box, 8½ x 4¼in (21.5 x 10.5cm).

**£10–15** John Smart ⊞

An Airfix 1st Duke of York's Bengal Lancer model kit, 1978, with box, 16¼ x 9in (41 x 23cm).

**£15–20** John Smart ⊞

A New Meccano No. 4 Outfit, with manuals, 1928, with box, 15 x 10in (38 x 25.5cm).

**£850–1,000** Vectis Auctions ⚒

A Meccano No. 0 aeroplane, late 1930s, 12in (30.5cm) wide.

**£130–155** Wallis & Wallis ⚒

A Meccano Accessory Outfit, c1930, 13in (33cm) wide.

**£35–40** Junktion ⊞

A Meccano Outifit No. 9, 1950s, with original two-drawer box, 18 x 15in (45.5 x 38cm).

**£170–200** Vectis ⚒

A Meccano factory model of a traction engine, slight damage, late 1950s–early 1960s, 12 x 9in (30.5 x 23cm).

**£340–400** Vectis ⚒

## EXPERT EYE PHOTON SLED

The box should be in good condition as this affects the overall value of the item.

These toys were made by Airfix during the 1970s under licence from the Meggo Corp of the USA.

An Airfix motorized Micronaut Photon Sled kit, c1980s, box 8in (20.5cm) wide.

**£25–30 Metropolis Toys** ⊞

The vehicles had small figures, just 3½in (9cm) high that came in a range of colours.

Collectors should look for complete items as vehicles had little parts that tended to get lost.

The Micronauts action figures were one of Airfix's more successful ranges. These are very affordable collectables and make a good entry level for those wishing to start a collection of science fiction toys. A large Space Lab, in mint condition with a mint box, would cost in the region of £100. Science fiction vehicles became popular in the late 1960s and 1970s, in the wake of growing interest in space exploration and boosted by films and television series that were set in space, although Micronauts were not merchandise from a film or TV series, but a generic range.

# CULT – ANIMATION

IF YOU TELL FRIENDS or relations that you collect toys you are likely to hear the typical respnse that includes words such as trains, dolls, teddy bears, Dinky and Meccano. However, times are changing and there are multitudes of collectors of all ages seeking more modern toys that break this stereotype. Much of this change has been driven by the popularity of what we would describe as 'cult' toys.

So what influenced this? Major advances in technology and increased investment in film production, along with every household owning a television, were important factors. These developments gave the population access to a vast array of new media, which was noted by shrewd toy manufacturers and some big new players in the market place appeared. The first of these was Kenner, catching Mattel and Hasbro by surprise, as both companies had previously dominated the market.

The influx of new manufacturers led to a revolution in the size of toys produced – from the traditional 12in (30.5cm) Hasbro Action Man, to 8in (20.5cm) Mego Superheroes and the 3½in (9cm) Kenner *Star Wars* figures. Gone were the days where a child was lucky to have one doll, a set of clothes and nothing else. The smaller scale meant less expense per item so they could afford several toys for the same price.

Today's collectors gravitate toward the merchandise they remember from childhood – specifically from animation, film and television. The most popular of these cult collectables is without doubt the toys produced for the *Star Wars* films, where collecting can pretty much suit the size of your wallet. A few loose figures can be bought for one or two pounds while a rare item can cost well into the thousands.

**Andrew Kitchen and Alex Beasley**

A Kenner Care Bears Tenderheart figure, 1984, 3in (7.5cm) high.

**£1–5 each  Toydreams** ⊞

*The American Greetings Card Co developed the concept of the Care Bears in the 1980s. They appeared in their own television show and even a couple of feature-length animated films.*

A Kenner Care Bears Professor Coldheart figure, 1985, 6in (15cm) high.

**£10–15  Toydreams** ⊞

A Knickerbocker *Lord of the Rings* Ringwraith figure, 1979, 4in (10cm) high.

**£110–125  Toydreams** ⊞

*This is one of the rarest and most sought-after figures. Knickerbocker produced a small toy line to accompany the 1979 animated Lord of the Rings movie, directed by Ralph Bakshi. The film's mix of animation combined with shadowy live-action footage was not a great success and subsequently the toys had little retail support. This factor, combined with the recent resurgence in popularity of Lord of the Rings fuelled by the blockbuster movies, has meant prices of this rare toy line have remained buoyant.*

A Knickerbocker *Lord of the Rings* Frodo action figure, 1979, 2½in (6.5cm) high.

**£45–50  Toydreams** ⊞

A Hasbro My Little Pony Baby Licorice, 1993, 2½in (6.5cm) wide.

**£40–45  Toydreams** ⊞

*This is one of the three rare UK-only Sweetie Babies and is highly sought after by US collectors.*

A Noddy Series Fun on Wheels Mr Plod, with original labels, 1958, 1½in (4cm) high, with box.

**£135–150  collectorsworld** ⊞

# ESSENTIAL REFERENCE MASTERS OF THE UNIVERSE

A Mattel *Masters of the Universe* He-Man action figure, with sword, axe, shield and body armour, 1982, 5in (12.5cm) high.

**£15–20 Toydreams** ⊞

A Mattel *Masters of the Universe* Skeletor action figure, with power punch action, 1982, 5in (12.5cm) high.

**£15–20 Toydreams** ⊞

A Mattel *Masters of the Universe* Castle Greyskull playset, 1982, 25in (63.5cm) wide.

**£200–300 Toydreams** ⊞

*The price of this item reflects the fact that it is in mint, unused condition in its box. This was a very popular playset and had many features such as laser cannons, a secret trapdoor and working drawbridge. It also doubled as a carry case for the figures.*

• Mattel's *Masters of the Universe*, which ran for a full ten years from 1982, was of their most successful toy lines.

• It was the first major toy line to incorporate action features into all its figures. Some squirted water, others breathed fiery sparks and one even fired caps.

• The line was developed when legislation dating from 1969 that prohibited children's television programmes from advertising and selling toys was oveturned. Mattel was the first manufacturer to take advantage of the revised law.

• Keen collectors seek the exclusive European-released figures of 'Laser Power He-Man' and 'Laser Light Skeletor', both commanding in excess of £150 for mint, loose complete examples.

• Mattel also created a massive playset named after He-man's planet – Eternia. This is truly rare and mint boxed examples can realize in excess of £1,000.

A bendy rubber Rupert Bear figure, 1969, 10in (25.5cm) high.

**£35–40 Reasons to be Cheerful** ⊞

A Kenner *Real Ghostbusters* Proton Pack,1986, 16in high.

**£50–60 Toydreams** ⊞

*The Real Ghostbusters cartoon was a spin-off from the Ghostbusters film. Proton packs were used to zap all the ghosts and ghouls encountered by the four heroes – Egon, Winston, Ray and Peter. Children could banish ghosts from their wardrobes and monsters from under their beds and get a good nights' sleep!*

A Peyo Smurf Astronaut figure, No. 20003, Hong Kong, 1969–86, 2in (5cm) high.

**£45–50 Mimi Fifi** ⊞

A Smurf Christmas Ornament figure, No. 51906, Hong Kong, 1981, 2in (5cm) high.

**£70–80 Mimi Fifi** ⊞

A Peyo Smurf Mushroom house, 1980s, 8in (20.5cm) high, with original box.

**£35–40 Toydreams** ⊞

A Playmates *Teenage Mutant Hero Turtles* Donatello figure, complete with battle staffs, 1988, 4in (10cm) high, on card.

**£40–45 Toydreams** ⊞

An LJN *Thundercats* Thundertank, 1985, in original box, 12in (30.5cm) long.

**£85–95 Toydreams** ⊞

*This vehicle was driven by Panthro in the cartoon and is a firm favourite with collectors as it made an appearance in nearly every episode.*

An LJN *Thundercats* Sword of Omens, 1986, 20in (50.8cm) long.

**£100–120 Toydreams** ⊞

*This rare sword has a light-up 'Eye of Thundera', activated by a button on the hilt, making the eye glow red. In the cartoon Sword gave Lion-O 'sight beyond sight', enabling him to see great distances and into the future.*

A LJN *Thundercats* Mumm-Ra figure, with electronic light-up eyes, 1985, 6in (15cm) high.

**£15–20 Toydreams** ⊞

*To have any collectable value this figure must be in good working condition with all the weapons and accessories.*

A set of Tintin and Snowy action figures, France, 1985, 9½in (24cm) high, boxed.

**£130–145 collectorsworld** ⊞

A *Tintin* Captain Haddock action figure, France, 1985, 10½in (26.5cm) high, boxed.

**£110–125 collectorsworld** ⊞

A Hasbro *Transformers* Superion Aerialbots gift set, 1986, 18in (45.7cm) tall.

**£155–175 Toydreams** ⊞

*This rare set allowed the child to have five separate transformers which could combine to form Superion the giant robot.*

A Marx Toys *Wombles* friction drive car with Tomsk figure, 1974, 6½in (16.5cm) long, with box.

**£55–65 MagicToy Box** ⊞

A Hasbro *Transformers* Megatron robot, 1984, 7in (17.8cm) high.

**£75–95 Toydreams** ⊞

*Megatron could be transformed into a superb replica Walther P-38 gun, complete with scope and shoulder rest. The pieces are very fragile and easily broken, hence the high value commanded by this figure which is both complete and in excellent condition.*

Seven HCF flock-covered *Wombles* figures, 1978, 2½in (6.5cm) high.

**£5–10 each MagicToy Box** ⊞

## EXPERT EYE    THUNDERCATS THUNDERWINGS LION-O

The head is a different mould, having solid eye sockets and is missing the electronics.

Standard

Thunderwings Lion-O did not come with the sword, glove or light ring accessories that were packaged with the standard Lion-O. The Thunderwings accessory is worth little – it is the figure itself that is important and where the value lies. A standard loose Lion-O figure is worth £15–20 in complete condition and £60–90 if mint on the original card. A loose Thunderwings Lion-O is worth £80–120 in complete condition and in excess of £300 if mint on the original card.

Thunderwings

Standard

The back of the Thunderwings Lion-O is the key difference from the standard production version. There are two things to note. Firstly, there is no 'battle-matic' action – the lever is completely missing. Secondly there is no metal contact ring for lighting Lion-O's eyes, as this version does not have the feature.

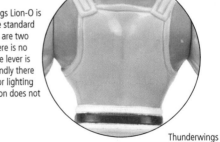

Thunderwings

Newcomers to toy collecting tend to collect the standard figures before learning about all the figure variations that are available. Some collectors like to seek the variations once they have completed their basic set. Variations are those figures that might be painted differently or have different physical features. The differences are due to the fact that figures were produced in more than one country during production runs, thus introducing different moulds and colours. In the LJN Thundercats toy series there is a major variation on each of the two main characters – Lion-O and Mumm-Ra. Here we concentrate on Lion-O, although the differences on the Mumm-Ra figure are similar. The rare version is known as the Thunderwings Lion-O, as the figure came packaged with the Thunderwings accessory that was normally sold separately.

**Andrew Kitchen and Alex Beasley**

# CULT – FILM

A Kenner *Aliens* EVAC Fighter spaceship, 1993, 14in (35.6cm) long, with box.

**£50–60** Toydreams ⊞

A Mattel *Battlestar Galactica* Colonial Viper star fighter, with figure and missile, 1978, 6in (15.2cm) long,

**£30–35** Toydreams ⊞

*A large number of these toys were recalled in January 1979, after a child in the US choked on one of the missiles and ten further injuries were reported. The toy was redesigned with a fixed non-firing missile for safety.*

A Mego *Buck Rogers in the 25th Century* Buck Rogers figure, 1979, 12in (30.5cm) high, boxed.

**£80–90** Magic Toy Box ⊞

*Mego's large figures suffer from plastic melt which changes the colour of the plastic and leaves it brittle.*

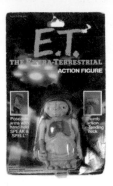

An LJN ET action figure, with poseable arms and thumb and hand-held 'Speak & Spell', America, c1982, 3½in (9cm) high.

**£25–30** collectorsworld ⊞

A Corgi Toys plastic James Bond Moon Buggy, No. 811, from *Diamonds are Forever*, 1973, 6in (15cm) high, boxed.

**£200–250** James Bond Toys ⊞

A Corgi Toys James Bond Aston Martin, No. 270, with tyre slashers, figures, lapel badge and instructions, 1973, 4in (10cm) long, with box.

**£170–190** J & S Haley ⊞

## ESSENTIAL REFERENCE INDIANA JONES

A Kenner Indiana Jones action figure, with whip and gun, 1982, 3½in (9cm) tall.

**£70–80** Toydreams ⊞

A Kenner Indiana Jones Marion Ravenwood figure, with figure and missile, 1982, 3½in (15.2cm) long.

**£400–450** Toydreams ⊞

A Kenner Indiana Jones Well of Souls action playset, from *Raiders of the Lost Ark*, 1982, 12¼in (31cm) wide.

**£155–175** Toys & Hobbies ⊞

• *Indiana Jones and the Raiders of the Lost Arc* was a surprise success in the early 1980s. The popularity of the main character grew with each film, making the Kenner toy line highly collectable.

• Unfortunately the toys and figures were never released in the UK but the development of the internet has made them more accessible.

• The figure line only ran for two series, mainly due to a marketing error in the way the figure assortments were shipped. The numbers of Toht and Cairo Swordsman figures were disproportionately high compared to the main characters, which led to the heroes of the film being impossible to find, resulting in rapid loss of interest from consumers and retailers.

• Marion Ravenwood is the most sought-after and valuable figure in the line because female action figures, never very popular with little boys, are produced in low numbers. This makes them rarer on the collectors market.

• Check the condition of your loose figures carefully, the thumbs are very fragile and are often broken. Also be aware of poor quality fake weapons which often appear shiny with rough edges.

## EXPERT EYE    INDIANA JONES CARDED FIGURES

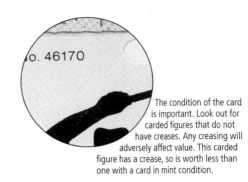

No. 46170

The hanger tab is important. It can be 'punched' where the tab part has been punched out, as in the picture. Look for carded figures that are 'unpunched', where the hanger tab is still present. These usually command slightly higher prices. It is also important to look out for rips in the hanger area as these would decrease value.

The condition of the card is important. Look out for carded figures that do not have creases. Any creasing will adversely affect value. This carded figure has a crease, so is worth less than one with a card in mint condition.

The bubble is equally as important as the cardback. If the bubble displays denting, like this carded figure, the resulting value will be reduced.

Sometimes bubbles can turn yellow due to hot temperatures or exposure to sunlight, which unfortunately deters many a collector from buying a carded figure. If the bubble is beginning to detach itself from the cardback (known as lifting) the value decreases. If it has been re-attached (known as resealing) the value will equate with that of a loose figure.

In worse scenarios bubbles can be cracked. Cracked bubbles radically affect the value of a carded figure and should be avoided – value will be reduced to almost that of a loose figure.

Look inside the bubble to check the figure has all the correct accessories and they are secured as originally manufactured. Most weapons are taped to the side of the bubble as shown.

Most carded figures have what is known as a proof of purchase (POP). You often had to send in proof of purchase symbols when manufacturers released mail-in offers. A good amount of carded figures display removed POPs, which substantially reduces value.

Take a look at the figure and ensure that it is in mint condition. Sometimes figures are badly painted or even damaged when they leave the factory and this does affect the value of the carded figure.

If you take those pieces of advice into account when assessing the condition of a figure you will not go far wrong with your collecting. This carded figure is worth £30–£40 due to the damage, whereas a mint version is worth £60–£90.

When purchasing a carded figure, that is one still attached to the original card back with the figure encased in a plastic bubble, there are many factors to be taken into account. Here we focus on an Indiana Jones German Mechanic carded figure but the principles are transferable to almost any carded figure in any toy line. Condition is everything and can make or break the value of the item. Fading, which occurs as a result of prolonged exposure to sunlight, is something to look our for and should be avoided.

**Andrew Kitchen and Alex Beasley**

A Kenner *Star Wars* Yak Face action figure, 1985, 3½in (8.9cm) high.

**£85–95 Toydreams** ⊞
*One of the hardest loose Star Wars figures to find, Yak Face was released right at the end of the toy line but never in the US.*

A Kenner *Star Wars* Darth Vader figure, with lightsaber 1978, 3½in (8.9cm) tall.

**£10–15 Toydreams** ⊞
*To have true collector value the fragile thin tip to the lightsaber must be present*

A Kenner *Star Wars* R2-D2 figure, 1978, 2in (5cm) tall.

**£20–30 Toydreams** ⊞
*This is a first release figure with a solid head.*

A Kenner *Star Wars* Han Solo figure, 1978, on 12-back card, 6in (15.2cm) high.

**£400–500 Toydreams** ⊞
*First release carded Star Wars figures were known as 12-backs, so-called because the backs of the cards displayed an artist's impression of the first 12 figures. These command large sums of money if in mint condition.*

A Kenner Star Wars 'Blue' Snaggletooth action figure, 1978, 3½in (8.9cm) tall.

**£130–150 Toydreams** ⊞
*This figure came in the 'Cantina Adventure Playset' released exclusively in the US by the Sears mail order company. It has cult status in the Star Wars collecting community as it is essentially an error as the toy designers were only given a head shot preproduction photo to work from. In the film the character was actually half the height, wore a red suit and had fur-covered hands and feet. When the error was spotted the figure was redesigned as the 'Red' Snaggletooth.*

A Kenner *Star Wars* Millennium Falcon spaceship, 1978, 20in (50.8cm) long.

**£70–85 Toydreams** ⊞
*This large vehicle was a very popular toy. The ship needs to have the easily lost light training bead to realize the highest price. There were various other features, including the smuggler's hatch, radar dish, entrance gantry struts and an electronic sound.*

---

## TIMELINE            STAR WARS PACKAGING LOGOS

The production dates of vintage *Star Wars* toys can be determined by which logo appears on the cards and boxes. Until 1985, when a new Power of the Force collector line and logo was introduced, the boxes displayed the logo of the most current film. Earlier figures were produced throughout the seven-year period, making it possible to collect most figures on all five different card backs, thus affecting value. For example, a Darth Vader figure on a 1978 *Star Wars* 12-back card is worth £250–350, while the same figure on a 1983 ROTJ – *Return of the Jedi* – card is worth a more modest £40–60.

Star Wars (SW): 1978–79
Look out for the first 12 figures, mint condition on SW 12-back cards, such as Luke Skywalker, as all sell in excess of £200 each and are the most sought-after versions.

The Empire Strikes Back (ESB): 1980–82
Look out for short release boxed items, such as the Patrol Dewback, released in ESB packaging for a short period. Most are worth at least twice as much as those in SW packaging.

A Kenner *The Empire Strikes Back* Jedi Master Yoda figure, 1980, on card, 1.5in (3.8cm) high.

**£150–170** Toydreams ⊞

A Kenner *The Empire Strikes Back* Cloud City playset, 1981, 9in (23cm) long, with box.

**£250–300** Toydreams ⊞
*This rare Sears USA-exclusive playset is difficult to find in a good condition. The boxes were often squashed or discarded and the actual playset is made from very thin card so is extremely fragile. This is one of the few sets that came with a selection of figures.*

A Kenner *The Empire Strikes Back* Back IG-88 doll, with all accessories, 1980, 15in (38cm) high.

**£100–175** Toydreams ⊞
*This is the rarest of the vintage Star Wars dolls.*

A Kenner *Return of the Jedi* Rancor Monster, 1984, 10in (25.4cm) high.

**£20–25** Toydreams ⊞

A Kenner *The Empire Strikes Back* AT-AT, 1980, 20in (50.8cm) long, with box.

**£120–150** Toydreams ⊞
*This vehicle is one of the biggest in the line and one of the most sought after by collectors. Look for the two clear moving chin guns, battery and bulb cover as these are often missing.*

A Kenner *Star Wars Return of the Jedi* Speederbike and Biker Scout rider, speederbike explodes, 1983, 6in (15.2cm) long.

**£15–20** Toydreams ⊞

A Kenner *Star Wars Return of the Jedi* Jabba the Hutt, 1983, 10in (25.4cm) long, in sealed box.

**£120–135** Toydreams ⊞

The Return of the Jedi (ROTJ): 1983–84
Look out for the Imperial Shuttle which was only released in a box with this logo. It is the largest spaceship ever created for the entire toy line and the retail price was very expensive even in 1983.

Tri-Logo: 1984
Look out for the General Madine figure on an ROTJ card which is worth £30–50. If you can find it on the rare Tri-Logo card shown it is worth in excess of £1,500 to the right collector.

The Power of the Force (POTF): 1985
Look out for any of the three POTF playpacks, such as Hoth Rescue. These were only released in Europe and are very hard to find. Each is worth in excess of £200 in a mint box.

A Kenner *Star Wars* Princess Leia figure, 1996, 6in (15.2cm) tall, on card.

**£1–5 Toydreams** ⊞

*This figure realized prices in excess of £80 when first released, as it was difficult to find, but once the supply problem was resolved the price dropped rapidly. The figure itself is a poor likeness to the actress Carrie Fisher and as soon as more appropriately sculpted figures were produced demand hit an all-time low and has never recovered.*

A Kenner *Star Wars* Luke and Wampa action figure set, 1997, 8in (20.3cm) long, with box.

**£20–25 Toydreams** ⊞

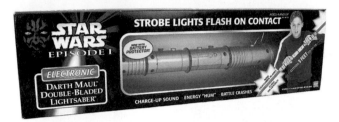

A Hasbro *Phantom Menace* Darth Maul double bladed lightsaber, 1998, 20in (50.8cm) tall, with box.

**£60–70 Toydreams** ⊞

A Hasbro *Phantom Menace* TC-14 protocol droid, 1998, 6in (15.2cm) tall, on card.

**£20–25 Toydreams** ⊞

*This is one of a handful of modern Star Wars related toys that actually exhibit inventment potential. This figure along with Amidala Ascension gun and R2-B1 are the most difficult to locate in the set of figures produced for this film.*

A Kenner *Star Wars* Darth Vader action figure, with removable helmet and freeze-frame slide, 1998, 6in (15.2cm) high, on card.

**£5–10 Toydreams** ⊞

A Hasbro *Phantom Menace* Naboo star fighter, 1997, 14in (35.6cm) tall, with box.

**£20–25 Toydreams** ⊞

## MARKET INFORMATION    STAR WARS

• After coins, *Star Wars* is the most popular subject for collecting. Between 1977 and 1985 250 million figures were sold from the original series and most children had at least one item from the films.

• In 1995 the licence was revived by Kenner (who were bought by Hasbro), leading to hundreds of new figures. There are now well over 500 different figures to collect.

• Prices for toys from the original series have recently been affected by an influx of fake accessories and the impact of The Action Figure Authority, or AFA, grading system. Values for loose items are generally falling while mint carded and sealed boxed toys are realizing greatly increased prices.

• After quite a buoyant start in1995, modern collectable prices have peaked and are now tailing off. However, collectors must take into account that the old toys were made for children and therefore played with, whereas the new toy line was created more for the adult collector and marketed as such. Unfortunately, the knowledge of old toys being worth good money in the original packet has precipitated the belief that the new toys will also see the same increase in value over time. Sadly this probably isn't going to be the case. This year has seen most figures available in the £2–5 price range.

• In the last couple of years there has been great interest in the figure variations produced ouside the US. This has lead to large price increases, especially with some of the paint variation figures available in the UK. Keep a look out for the dark boots Rebel Soldier and orange hair Luke Skywalker Bespin outfit, among others.

A Dinky Toys diecast and plastic model of U.S.S. *Enterprise,* from *Star Trek,* 1975, 9in (23cm) long, with box.

**£60–70  J & S Haley** ⊞

A Mego *Star Trek* Klingon action figure, 1979, 12½in (32cm) high, with box.

**£70–80  Magic Toy Box** ⊞

A Kenner *Terminator* electronic talking doll, 1992, 12in (30.5cm) high, with box.

**£50–60  Toydreams** ⊞
*The Terminator was brought to life by former Mr Universe Arnold Schwarzenegger in the 1984 blockbuster of the same name. The 1992 film was aimed at a younger audience so a toy line was produced off the back of this. This superb figure spoke authentic phrases from the film and really looked impressive.*

Two Mego Wizard of Oz action figures, Tin Man and Cowardly Lion, 1974, 8in (20.5cm) high, boxed.

**£20–25  Magic Toy Box** ⊞

## ESSENTIAL REFERENCE  TOY STORY

A Thinkway Toys *Toy Story* electronic talking Buzz Lightyear toy, 1995, 10in (25.4cm) tall, boxed.

**£40–50  Toydreams** ⊞

A Thinkway Toys *Toy Story* Woody action Figure, complete with sheriff badge stand, 4in (10.2cm) tall.

**£5–10  Toydreams** ⊞

A Thinkway Toys *Toy Story* 2 Rex action figure, complete with three alphabet blocks, 1996, 4in (10.2cm) tall.

**£5–10  Toydreams** ⊞

• The ground-breaking movie *Toy Story* was the first feature-length film that was fully computer generated. The combination of cartoon-like graphics, Hollywood Stars performing voice-overs and a layered script made it an instant hit with children and adults alike. The merchandise just couldn't fail.

• When the electronic Buzz Lightyear action figure hit the shelves in late 1995, it became the must-have toy for every little boy at Christmas. The toy had opening wings, glow-in-the-dark trim, sliding helmet, wrist laser and sounds. It retailed at £30, but as Christmas approached they exchanged hands in excess of £200.

• Look out for the smaller 6in (15cm) figures made for both *Toy Story* films. Figures such as Baby Face, Rex and Emperor Zurg were made in small quantities and have recently increased in value.

• The spring-loaded wing mechanism on the 12in (30.5cm) Buzz Lightyear figure is extremely prone to breaking – be sure to test it before buying your figure.

• *Toy Story* helped to breathe new life into other classic toys such as Playskools' Mr Potato head, which has enjoyed a resurgence in popularity since the film's release.

# CULT – TELEVISION

An HCF flock-covered model of Basil Brush,
1970s, 6in (15cm) high.

**£5–10** Magic Toy Box ⊞

A Corgi diecast model of Basil Brush and his car, No. 808, 1971, 3½in (9cm) long, with box.

**£85–95** Magic Toy Box ⊞

## ESSENTIAL REFERENCE  A-TEAM

An Arco *A-Team* M-24 Assault Rifle target game set, No. 197,
c1983, 231/2in (59.5cm) long.

**£85–95** Metropolis Toys ⊞

An Ertl diecast *A-Team* BA's van, with sliding door, 1984,
8in (20.5cm) long.

**£40–50** Toydreams ⊞

• Everyone remembers the voice-over at the begining of each episode – and
every child did indeed want to hire them!

• Manufacturer Galoob landed the licence to manufacture the action figure
toy line in 1984, although Ertl produced a small range of large diecast toys
including Murdock's Helicopter, BA's van and Face's Corvette.

• BA Baracus or 'Mr T' was by far the most popular character in the line and,
as the character would have said, 'I pity the fool' who didn't buy his figure!

• The rarest toy in the line is the Galoob boxed Command Centre. The toy is
huge, about 30in (76cm) high and made from hardboard and plastic. It is a
difficult item to value as they rarely come up for sale and some guides even
list the item as 'never produced'.

• Look out for the rare outfit colour variations on the large 6in (15cm) *A-
Team* figures and also for the elusive female figure of Amy Allen.

A Galoob plastic *A-Team* Sgt Bosco
'Bad Attitude' Baracus figure, 1984, on
card, 10in (25.5cm) high.

**£35–45** Toydreams ⊞

A Marx plastic Dr Mopp friction drive car, from
*Camberwick Green*, 1967, 3in (7.5cm) long, with box.

**£55–65** Magic Toy Box ⊞

A Codeg plastic village set with figures, from *Camberwick Green*, 1966,
17in (43cm) long, with box.

**£250–280** Magic Toy Box ⊞

## ESSENTIAL REFERENCE — BATMAN CORGI BATMOBILE

A Corgi Juniors Batmobile, No. 69, 1974, 6in (15cm) long, on card.

**£30–35  J & S Haley**

Palitoy plastic talking Batmobile, 1977, 9½in (24cm) long, with box.

**£160–180  Metropolis Toys** ⊞

A Corgi Toys diecast Rocket Firing Batmobile, with Batboat and trailer, first issue, 1967, 12in (30.5cm) long, with box.

**£1,100–1,250  Militaryman** ⊞

• The first Corgi models appeared in 1956. One of their top selling models of all time is the 1966 Batmobile, of which they sold five million. It was an exceedingly accurate representation of the vehicle in the hit television series and every child wanted it.

• The Batmobile diecast toy had a working chain slasher blade, working triple rocket tubes (with original rockets) and working turbine jet exhaust. The figures of Batman and Robin were also included with most models and they can sit in the seats of the vehicle.

• The model was produced from 1966 to 1980 and can be found in eight different versions, although the changes were generally minor, such as different coloured wheel hubs.

• To accompany the Batmobile Corgi produced the BatBike and Batboat, which comes with its own trailer that couples to the Batmobile.

• Be very wary when looking to purchase early examples of the Corgi Batmobile. There are very high-quality reproduction parts available now and even whole new sets of packaging can be sourced to make the toy look as new. Due to the nature of diecast toys Batmobile toys can become badly scratched. It is quite common to see toys that have been completely repainted; these look good but have little value.

A set of six Codeg plastic Village Folk dolls, from *Camberwick Green*, 1967, 5½in (14cm) high, boxed.

**£220–250  Magic Toy Box** ⊞

A set of Codeg plastic Pippin Fort Soldier Skittles, from *Camberwick Green*, 1966, 5½in (14cm) high, with box.

**£110–125  Magic Toy Box** ⊞

**CULT – TELEVISION**

## MARKET INFORMATION  CAPTAIN SCARLET

• *Captain Scarlet* has a large collector following, most of whom also collect some of Gerry Anderson's other famous television-related toys, such as *Thunderbirds* or *Stingray*.

• Collectors have a wide range of different items to choose from, ranging from early Dinky and J. Rosenthal toys to Timpo soldiers and more modern action figures from Vivid Imaginations.

• Mint example Dinky toys of the SPV, MSV and SPC regularly command high prices. J. Rosenthal toys are generally more expensive to acquire and somewhat larger in size. A mint example of the Spectrum Patrol Car by this manufacturer regularly sells for £400–600.

• Pedigree produced a beautiful Captain Scarlet doll in 1967 that is becoming increasingly rare. Mint examples with original boxes are this year approaching the £1,000 mark.

• Individual Timpo 'soldier'-style figures of Captain Scarlet characters have recently been selling for £20–30.

• Vivid Imaginations produced a very good line of *Captain Scarlet* toys in 1993/94. Most are relatively common but the second line of figures is far rarer. These include Captain Black as a Spy, Harmony Angel, Captain Magenta and Captain Scarlet in Spectrum Astronaut kit. Unfortunately prices have significantly lowered this year, in some cases by more than half. Mint carded Captain Scarlet figures in Spectrum Astronaut kit used to fetch upwards of £100, but can now regularly be found for less than £50.

A Vivid Imaginations *Captain Scarlet* Spectrum Pursuit Vehicle, 1993, 12in (30.5cm) long.

**£15–20  Toydreams** ⊞

A Vivid Imaginations Captain Scarlet action figure, in Spectrum Astronaut kit, 1994, on card, 5in (12.5cm) high.

**£50–60  Toydreams** ⊞

A Vivid Imaginations *Captain Scarlet* action figure, 1993, 12in (30.5cm) high.

**£10–15  Toydreams** ⊞

A Palitoy plastic talking K-9, from *Dr Who*, 1978 , 6in (15cm) high, with box.

**£85–95  Magic Toy Box** ⊞
*The talking mechanism is operated by rubber bands; it is unusual to find one still in working order.*

A Denys Fisher Cyberman figure, from *Dr Who*, 1976, 10¼in (26cm) high, with box.

**£400–450  Metropolis Toys** ⊞

A Denys Fisher Dr Who action figure, 1976, 6in (15cm) high.

**£35–40  Toydreams** ⊞

A Palitoy talking Dalek, from *Dr Who*, 1976, 6in (15cm) high.

**£70–80  Toydreams** ⊞

A Denys Fisher plastic Giant Robot, from *Dr Who*, 1976, 9¾in (25cm) high.

**£300–350  Metropolis Toys** ⊞

A Mego poseable action figure of Bo, from *The Dukes of Hazard*, 1980, 8in (20.5cm) high, on card.

**£55–65 Magic Toy Box** ⊞

A Mego poseable action figure of Boss Hogg, from *The Dukes of Hazard*, 1980, 8in (20.5cm) high, on card.

**£55–65 Magic Toy Box** ⊞

A Corgi model of Green Hornet's Black Beauty, 1966, 5in (12.5cm) long, with box.

**£195–235 Mastro Auctions** ✦

A Mego poseable action figure of Richie, from *Happy Days*, 1976, 8in (20.5cm) high, on card.

**£55–65 Magic Toy Box** ⊞

A Mego poseable action figure of Fonzie, c1970, 8in (20.5cm) high.

**£15–20 Upstairs Downstairs** ⊞

A Mego World's Greatest Hereos Super Torch figure, 1975, 8in 920.5cm) high.

**£15–20 Toydreams** ⊞

A Palitoy plastic *Incredible Hulk* figure, 1979, 9in (23cm) high, boxed.

**£50–55 James Hardwick** ⊞

## ESSENTIAL REFERENCE KNIGHT RIDER

A Kenner *Knight Rider* 2000 Voice Car, 1983, 15in (38cm) long.

**£100–120 Toydreams** ⊞

• The hit 1982 show *Knight Rider* was huge in the UK but few toys were actually released.

• The Knight 2000 car or KITT was the icon from the show and every child wished their dad's car would talk to them. Alas this sadly wasn't going to be the case! KITT could be purchased as an Ertl diecast model, an LJN Rough Riders toy or even a radio-controlled car.

• Kids in the US were treated to the Kenner talking Knight 2000 car with the Michael Knight figure as pictured here. The car works by pressing the back number plate down to activate a miniature battery-operated record playing mechanism which plays a phrase from the show.

A Kenner *Knight Rider* Michael Knight figure, 1983, 5in (12.5cm) high.

**£5–10 Toydreams** ⊞

A Corgi *Kojak* Buick car and figures, 1976, with box, 8in (20.5cm) wide.
**£85–95 Metropolis Toys ⊞**

A Marx Toys *Lone Ranger* Tonto action figure, 1973, 9½in (24cm) high, with box.
**£115–125 Magic Toy Box ⊞**

A tin *Magic Roundabout* kaleidoscope, 1996, 9in (23cm) long.
**£5–10 John Smart ⊞**

A Clodrey poseable Dylan doll, wearing felt clothes, France, 1966, 13in (33cm) high.
**£130–145 Magic Toy Box ⊞**

A Marx Lone Ranger figure, 1973, 9½in (24.5cm) lhigh.
**£25–30 Toydreams ⊞**
*The Lone Ranger was a hit show and a very good line of toys were produced including buildings, wagons, horses and other such accessories. Butch Cavendish was his arch enemy.*

A rubber Brian toy, France, 1968, 5in (12.5cm) long, with box.
**£110–125 Magic Toy Box ⊞**

LE MANEGE ENCHANTE

A set of five JIM plastic *Magic Roundabout* characters, 1968, 2½in (6.5cm) high, with box.
**£155–175 Magic Toy Box ⊞**

A Teach-a-Tot plastic *Magic Roundabout* Tune-O-Vision clockwork musical box, 1968, 8in (20.5cm) wide.
**£55–65 Magic Toy Box ⊞**

A Corgi diecast *Magic Roundabout* Dougal's car, No. 807, with plastic figures, 1971, 4in (10cm) long, with box.
**£110–125 Magic Toy Box ⊞**

A Corgi *Man from U.N.C.L.E.* car, No. 497, Waverley ring missing, 1966, 6in (15cm) long, with box.
**£165–180 J & S Haley ⊞**
*Complete with Waverley ring, this car would be worth £200–230.*

## ESSENTIAL REFERENCE MORK AND MINDY

A Mattel poseable talking Mork action doll, from *Mork and Mindy*, 1979, 9in (23cm) high, with box.
**£95–105 Magic Toy Box** ⊞

A Mattel poseable Mindy action doll, from *Mork and Mindy*, 1979, 9in (23cm) high, with box.
**£40–50 Magic Toy Box** ⊞

A Mork Eggship, from *Mork and Mindy*, Hong Kong, c1979, 4½in (11.5cm) high.
**£20–25 collectorsworld** ⊞

• From 1978 to 1982 the *Mork and Mindy* show was made famous by the comic genius of Robin Williams, who played the alien 'Mork from Ork' to perfection.

• To emphasize the weirdness of the Mork character, Mattel decided to package the 9in (23cm) toy figure upside down in the box. The spacepack that came with the figure will let you hear 'Na-no, Na-no!' and seven other famous Mork phrases.

• The 4in (10cm) Mattel figure is difficult to find complete with the egg spaceship as these were often lost or discarded over the years.

• Very few toys were available for this popular television show, but you can find Viewmaster reals and a board game for very reasonable prices.

A Bandai *Power Rangers* Saba Talking Tiger, 1994, 20in (51cm) high, with box.
**£25–30 Toydreams** ⊞

A Bandai *Power Rangers* Lost Galaxy Megazord action figure, 1999, 20in (51cm) high.
**£10–15 Toydreams** ⊞
*The Power Rangers fit the bill for being a collectable of the future – the toy line is diverse, colourful and has a huge following due to the success of the television programme.*

A Kenner *Six Million Dollar Man* Maskatron figure, 1976, 14in (35.5cm) high, with box.
**£85–95 Metropolis Toys** ⊞

A Denys Fisher *Six Million Dollar Man* figure, 1975, 12in (30.5cm) high, with original box.
**£75–85 Magic Toy Box** ⊞

A Dinky Toys *Space 1999* Eagle Transporter, c1976, 10in (25.5cm) long, with box.
**£90–100 J & S Haley** ⊞

A Mego Spiderman action figure, 1973, 8in (20.5cm) long.

**£25–30** Toydreams ⊞

A Mego Lizard action figure, from *Spiderman*, 1975, 8in (20.5cm) high.

**£65–80** Toydreams ⊞

A Matchbox *Stingray* Phones action figure, 1992, 10in (25.5cm) long, on card.

**£10–15** Toydreams ⊞

*Phones, the co-pilot of the Stingray submarine, is the hardest Matchbox figure to find as it was produced in low numbers. All the other figures – Marina, Troy Tempest, Titan and Sam Shore – are relatively easy to locate.*

A J. Rosenthal plastic battery-operated Thunderbird 4, 1967, 10¼in (26cm) long, with box.

**£175–195** Metropolis Toys ⊞

A J. Rosenthal *Thunderbirds* Lady Penelope's FAB 1 car, 1967, 10in (25.5cm) long, with box.

**£145–165** Metropolis Toys ⊞

A Matchbox *Thunderbirds* electronic Tracey Island playset, 1992, 20in (51cm) wide.

**£85–95** Toydreams ⊞

*This playset was in very short supply during Christmas 1992. Anxious parents queued at toy shops but demand outstripped supply and the playsets began to exchange hands for upwards of £200. The childrens' television show Blue Peter even broadcast a build-your-own Tracey Island guide for the unlucky ones.*

A Matchbox *Thunderbirds* Lady Penelope action figure, 1992, 8in (20.5cm) high, boxed.

**£10–15** Reasons to be Cheerful ⊞

A Matchbox diecast *Thunderbirds* gift set, 1993, 10in (25.5cm) long.

**£25–30** Toydreams ⊞

A Matchbox electronic talking Thunderbird 2 with Thunderbird 4, 1993, 13in (51cm) long.

**£25–30** Toydreams ⊞

A Bradgate plastic battery-operated talking *Trumpton* Fire Engine, 1968, 9in (23cm) long, with box.

**£110–125** Magic Toy Box ⊞

A Marx Toys tinplate *Trumpton* Fireman bell, 1967, 24in (61cm) high, with box.

**£110–125** Magic Toy Box ⊞

## EXPERT EYE    WWF LOOSE FIGURES

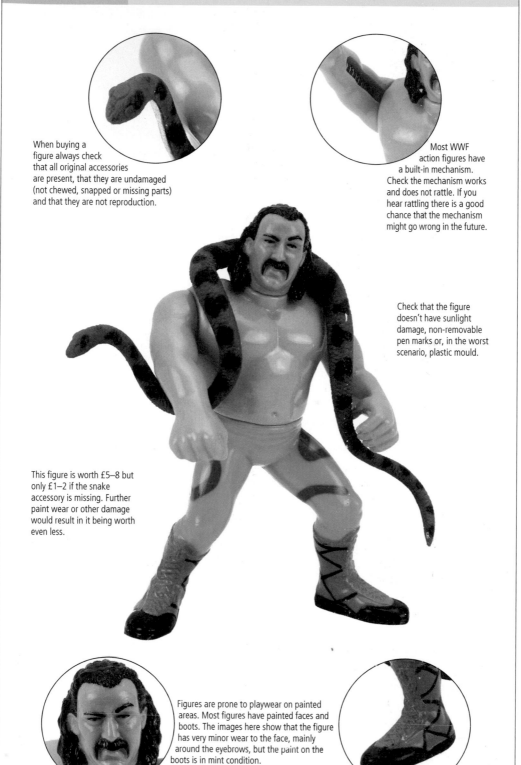

When buying a figure always check that all original accessories are present, that they are undamaged (not chewed, snapped or missing parts) and that they are not reproduction.

Most WWF action figures have a built-in mechanism. Check the mechanism works and does not rattle. If you hear rattling there is a good chance that the mechanism might go wrong in the future.

Check that the figure doesn't have sunlight damage, non-removable pen marks or, in the worst scenario, plastic mould.

This figure is worth £5–8 but only £1–2 if the snake accessory is missing. Further paint wear or other damage would result in it being worth even less.

Figures are prone to playwear on painted areas. Most figures have painted faces and boots. The images here show that the figure has very minor wear to the face, mainly around the eyebrows, but the paint on the boots is in mint condition.

Collecting loose figures can be great fun and finding all the accessories quite a challenge. Many collectors ask us what they should look for when buying loose figures. Here we cover the key points to look for when spending your hard-earned money on a World Wrestling Federation (WWF) Jake 'The Snake' Roberts figure by Hasbro.

**Andrew Kitchen and Alex Beasley**

A selection of plastic Diddymen figures, 1970s, 6in (15cm) high.

**£25–30 each** Magic Toy Box ⊞

A Mattel Jimmy Osmond doll, from *The Donnie and Marie Show*, 1978, 10in (25.5cm) high, with box.

**£65–75** Magic Toy Box ⊞

A Milton Bradley Electronics Star Bird electronic spaceship, 1978, 15in (38cm) long, with box

**£45–50** Toydreams ⊞

A Galoob The Animal battery-operated truck, with extending claw wheels, 1984, 10in (25.5cm) long.

**£25–30** Toydreams ⊞

A Milton Bradley Electroncis Big Trak space tank, 1979, 12in (30.5cm) long.

**£30–35** Toydreams ⊞

*Big Trak was a hugely popular toy at the turn of the 1980s. It was a fully mobile, electronically programmable tank that would drive around the house, following every command you gave it, whether to go straight ahead, turn left or fire the laser cannon. Tremendous fun, even for the adults, who never admitted that it was really bought for them.*

An LJN vinyl Michael Jackson doll, wearing 'Thriller' costume, 1984, 14in (35.5cm) high, with box.

**£25–30** Magic Toy Box ⊞

*This is one of a series of four dolls that originally retailed for £7.50.*

A Corinthian David Beckham doll, wearing England kit, 1994, 12in (30.5cm) high.

**£10–15** Toydreams ⊞

A Galoob Spice Girls Posh Spice doll, 1998, 12in (30.5cm) high, with box.

**£10–15** Toydreams ⊞

# DIECAST – CORGI

A Corgi Toys Smiths Karrier Bantam mobile shop, No 413, late 1950s, 4in (10cm) long, with original box.
**£80–90   J & S Haley** ⊞

A Corgi Toys Tour de France Gift Set, No. 13, with Paramount film unit, Renault 16 with camera man and a cyclist, 1960s, with original box, 8in (20.5cm) long.
**£140–170   Wallis & Wallis** ⚒

A Corgi Toys Major Euclid TC12 Tractor with Dozer Blade, No. 1102, early 1960s, with original box, 6in (15cm) long.
**£140–170   Wallis & Wallis** ⚒

A Corgi Toys Austin Healey sports car, No. 300, c1960, 3in (7.5cm) long, with original box.
**£110–125   J & S Haley** ⊞

A Corgi Toys Major racing car transporter, 1961, 7in (18cm) long, with original box.
**£360–400   Militaryman** ⊞

A Corgi Toys Aston Martin DB4, No. 218, c1963, 4in (10cm) long, with original box.
**£75–85   J & S Haley** ⊞

A Corgi Toys Mercedes Benz 220 SE Coupé, No 230, 1960s, 3½in (9cm) long, with original box.
**£50–60   J & S Haley** ⊞

A Corgi Toys Volkswagen Delivery Van, No 433, 1960s, 3½in (9cm) long, with original box.
**£75–85   J & S Haley** ⊞

A Corgi Toys Monkees Monkeemobile, 1967, with box, 4½in (11.5cm) long.

**£430–500  Mastro Auctions** 🔨

A Corgi Toys Rocket Age gift set, No. GS6, comprising a Bristol Bloodhound Guided Missile with Launching Ramp and Loading Trolley, RAF Land Rover, Electric Thunderbird Guided Missile on Trolley, Radar Unit, RAF Staff Car and Decca Airfield Radar Scanner, 1959–62.

**£500–600  Vectis** 🔨

A Corgi Toys Rockets car, 1969, 2½in (6.5cm) wide, with original packaging.

**£30–35**
**Dave's Classic Toys** ⊞

A Corgi Toys Simon Snorkel fire engine, 1968–72, 11¼in (28.5cm) long, with original box.

**£35–40  Metropolis Toys** ⊞

## ESSENTIAL REFERENCE    PRISTINE Vs USED

A Corgi Toys Austin A60 De Luxe Saloon Motor School car, No 236, 1960s, 4in (10cm) long, with original box.

**£80–90  J & S Haley** ⊞
*This model is in very good condition.*

A Corgi Toys Austin A60 De Luxe Saloon Motor School car, No 236, 1960s, 4in (10cm) long, with original box.

**£45–50  J & S Haley** ⊞
*This model is in used condition.*

• This Corgi Austin A60 was introduced in 1963 in two versions: light blue, right-hand drive for the home market and dark blue, left-hand drive for export. The light blue model is much easier to find in the UK than the dark blue one.

• In mint condition a light blue boxed model is worth £90, £55 if used. A car without a box is worth £5 for a poor example or £25 for one that is in mint condition.

• The dark blue model in boxed mint condition is worth £140 whereas a good, but used boxed model £75. A loose model will command £10 for a poor example or £55 for one in near mint condition. All these prices increase by 15 per cent if the Corgi Junior Highway Code leaflet is present.

• The wheel on the top of the car turns the front wheels and the car has front and rear 'L' plates.

**Simon Haley, J & S Haley**

# DIECAST – DINKY

A Dinky Toys convertible car, 1930s,
4in (10cm) long.

**£115–130** Dave's Classic Toys ⊞

A Dinky Toys Camion Militaire Berliet Tous
Terrains, No. 818, France, 1960–70,
5½in (14cm) wide, with original box.

**£90–100** Dave's Classic Toys ⊞

A Dinky Toys Camion G.M.C. Militaire
Depannage, 1972, 7in (18cm) long,
with original box.

**£450–500** Militaryman ⊞

A Dinky Toys aircraft set, No. 60, containing
Mystère IV, Vautour, Sikorsky S.58 Sabena
and Vickers Viscount, France, 1950s, with
original box and insert, 10in (25.5cm) square.

**£1,300–1,600** Wallis & Wallis ⚒

## ESSENTIAL REFERENCE  DINKY SUPERTOYS

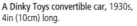

A Dinky Supertoys Foden eight-wheeled
Flat Truck, No. 502, 1949, 8in (20.5cm)
long, with original box.

**£340–380** Dave's Classic Toys ⊞

A Dinky Supertoys Slumberland Guy van,
No. 514, 1952, with box.

**£380–460** Wallis & Wallis ⚒

A Dinky Supertoys Big Bedford Heinz van,
1960, with box.

**£250–300** Wallis & Wallis ⚒

- Dinky Supertoys are aeroplanes or commercial vehicles that were manufactured between 1947 and 1970. The early issues are 500 series; when reintroduced after being out of production for some time they became 900 series.

- With a few exceptions, both Supertoys and orginal Dinky toys approximate to 1:48 scale.

- As with most toys, few have survived in good condition. For collectors, condition is all-important and determines value.

- The existence of a box does add to value, but its condition will influence the combined value of the items. Broadly speaking a box will double the value of an unboxed toy, mint or otherwise. Box types and styles of boxes changed over the years, so make sure you have the correct one for your vehicle.

- Reproduction castings were produced but most of these are identified as such by the maker; repainted and restored examples can also be found.

- Reproduction boxes are now readily available. The type of cardboard used is often a giveaway, as is the quality of the printing, although the latter is improving all the time.

**Wallis & Wallis**

# DIECAST – MATCHBOX

A Matchbox Bedford Milk Float, No 29, 1950s, 2in (5cm) long, with original box.
**£20–25** J & S Haley ⊞

A Matchbox Major M-10 Pack dumper, 1960s, 4in (10cm) long, with original box.
**£35–40** J & S Haley ⊞

A Matchbox Ford Thunderbird, No. 75, 1960s, 3½in (9cm) long, with original box.
**£30–35** J & S Haley ⊞

A Matchbox Superfast Road Dragster, No. 19, c1971, 3in (7.5cm) long, with original box.
**£10–15** J & S Haley ⊞

A Matchbox scout car, No 61, 1950s–60s, 2in (5cm) long, with original box.
**£15–20** J & S Haley ⊞

A Matchbox Tank Transporter and Tank, c1960s, 6in (15cm) long.
**£15–20** J & S Haley ⊞

A Matchbox Superfast Ford Capri, No. 54, 1970, 3in (7.5cm) long, with original box.
**£10–15** J & S Haley ⊞

A Matchbox Superfast Blue Shark, No. 61, c1971, 3in (7.5cm) long, with original box.
**£10–15** J & S Haley ⊞

GAMES

An Aviarieties party game, No. G684, from Dennis's 'Dainty' Series, 1920s, 6in (15cm) high.

**£10–15 Junktion** ⊞

A Glevum Games Tidley Skittles game, 1930s, 7½in (19cm) wide.

**£25–30 Noble Gold** ⊞

A Pepys Dan Dare card game, 1950s, 3¾in (9.5cm) high.

**£30–35 Toys & Hobbies** ⊞
*The association with Dan Dare boosts the price of these playing cards.*

A Chad Valley Concentration game, from the Granada Television series, 1959, 15¼ x 13½in (39 x 34cm).

**£5–10 John Smart** ⊞

A Bell Toys & Games Four Feather Falls board game, box lid damaged, 1960, 14¼in (36cm) square.

**£60–70 John Smart** ⊞

An Avalon Hill's Game Co Tactics II game, America, 1961, 14½in (37cm) wide.

**£15–20 Noble Gold** ⊞

A Peter Pan Playthings Frustration game, 1965, 10¾in (27.5cm) wide.

**£10–15 Vintage Toybox** ⊞

A John Waddington Whot card game, 1968, 7½in (19cm) wide.

**£5–10 Vintage Toybox** ⊞

A Spears Games Tell Me quiz game, 1960s, 7½in (19cm) wide.

**£1–5 Collectables** ⊞

An Invicta Space Lines game, 1969, 13½in (34.5cm) high.

**£5–10 John Smart** ⊞

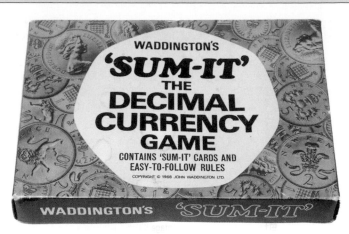

A Waddington's Sum-it Decimal Currency Game, c1970, 7in (18cm) wide.

**£1–5 Collectables** ⊞

*The official switch to decimal currency in the UK took place on 15 February 1971. Board game maker Waddington's adapted their classic Sum-It game to go some way to sorting out the confusion.*

A Waddington's Tennis and Badminton Game, c1970, 7in (18cm) wide.

**£1–5 Collectables** ⊞

A Waddington's Click dice game, 1970s, 7in (18cm) wide.

**£1–5 Collectables** ⊞

A Denys Fisher Miss UK board game, 1975, 18in (45.5cm) wide.

**£25–30 Vintage Toybox** ⊞

A Milton Bradley Pac-Man board game, 1982, 19in (48.5cm) wide.

**£10–15 Vintage Toybox** ⊞

A Parker Brothers Q*bert board game, 1983, 15in (38cm) wide.

**£10–15 Vintage Toybox** ⊞

A Ravensburger Labyrinth board game, 1992, 14½in (37cm) wide.

**£15–20 Vintage Toybox** ⊞

A Milton Bradley Curse of the Idol board game, 1992, 20in (51cm) wide.

**£10–15 Vintage Toybox** ⊞

# PUPPETS

A Fairylite Bill or Ben rubber and cloth glove puppet, 1954–55, 10in (25.5cm) high.

**£45–50** Magic Toy Box ⊞

A Pelham Andy Pandy string puppet, 1956, 12in (30.5cm) high, with original box.

**£90–100** Magic Toy Box ⊞

A Pelham Cowboy and Cowgirl string puppet, 1950s, 12in (30.5cm) high, with original boxes.

**£55–65**
Alvin's Vintage Games & Toys ⊞

A Pelham Skeleton shop display string puppet, 1950s, 30in (76cm) high.

**£360–400**
Alvin's Vintage Games & Toys ⊞

A Pelham Mexican Girl string puppet, 1950s, 12in (30.5cm) high, with original box.

**£65–75**
Alvin's Vintage Games & Toys ⊞

A Pelham Twizzle string puppet, c1960, 12in (30.5cm) high, with original box.

**£180–200**
Alvin's Vintage Games & Toys ⊞

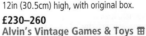

A Pelham Crow string puppet, 1963, 12in (30.5cm) high, with original box.

**£230–260**
Alvin's Vintage Games & Toys ⊞

A Pelham Zebedee string puppet, with a plastic rod, 1972, 11in (28cm) high, with original box.

**£90–100** Magic Toy Box ⊞

A Pelham ventriloquist caterpillar puppet, with moving eyes, 1975, 19in (48.5cm) high.

**£135–150** Magic Toy Box ⊞

A Pelham Kermit string puppet, 1970s, 12in (30.5cm) high, with original box.

**£180–200**
Alvin's Vintage Games & Toys ⊞

A Tri-ang Minic searchlight lorry, No. 49ME, 1930s, 5½in (14cm) long.

**£370–430 Militaryman** ⊞

A Tri-ang pressed-steel Shell BP tanker, 1950s, 23in (58.5cm) long.

**£180–200 Beaulieu Autojumble** ⊞

A Tri-ang plastic racing car, 1950s, 8in (20.5cm) long, with original box.

**£25–30 Beaulieu Autojumble** ⊞

A Tri-ang plastic milk truck, with milk bottles, 1950s, 13in (33cm) long, with original box.

**£65–75 Mr & Mrs Hill** ⊞

A Tri-ang diecast outboard motor, 1950s, 6in (15cm) wide, with original box.

**£55–65 Beaulieu Autojumble** ⊞

A Tri-ang metal Happy Washdays electric washing machine, 1950s, 12in (30.5cm) high, with original box.

**£45–50 Beaulieu Autojumble** ⊞

A Tri-ang pressed-steel ride-on toy lorry, 1950s, 18½in (47cm) long.

**£75–85 Beaulieu Autojumble** ⊞

A Tri-ang plastic Motor Roar Grand Prix Sound toy, 1960s, 7½in (19cm) long, with original box.

**£20–25 Beaulieu Autojumble** ⊞

A Tri-ang pressed-steel Air Force rocket launcher, late 1960s, 25in (63.5cm) long.

**£120–140 Beaulieu Autojumble** ⊞

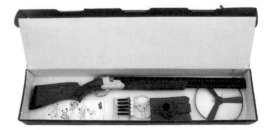

A Tri-ang plastic and metal Flying Shot toy, late 1960s, 36½in (92.5cm) long.

**£40–45 Beaulieu Autojumble** ⊞

A Tri-ang Minic clockwork mouse, 1960s, 4in (10cm) long, with original box.

**£5–10 Metropolis Toys** ⊞

A Tri-ang plastic Real Estate building set, 1960s, 8in (20.5cm) wide, with original box.

**£30–35 Beaulieu Autojumble** ⊞

# TRAINS

A Bing Deutsche Reichsbahn open wagon, Germany, pre-WWII, 6in (15cm) long.

**£25–30** J & S Haley ⊞

A Märklin tinplate and cast-metal live steam locomotive and tender, front bogey missing, Germany, pre-WWI, 16in (40.5cm) long.

**£800–900** J & S Haley ⊞

*The price reflects the rarity of this piece, and a complete example would be worth as much as £1,500.*

A tinplate clockwork train set, comprising an engine and one car, early 1950s, track 18in (45.5cm) long.

**£15–20** Mr & Mrs Hill ⊞

A Fleischmann twin pantograph electric mainline locomotive, Switzerland, 1970s, 12in (30.5cm) long, with box.

**£75–85** Wheels of Steel ⊞

A Wrenn Railways W2268 4–6–2 BR Streamlined West Country Class locomotive, No. 34004, 'Yeovil', 1986, 14in (35.5cm) long, with box.

**£360–440** Vectis ⚒

# ESSENTIAL REFERENCE TRIX

A Trix Twin Railway Pullman saloon car, 1930–50, 9in (23cm) long, with box.

**£25–30** John & Simon Haley ⊞

*This Trix Twin Pullman coach is classed as a scale-length coach. Later 1960s versions were named 'Sheila', 'Zena' or 'Car No. 34' and had moulded interiors.*

A Trix Twin Railway dining car, 1940s, 7in (18cm) long, with box.

**£45–50** J & S Haley ⊞

• Trix began in Germany around 1934, with the Trix Express range. It was distributed and sold in Britain by Basset-Lowke from Christmas 1935.

• The Trix Twin Railway, also known as TTR, was formed in England in late 1936.

• The most desirable engines are 'Princess Coronation Nord' and 'Scotsman'.

• Different versions of the couplings are diecast block with wire drop prior to WWII, then bent tin during the post-WWII years.

• Trix can be very affordable, with wagons starting at £5 and engines at £25.

A Trix Twin Railway diecast Continental-style locomotive and tender, post-WWII, 7in (18cm) long.

**£70–80** J & S Haley ⊞

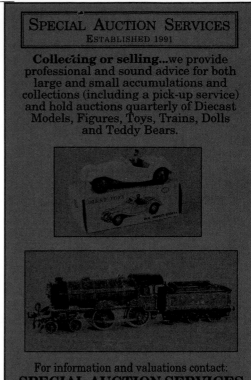
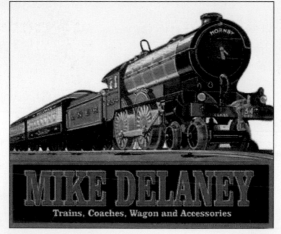

A Hornby 0 gauge Pratts petrol tanker, 1920s, 6in (15cm) long.
**£45–50 J & Haley** ⊞

A Hornby 0 gauge tinplate petrol tanker, pre-WWII, 5in (12.5cm) long.
**£40–45 Junktion** ⊞

Hornby 0 gauge 20v No.2 special tank set, pre-WWII, in a box 18in (45.5cm) wide.
**£450–500 J & S Haley** ⊞

A Hornby 0 gauge cement wagon, 1920–30, 6in (15cm) long.
**£35–40 J & S Haley** ⊞

A Hornby 0 gauge tinplate Arcadia No. 2 Pullman coach, 1930, 14in (35.5cm) long, with box.
**£110–130 Vintage Toys** ⊞

A Hornby 0 gauge tinplate Fyffes banana van, 1931–34, 6¼in (16cm) long, with box.
**£100–110 Vintage Toys** ⊞

A Hornby 0 gauge 4–4–0 No. 2 Special LMS clockwork locomotive and tender, No. 1185, 'Compound', 1932–34, 12in (30.5cm) long.
**£240–290 Vectis** ⚒

A Hornby 0 gauge open wagon 'B', No. RS694, 1934, 7in (18cm) long, with box.
**£50–55 Gloucester Toy Mart** ⊞

A Hornby 0 gauge tinplate fish van, 1935, 5½in (14cm) long, with box.
**£65–75 Vintage Toys** ⊞

A Hornby 0 gauge 0–4–0 LMS late version tank locomotive, No. 2115, 1935–38, 7in (18cm) long.
**£220–270** Vectis

A Hornby 0 gauge 4–4–2 No. 2 Special LMS tank locomotive, No. 6954, rear bunker tabs broken, 1936–38, 13in (33cm) long, with box.
**£280–340** Vectis

A Hornby 0 gauge 0–4–0 LNER tank locomotive, No. 2162, 1936–38, 8in (20.5cm) long.
**£300–360** Vectis

A Hornby 0 gauge 4–4–0 No. 2 Special LNER locomotive and tender, No. 201, 'The Bramham Moor', 1936–38, 12in (30.5cm) long.
**£700–800** Vectis

A Hornby 0 gauge 0–4–0 clockwork No. 1 LMS locomotive and tender, No. 5600, 1937–39, 8in (20.5cm) long, with original boxes and guarantee slip.
**£120–145** Vectis

A Hornby 0 gauge tinplate Manchester Oil Refinery tanker, c1950, 8in (20.5cm) long, with box.
**£35–40** Dave's Classic Toys ▦

A Hornby 0 gauge 4–4–4 clockwork No. 2 LNER tank locomotive, early 1950s, 18in (45.5cm) long.
**£110–135** Vectis

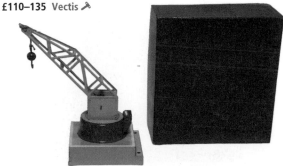

A Hornby 0 gauge platform crane, post-WWII, 7in (18cm) high.
**£20–25** J & S Haley ▦

A Hornby 0 gauge water tanker, post-WWII, 7in (18cm) high.
**£15–20** J & S Haley ▦

Two Hornby Dublo three-rail boxes for EDL LNER Gresley locomotive and tender, 1938–39, 10 x 4in (25.5 x 10cm).

**£2,600–3,000  Vectis** ⚒

*These boxes are in exceptional condition. Only 150 were made and the tender box is one of a very few survivors. They are bought by collectors who wish to store their locomotives and tenders in the appropriate boxes.*

A Hornby Dublo three-rail EDL7 0–6–2 SR tank locomotive, 1949–50, 6in (15cm) long, with box.

**£200–240  Vectis** ⚒

A Hornby Dublo three-rail EDP2 passenger train set, early 1950s, in a box 20 x 14in (51 x 35.5cm).

**£1,300–1,600  Vectis** ⚒

A Hornby Dublo three-rail 3217 0–6–2 BR early crest N2 Class tank locomotive, No. 69567, with instruction booklet, 1959, 6in (15cm) long, with box.

**£300–360  Vectis** ⚒

A Hornby Dublo diecast metal through station, 1950s, 23in (58.5cm) long, with original box.

**£30–35  J & S Haley** ⊞

A Hornby Dublo teak three-rail D2 LNER articulated coach set, with centre bogie, corridor connection missing, 1938–39, 18in (45.5cm) long.

**£200–240  Vectis** ⚒

A Hornby Dublo diecast engine and tender, 'Duchess of Atholl', 1940–50, 12in (30.5cm) long.

**£70–75  J & Haley** ⊞

*A number of versions of this engine were produced – all were the same colour and had the same number on the cab. The main differences are the nameplate, either long or short, with various colourings of the letters of the name. The rarest example has a cream background to the nameplate with maroon lettering. Another late rare version has smoke deflectors on the front of the engine. Prices can vary from £450 to £500 for one of the rarer versions (cream background nameplate or smoke deflector versions).*

A Hornby Dublo diecast tank engine, c1950, 7in (18cm) long.

**£45–50  J & S Haley** ⊞

A Hornby Dublo three-rail EDL2 4–6–2 LMS Princess Coronation Class locomotive and tender, No. 6231, 1950–51, 14in (35.5cm) long, with boxes.

**£400–480  Vectis** ⚒

A Hornby Dublo three-rail Co-Co BR diesel locomotive, 1959–63, 10in (25.5cm) long, with box.

**£110–135  Vectis** ⚒

# EXPERT EYE   HORNBY DUBLO – CITY OF LONDON

**A Hornby Dublo train set,** with diecast 'City of London' engine and tin coaches, early 1960s, with original box 21in (53.5cm) wide.

**£180–200 J & S Haley** ⊞

This set is an immaculate condition, although it is not particularly rare. Collectors can obtain a good example for a relatively modest outlay.

The condition of the box is important. A poor box will reduce the value to less than £100, whereas an immaculate example could raise the overall worth to £200.

There was a whole class of trains named after various cities in the British Isles.

During the 1960s Hornby faced competition from rival companies who produced trains that were cheaper to buy and, although not of the same quality, found favour with buyers. Some of the most sought-after Hornby trains are the last of the Dublo three-rail system, which includes the set shown above. Among other late additions is the 'City of Liverpool' which, if in excellent condition and with its box, can fetch £400. After several changes in its fortunes, including being part of Tri-ang, the Hornby name lives on as Hornby Railways.

**Simon Haley  J & S Haley**

A Hornby Dublo D22 corridor coach, 1950s, 9in (23cm) long, with box.
**£10–15 J & S Haley** ⊞

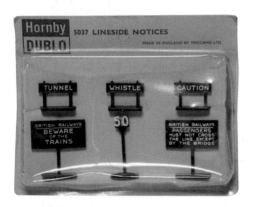

A Hornby Dublo two-rail 4–6–2 BR Princess Coronation Class locomotive, No. 46245, 'City of London', 1960, 12in (30.5cm) long, with box and instruction booklet.
**£80–100 Vectis** 🔨

A set of Hornby Dublo plastic lineside notices, early 1960s, in original packet, 5in (12.5cm) wide.
**£40–45 J & S Haley** ⊞

A Hornby Dublo product catalogue, 1961, 10in (25.5cm) wide.
**£10–15 J & S Haley** ⊞

A Hornby Dublo two-rail BR restaurant car, 1963–64, 11in (28cm) long, with box.
**£110–135 Vectis** 🔨

A Hornby Dublo three-rail tank engine, 1950s, 8in (20.5cm) long, with box.
**£55–60 J & Haley** ⊞

A Hornby Dublo two-rail 2235 4–6–2 BR West Country Class locomotive, No. 34005, 'Barnstaple', 1960–63, 14in (35.5cm) long, with box.
**£120–145 Vectis** 🔨

A Hornby Dublo 5003 terminal/through station composite kit, 1960–64, with box, 24 x 16in (61 x 40.5cm).
**£500–600 Vectis** 🔨

A Hornby Dublo three-rail Co-Co BR two tone Deltic Class locomotive, No. D9001, 'St Paddy', 1962–63, 10in (25.5cm) long, with box.
**£220–270 Vectis** 🔨

A Hornby Dublo three-rail 4–6–0 BR Castle locomotive, 'Ludlow Castle', 1963–64, 14in (35.5cm) long, with box.
**£380–430 Vectis** 🔨

# WATCHES & CLOCKS

A silver wristwatch, with a leather strap, c1915, 1⅜in (3.5cm) diam.

**£400–450 Harpers Jewellers** ⊞

An Omega Seamaster Automatic wristwatch, Switzerland, 1950s.

**£230–260 Tony Durante** ⊞

A Cyma stainless steel wristwatch, No. 25663, with subsidiary seconds dial, c1960.

**£45–55 Charterhouse** 🔨

A Jaeger-LeCoultre Automatic 9ct gold wristwatch, signed, Switzerland, c1970.

**£280–330 Charterhouse** 🔨

A Rolex white metal digital jump hour/wandering hours and minutes wristwatch, by Anton Schild, Switzerland, 1920s.

**£630–700 Fossack & Furkle** ⊞
*At this time Rolex were known to be using AS movements and the case design and specification of this piece are identical to one found in a late 1920s Rolex Bucherer catalogue.*

A Lucerne wristwatch, signed, Switzerland,1970s.

**£35–40 www.collectorsworld** ⊞

A Rolex Oyster Royal stainless steel wristwatch, No. 49771, with a 15 jewel movement, signed, Switzerland, 1930s.

**£240–290 Charterhouse** 🔨

An Omega Seamaster Cosmic stainless steel automatic wristwatch, with a day/date window, signed, Switzerland, c1970.

**£120–145 Charterhouse** 🔨

An Omega 18ct gold bracelet wristwatch, the bezel inset with 20 diamonds, signed, Switzerland, 1980s, with box.

**£460–550 Charterhouse** 🔨

An oak and chrome mantel clock, 1930s, 6½in (16.5cm) wide.
**£40–45** Hemswell Antiques Centre ⊞

A Maple & Co oak wall clock, the dial with brass numerals, with a Zenith 18-day movement, 1930s, 13½in (34cm) diam.
**£460–550** Wellers Auctioneers ⚒

A Coral plastic alarm clock, 1960–70, 6in (15cm) high.
**£25–30** Attica ⊞

A Blessing plastic alarm clock, Germany, 1960–70, 8½in (21.5cm) high.
**£40–45** Attica ⊞

A Seth Thomas plastic alarm clock, America, 1960s, 4¾in (12cm) high.
**£45–50** Vintage Swank ⊞

A Westclox tin and plastic wind-up alarm clock, 1970s, 5in (12.5cm) high.
**£10–15** Attica ⊞

A General Electric wall clock, No. 2150, in the form of a flower, 1970s, 7in (18cm) high.
**£20–25** Vintage Swank ⊞

# COLLECTABLES OF THE FUTURE

A jar of Guinness Marmite, 2007, 3½in (9cm) high.

**£1–5 Fabjo's Jars** ⊞

*In 2007 Marmite and Guinness collaborated to produce a limited edition of 300,000 250g jars of Marmite made with 30 per cent Guinness. The jars were given a distinctive black and white label.*

A pair of Top Shop denim hotpants, designed by Kate Moss, 2007.

**£25–30 Baggage Collectables** ⊞

*In 2007 the supermodel Kate Moss collaborated with the High Street fashion chain Top Shop to produce a range of clothing, including these colourful hotpants.*

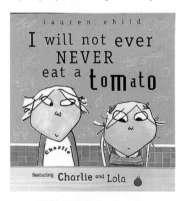

Lauren Child, *I Will Not Ever Never Eat a Tomato*, published by Orchard Books, 2001, 26½in (67.5cm) high.

**£5–10 Orchard Books** ⊞

*This is Lauren Child's second book for Orchard. Charlie and Lola deal with difficult issues for children and they have appeared on television in their own series as well as items as diverse as birthday cards and lunch boxes.*

An Anya Hindmarch cotton bag, I'm Not A Plastic Bag, 2007, 13½in (34.5cm) high.

**£5–10 Anya Hindmarch** ⊞

*I'm Not A Plastic Bag was designed by leading accessories designer Anya Hindmarch in partnership with global social change movement We Are What We Do and creative agency Antidote. Anya wanted to use her influence as a luxury fashion brand to make it fashionable not to use plastic bags and to encourage people to make small changes in their behaviour.*

Crown Copyright

A silver and gold-plated proof £2 coin, inscribed 'An Act for the Abolition of the Slave Trade, 2007', 1in (2.5cm) diam.

**£25–30 Royal Mint Collectors' Club** ⊞

*This coin features the simple yet powerful design by David Gentleman. He chose to depict the imagery of chains with one link broken representing a 'release from subjection' which also doubles as the anniversary date of 1807. The portrait of the Queen by Ian Rank-Broadley appears on the obverse framed by the contrasting outer ring. The edge inscription is taken from the anti-slavery seal by Josiah Wedgwood which reads 'Am I Not a Man and A Brother'. Just 10,000 of these coins were minted,*

A brass Zaida necklace, by Pippa Small for MADE, 2007, 8in (20.5cm).

**£45–50 Made** ⊞

*Pippa started making jewellery to fund her degree and soon attracted the attention of the fashion world, including Gucci, Nicole Farhi and Chloe. MADE accessories incorporate Fair Trade materials and craftsmanship into their pieces. The original designs are sourced in developing African countries before being reworked by UK designers such as Pippa Small. The final designs are then handmade by the original developing country producers using sustainable local resources – precious metals, stones and indigenous materials that are familiar to the craftsmen – to create distinctive and original jewellery, bags, belts and shoes.*

*This picture is the property of Pippa Small for MADE Fair Trade jewellery. www.made.uk.com*

# COLLECTING BY STYLE

## FIFTIES

A Fritz Hansen Pot chair, by Arne Jacobsen, 1958.
**£580–650 Modern Warehouse** ⊞

A Fritz Hansen Egg chair, by Arne Jacobsen, designed 1958.
**£1,200–1,450**
**Special Auction Services** ⚒

A chrome Sputnik ashtray, 1950s, 16in (40.5cm) high.
**£25–30 Attica** ⊞

A Piero Fornasetti enamelled tin tray, 1950s, 23 x 10in.
**£155–175 20th Century Marks** ⊞

A Washington Pottery Planets tea plate, 1950s, 11in (28cm) diam.
**£15–20 Pineapple Ice Bucket** ⊞

A set of four Federal Glass Patio snack sets, America, Ohio, 1950s, plate 10in (25.5cm) wide, with original box.
**£15–20 Retro2Go** ⊞

A Carlton Ware Orbit jam pot, 1950s, 5in (12.5cm) high.
**£20–25 Chinasearch** ⊞

# SIXTIES

A **Flare plastic drinks stand**, 1960, 23in (58.5cm) high.
**£35–40 Attica ⊞**

*Time* magazine, 'London the Swinging City' issue, includes photographs of Julie Christie, Jean Shrimpton, Terence Stamp and Cathy McGowan, with mailing address label, 15 April 1966, 11in (28cm) high.
**£30–35 BeatBooks ⊞**

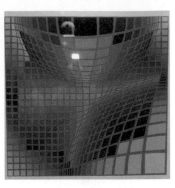

A **silk screen print artist's proof**, by Victor Vasarely, entitled 'Convex Concave', Hungary, 1968, 28in (71cm) square.
**£1,350–1,500 Boom Interiors ⊞**

A **pair of chrome armchairs**, with padded backs and seats, 1960s.
**£1,000–1,150 Dorchester Antiques ⊞**

A **pair of cotton curtains**, screen-printed with an abstract pattern, 1960s, 46½ x 84¼in (118 x 214cm).
**£15–20 Special Auction Services ⚒**

A **painted metal ashtray**, with a plastic plunger, 1960s, 21½in (54.5cm) high.
**£15–20 Bentley's ⚒**

## SEVENTIES

A Joe Colombo plastic Boby trolley, early 1970s, 21in (53.5cm) high.

**£160–175  Attica** ⊞

A Verner Panton plastic wall panel, decorated with nine domes, early 1970s, 23in (58.5cm) wide.

**£45–50  Twinkled** ⊞

A plastic wall coat rack and mirror, 1970s, 32¾in (83cm) high.

**£30–35  Special Auction Services** 🔨

A plastic drinks wall cabinet, by Boris Parlov, 1970s, 21in (53.5cm) wide.

**£70–80  Twinkled** ⊞

A  Waiting chair, by Rudolfo Dordoni for Muroso, part of a suite, Italy, 1970s.

**£360–400  20th Century Marks** ⊞

A chrome occasional table, 1970s, 22in (56cm) high.

**£500–550  Dorchester Antiques** ⊞

A Verner Panton System 1-2-3 chair, c1975.

**£780–880  20th Century Marks** ⊞

A Verner Panton steel Peacock chair, 1970s.

**£400–450  High Street Retro** ⊞

An M. Myers plastic LP record stand, 1970s, 7½in (19cm) high.

**£15–20  Twinkled** ⊞

A teak sculpture, by Brian Willsher, signed, 1978, 11in (28cm) high.

**£270–300  Fragile Design** ⊞

# DIRECTORY OF SPECIALISTS

If you wish to be included in next year's directory, or if you have a change of address or telephone number, please contact Miller's Advertising Department by May 2008. We advise readers to make contact by telephone before visiting a dealer, therefore avoiding a wasted journey.

## 20TH CENTURY
### U.S.A.
ModCats.com
info@modcats.com
www.modcats.com
*Mid century modern design*

### U.K.
### Berkshire
Retro Centre Tel: 0118 950
7224 al@retro-centre.co.uk
www.retro-centre.co.uk
*20thc design, homewares, collectables*

### London
Twinkled, 1.5 Kingly Court,
Carnaby Street
Tel: 020 7734 1978
07940 471569  07940 471574
info@twinkled.net
www.twinkled.net
*Original 50s–80s furniture,
homewares & vintage clothing*

The Modern Warehouse,
243b Victoria Park Road,
E9 Tel: 020 8986 0740
www.themodernwarehouse.com

Richard Wallis Antiks
Tel: 020 8529 1749
www.richardwallisantiks.com
*20th century Scandinavian ceramics,
glass & design. Specialists in the
works of Bjorn Wiinblad*

### Nottinghamshire
Luna, 139 Lower Parliament
Street, Nottingham
Tel: 0115 924 3267
www.luna-online.co.uk
*20th century objects for the home*

### East Sussex
High Street Retro,
39 High Street, Old Town,
Hastings Tel: 01424 460068
www.highstreetretro.co.uk
*20th century design furniture,
lighting, clothing and accessories*

### Tyne & Wear
Pure Imagination, P.O. Box 140,
South Shields, NE33 3WU
Tel: 0191 4169090 or
0771 5054919
www.pureimaginations.co.uk

### West Midlands
Fragile Design, 8 The Custard
Factory, Digbeth,
Birmingham, B9 4AA
Tel: 0121 693 1001
www.fragiledesign.com

## ACCESSORIES
### U.K.
### London
Tony Durante, Alfie's Antique
Market, Unit G047-G048
Ground Floor,
13–25 Church Street
Tel: 020 7723 0449 or
07989 446569
durantetony@hotmail.com
*Accessories, 20th century costume
jewellery and handbags*

## ADVERTISING
### U.S.A.
AwsumAdvertising,
P.O. Box 1782, Linden,
NJ 07036
Tel: 732 331 2951
awsumadvertising@aol.com
*Advertising, Disneyana, collectibles,
toys, Pez & character memorabilia*

### U.K.
### Lincolnshire
Junktion, The Old Railway
Station, New Bolingbroke,
Boston Tel: 01205 480068 or
07836 345491
junktionantiques@hotmail.com
*Advertising and packaging,
automobilia, slot machines, pedal
cars, etc*

### London
The Advertising Archives,
Larry Viner,
45 Lyndale Avenue
Tel: 020 7435 6540
larry@advertisingarchives.co.uk
www.advertisingarchives.co.uk

Dantinman Old Advertising,
Lipka Arcade (Portobello Road),
Unit 13-14 Lower Ground,
282 Westbourne Grove
Tel: 01761 462477 or
07768 166808
www.dantinman.com
*Decorative printed tins, signs and
packaging 1880–1939*

### North Yorkshire
The Tin Shop, Market Vaults,
Scarborough
Tel: 01723 351089
www.tinshop.co.uk
*Collectable tins and advertising
memorabilia*

## AERONAUTICA
### U.K.
### Yorkshire
Aeroclocks, Circadian (UK) Ltd,
Barnsdale House,
Barnsdale Mews,
Campsall, Doncaster
Tel: 01302 707553 or
07774 120692
www.aeroclocks.com

### Lincolnshire
Junktion,
The Old Railway Station,
New Bolingbroke, Boston
Tel: 01205 480068 or
07836 345491
junktionantiques@hotmail.com
*Advertising and packaging,
automobilia, slot machines, pedal
cars, etc*

## AMUSEMENT MACHINES
### U.K.
### Hampshire
Classic Amusements
Tel: 01425 472164
pennyslot@aol.com
www.classicamusements.net
*Vintage slot machines*

### Lincolnshire
Junktion, The Old Railway
Station, New Bolingbroke,
Boston Tel: 01205 480068 or
07836 345491
junktionantiques@hotmail.com
*Advertising and packaging,
automobilia, slot machines, pedal
cars, etc*

## ANIMATION ART
### U.S.A.
Wonderful World of Animation,
9517 Culver Blvd, Culver City,
CA 90232 Tel: 310 836 4992
www.wonderfulworldof
animation.com
*Animation and pop culture art*

## ARCHITECTURAL ANTIQUES
### U.K.
### Somerset
Robert Mills Ltd,
Narroways Road, Eastville,
Bristol Tel: 0117 955 6542
info@rmills.co.uk
www.rmills.co.uk

## ARMS & MILITARIA
### U.K.
### Gloucestershire
Q & C Militaria,
22 Suffolk Road, Cheltenham
Tel: 01242 519815 or
07778 613977
qcmilitaria@btconnect.com
www.qcmilitaria.com
*Orders, decorations, medals,
uniforms, militaria, Trench Art*

### Hampshire
Jim Bullock Militaria,
P.O. Box 217, Romsey
Tel: 01794 516455
jim@jimbullockmilitaria.com
www.jimbullockmilitaria.com
*War medals, decorations and militaria*

### Kent
Tussie Mussies, The Old Stables,
2b East Cross, Tenterden
Tel: 01580 766244
tussiemussies@btinternet.com
www.tussiemussies.co.uk
*Arms & militaria, brocante antiques,
collectables, glass & pottery,
decorative items and local crafts*

### London
Chelsea Military Antiques,
Antiquarius,
131/141 Kings Road,
Chelsea Tel: 020 7352 0308
www.chelseamilitaria.co.uk
*WWI, WWII memorabilia, military
medals, orders, decorations,
Campaign medals*

### Northamptonshire
The Old Brigade,
10A Harborough Road,
Kingsthorpe, Northampton
Tel: 01604 719389
theoldbrigade@btconnect.com
stewart@theoldbrigade.co.uk
www.theoldbrigade.co.uk

### Nottinghamshire
Michael D Long Ltd,
96-98 Derby Road,
Nottingham
Tel: 0115 941 3307
www.michaeldlong.com
*Militaria and arms & armour*

### Somerset
Grimes Militaria,
13 Lower Park Row,
Bristol Tel: 0117 929 8205

### Surrey
West Street Antiques,
63 West Street,
Dorking Tel: 01306 883487
www.antiquearmsandarmour.com
*Fine antique arms & armour*

### East Sussex
Wallis & Wallis,
West Street Auction Galleries,
Lewes
Tel: 01273 480208
auctions@wallisandwallis.co.uk
www.wallisandwallis.co.uk
*Arms & armour, militaria auctions*

## AUCTIONEERS
### U.S.A.
Heritage Auction Galleries,
3500 Maple Avenue,
17th Floor, Dallas,
Texas 75219-3941
Tel: 214 528 3500/
800 872 6467
www.HeritageAuctions.com
*Collectibles auctions*

Hunt Auctions, Inc.,
75 E. Uwchlan Avenue,
Suite 130, Exton,
Pennsylvania 19341
Tel: 610 524 0822
www.huntauctions.com
*Historical baseball and football
memorabilia auctions*

James D Julia, Inc.,
P. O. Box 830, Rte.201,
Skowhegan Road, Fairfield,
ME 04937
Tel: 207 453 7125
www.juliaauctions.com
*Americana, firearms, lamps and glass,
advertising, toys and dolls auctions*

Mastro Auctions,
7900 South Madison Street,
Burr Ridge,
Illinois 60527
Tel: 630 472 1200
www.mastroauctions.com
*Sports and Americana collector auctions*

PBA Galleries,
133 Kearny Street,
4th Floor, San Francisco,
California 94108
Tel: 415 989 2665
www.pbagalleries.com
*Auctions of rare books and
manuscripts, maps and atlases and
photographs*

Rago Arts & Auction Center,
333 North Main Street,
Lambertville, New Jersey 08530
Tel: 609 397 9374
www.ragoarts.com
*Decorative arts and furnishings, fine
art, jewelry, etc*

Skinner Inc,
357 Main Street, Bolton,
MA 01740
Tel: 978 779 6241
www.skinnerinc.com
*Antiques, fine art and collectibles
auctions*

Skinner Inc,
The Heritage On The Garden,
63 Park Plaza, Boston,
MA 02116
Tel: 617 350 5400
www.skinnerinc.com
*Antiques, fine art and collectibles
auctions*

Sotheby's,
1334 York Avenue at 72nd St,
New York, NY 10021
Tel: 212 606 7000
www.sothebys.com
*Antiques, fine art and collectibles
auctions*

### U.K.
### Berkshire
Dreweatt Neate, Donnington
Priory, Donnington, Newbury
Tel: 01635 553553
www.dnfa.com/donnington

Special Auction Services,
Kennetholme, Midgham,
Reading Tel: 0118 971 2949
www.specialauctionservices.com
*Commemoratives, pot lids &
Prattware, Fairings, Goss & Crested,
Baxter & Le Blond prints. Also toys for
the collector*

### Cleveland
Vectis Auctions Ltd and Vectis
Direct, Fleck Way, Thornaby,
Stockton-on-Tees
Tel: 01642 750616 and
01642 764455
admin@vectis.co.uk and
admin@vectisdirect.co.uk
www.vectis.co.uk and
www.vectisdirect.co.uk
*Toy auctions*

### Devon
Bearnes, St Edmund's Court,
Okehampton Street,
Exeter
Tel: 01392 207000
www.bearnes.co.uk

### Dorset
Onslow's Auctions Ltd,
The Coach House, Manor Road,
Stourpaine, Blandford Forum
Tel: 01258 488838
onslowauctions@btinternet.com
*19th and 20th century posters,
railwayana, motoring, aviation, Titanic
and ocean liner collectors items*

### Essex
Sworders, 14 Cambridge Road,
Stansted Mountfitchet
Tel: 01279 817778
www.sworder.co.uk

### Kent
The Canterbury Auction
Galleries, 40 Station Road West,
Canterbury
Tel: 01227 763337
www.thecanterburyauction
galleries.com

Lambert & Foster,
102 High Street,
Tenterden
Tel: 01580 762083
saleroom@lambertandfoster.co.uk
www.lambertandfoster.co.uk

### London
Bloomsbury Auctions,
Bloomsbury House,
24 Maddox Street
Tel: 020 7495 9494
www.bloomsburyauctions.com
*Books, manuscripts, art, prints,
collectables auctions*

Graham Budd Auctions Ltd
Tel: 020 8366 2525 or
07974 113394
www.grahambuddauctions.co.uk
*Sporting memorabilia auctions*

Dix Noonan Webb,
16 Bolton Street, Piccadilly
Tel: 020 7016 1700
www.dnw.co.uk
*Auctioneers and valuers of orders,
decorations and medals, coins,
tokens and banknotes*

### Nottinghamshire
International Autograph
Auctions Ltd., Foxhall Business
Centre, Foxhall Road,
Nottingham, NG7 6LH
Tel: 0115 845 1010
info@autographauctions.co.uk
www.autographauctions.co.uk

T. Vennett-Smith,
11 Nottingham Road,
Gotham Tel: 0115 983 0541
info@vennett-smith.com
www.vennett-smith.com
*Ephemera and sporting memorabilia
auctions*

### Shropshire
Mullock's Specialist Auctions &
Valuers, The Old Shippon,
Wall-under-Heywood,
Nr Church Stretton
Tel: 01694 771771 or
01584 841 428
www.mullocksauctions.co.uk
*Sporting memorabilia auctions*

### East Sussex
Gorringes,
15 North Street, Lewes
Tel: 01273 478221
www.gorringes.co.uk

Wallis & Wallis,
West Street Auction Galleries,
Lewes Tel: 01273 480208
auctions@wallisandwallis.co.uk
www.wallisandwallis.co.uk
*Tinplate and diecast toys and arms &
armour, militaria auctions*

### Warwickshire
Locke & England,
18 Guy Street,
Leamington Spa
Tel: 01926 889100
www.auctions-online.com/locke

### West Midlands
Fieldings Auctioneers Ltd,
Mill Race Lane, Stourbridge,
DY8 1JNTel: 01384 444140
www.fieldingsauctioneers.co.uk

### Wiltshire
Woolley & Wallis,
Salisbury Salerooms,
51-61 Castle Street, Salisbury
Tel: 01722 424500/411854
www.woolleyandwallis.co.uk

### Worcestershire
Gloucestershire Worcestershire
Railwayana Auctions LLP,
The Willows, Badsey Road,
Evesham
Tel: 01386 421324 or
01684 773487
master@gwra.co.uk
www.gwra.co.uk
*Railwayana & transport collectables
auctions*

### Yorkshire
Hartleys,
Victoria Hall Salerooms,
Little Lane, Ilkley
Tel: 01943 816363
www.hartleysauctions.co.uk

## AUTOGRAPHS
### U.K.
The Signature Connection
Tel: 07919 092991
steve@thesignatureconnection.
co.uk
www.thesignatureconnection.co.uk

Special Signings Limited
Tel: 01438 714728
sales@specialsignings.com
www.specialsignings.com
*Autographs and autographed
memorabilia*

### Nottinghamshire
The Autograph Collectors
Gallery, 7 Jessops Lane,
Gedling, Nottingham
Tel: 0115 961 2956/987 6578
www.autograph-gallery.co.uk

International Autograph
Auctions Ltd., Foxhall Business
Centre, Foxhall Road,
Nottingham, NG7 6LH
Tel: 0115 845 1010
info@autographauctions.co.uk
www.autographauctions.co.uk
*Autograph auctions*

## AUTOMOBILIA
### U.K.
Automobilia Planet, P.O. Box 624,
Yarm Tel: 01642 658454
www.automobiliaplanet.com

### Leicestershire
Pooks Motor Books, Fowke
Street, Rothley
Tel: 0116 237 6222
pooks.motorbooks@virgin.net
www.pooksmotorbooks.co.uk
*Motoring books and automobilia*

## BAROGRAPHS
### U.K.
### Somerset
Richard Twort Tel: 01934 612439
or 07711 939789
*Barographs and all types of
meteorological instruments*

## BOOKS
### U.S.A.
PBA Galleries,
133 Kearny Street, 4th Floor,
San Francisco, California 94108
Tel: 415 989 2665
www.pbagalleries.com
*Auctions of rare books and manuscripts,
maps and atlases and photographs*

### U.K.
### Dorset
Books Afloat,
66 Park Street, Weymouth
Tel: 01305 779774
*Books on all subjects, liner and naval
memorabilia, shipping company
china, ships bells, old postcards,
models, paintings*

**Herefordshire**
Addyman Books,
39 Lion Street,
Hay-on-Wye
Tel: 01497 821136

**London**
Biblion, Grays Antique Market,
1-7 Davies Mews
Tel: 020 7629 1374
www.biblionmayfair.com
*Antiquarian books, maps & prints*

Bloomsbury Auctions,
Bloomsbury House,
24 Maddox Street
Tel: 020 7495 9494
www.bloomsburyauctions.com
*Books, manuscripts, art, prints, collectables auctions*

Nigel Williams Rare Books,
25 Cecil Court
Tel: 020 7836 7757
www.nigelwilliams.com
*Books - first editions, illustrated, childrens and detective*

**Northumberland**
Barter Books, Alnwick Station,
Alnwick Tel: 01665 604888
www.barterbooks.co.uk
*One of the largest secondhand bookshops in Britain*

**Scotland**
Robert Mullin, The Wee Web,
61 (Flat 2) Rosevale Terrace,
Edinburgh
Tel: 0131 467 7147
www.theweeweb.co.uk
*Ladybird books*

**BOTTLES**
**U.K.**
**Staffordshire**
Gordon Litherland,
25 Stapenhill Road,
Burton on Trent
Tel: 01283 567213 or
07952 118987
gordon@jmp2000.com
*Bottles, breweriana and pub jugs, advertising ephemera and commemoratives*

**BREWERIANA**
**U.K.**
**Lincolnshire**
Junktion,
The Old Railway Station,
New Bolingbroke,
Boston
Tel: 01205 480068 or 07836
345491
junktionantiques@hotmail.com
*Advertising and packaging, automobilia, slot machines, pedal cars*

**Staffordshire**
Gordon Litherland,
25 Stapenhill Road,
Burton on Trent
Tel: 01283 567213 or
07952 118987
gordon@jmp2000.com
*Bottles, breweriana and pub jugs, advertising ephemera and commemoratives*

**CAMERAS**
**U.K.**
**Lincolnshire**
Antique Photographic Company
Ltd Tel: 01949 842192
alpaco47@aol.com
www.rubylane.com/shops/
woodstoneantiques
*Vintage photographica, optical toys, magic lanterns, stereo, scientific, bakelite and unusual items*

**West Sussex**
Arundel Photographica,
The Arundel Antiques and
Collectors Centre,
51 High Street, Arundel
Tel: 01903 885540
www.arundel-photographica.
co.uk
*Antique and classic cameras, everything associated with photography and cinematography and items of optical interest*

**West Yorkshire**
The Camera House,
65 Oakworth Hall, Oakworth,
Keighley Tel: 01535 642333
www.the-camera-house.co.uk
*Cameras & photographic equipment from 1850*

**CERAMICS**
**U.S.A.**
Mary's Memories, P.O. Box 2342,
Centreville, VA 20122
mcmonet@hughes.net
www.tias.com/stores/mm

Pascoe & Company,
253 SW 22nd Avenue,
Miami, Florida 33135
Tel: 800 872 0195/
305 643 2550
www.pascoeandcompany.com
*Hand-crafted porcelain collectibles and Art Pottery from Royal Doulton and other renowned european potteries*

**U.K.**
AntiquesAdvertiser.co.uk
info@antiquesadvertiser.co.uk
www.antiquesadvertiser.co.uk
*Classified advertising website*

www.retroselect.com
info@retroselect.com
*Retro ceramics and glass from the 1950s to 1980s*

**Dorset**
Shibusa Gallery, The Sub Post
Office, Rear of 14 Dunyeats Road,
Broadstone Tel: 07931 298584
www.shibusa-gallery.co.uk
*20thC Studio Pottery and art and design*

**Essex**
Hazle Ceramics Limited,
33-35 Barleylands Craft Centre,
Barleylands Road, Billericay
Tel: 01268 270892
www.hazle.com
*Collectible ceramic wall plaques*

The Poole Room
info@pooleroom.co.uk
www.pooleroom.co.uk
*Antique and collectable Poole pottery*

**Kent**
ReMemories Antiques,
74 High Street, Tenterden
Tel: 01580 763416
*Doulton & Beatrix Potter specialist*

Serendipity,
125 High Street, Deal
Tel: 01304 369165/01304
366536 dipityantiques@aol.com
www.serendipityantiques.co.uk
*Staffordshire pottery*

**London**
Beth, GO 43-44 Alfies Antique
Market, 13-25 Church Street,
Marylebone
Tel: 020 7723 5613/
0777 613 6003
*Glass & ceramics, porcelain, vases, bowls, jars, English china*

Beverley, 30 Church Street,
Marylebone Tel: 020 7262 1576
or 07776136003
*Glass & ceramics, porcelain, vases, bowls, jars, English china*

John English Gifts,
6 Prices Arcade, Picadilly
(closed during Feb)
Tel: 020 7437 2082
www.johnenglishgifts.com
*Worldwide suppliers of collectables*

KCS Ceramics International
Tel: 020 8384 8981
www.kcsceramics.co.uk
*Poole, Lladro, Doulton, Troika, Carlton ware*

**Norfolk**
Cat Pottery, 1 Grammar School
Road, North Walsham
Tel: 01692 402962
*Winstanley cats*

**Oxfordshire**
The Ceramic Studio,
2 Potters Hill Farm Cottages,
Langley, Witney
www.theceramicstudio.co.uk
*Studio pottery*

**Surrey**
A1 Collectables Ltd,
Hampton Wick Antique Market,
97B High Street, Hampton Wick
Tel: 020 8977 7230
www.a1-collectables.co.uk
*Gifts, collectables, jewellery, silverware, retro items and vintage games and jigsaws*

**East Sussex**
Tony Horsley, P.O. Box 3127,
Brighton Tel: 01273 550770
*Candle extinguishers, Royal Worcester and other porcelain*

**Tyne & Wear**
www.cornishware.biz
Vintage-Kitsch, 1 Crown &
Anchor Cottages, Horsley,
Newcastle
Tel: 07979 857599
info@cornishware.biz
www.cornishware.biz
*Vintage T G Green Cornish kitchen ware and related ranges*

**Wales**
Islwyn Watkins, Offa's Dyke
Antique Centre, 4 High Street,
Knighton, Powys
Tel: 01547 520145
*18th and 19th century pottery, 20th century country and Studio Pottery, small country furniture, Treen and bygones*

**Warwickshire**
Chinasearch, P.O. Box 1202,
Kenilworth
Tel: 01926 512402
info@chinasearch.co.uk
www.chinasearch.co.uk
*Discontinued dinner, tea and collectable ware bought and sold*

Cornishware Search,
Henley Street Antiques Centre,
Henley Street,
Stratford-upon-Avon
Tel: 01926 427069
www.cornishwaresearch.co.uk
*Specialists in vintage TG Green items*

**CIGARETTE CARDS**
**U.K.**
**Gloucestershire**
M&C Cards,
Unit 30/32 Antique Centre,
Severn Road,
Gloucester
Tel: 01452 506361
www.mandccards.co.uk
*Cigarette, trade cards and postcards*

**London**
Murray Cards (International)
Ltd, 51 Watford Way,
Hendon Central
Tel: 020 8202 5688
www.murraycard.com/
*Cigarette & trade cards*

**Somerset**
London Cigarette Card Co Ltd,
Sutton Road, Somerton
Tel: 01458 273452
cards@londoncigcard.co.uk
www.londoncigcard.co.uk
*Cigarette and trade cards*

**Suffolk**
W. L. Hoad,
9 St. Peter's Road,
Kirkley, Lowestoft
Tel: 01502 587758
william@whoad.fsnet.co.uk
www.cigarettecardsplus.co.uk

**COINS**
**U.K.**
**London**
Coincraft,
44 & 45 Great Russell Street
Tel: 020 7636 1188 &
020 7637 8785
www.coincraft.com
*Coins, banknotes, medallions, ancient coins and antiquities*

**Hampshire**
A B Coins & Medals,
23-25 'Old' Northam Road,
Southampton
Tel: 023 8023 3393 or
07759 655739/07770 671832

# DIRECTORY OF SPECIALISTS

**London**
Dix Noonan Webb,
16 Bolton Street, Piccadilly
Tel: 020 7016 1700
www.dnw.co.uk
*Auctioneers and valuers of orders,
decorations and medals, coins,
tokens and banknotes*

## COLLECTIBLES
**U.S.A.**
British Collectibles,
917 Chicago Avenue,
Evanston, Illinois 60202
Tel: 800 634 0431
kevin@britishcollectibles.com
sheila@britishcollectibles.com
britcol@msn.com
*David Winter cottages, Kevin Francis
face pots and ceramics. Figurines as
well as many other fine British made
gifts and collectibles*

Don and Chris' Old Stuff,
Wholesale Vintage Antiques
and Collectibles,
1242 Shawnee Run Drive,
Maineville, OH 45039
Tel: 513 677 3351
www.oldstuffonly.com
*Vintage antiques and collectibles*

The Knick Knack Nook,
W. Pratt Boulevard, Chicago,
IL 60626 Tel: 773 274 9511
www.knickknacknook.com
*Collectible and decorative items*

Owen Collectibles,
Dallas, TXTel: 214 680 4960
www.owencollectibles.com

**U.K.**
**Devon**
Collectables, 134B High Street,
Honiton, Devon, EX14 1JP
Tel: 01404 47024
chris@collectableshoniton.co.uk
www.collectableshoniton.co.uk
*Open Tues, Wed, Fri, Sat 10am–4.30pm.
Annuals, breweriana, cameras,
cigarette & phone cards, commemorative*

## COMICS
**U.K.**
**Oxfordshire**
Comic Connections,
4a Parsons Street, Banbury
Tel: 01295 268989
www.american-comics.net/

## COMMEMORATIVES
**U.K.**
**Berkshire**
Special Auction Services,
Kennetholme, Midgham,
Reading Tel: 0118 971 2949
www.specialauctionservices.com
*Commemoratives, pot lids & Prattware,
Fairings, Goss & Crested, Baxter & Le
Blond prints. Also toys for the collector*

**Devon**
Commemorabilia,
15 Haroldsleigh Avenue,
Crownhill, Plymouth
Tel: 01752 700795
www.commemorabilia.co.uk
*Commemorative items including royal
memorabilia*

## DECORATIVE ARTS
**U.K.**
Steven Bishop Antiques &
Decorative Arts
Tel: 07761563095
meridian34all@btinternet.com
www.meridiangallery.co.uk
*British Art Pottery & applied
decorative art & design*

**Kent**
The Design Gallery 1850–1950,
5 The Green,
Westerham
Tel: 01959 561234 or
07974 322858
www.designgallery.co.uk
*Quality original items 1850-1950*

**London**
Banana Dance Ltd,
155A Northcote Road,
Battersea
Tel: 01634 364539 or
07976 296987
www.bananadance.com
*Decorative Arts of the 1920s and the
1930s*

Mike Weedon,
7 Camden Passage,
Islington
Tel: 020 7226 5319 or
020 7609-6826
www.mikeweedonantiques.com
*Art Deco and Art Nouveau antiques*

**Shropshire**
Decorative Antiques,
47 Church Street,
Bishop's Castle
Tel: 01588 638851
www.decorative-antiques.co.uk
*Decorative objects of the 19th and
20thc*

**Staffordshire**
AD Antiques,
P.O. Box 2407,
Stone Tel: 07811 783518
www.adantiques.com
*Ceramics, glass and metals from the
Art Nouveau, Arts & Crafts and
Secessionist Movements*

**Worcestershire**
Art Nouveau Originals,
The Bindery Gallery,
69 High Street, Broadway
Tel: 01386 854645 or
07774 718 096
www.artnouveauoriginals.com

**West Yorkshire**
Muir Hewitt Art Deco Originals,
Redbrick Mill,
218 Bradford Road, Batley
Tel: 01813 685990
muirhewitt@hotmail.com
www.muirhewitt.com

## DOLLS
**U.S.A.**
All Dolled Up
Tel: 519 745 2122
jenn@alldolledup.ca
www.alldolledup.ca
*Vintage Barbie dolls and friends from
1959 to 1976*

**U.K.**
**Kent**
Lolli Dollies Online,
8 Athol Terrace, Dover
www.lolli-dollies-online.co.uk
*Vintage and modern dolls, clothes
and accessories*

**West Sussex**
Pollyanna,
34 High Street, Arundel
Tel: 01903 885198 or
07949903457

## EPHEMERA
**U.S.A.**
Kit Barry Ephemera & Supplies,
74 Cotton Mill Hill,
#A252, Brattleboro,
VT 05301

**U.K.**
**London**
BeatBooks.com,
32 St Paul's View,
15 Amwell Street
Tel: 020 7278 5034
www.beatbooks.com
*Rare and used books, magazines and
ephemera from the Beat Generation,
the Sixties CounterCulture, and the
Avant-Gardes*

## EXHIBITIONS & FAIRS
**U.K.**
**West Midlands**
Memorabilia, NEC, Birmingham
Tel: 0870 224 8615
www.memorabilia.co.uk
*Europe's largest collector's fair for sci-
fi, fantasy, cult film & TV, comics,
sport and pop culture collectables.
November 24 & 25 2007, March 29 &
30 2008, Summer show - please see
website for details*

## FISHING
**U.K.**
**Kent**
The Old Tackle Box, P.O. Box
55, High Street, Cranbrook
Tel: 01580 713979 or 07729
278 293 tackle.box@virgin.net
*Old fishing tackle*

## GLASS
**U.S.A.**
City Scavenger Vintage Glass &
Goods, 563N 66th Street,
Wallwatosa, WI 53213
Tel: 414 763 5734
www.justglassmall.com/stores/b
allerinalady
*Vintage merchandise for designers,
set decorators and the public. Home
of depression, 40s, 50s, 60s, Art
glass, kitchen glass and vintage goods*

Retro Art Glass, California
Tel: 951 639 3032
www.retroartglass.com

**U.K.**
**Cumbria**
Just Glass, Cross House,
Market Place, Alston,
CA9 3HS
Tel: 01434 381263 or
0783 3994948

**Gloucestershire**
Grimes House Antiques,
High Street, Moreton-in-Marsh
Tel: 01608 651029
grimes_house@cix.co.uk
www.grimeshouse.co.uk
www.cranberryglass.co.uk
*Cranberry glass*

**Shropshire**
Jonathan Harris Studio Glass
Ltd, Woodland House,
24 Peregrine Way, Apley Castle,
Telford, TF1 6TH
Tel: 01952 246381/588441
www.jhstudioglass.com

**Somerset**
Frank Dux Antiques,
33 Belvedere, Bath, BA1 5HR
Tel: 01225 312367
www.antique-glass.co.uk

**East Sussex**
Glass etc, 18–22 Rope Walk, Rye,
TN31 7NA Tel: 01797 226600
decanterman@freezone.co.uk
www.decanterman.com

## GOLF
**U.K.**
**Scotland**
Rhod McEwan - Golf Books,
Glengarden, Ballater,
Aberdeenshire
Tel: 013397 55429
teeoff@rhodmcewan
www.rhodmcewan.com
*Rare and out-of-print golfing books*

## HORSE RACING
**U.K.**
**Staffordshire**
Gordon Litherland,
25 Stapenhill Road,
Burton on Trent
Tel: 01283 567213 or
07952 118987
gordon@jmp2000.com
*Bottles, breweriana and pub jugs,
advertising ephemera and
commemoratives*

## JEWELLERY
**U.S.A.**
Vintique Vintage Jewelry,
Lakeville, MN 55044
Tel: 612 968 4600
www.rubylane.com/shops/spark
les/ilist/ is=o.html

**U.K.**
**Lancashire**
Arlene De Vries Antiques
Tel: 07850 100249
brightthingsrevisited@
btinternet.com
www.brightthingsrevisited.com
*Jewellery, silver and objets de vertu*

## KITCHENWARE
**U.K.**
**East Sussex**
Jane Wicks Kitchenalia,
'Country Ways', Strand Quay,
RyeTel: 01424 713635 or
07754 308269
janes_kitchen@hotmail.com
*Kitchen, garden and textiles
collectables*

## LIGHTING
### U.S.A.
Chameleon Fine Lighting,
223 East 59th Street,
New York, NY 10022
Tel: 212 355 6300
mail@chameleon59.com
www.chameleon59.com
*Antique and replica lighting*

## MAGAZINES
### U.K.
**London**
The Advertising Archives,
Larry Viner, 45 Lyndale Avenue
Tel: 020 7435 6540
larry@advertisingarchives.co.uk
www.advertisingarchives.co.uk

## MODERN TECHNOLOGY
### U.S.A.
Harry Poster,
1310 Second Street,
Fair Lawn, NJ 07410
tvs@harryposter.com
www.harryposter.com
*Vintage TVs, electronic items and radios*

### U.K.
**Hampshire**
Pepe Tozzo pepe@tozzo.co.uk
*Collectable technology*

**Lincolnshire**
Junktion, The Old Railway
Station, New Bolingbroke,
Boston Tel: 01205 480068 or
07836 345491
junktionantiques@hotmail.com
*Advertising and packaging, automobilia, slot machines, pedal cars, etc*

## MONEY BOXES
### U.K.
**Yorkshire**
John & Simon Haley,
89 Northgate, North Bridge,
Halifax Tel: 01422 360434
collectorsoldtoy@aol.com
www.collectorsoldtoyshop.com
*Old toys and money boxes*

## MUSICAL INSTRUMENTS
**Somerset**
Vintage & Rare Guitars (Bath) Ltd,
7-8 Saville Row, Bath, BA1 2QP
Tel: 01225 330 888
www.vintageandrareguitars.com

**London**
Vintage & Rare Guitars
(London), 6 Denmark Street,
WC2H 8LX
Tel: 020 7240 7500
www.vintageandrareguitars.com

## NAUTICAL
### U.K.
**Somerset**
Oldnautibits,
P.O. Box 67, Langport
Tel: 01458 241816 or
07947 277833
www.oldnautibits.com
*Nautical antiques, aeronautical and aviation collectables, naval and aviation memorabilia, maritime antiques and items of militaria*

## PAPER MONEY
### U.K.
**Surrey**
British Notes, P.O. Box 257,
Sutton Tel: 020 8641 3224
pamwestbritnotes@aol.com
www.britishnotes.co.uk
*Banking collectables*

## PAPERWEIGHTS
### U.K.
**Cheshire**
Sweetbriar Gallery Ltd,
29 Beechview Road, Kingsley,
Frodsham Tel: 01928 788225
sales@sweetbriar.co.uk
www.sweetbriar.co.uk
www.sweetbriarartglass.co.uk
*Paperweights*

## PENS
### U.S.A.
Vintage Pens, P.O. Box 41452,
Providence, RI 02940-1452
Tel: 401 351 7607
pen.info@vintagepens.com
www.vintagepens.com

### U.K.
**East Sussex**
Hans's Vintage Fountain Pens
Tel: 01323 765398 or
07850 771183
HSeiringer@aol.com
www.hanspens.com

## PHONECARDS
### U.S.A.
KARS Unlimited,
P.O. Box 895340, Leesburg,
FL 34789-5340 Tel: 352 365 0229
karsunltd@aol.com
www.kars-unlimited.com

### U.K.
**Devon**
Collectables, 134B High Street,
Honiton, Devon, EX14 1JP
Tel: 01404 47024
chris@collectableshoniton.co.uk
www.collectableshoniton.co.uk
*Open Tues, Wed, Fri, Sat 10.00am–4.30pm. Annuals, breweriana, cameras, cigarette & phone cards, commemorative*

## POSTCARDS
### U.K.
**London**
Memories Collectors Shop,
130-132 Brent Street,
Hendon Tel: 020 8203 1500
www.memoriespostcards.co.uk
*Picture library, framing and postcards*

**Somerset**
S&D Postcards, Bartlett Street
Antique Centre, 5-10 Bartlett
Street, Bath Tel: 07979 506415
wndvd@aol.com

## POSTERS
### U.K.
**Buckinghamshire**
Briggs Rock & Pop Memorabilia,
Loudwater House, London Road,
Loudwater, High Wycombe
Tel: 01494 436644
music@usebriggs.com
www.usebriggs.com

**Dorset**
Onslow's Auctions Ltd,
The Coach House, Manor Road,
Stourpaine, Blandford Forum
Tel: 01258 488838
onslowauctions@btinternet.com
*19th and 20th century posters, railwayana, motoring, aviation, Titanic and ocean liner collectors items*

**London**
Limelight Movie Art,
135 King's Road, Chelsea
Tel: 020 7751 5584
www.limelightmovieart.com
*Original film posters and lobby cards*

## POWDER COMPACTS
### U.K.
**Devon**
Sue Wilde at Wildewear
Tel: 01395 577966
compacts@wildewear.co.uk
www.wildewear.co.uk
*Fashion accessories 1900-1950 including beaded and leather bags, purses, hats, powder compacts, buttons and jewellery*

## PROPS
### U.K.
**London**
The Prop Store of London
www.propstore.com
*One of the world's leading vendors of movie props and costumes as collectable items*

## RADIOS
### U.K.
**Cheshire**
On The Air,
The Vintage Technology Centre,
The Highway,
Hawarden,
(Nr Chester), Deeside
Tel: 01244 530300 or
07778 767734
www.vintageradio.co.uk

**Somerset**
Philip Knighton,
1c South Street,
Wellington, TA21 8NS
Tel: 01823 661618
philip.knighton@btconnect.com
*Vintage radio and gramophone repairs*

## RAILWAYANA
### U.K.
**Bedfordshire**
Sheffield Railwayana Auctions,
4 The Glebe, Clapham,
Bedford
Tel: 01234 325341
SheffRailwayana@aol.com
www.sheffieldrailwayana.co.uk

**Worcestershire**
Gloucestershire Worcestershire
Railwayana Auctions LLP,
The Willows, Badsey Road,
Evesham
Tel: 01386 421324 or
01684 773487
master@gwra.co.uk
www.gwra.co.uk
*Railwayana & transport collectables auctions*

## ROCK & POP
### U.K.
**Buckinghamshire**
Briggs Rock & Pop Memorabilia,
Loudwater House,
London Road, Loudwater,
High Wycombe
Tel: 01494 436644
music@usebriggs.com
www.usebriggs.com

**Cheshire**
Collectors Corner,
P.O. Box 8, Congleton
Tel: 01260 270429
dave.popcorner@ukonline.co.uk
*Beatles and pop memorabilia*

**Hampshire**
Spinna Disc Records,
2B Union Street,
Aldershot, GU11 1EG
Tel: 01252 327261
www.spinnadiscrecords.com
*Vinyl albums, LPs, CDs, 12"s and 7"s. Specialising in rock, punk, heavy metal, progressive, folk, blues, pop, alternative, indie*

Sweet Memories Vinyl Records
UK www.vinylrecords.co.uk
*Vinyl records from the 50s, 60s, 70s, 80s & 90s*

**Lancashire**
Tracks, P.O. Box 117,
Chorley Tel: 01257 269726
sales@tracks.co.uk
www.tracks.co.uk
*Beatles and pop memorabilia*

**London**
Beanos, Middle Street,
Croydon, CR0 1RE
Tel: 020 8680 1202
www.beanos.co.uk
*Records, CDs, DVDs, videos, books, record accessories and pop memorabilia*

## SCIENTIFIC INSTRUMENTS
### U.K.
**Cheshire**
Charles Tomlinson,
Chester
Tel: 01244 318395
charlestomlinson@tiscali.co.uk

## SHIPPING
### U.K.
**Hampshire**
Cobwebs,
78 Northam Road,
Southampton, Hampshire
Tel: 023 8022 7458
www.cobwebs.uk.com
*Ocean liner memorabilia. Also naval and aviation items*

## SPORT
### U.S.A.
Hunt Auctions, Inc.,
75 E. Uwchlan Avenue,
Suite 130, Exton,
Pennsylvania 19341
Tel: 610 524 0822
www.huntauctions.com
*Historical baseball and football memorabilia auctions*

Mastro Auctions,
7900 South Madison Street,
Burr Ridge, Illinois 60527
Tel: 630 472 1200
www.mastroauctions.com
*Sports and Americana collector
auctions*

**U.K.**
**London**
Graham Budd Auctions Ltd
Tel: 020 8366 2525 or
07974 113394
www.grahambuddauctions.co.uk
*Sporting memorabilia auctions*

**Nottinghamshire**
T. Vennett-Smith,
11 Nottingham Road,
Gotham
Tel: 0115 983 0541
info@vennett-smith.com
www.vennett-smith.com
*Sporting memorabilia auctions*

**Oxfordshire**
Manfred Schotten,
109 High Street,
Burford
Tel: 01993 822302
www.schotten.com
*Sporting antiques, memorabilia and
collectibles*

**Shropshire**
Mullock's Specialist Auctions &
Valuers, The Old Shippon,
Wall-under-Heywood,
Nr Church Stretton
Tel: 01694 771771 or
01584 841 428
info@mullocksauctions.co.uk
www.mullocksauctions.co.uk
*Sporting memorabilia auctions*

**TEDDY BEARS**
**U.K.**
**Oxfordshire**
Teddy Bears of Witney,
99 High Street,
Witney
Tel: 01993 706616
bears@witneybears.co.uk
www.teddybears.co.uk

**West Yorkshire**
Bears of Windy Hill,
P.O. Box 51, Shipley
Tel: 01274 599175 or
07768 240158
www.bearsofwindyhill.co.uk

**TELEPHONES**
**U.K.**
Retrobrick www.retrobrick.com
*Vintage and retro mobile phones*

**Gloucestershire**
Telephone Lines Ltd,
304 High Street, Cheltenham
Tel: 01242 583699
info@telephonelines.net
www.telephonelines.net

**Kent**
Candlestick & Bakelite,
P.O. Box 308, Orpington
Tel: 020 8467 3743
candlestick.bakelite@mac.com
www.candlestickandbakelite.co.uk

**TEXTILES**
**U.S.A.**
Vintage Swank, 212 East Main
Street, Front Royal, VA 22630
Tel: 540 636 0069
www.vintageswank.com
*Vintage clothing, housewares,
furniture and lighting*

**U.K.**
**Kent**
Castle Antiques,
1 London Road, Westerham
Tel: 01959 562492
(Thurs or Sat)
*Linen: Good quality, ready to sell bulk
linen. Lots for trade buyers. Costume
and fashion accessories. Affordable
chandeliers. Also odd unusual
antiques and collectables*

**Lancashire**
Decades,
20 Lord St West,
Blackburn Tel: 01254 693320
*Original Victorian to 1970s clothing,
accessories, jewellery, decorative
textiles and more*

**London**
299,
299 Lillie Road
Tel: 07860 223707
*Period & vintage costume &
accessories. Antique textiles &
haberdashery*

Rokit Ltd,
101 & 107 Brick Lane
Tel: 020 7375 3864
*Vintage clothing and accessories*

Sparkle Moore,
Alfies Antique Market,
G100 & G116 Ground Floor,
13-25 Church Street,
Marylebone
Tel: 020 7724 8984 or
07958 515614
www.sparklemoore.com
*20thC pin-up & period clothing,
accessories & collectables for sale and
hire. Vintage men's clothing and top
drawer accessories*

Steinberg & Tolkien Vintage &
Designer Clothing,
193 Kings Road
Tel: 020 7376 3660

**East Sussex**
First Call, Module B2 Enterprise
Point, Melbourne Street,
Brighton
Tel: 01273 202201
*Vintage clothing and accessories*

Wardrobe,
51 Upper North Street,
Brighton
Tel: 01273 202201
*Vintage clothing and accessories*

**Wales**
Ashmans Vintage Clothing &
Accessories Makers,
Park Lane House,
7 & 11 High Street,
Welshpool
Tel: 01938 554505

**Yorkshire**
Echoes,
650a Halifax Road,
Eastwood, Todmorden
Tel: 01706 817505
*Antique costume, textiles including
linen, lace and jewellery*

Steptoes Dog Antiques
Tel: 07731475164
steptoes.dog@virgin.net
www.steptoesantiques.co.uk
*Vintage retro & antique clothing &
collectables*

**TOYS**
**U.K.**
Toydreams
sales@toydreams.co.uk
www.toydreams.co.uk

Toys & Hobbies
Tel: 0161 794 5360
toysandhobbies@btinternet.co
m www.toysandhobbies.net

**Berkshire**
Special Auction Services,
Kennetholme,
Midgham, Reading
Tel: 0118 971 2949
www.specialauctionservices.com
*Toys for the collector*

**Cleveland**
Vectis Auctions Ltd and Vectis
Direct, Fleck Way,
Thornaby,
Stockton-on-Tees
Tel: 01642 750616 and
01642 764455
admin@vectis.co.uk and
admin@vectisdirect.co.uk
www.vectis.co.uk and
www.vectisdirect.co.uk
*Toy auctions*

**Gloucestershire**
Dave's Classic Toys,
Antiques Centre Gloucester,
1 Severn Road,
The Historic Docks,
Gloucester
Tel: 01452 529716

**Hampshire**
The Magic Toy Box,
210 Havant Road,
Drayton, Portsmouth
Tel: 02392 221307
www.magictoybox.co.uk
www.sindy-dolls.co.uk
*Toys, dolls and china figurines,
Pelham Puppets, plastic kits and
models*

**Isle of Wight**
Nostalgia Toy Museum,
High Street,
Godshill, Ventnor
Tel: 01983 522148
toyman@nostalgiatoys.com
www.nostalgiatoys.com
*Diecast toys specialist and museum*

**Lincolnshire**
Junktion,
The Old Railway Station,
New Bolingbroke,
Boston Tel: 01205 480068 or

07836 345491
junktionantiques@hotmail.com
*Advertising and packaging,
automobilia, slot machines, pedal
cars, etc*

Vintage Toybox, Gainsborough
contact@vintagetoybox.co.uk
www.vintagetoybox.co.uk

**London**
Mimi Fifi, 27 Pembridge Road,
Notting Hill Gate
Tel: 020 7243 3154
www.mimififi.com
*Vintage and collectible toys*

**Oxfordshire**
Mike Delaney
Tel: 01993 840064 or
07979 910760
mike@vintagehornby.co.uk
www.vintagehornby.co.uk
*Vintage Hornby 0 gauge & other toy
trains*

**Staffordshire**
Metropolis Toys,
31 Derby Street,
Burton on Trent
Tel: 01283 740400
www.metropolistoys.co.uk
*Vintage collectables, particularly TV
and film related toys, Action Man and
other action figures, also selling
Dinky, Corgi and model railways*

**Suffolk**
Militaryman
Tel: 01473 274367
militaryman@peace41.fsnet.co.uk
www.dinkycollector.com
*Pre and post war toys from all leading
manufacturers including Dinky, Corgi,
Britains and Solido*

**East Sussex**
Wallis & Wallis,
West Street Auction Galleries,
Lewes Tel: 01273 480208
auctions@wallisandwallis.co.uk
www.wallisandwallis.co.uk
*Tinplate and diecast toys auctions*

**Yorkshire**
Gerard Haley,
Hippins Farm,
Black Shawhead,
Nr Hebden Bridge
Tel: 01422 842484
gedhaley@yahoo.co.uk
*Toy soldiers*

John & Simon Haley,
89 Northgate,
North Bridge, Halifax
Tel: 01422 360434
collectorsoldtoy@aol.com
www.collectorsoldtoyshop.com
*Old toys and money boxes*

**West Yorkshire**
Andrew Clarke Models,
Unit 13 Baildon Mills,
Northgate, Baildon,
Shipley, BD17 6JX
Tel: 01274 594552
andrew@andrewclarkemodels.com
*Dinky, Corgi, Matchbox, Spot-On,
tinplate toys, Britains, trains, etc*

# DIRECTORY OF COLLECTORS' CLUBS

With new Collectors' Clubs emerging every day this directory is by no means complete. If you wish to be included in next year's directory or if you have a change of details, please inform us by May 2008.

**A.C.O.G.B (Autograph Club of Great Britain),** SAE to Mr R. Gregson, 47 Webb Crescent, Dawley, Telford, Shropshire, TF4 3DS Tel: 01952 410332 gregson@blueyonder.co.uk www.acogb.co.uk

**The Action Soldier Collectors Club,** 30 New Street, Deinolen, Gwynedd, North Wales, LL55 3LH

**Alice in Wonderland Collectors Network,** Joel Birenbaum, 2765 Shellingham Drive, Lisle, IL 60532-4245, U.S.A.

**American Art Pottery Association,** Patti Bourgeois, P.O. Box 834, Westport, MA 02790, U.S.A. Tel: 508 679 5910 patspots1997@aol.com www.amartpot.org

**American Business Card Club UK,** Robin Cleeter, 38 Abbotsbury Road, Morden, Surrey, SM4 5LQ

**American Business Card Club US,** Avery N. Pitzak, P.O. Box 460297, Aurora, CO 80046-0297, U.S.A.

**American Ceramic Circle,** Nancy K Lester, 520 16th St, Brooklyn, NY 11215, U.S.A. nlester@earthlink.net

**American Credit Card Collectors Society,** Bill Wieland, President, P.O. Box 2465, MI 48641, U.S.A. acccs1@charter.net www.creditcollectibles.com

**American Fish Decoy Collectors Association,** P.O. Box 252, Boulder Junction, WI 54512, U.S.A.

**American Hatpin Society,** Virginia Woodbury, 20 Montecillo Drive, Rolling Hills Estates, CA 90274, U.S.A. www.americanhatpinsociety.com

**American Lock Collectors Association,** 36076 Grennada, Livonia, MI 48154, U.S.A.

**American Matchcover Collecting Club,** P.O. Box 18481, Asheville, NC 28814, U.S.A.

**American Society of Camera Collectors, Inc.,** c/o Sam Rosenfeld, VP, 6570 Kelvin Ave, Canoga Park, CA 91306-4021, U.S.A.

**American Toy Emergency Vehicle (ATEV) Club,** Jeff Hawkins, President, 11415 Colfax Road, Glen Allen, Virginia 23060, U.S.A.

**Antiquarian Horological Society,** New House, High Street, Ticehurst, East Sussex, TN5 7AL Tel: 01580 200 155 secretary@ahsoc.demon.co.uk www.ahsoc.demon.co.uk

**Antique Bottles & Collectibles Club,** Willy Young, P.O. Box 1061, Verdi, NV 89439, U.S.A.

**Antique Fan Collectors' Association,** P.O. Box 5473, Sarasota, FL 34277-5473, U.S.A. Tel: 941 955 8232 membership@fancollectors.org www.fancollectors.org

**Antique Wireless Association (AWA),** Box E, Breesport, New York 14816, U.S.A.

**The Aviation Postcard Club Int. & USA,** Phil Munson, 25 Kerill Avenue, Old Coulsdon, Surrey, CR5 1QB

**Badge Collectors' Circle,** c/o Frank Setchfield, 57 Middleton Place, Loughborough, Leicestershire, LE11 2BY Tel: 01509 569270 f.setchfield@ntlworld.com www.badgecollectorscircle.co.uk

**Barbie Collectors Club of Great Britain,** Elizabeth Lee, 17 Rosemont Road, Acton, London, W3 9LU

**Barbie Lover's Club,** Amy Reed, 399 Winfield Road, Rochester, New York 14622, U.S.A.

**The Beano & Dandy Collectors' Club,** P.O. Box 3433, Brighton, East Sussex, BN50 9JA Tel: 01273 673462 phil@phil-comics.com www.phil-comics.com

**Bearly Ours Teddy Club,** Linda Harris, 54 Berkinshaw Crescent, Don Mills, Ontario, M3B 2T2, Canada

**Beer Can Collectors of America,** Don Hicks, 747 Merus Court, Fenton, MO 63026-2092, U.S.A.

**Beswick Collectors Club,** Barry Hill, P.O. Box 310, Richmond, Surrey, TW10 7FU Tel: barryjhill@hotmail.com www.collectingdoulton.com/

**Black Memorabilia Collectors Association,** Sharon Hart, 2482 Devoe Terrace, Bronx, NY 10468, U.S.A.

**Borsato Collectors Club,** Allan Koskela, P.O. Box 104, Webster City, IA 50595, U.S.A. Tel: 515 832 2437 alankoskela@wmconnect.com www.borsato.20m.com/

**The British Beermat Collectors' Society,** Hon Sec, 69 Dunnington Avenue, Kidderminster, Worcestershire, DY10 2YT www.britishbeermats.org.uk

**British Button Society,** Rex Butler, Membership Secretary, 12 Middlefield, Gnosall, Stafford, ST20 0LS Tel: 01785 824426 rexbbs@tailend.fsnet.co.uk www.britishbuttonsociety.org

**The British Compact Collectors' Society,** P.O. Box 131, Woking, Surrey, GU24 9YR www.compactcollectors.co.uk

**British Diecast Model Collectors Association,** P.O. Box 11, Norwich, NR7 0SP www.swapmeet.freeserve.co.uk

**British Model Soldier Society,** Hon Treasurer, 12 Savay Lane, Denham Green, Denham, Buckinghamshire, UB9 5NH Tel: 01895 832757 bmss.treasurer@btinternet.com

**British Postmark Society,** General Secretary John A. Strachan, 12 Dunavon Park, Strathaven, ML10 6LP Tel: 01357 522430 johlen@stracml10.freeserve.co.uk www.britishpostmarksociety.org.uk

**The British Smurf Collectors Club,** P.O. Box 96, Deeping St James, Peterborough, Cambridgeshire, PE6 8YN Tel: 01778 349426 www.kittyscavern.com

**Brooklands Automobilia & Regalia Collectors' Club,** P.O. Box No 4, Chapel Terrace Mews, Kemp Town, Brighton, East Sussex, BN2 1HU Tel: 01273 622722 www.barcc.co.uk www.brmmbrmm.com/barc

**Bubble Gum Charm Collectors,** Maureen McCaffrey, 24 Seafoam Street, Staten Island, NY 10306, U.S.A.

**The Burleigh Ware International Collectors Circle** Tel: 01664 454570

**Butter Pats International Collectors Club,** Alice Black, 38 Acton Street, Maynard, MA 01754, U.S.A.

**Caithness Glass Paperweight Collectors' Society,** Caithness Glass, Inveralmond, Perth, Scotland, PH1 3TZ Tel: 01738 637373 rburns@caithnessglass.co.uk www.caithnessglass.co.uk

**Carlton Ware Collectors International,** Carlton Factory Shop, Carlton Works, Copeland Street, Stoke on Trent, Staffordshire, ST4 1PU Tel: 01782 410504

**Carnival Glass Society (UK),** P.O. Box 14, Hayes, Middlesex, UB3 5NU www.carnivalglasssociety.co.uk

**Cash Register Collectors Club,** P.O. Box 20534, Dayton, OH 45420-0534, U.S.A. Tel: 937 433 3529 www.crcci.org

**Cat Collectables,** 297 Alcester Road, Hollywood, Birmingham, West Midlands, B47 5HJ Tel: 01564 826277 cat.collectables@btinternet.com www.cat-collectables.co.uk

**Cigarette Case Collectors' Club,** Colin Grey, 19 Woodhurst North, Raymead Road, Maidenhead, Berkshire, SL6 8PH Tel: 01628 781800

**Cigarette Pack Collectors Association,** Richard Elliot, 86 Plymouth Grove Drive, Kennebunk, ME 04043, U.S.A.

**Cigarette Packet Collectors Club of GB,** Barry Russell, Talisker, Vines Cross Road, Horam, Heathfield, East Sussex, TN21 0HF Tel: 01435 812453

**Clarice Cliff Collectors' Club,** P.O. Box 2706, Eccleshall, Stafford, ST21 6WY

**The Coca-Cola Collectors Club,** Membership Director, 4780 Ashford-Dunwoody Road, Suite. A, Atlanta, Georgia 30338, U.S.A. www.cocacolaclub.org

**Commemorative Collectors' Society and Commemoratives Museum,** c/o Steven Jackson, Lumless House, 77 Gainsborough Road, Winthorpe, Newark, Nottinghamshire, NG24 2NR Tel: 01636 671377 commemorativecollectorssociety@hotmail.com

**Compact Collectors Club International,** Roselyn Gerson, P.O. Box 40, Lynbrook, NY 11563, U.S.A.

**Corgi Collector Club,** c/o Corgi Classics Ltd, Meridian East, Meridian Business Park, Leicester, LE19 1RL Tel: 0870 607 1204 susie@collectorsclubs.org.uk

**Cornish Collectors Club,** P.O. Box 58, Buxton, Derbyshire, SK17 0FH

**The Costume Society,** St Paul's House, Warwick Lane, London, EC4P 4BN www.costumesociety.org.uk

**The Crested Circle,** 42 Douglas Road, Tolworth, Surbiton, Surrey, KT6 7SA

**Crunch Club (Breakfast Cereal Collectables),** John Cahill, 9 Weald Rise, Tilehurst, Reading, Berkshire, RG30 6XB ChCrnch@aol.com

**Danesby Collectors Club,** P.O. Box 2706, Eccleshall, Stafford, ST21 6WY

**The Dean's Collectors Club,** Euro Collectibles, P.O. Box 370565, 49 NE 39th Street, Miami FL33 137, U.S.A. Tel: US toll free 1 800 309 8336 www.deansbears.com

**The Dean's Collectors Club,** Pontypool, Gwent, NP4 6YY Tel: 01495 764881 www.deansbears.com

**Devon Pottery Collectors' Group,** Mrs Joyce Stonelake, 19 St Margarets Avenue, Torquay, Devon, TQ1 4LW

**Die Cast Car Collectors Club,** c/o Jay Olins (Chairman), P.O. Box 67226, Los Angeles, California 90067-0266, U.S.A. Tel: 310 629 7113 jay@diecast.org www.diecast.org

**Dinky Toy Club of America,** c/o Jerry Fralick, P.O. Box 5192, Chapel Hill, North Carolina 27517, U.S.A. www.dinkytoyclub.net

**Dinosaur Collectors Club,** Mike Howgate, 71 Hoppers Road, Winchmore Hill, London, N21 3LP

**E.T.B. Radford Collectors' Club,** 27 Forest Mead, Denmead, Waterlooville, Hampshire, PO7 6UN www.radfordcollect.com

**The Eagle Society,** Membership Secretary Keith Howard, 25a Station Road, Harrow, Middlesex, HA1 2UA

**Egg Cup Collectors' Club of GB,** Sue Wright, Subs Secretary, P.O. Box 39, Llandysul, Wales, SA44 5ZD suewright@suecol.freeserve.co.uk www.eggcupworld.co.uk

**The English Playing Card Society,** John Sings, Secretary, P.O. Box 29, North Walsham, Norfolk, NR28 9NQ Tel: 01692 650496 Secretary@EPCS.org www.wopc.co.uk/epcs

**The Enid Blyton Society,** Tony Summerfield, 93 Milford Hill, Salisbury, Wiltshire, SP1 2QL

**Ephemera Society of America, Inc.,** P.O. Box 95, Cazenovia, NY 13035, U.S.A. Tel: 315 655 9139 info@ephemerasociety.org www.ephemerasociety.org

**The Ephemera Society,** P.O. Box 112, Northwood, Middlesex, HA6 2WT Tel: 01923 829 079 info@ephemera-society.org.uk www.ephemera-society.org.uk

**The European Honeypot Collectors' Society,** John Doyle, The Honeypot, 18 Victoria Road, Chislehurst, Kent, BR7 6DF Tel: 020 8289 7725 johnhoneypot@hotmail.com www.geocities.com/tehcsuk

**Fan Circle International,** Sec: Mrs Joan Milligan, "Cronk-y-Voddy", Rectory Road, Coltishall, Norwich, NR12 7HF

**Festival of Britain Society,** c/o George Simner, 23 Langton Avenue, East Ham, London, E6 6AN fofbs@tiscali.co.uk www.festivalofbritain.org

**Fieldings Crown Devon Collectors' Club,** P.O. Box 462, Manvers, Rotherham, S63 7WT Tel: 01709 874433 FCDCC2003@talktalk.net www.fieldingscrowndevclub.com

**The Followers of Rupert,** Mrs S. Reeves, The Membership Secretary, 31 Whiteley, Windsor, Berkshire, SL4 5PJ Tel: 01753 865562 followersofrupert@hotmail.com www.rupertthebear.org.uk

**Friar Tuck Collectors Club,** c/o Jim and Barbara, Chilcutt 903 Western Air Drive, Jefferson City, MO 65109-0617, U.S.A.

**Friends of Blue Ceramic Society,** Terry Neale-Sheppard, P.O. Box 247, Aylesbury, Buckinghamshire, HP20 1JZ www.fob.org.uk

**The Furniture History Society,** c/o Dr. Brian Austen, 1 Mercedes Cottages, St. John's Road, Haywards Heath, West Sussex, RH16 4EH Tel: 01444 413845 furniturehistorysociety@hotmail.com www.furniturehistorysociety.com

**The Glass Gallery,** L.H. Selman Ltd., 123 Locust Street, Santa Cruz, CA 95060-3907, U.S.A. Tel: 831 427 1177 www.glassgallery.com

**The Glove Collector Club,** Joe Phillips, 14057 Rolling Hills Lane, Dallas, TX 75240, U.S.A.

**The Happy Pig Collectors Club,** Gene Holt, P.O. Box 17, Oneida, IL 61467-0017, U.S.A.

**Historical Model Railway Society,** 59 Woodberry Way, London, E4 7DY

**Honiton Pottery Collectors' Society,** Janet Mills (Secretary), Ships View, The Quay, Osmonds Lane, Teignmouth, Devon, TQ14 8DB Tel: 01626 774497 hpcs@shipsview.co.uk

**Hornby Collectors Club,** P.O. Box 25, Melton Mowbray, Leicestershire, LE13 1ZG Tel: 0870 062 4001 alexmckenzie@collectorsclubs.org.uk

**The Hornby Railway Collectors' Association,** David Embling, 77 Station Road, Rayleigh, Essex, SS6 8AR davidembling@btinternet.com

**Hornsea Pottery Collectors' and Research Society,** c/o Dorothy Tennant, 128 Devonshire Street, Keighley, West Yorkshire, BD21 2QJ hornsea@pdtennant.fsnet.co.uk www.hornseacollector.co.uk

**Inn Sign Society,** Chairman Mr R. P. Gatrell, Flat 19, Stamford Grange, Dunham Road, Altrincham, Cheshire, WA14 4AN Raymond@gatrell65.freeserve.co.uk www.bjcurtis.force9.co.uk

**International Association of Calculator Collectors,** P.O. Box 345, Tustin, CA 92781-0345, U.S.A.

**International Bank Note Society,** c/o Milan Alusic, P.O. Box 1642, Racine, WI 53401, U.S.A.

**International Bond & Share Society, American Branch,** Ted Robinson, Vice President, P.O. Box 814, Richboro, PA, U.S.A. Tel: 215 357 6820 fandr@voicenet.com

**International Bond and Share Society,** c/o Peter Duppa-Miller, Beechcroft, Combe Hay, Bath, Somerset, BA2 7EG

**International Map Collectors Society (IMCoS),** Secretary Yasha Beresiner, 43 Templars Crescent, London, N3 3QR

**The International Owl Collectors Club,** 54 Tiverton Road, Edgware, Middlesex, HA8 6BE

**International Perfume Bottle Association,** Details from Lynda Brine, Assembly Antique Centre, 6 Saville Row, Bath, Somerset, BA1 2QP Tel: 01225 448488 lyndabrine@yahoo.co.uk www.scentbottlesandsmalls.co.uk

**International Perfume Bottle Association,** c/o Membership Secretary, P.O. Box 1299, Paradise, CA 95967, U.S.A.

**International Playing Card Society,** PR Officer Yasha Beresiner, 43 Templars Crescent, London, N3 3QR

**International Society for Apple Parer Enthusiasts,** G.W. Laverty, 735 Cedarwood Terrace, Apt 735B, Rochester, NY 14609, U.S.A.

**The International Society of Meccanomen,** Adrian Williams, Bell House, 72a Old High Street, Headington, Oxford, OX3 9HW www.internationalmeccanomen.org.uk

**International Swizzle Stick Collectors Association,** Ray P. Hoare, P.O. Box 1117, Bellingham, WA 98227-1117, U.S.A. veray.issca@shaw.com

**The James Bond Collectors Club,** P. O. Box 1570, Christchurch, Dorset, BH23 4XS Tel: 0870 4423007 solopublishing@firenet.uk.com

**James Sadler International Collectors Club,** Customer Services, Churchill China PLC, High Street, Tunstall, Stoke on Trent, Staffordshire, ST6 5NZ Tel: 01782 577566 diningin@churchillchina.plc.uk www.james-sadler.co.uk

**Jonathan Harris Studio Glass Ltd,** Woodland House, 24 Peregrine Way, Apley Castle, Telford, Shropshire, TF1 6TH Tel: 01952 246381/588441 jonathan@jhstudioglass.com www.jhstudioglass.com

**Just Golly! Collectors Club,** SAE to Mrs A. K. Morris, 9 Wilmar Way, Seal, Sevenoaks, Kent, TN15 0DN www.gollycorner.co.uk

**Kevin Francis Toby Jug Collectors Guild,** 917 Chicago Avenue, Evanston, IL 60202, U.S.A. Tel: 800 634 0431 or 847 570 4867 Britcol@msn.com www.britishcollectibles.com/

**Kewpie Traveler,** Rose Morgan, P.O. Box 4032, Portland, OR 97208-4032, U.S.A. origppress@aol.com

**King George VI Collectors' Society (Philately),** Secretary, 17 Balcaskie Road, Eltham, London, SE9 1HQ www.kg6.info

**The Lace Guild,** Charity Reg No 274397, The Hollies, 53 Audnam, Stourbridge, West Midlands, DY8 4AE Tel: 01384 390739 hollies@laceguild.org www.laceguild.org

**Legend Products International Collector's Club,** Sheila Cochrane (Owner and Club Founder), 1 Garden Villas, Wrexham Road, Cefn Y Bedd, Flintshire, LL12 9UT Tel: 01978 760800 sheila@legend-lane.demon.co.uk www.legendproducts.co.uk

**Lilliput Lane Collectors' Club,** P.O. Box 498, Itasca, IL 60143-0498, U.S.A.

**Lock & Key Collectors' Club,** Mr Richard Phillips, "Merlewood", The Loan, West Linton, Peeblesshire, Scotland, EH46 7HE Tel: 01968 661039 rphillips52@btinternet.com

**Marble Collectors' Society of America MCSA,** P.O. Box 222, Trumball, CT 06611, U.S.A.

**Matchbox International Collectors Association (MICA) of North America,** c/o Stewart Orr and Kevin McGimpsey, P.O. Box 28072, Waterloo, Ontario, N2L 6J8, Canada

**The Matchbox Toys International Collectors' Association,** Editor Kevin McGimpsey, P.O. Box 120, Deeside, Flintshire, CH5 3HE Tel: 01244 539414 kevin@matchboxclub.com www.matchboxclub.com

**Mauchline Ware Collectors Club,** Secretary Mrs Christabelle Davey, P.O. Box 158, Leeds, LS16 5WZ contact@mauchlineware.com www.mauchlineware.com

**Memories UK Mabel Lucie Attwell Club,** Abbey Antiques, 63 Great Whyte, Ramsey, Nr Huntingdon, Cambridgeshire, PE26 1HL www.mabellucieatwellclub.com

**Merrythought International Collector's Club,** Club Sec Peter Andrews, Ironbridge, Telford, Shropshire, TF8 7NJ Tel: 01952 433116 Ext21 contact@merrythought.co.uk

**Merrythought International Collector's Club,** P.O. Box 577, Oakdale, California 95361, U.S.A.

**Milk Bottle News,** Paul & Lisa Luke, 60 Rose Valley Crescent, Stanford-le-Hope, Essex, SS17 8EF mbneditor@blueyonder.co.uk www.milkbottlenews.org.uk

**The Model Railway Club,** The Hon Sec, Keen House, 4 Calshot Street, London, N1 9DA www.themodelrailwayclub.org

**Moorcroft Collectors' Club,** W. Moorcroft PLC, Sandbach Road, Burslem, Stoke-on-Trent, Staffordshire, ST6 2DQ www.moorcroft.com

**Muffin the Mule Collectors' Club,** 12 Woodland Close, Woodford Green, Essex, IG8 0QH adrienne@hasler.gotadsl.co.uk www.muffin-the-mule.com

**Keith Murray Collectors Club,** (Patron Constance Murray), P.O. Box 2706, Eccleshall, Stafford, ST21 6WY

**Musical Box Society of Great Britain,** P.O. Box 373, Welwyn, AL6 0WY Tel: Membership enquiries 01536 726759 mail@mbsgb.org.co.uk www.mbsgb.org.co.uk

**Myott Collectors Club,** P.O. Box 110, Sutton, Surrey, SM3 9YQ Tel: 07986 437 904 martin@setforthenet.com www.myottcollectorsclub.com

**National Association of Avon Collectors,** Connie Clark, President, P.O. Box 7006, Kansas City, MO 64113, U.S.A.

**National Button Society,** Lois Pool, Secretary, 2733 Juno Pl., Apt 4, Akron, Ohio 44333-4137, U.S.A. Tel: 330 864 3296

**National Doll & Teddy Bear Collector,** Rose Morgan, P.O. Box 4032, Portland, OR 97208-4032, U.S.A.

**National Fishing Lure Collectors Club,** Secretary-Treasurer NFLCC, 197 Scottsdale Circle, Reeds Springs, MO 65737, U.S.A.

**National Shelley China Club,** Rochelle Hart, 591 West 67th Ave, Anchorage, AK 99518-1555, U.S.A. Tel: 907 562 2124 imahart@alaska.net www.nationalshelleychinaclub.com/

**National Society of Lefton Collectors,** Loretta DeLozier, P.O. Box 50201, Knoxville, TN 37950 0201, U.S.A.

**New Baxter Society,** Membership Secretary, 205 Marshalswick Lane, St Albans, Hertfordshire, AL1 4XA Tel: 01727 857945 www.rpsfamily.demon.co.uk

**NFFC - The Club for Disneyana Enthusiasts,** P.O. Box 19212, Irvine, CA 92623-9212, U.S.A. Tel: 714 731 4705 www.nffc.org

**Observer's Pocket Series Collectors Society (OPSCS),** Alan Sledger, Secretary, 10 Villiers Road, Kenilworth, Warwickshire, CV8 2JB Tel: www.observersbooksociety.co.uk

**The Official Betty Boop Fan Club,** Ms Bobbie West, 10550 Western Avenue #133, Stanton, CA 90680-6909, U.S.A. BBOOPFANS@aol.com

**The Official International Wade Ceramics Collectors Club,** Royal Victoria Pottery, Westport Road, Burslem, Stoke on Trent, Staffordshire, ST6 4AG www.wade.co.uk

**Official Popeye Fan Club,** 1001 State St, Chester, IL 62233, U.S.A.

**Old Appliance Club,** P.O. Box 65, Ventura, CA 93002, U.S.A.

**Old Bottle Club of Great Britain,** Alan Blakeman, c/o BBR, Elsecar Heritage Centre, Nr Barnsley, Yorkshire, S74 8HJ Tel: 01226 745156 sales@onlinebbr.com www.onlinebbr.com

**The Old Hall Stainless Steel Tableware Collectors Club,** Nigel Wiggin, Sandford House, Levedale, Stafford, ST18 9AH Tel: 01785 780376 oht@gnwiggin.freeserve.co.uk www.oldhallclub.co.uk

**On the Lighter Side (OTLS),** P.O. Box 1733, Quitman, TX 75783-1733, U.S.A. Tel: 903 763 2795 info@otls.com

**Ophthalmic Antiques International Collectors' Club,** Mr Frank Barraclough, Chairman, Beaulieu Lodge, 10 Beaulieu Road, Cooden, Bexhill-on-Sea, East Sussex, TN39 3AD www.oaicclub.org

**Paperweight Collectors Circle,** P.O. Box 941, Comberton, Cambridgeshire, CB23 7GQ

**Peanuts Collector Club, Inc.,** 539 Sudden Valley, Bellingham, WA 98229-4811, U.S.A.

**Pedal Car Collectors' Club (P.C.C.C.),** Hon Sec A. P. Gayler, P.O. Box No4, Chapel Terrace Mews, Kemp Town, Brighton, East Sussex, BN2 1HU Tel: 01273 622722 cars@kemptown-brighton.freeserve.co.uk www.brmmbrmm.com/pedalcars

**Pelham Puppets Collectors Club,** Sue Valentine, 46 The Grove, Bedford, MK40 3JN Tel: 01234 363336 sue.valentine@ntlworld.com

**Pen Delfin Family Circle,** P.O. Box 431, Burnley, Lancashire, BB10 2WT

**The Pewter Society,** Llananant Farm, Penallt, Monmouth, NP25 4AP secretary@pewtersociety.org www.pewtersociety.org

**The Photographic Collector's Club of Great Britain,** Membership Office, The Photographic Collector's Club International Ltd., 5 Buntingford Road, Puckeridge, Ware, Hertfordshire, SG11 1RT Tel: 01920821611 www.pccgb.com

**Pilkington's Lancastrian Pottery Society,** Wendy Stock, Sullom Side, Barnacre, Garstang, Preston, Lancashire, PR3 1GH

**Poole Pottery Collectors Club,** Poole Pottery Limited, Sopers Lane, Poole, Dorset, BH17 7PP Tel: 01202 666200 sales@poolepottery.co.uk www.poolepottery.co.uk

**Postcard Club of Great Britain, Est 1960,** c/o Mrs D. Brennan, 34 Harper House, St James Crescent, London, SW9 7LW Tel: 020 7771 9404

**The Pot Lid Circle,** c/o Ian Johnson, Collins House, 32/38 Station Road, Gerrards Cross, Buckinghamshire, SL9 8EL Tel: 01753 279001 ian.johnson@bpcollins.co.uk www.thepotlidcircle.co.uk

**Potteries of Rye Society,** Membership Secretary Barry Buckton, 2 Redyear Cottages, Kennington Road, Ashford, Kent, TN24 0TF

**Road Map Collectors Association,** P.O. Box 158, Channelview, TX 77530-0158, U.S.A.

**Royal Doulton International Collectors' Club,** Barlaston, Stoke-on-Trent, Staffordshire, ST12 9ES Tel: 01782 404046 www.royaldoulton.com

**Royal Mint Coin Club,** P.O. Box 500, Pontyclun, CF1 1HA Tel: 0845 6088300 www.royalmint.com

**The Royal Numismatic Society,** Hon Sec, Vesta Sarkhosh Curtis, c/o Department of Coins and Medals, The British Museum, London, WC1B 3DG www.numismatics.org.uk

**Rugby Memorabilia Society,** P.O. Box 57, Hereford, HR1 9DR www.rugby-memorabilia.co.uk

**Scientific Instrument Society,** Registered Charity No 326733, 31 High Street, Stanford in the Vale, Faringdon, Oxon, SN7 8LH Tel: 01367 710223 www.sis.org.uk

**The Shelley Group, (for collectors of Shelley and Wileman wares),** Ruskin, 47 St Andrew's Drive, Perton, Staffordshire, WV6 7YL Tel: 01902 754245 shelley.group@shelley.co.uk www.shelley.co.uk

**Silhouette Collectors' Club,** c/o Miss Diana B. Joll, Flat 5, 13 Brunswick Square, Hove, East Sussex, BN3 1EH

**Smurf Collectors Club International,** Dept 115 NR, 24 Cabot Road West, Massapeque, New York 11758, U.S.A.

**The Soviet Collectors Club,** P.O. Box 56, Saltburn by the Sea, TS12 1YD collect@sovietclub.com

**Steiff Club - North America,** Rebekah Kaufman, Steiff North America, Inc., 425 Paramount Drive, Raynham, MA 02767, U.S.A. www.steiffusa.com

**The SylvaC Collectors Circle,** 174 Portsmouth Road, Horndean, Waterlooville, Hampshire, PO8 9HP Tel: 02392 591725 www.sylvacclub.com

**TEAMS Club - The official club for Brooke Bond Card Collectors,** P.O. Box 1672, Croydon, Surrey, CR9 4XW

**Toaster Collector Association,** P.O. Box 485, Redding Ridge, CT 06876, U.S.A.

**Tobacco Jar Society,** Colin Grey, 19 Woodhurst North, Raymead Road, Maidenhead, Berkshire, SL6 8PH Tel: 01628 781800

**Tools and Trades History Society,** Membership Secretary, Woodbine Cottage, Budleigh Hill, East Budleigh, Devon, EX9 7DT Tel: 01395 443030 membership@taths.org.uk www.taths.org.uk

**Totally Teapots, The Novelty Teapot Collectors Club,** Vince McDonald, Euxton, Chorley, Lancashire, PR7 6EY Tel: 01257 450366 vince@totallyteapots.com www.totallyteapots.com

**Toy Story Collectors' Club,** Paul Cross, 20 Thurstons Barton, Whitehall, Bristol, Gloucestershire, BS5 7BQ

**Trade Card Collector's Association,** P.O. Box 284, Marlton, NJ 08053, U.S.A.

**Train Collectors Society,** James Day, Membership Secretary, P.O. Box 20340, London, NW11 6ZE tcsinformation@btinternet.com www.traincollectors.org.uk

**The Transport Ticket Society,** Membership Secretary Steve Skeavington, 6 Breckbank, Forest Town, Mansfield, NG19 0PZ stephenskeavington@msn.com

**Treasures for Little Chldren,** c/o Gail Ryan, 6885 S. Mingus Drive, Chandler, AZ 85249, U.S.A. www.treasuresforlittlechildren.com

**Treasury of Christmas Ornaments Collectors' Club,** P.O. Box 277, Itasca, IL 60143-0277, U.S.A.

**Trix Twin Railway Collectors' Association,** c/o Mr C B Arnold, 6 Ribble Avenue, Oadby, Leicester, LE2 4NZ www.ttrca.co.uk

**UK 1/6th Collectors Club,** Adrian Pitman, 1 St Cadocs Rise, Barry, Vale of Glamorgan, South Wales, CF63 2FG www.onesixthcollectors.co.uk

**UK Football Programme Collectors Club,** P.O. Box 3236, Norwich, NR7 7BF Tel: 01603 449237 progm@hotmail.com

**UK Headscarf Collectors Society,** 19 Poulton Old Road, Blackpool, Lancashire, FY3 7LD

**UK McDonald's & Fast Food Collectors Club,** c/o Lawrence Yap, 110 Tithelands, Harlow, Essex, CM19 5ND

**UK Sucrologists Club,** The Membership Secretary, 14 Marisfield Place, Selsey, Chichester, West Sussex, PO20 0PD uksucsugar@hotmail.co.uk www.uksucrologistsclub.org.uk

**United Kingdom Spoon Collectors Club,** David Cross, General Secretary, 72 Edinburgh Road, Newmarket, Suffolk, CB8 0DQ Tel: 01638 665457 david.cross340@ntlworld.com

**Universal Autograph Collectors Club,** Michael Hecht, President UACC, P.O. Box 1392, Mt. Dora, FL 32756-1392, U.S.A. www.uacc.org

**Unofficial McDonalds Collectors Newsletter,** c/o Ian Smith, 14 Elkstone Road, Chesterfield, Derbyshire, S40 4UT

**The Victorian Military Society,** P.O. Box 5837, Newbury, Berkshire, RG14 3FJ Tel: 01635 48628 vmsdan@msn.com www.vms.org.uk

**Vintage Fashion & Costume Jewelry Club,** P.O. Box 265, Glen Oaks, NY 11004, U.S.A.

**Vintage Model Yacht Group,** Hon Membership Secretary Alistair Roach, Windy Corner, Weston Town, Evercreech, Somerset, BA4 6JG www.vmyg.org.uk

**Vintage Tupperware Collectors** http://groups.yahoo.com/group/vintagetupperware/

**The Washington Historical Autograph and Certificate Organization - Whaco!,** P.O. Box 2428, Springfield, VA 22152-2428, U.S.A.

**The Writing Equipment Society,** c/o Sec Mr John S. Daniels, 33 Glanville Road, Hadleigh, Ipswich, Suffolk, IP7 5SQ www.wesoc.co.uk

**Zippo Click Collectors Club,** Zippo Manufacturing Company, 33 Barbour Street, Bradford, PA 16701, U.S.A. Tel: 814 368 2725 kjones@zippo.com www.zippo.com www.zippoclick.com

# DIRECTORY OF MARKETS & CENTRES

## U.S.A.

Alhambra Antiques Center, 3640 Coral Way,
Coral Cables, Florida
Tel: 305 446 1688

Antique Center I, II, III at Historic Savage Mill,
Savage, Maryland
Tel: 410 880 0918 or 301 369 4650

Antique Village, North of Richmond, Virginia,
on Historic US 301, 4 miles North of 1-295
Tel: 804 746 8914

Antiques at Colony Mill Marketplace, 222 West Street,
Keene, New Hampshire 03431
Tel: 603 358 6343

The Coffman's Antiques Market, at Jennifer House Commons,
Stockbridge Road, Route 7, P.O. Box 592,
Great Barrington, MA 01230
Tel: 413 528 9282/9602
www.coffmansantiques.com

Fern Eldridge & Friends, 800 First NH Turnpike (Rte. 4),
Northwood, New Hampshire 03261
Tel: 603 942 5602/8131

Goodlettsville Antique Mall, 213 N. Main St,
Germantown, Tennessee
Tel: 615 859 7002

The Hayloft Antique Center, 1190 First NH Turnpike (Rte. 4),
Northwood, New Hampshire 03261
Tel: 603 942 5153

Hermitage Antique Mall, 4144-B Lebanon Road,
Hermitage, Tennessee
Tel: 615 883 5789

Madison Antique Mall, 320 Gallatin Rd, S. Nashville, Tennessee
Tel: 615 865 4677

Michiana Antique Mall, 2423 S. 11th Street,
Niles, Michigan 49120
www.michianaantiquemall.com

Morningside Antiques, 6443 Biscayne Blvd., Miami, Florida
Tel: 305 751 2828

Nashville Wedgewood Station Antique Mall,
657 Wedgewood Ave., Nashville, Tennessee
Tel: 615 259 0939

Parker-French Antique Center, 1182 First NH Turnpike (Rt. 4),
Northwood, New Hampshire 03261
Tel: 603 942 8852

Quechee Gorge Antiques & Collectibles Center,
Located in Quechee Gorge Village
Tel: 800 438 5565

Showcase Antique Center, P.O. Box 1122,
Sturbridge MA 01566
Tel: 508 347 7190
www.showcaseantiques.com

Tennessee Antique Mall, 654 Wedgewood Ave., Nashville,
Tennessee Tel: 615 259 4077

## UK
### Berkshire
Stables Antiques Centre, 1a Merchant Place (off Friar Street),
Reading, RG1 1DT Tel: 0118 959 0290

### Buckinghamshire
Jackdaw Antiques Centres Ltd, 25 West Street,
Marlow, SL7 2LS
Tel: 01628 898285

Marlow Antique Centre, 35 Station Road,
Marlow, SL7 1NW
Tel: 01628 473223

### Derbyshire
Alfreton Antique Centre, 11 King Street, Alfreton, DE55 7AF
Tel: 01773 520781
*30 dealers on 2 floors. Antiques, collectables, furniture, books, militaria, postcards, silverware. Open 7 days Mon–Sat 10am–4.30pm, Sundays 11am–4.30pm. Customer car park.*

Chappells Antiques Centre - Bakewell, King Street,
Bakewell, DE45 1DZ
Tel: 01629 812496 www.chappellsantiquescentre.com

Heanor Antiques Centre, 1–3 Ilkeston Road, Heanor, DE757AE
Tel: 01773 531181/762783
www.heanorantiquescentre.co.uk

Matlock Antiques & Collectables, 7 Dale Road,
Matlock, DE4 3LT
Tel: 01629 760808
www.matlock-antiques-collectables.cwc.net
*Over 70+ dealers selling a wide range of items including collectables, mahogany, pine, oak, pictures, books, linen, kitchenalia, china, clocks, clothes, jewellery. Call in to buy, sell or browse. Open 7 days a week 10am–5pm.*

### Devon
Quay Centre, Topsham, Nr Exeter, EX3 0JA
Tel: 01392 874006
www.quayantiques.com
*80 dealers on 3 floors. Antiques, collectables and traditional furnishings. Ample parking. Open 7 days, 10am–5pm. All major cards accepted.*

### Essex
Debden Antiques, Elder Street, Debden,
Saffron Walden, CB11 3JY
Tel: 01799 543007
www.debden-antiques.co.uk

### Gloucestershire
Antiques Centre Gloucester, 1 Severn Road, The Historic
Docks, Gloucester, GL1 2LE Tel: 01452 529716
www.antiques.center.com

Church Street Antiques Centre, 3-4 Church Street,
Stow on-the-Wold, GL54 1BB
Tel: 01451 870186

Durham House Antiques, Sheep Street, Stow-on-the-Wold,
GL54 1AA Tel: 01451 870404
www.DurhamHouseGB.com

The Top Banana Antiques Mall, 1 New Church Street, Tetbury,
GL8 8DS Tel: 0871 288 1102
www.topbananaantiques.com

**Hampshire**
Dolphin Quay Antique Centre, Queen Street,
Emsworth, PO10 7BU
Tel: 01243 379994

Lymington Antiques Centre, 76 High Street,
Lymington, SO41 9AL
Tel: 01590 670934

Squirrel Collectors Centre, 9 New Street,
Basingstoke, RG21 1DE
Tel: 01256 464885

**Herefordshire**
Mulberry's Antiques & Vintage Costumes,
Hereford, HR1 2NN
Tel: 01432 350101

**Hertfordshire**
By George Antique Centre, 23 George Street,
St Albans, AL3 4ES
Tel: 01727 853032

Riverside Antiques Centre, The Maltings, Station Road,
Sawbridgeworth, CM21 9JX
Tel: 01279 600985 or 07956 844792

**Kent**
Burgate Antiques Centre, 23A Palace Street,
Canterbury, CT1 2DZ
Tel: 01227 456500

Castle Antiques, 1 London Road, Westerham,
TN16 1BB Tel: 01959 562492 (Thurs only)
*Open 10am–5pm 7 days. 4 rooms of antiques, small furniture,
collectables, rural bygones, costume, glass, books, linens, jewellery,
chandeliers, die cast models, chair caning, theatre memorabilia. Services:
advice, valuations, theatre props, house clearance, talks on antiques.*

Copperfields Antiques & Craft Centre, 3c-4 Copperfields,
Spital Street, Dartford, DA9 2DE
Tel: 01322 281445

Nightingales, 89-91 High Street, West Wickham,
BR4 0LS Tel: 020 8777 0335

Tenterden Antiques Centre, 66-66A High Street,
Tenterden, TN30 6AU
Tel: 01580 765655/765885

**Lancashire**
The Antique & Decorative Design Centre,
56 Garstang Road, Preston, PR1 1NA
Tel: 01772 882078
www.paulallisonantiques.co.uk

GB Antiques Centre, Lancaster Leisure Park, (the former
Hornsea Pottery), Wyresdale Road, Lancaster, LA1 3LA
Tel: 01524 844734
*140 dealers in 40,000 sq. ft. of space. Porcelain, pottery, Art Deco, glass,
books, linen, mahogany, oak and pine furniture. Open 7 days
10am–5pm.*

Kingsmill Antique Centre, Queen Street, Harle Syke, Burnley,
BB10 2HX Tel: 01282 431953
www.kingsmill.demon.co.uk

**Lincolnshire**
Hemswell Antique Centres, Caenby Corner Estate,
Hemswell Cliff, Gainsborough, DN21 5TJ
Tel: 01427 668389
enquiries@hemswell-antiques.com
www.hemswell-antiques.com
*Over 300 dealers in 3 buildings with the largest choice of antiques and
collectables in Europe.*

St Martins Antiques Centre, 23a High St, St Martins, Stamford,
PE9 2LF Tel: 01780 481158
www.st-martins-antiques.co.uk

Sue's Collectables, 61 Victoria Road, Mablethorpe, LN12 2AF
Tel: 01507 472406

**London**
Alfie's Antique Market, 13 Church Street, Marylebone,
NW8 8DT Tel: 020 7723 6066
www.alfiesantiques.com

Bermondsey Antiques Market, Corner of Long Lane &
Bermondsey Street, SE1 5QH
Tel: 020 7351 5353

Bond Street Antiques Centre,
124 New Bond Street, W1Y 9AE
Tel: 020 7351 5353

Bourbon-Hanby Arcade Antiques & Interiors,
151 Sydney Street, Chelsea, SW3 6NT
Tel: 0870 1423403
www.bourbonhanby.co.uk
www.antiqueschelsea.co.uk

Covent Garden Antique Market, Jubilee Hall,
Southampton Street, Covent Garden, WC2
Tel: 020 7240 7405
*Every Monday from 6am*

Grays Antique Markets, South Molton Lane, W1K 5AB
Tel: 020 7629 7034
www.graysantiques.com

Kensington Antique Centre,
58-60 Kensington Church Street,
W8 4DB Tel: 020 7376 0425

The Mall Antiques Arcade, Camden Passage,
359 Upper Street, Islington, N1 8DU
Tel: 020 7351 5353

Northcote Road Antique Market, 155a Northcote Road,
Battersea, SW11 6QB
Tel: 020 7228 6850
www.spectrumsoft.net/nam.htm

Palmers Green Antiques Centre, 472 Green Lanes,
Palmers Green, N13 5PA
Tel: 020 8350 0878

Spitalfields Antique Market,
Commercial Street, E1
Tel: 020 7240 7405
*Every Thursday from 7am*

St James's Antiques Market,
197 Piccadilly, W1V 0LL
Tel: 020 7734 4511/020 74377688

**Norfolk**
Tombland Antiques Centre, Augustine Steward House,
14 Tombland, Norwich, NR3 1HF
Tel: 01603 761906 or 619129
www.tomblandantiques.co.uk

**Northamptonshire**
Magpies Antiques and Collectables Centre,
1 East Grove, Rushden, NN10 0AP
Tel: 01933 411404

**Nottinghamshire**
Castlegate Antiques Centre, 55 Castlegate,
Newark, NG24 1BE
Tel: 01636 700076

Newark Antiques Centre, Regent House, Lombard Street,
Newark, NG24 1XP
Tel: 01636 605504

Occleshaw Antiques Centre, The Old Major Cinema,
11 Mansfield Road, Edwinstowe, NG21 9NL
Tel: 01623 825370

Top Hat Antiques Centre, 70-72 Derby Road, Nottingham,
NG1 5FD Tel: 0115 941 9143

## Oxfordshire
Deddington Antiques Centre, Laurel House,
Market Place, Bull Ring, Deddington, Nr Banbury, OX15 0TT
Tel: 01869 338968

Lamb Arcade Antiques Centre, High Street,
Wallingford, OX10 0BX
Tel: 01491 835166

The Quiet Woman Antiques Centre, Southcombe,
Chipping Norton, OX7 5QH
Tel: 01608 646262

The Swan at Tetsworth, High Street, Tetsworth, Nr Thame,
OX9 7AB Tel: 01844 281777
www.theswan.co.uk

## Scotland
Rait Village Antiques Centre, Rait, Perthshire, PH2 7RT

Scottish Antique and Arts Centre, Carse of Cambus,
Doune, Perthshire, FK16 6HG
Tel: 01786 841203
www.scottish-antiques.com

Scottish Antique and Arts Centre, Abernyte,
Perthshire, PH14 9SJ
Tel: 01828 686401
www.scottish-antiques.com

## Shropshire
Shrewsbury Antique Market,
Frankwell Quay Warehouse, Shrewsbury, SY3 8LG
Tel: 01743 350916

Stretton Antiques Market, Sandford Avenue, Church Stretton,
SY6 6BH Tel: 01694 723718

## Somerset
Assembly Antiques, 6 Saville Row, Bath, BA1 2QP
Tel: 01225 448488

Bartlett Street Antique Centre, 5-10 Bartlett Street, Bath,
BA1 2QZ Tel: 01225 466689
www.antiques-centre.co.uk

Bath Antiques Market, Guinea Lane, (off Landsdown Rd), Bath,
BA1 5NB Tel: 07787 527527

## Staffordshire
Potteries Antique Centre, 271 Waterloo Road,
Cobridge, Stoke on Trent, ST6 3HR
Tel: 01782 201455
www.potteriesantiquecentre.com
*Open Mon–Sat 9am–5.30pm*

Rugeley Antique Centre, 161 Main Road,
Brereton, Nr Rugeley, WS15 1DX
Tel: 01889 577166

## Suffolk
Snape Maltings Antique & Collectors Centre,
Saxmundham, IP17 1SR
Tel: 01728 688038

## Surrey
Great Grooms Antiques Centre, 51/52 West Street,
Dorking, RH4 1BU
Tel: 01306 887076
www.greatgrooms.co.uk

Kingston Antiques Centre, 29-31 London Road,
Kingston-upon-Thames, KT2 6ND
Tel: 020 8549 2004/3839
www.kingstonantiquescentre.co.uk

Serendipity Antique Centre, 7 Petworth Road, Haslemere
GU27 2JB Tel: 01428 642682

## East Sussex
The Brighton Lanes Antique Centre, 1
2 Meeting House Lane, Brighton, BN1 1HB
Tel: 01273 823121

Church Hill Antique Centre, 6 Station Street, Lewes,
BN7 2DA Tel: 01273 474842

The Emporium Antique Centre Too, 24 High Street, Lewes,
BN7 2 LU Tel: 01273 477979

Lewes Antique Centre, 20 Cliffe High Street, Lewes, BN7 2AH
Tel: 01273 476148

## West Sussex
Antiques & Collectors Market, Old Orchard Building,
Old House, Adversane, Nr Billingshurst, RH14 9JJ
Tel: 01403 782186

Arundel Antiques Centre, 51 High Street, Arundel,
BN18 9AJ Tel: 01903 882749

## Wales
Afonwen Antiques, Gift & Craft Centre,
Afonwen, Nr Caerwys, Nr Mold, Flintshire, CH7 5UB
Tel: 01352 720965
www.afonwen.co.uk

Offa's Dyke Antique Centre, 4 High Street,
Knighton, Powys, LD7 1AT
Tel: 01547 528635/ 520145
*Open Mon–Sat 10am–5pm. Wide ranging stock. Specialists in ceramics and glass, fine art of the 19th & 20th centuries. Country antiques and collectables.*

Second Chance Antiques & Collectables Centre, Ala Road,
Pwllheli, Gwynedd, LL53 5BL
Tel: 01758 612210

## Warwickshire
Stratford-upon-Avon Antique Centre, 60 Ely Street,
Stratford-upon-Avon
Tel: 020 7240 7405
*7 days a week 10am–5pm*

## West Midlands
Birmingham Antique Centre, 1407 Pershore Road,
Stirchley, Birmingham, B30 2JR
Tel: 0121 459 4587

## Worcestershire
Worcester Antiques Centre, Reindeer Court,
Mealcheapen Street, Worcester, WR1 4DF
Tel: 01905 610680
www.worcesterantiquecentre.com

## Yorkshire
The Antiques Centre York, Allenby House,
41 Stonegate, York, YO1 8AW
Tel: 01904 635888
www.theantiquescentreyork.com
*Open Mon–Sat 9am–5.30pm Sun 9am–4pm*

Cavendish Antique & Collectors Centre,
44 Stonegate, York, YO1 8AS
Tel: 01904 621666
www.cavendishantiques.com

The Collectors Centre, 35 St Nicholas Cliff,
Scarborough, YO11 2ES
Tel: 01723 365221/374175
www.collectors.demon.co.uk

Stonegate Antiques Centre, 41 Stonegate, York, YO1 8AW
Tel: 01904 613888

York Antique Centre, 2a Lendel, York
Tel: 020 7240 7405
*Monday–Saturday 10am–5pm*

# KEY TO ILLUSTRATIONS

Each illustration and descriptive caption is accompanied by a letter code. By referring to the following list of auctioneers (denoted by ➤) and dealers (⊞) the source of any item may be immediately determined. Inclusion in this edition in no way constitutes or implies a contract or binding offer on the part of any of our contributors to supply or sell the goods illustrated, or similar articles, at the prices stated. Advertisers in this year's directory are denoted by †.

If you require a valuation for an item, it is advisable to check whether the dealer or specialist will carry out this service and if there is a charge. Please mention Miller's when making an enquiry. Having found a specialist who will carry out your valuation it is best to send a photograph and description of the item to the specialist together with a stamped addressed envelope for the reply. A valuation by telephone is not possible.

Most dealers are only too happy to help you with your enquiry; however, they are very busy people and consideration of the above points would be welcomed.

**20th Century Marks**
⊞ 20th Century Marks, 'The Office', Whitegates, Rectory Road, Little Burstead, Essex, CM12 9TR Tel: 01268 411 000 or 07831 778992 info@20thcenturymarks.co.uk www.20thcenturymarks.co.uk

**299**
⊞ 299, 299 Lillie Road, London, SW6 7LL Tel: 07860 223707

**A B Coins & Medals**
⊞ A B Coins & Medals, 23-25 'Old' Northam Road, Southampton, Hampshire, SO14 Tel: 023 8023 3393 or 07759 655739/07770 671832

**A D Antiques**
⊞ AD Antiques, P.O. Box 2407, Stone, Staffordshire, ST15 9WY Tel: 07811 783518 www.adantiques.com

**Ad-Age**
⊞ Ad-Age Antique Advertising Tel: 01622 670595

**Addyman Books**
⊞ Addyman Books, 39 Lion Street, Hay-on-Wye, Herefordshire, HR3 5AD Tel: 01497 821136

**Aeroclocks**
⊞ Aeroclocks, Circadian (UK) Ltd, Barnsdale House, Barnsdale Mews, Campsall, Doncaster, DN6 9RH Tel: 01302 707553 or 07774 120692 aeroclocks@btinternet.com www.aeroclocks.com

**Afford Decorative Arts**
⊞ Afford Decorative Arts Tel: 01827 330042 or 07831 114909 afforddecarts@fsmail.net

**Afonwen Centre**
⊞ Afonwen Craft & Antique Centre, Afonwen, Nr Caerwys, Nr Mold, Flintshire, Wales, CH7 5UB Tel: 01352 720965 www.afonwen.co.uk

**Alan Pezaro**
⊞ Alan Pezaro, 32 Long Street, Tetbury, Gloucestershire, GL8 8AQ

**Alexander von Tutschek**
⊞ Alexander von Tutschek Tel: 01225 465532 vontutschek@onetel.co.uk

**All Dolled Up**
⊞ All Dolled Up Tel: 519 745 2122 jenn@alldolledup.ca www.alldolledup.ca

**Alvin's Vintage Games & Toys**
⊞ Alvin's Vintage Games & Toys alvin@vintage-games.co.uk www.vintage-games.co.uk

**Andrew Hartley**
➤ Hartleys, Victoria Hall Salerooms, Little Lane, Ilkley, Yorkshire, LS29 8EA Tel: 01943 816363 info@hartleysauctions.co.uk www.hartleysauctions.co.uk

**Andrew Muir**
⊞ Andrew Muir Tel: 07976 956208 andrewmuir@blueyonder.co.uk www.andrew-muir.com

**Anthony Welling**
⊞ Anthony Welling, Broadway Barn, High Street, Ripley, Surrey, GU23 6AQ Tel: 01483 225384 ant@awelling.freeserve.co.uk www.antique-oak-furniture.com

**Antique Garden**
⊞ The Antique Garden, Grosvenor Garden Centre, Wrexham Road, Belgrave, Chester, CH4 9EB Tel: 01244 629191/07976 539 990 antigard@btopenworld.com www.antique-garden.co.uk

**Antique Mystique**
⊞ Antique Mystique Tel: 308 532 3404 sales@antiquemystique.com www.antiquemystique.com

**Antique Photographic**
⊞ Antique Photographic Company Ltd Tel: 01949 842192 alpaco47@aol.com www.rubylane.com/shops/woodstoneantiques

**Anya Hindmarch**
⊞ Anya Hindmarch, The Stable Block, Plough Brewery, 516 Wandsworth Road, London, SW8 3JX Tel: 020 7501 0177 www.anyahindmarch.com

**Argyll Etkin**
⊞ Argyll Etkin Ltd, 1-9 Hills Place, Oxford Circus, London, W1F 7SA Tel: 020 7437 7800 philatelists@argyll-etkin.com www.argyll-etkin.com

**Arlene De Vries**
⊞ Arlene De Vries Antiques Tel: 07850 100249 brightthingsrevisited@btinternet.com

**Art Nouveau Originals**
⊞ Art Nouveau Originals, The Bindery Gallery, 69 High Street, Broadway, Worcestershire, WR12 7DP Tel: 01386 854645 or 07774 718 096 cathy@artnouveauoriginals.com www.artnouveauoriginals.com

**Arundel Photographica**
⊞ Arundel Photographica, The Arundel Antiques and Collectors Centre, 51 High Street, Arundel, West Sussex, BN18 9AJ Tel: 01903 885540 cameras@arundel-photographica.co.uk www.arundel-photographica.co.uk

**Ashmans Vintage Clothing**
⊞ Ashmans Vintage Clothing & Accessories, Makers Park, Lane House, 7 & 11 High Street, Welshpool, SY21 7JE Tel: 01938 554505

**Attica**
⊞ Attica, 2 Old George Yard, off Highbridge, Newcastle upon Tyne, Tyne & Wear, NE1 1EZ Tel: 0191 261 4062

**Autograph Collectors Gallery**
⊞ The Autograph Collectors Gallery, 7 Jessops Lane, Gedling, Nottingham, NG4 4BQ Tel: 0115 961 2956/987 6578 www.autograph-gallery.co.uk

**Bac to Basic**
⊞ Bac to Basic Antiques Tel: 07787 105609 bcarruthers@waitrose.com

**Banana Dance**
⊞ Banana Dance Ltd, 155A Northcote Road, Battersea, London, SW11 6QT Tel: 01634 364539 or 07976 296987 jonathan@bananadance.com www.bananadance.com

**Barbara Ann Newman**
⊞ Barbara Ann Newman Tel: 07850 016729

**Barter Books**
⊞ Barter Books, Alnwick Station, Alnwick, Northumberland, NE66 2NP Tel: 01665 604888 www.barterbooks.co.uk

**BBA** see Bloomsbury

**Beanos**
⊞ Beanos, Middle Street, Croydon, London, CR0 1RE Tel: 020 8680 1202 enquiries@beanos.co.uk www.beanos.co.uk

**Bearnes**
⚒ Bearnes, St Edmund's Court, Okehampton Street, Exeter, Devon, EX4 1DU Tel: 01392 207000 enquiries@bearnes.co.uk www.bearnes.co.uk

**Bears of Windy Hill**
⊞ Bears of Windy Hill, P.O. Box 51, Shipley, West Yorkshire, BD18 2YH Tel: 01274 599175 or 07768 240158 info@bearsofwindyhill.co.uk www.bearsofwindyhill.co.uk

**BeatBooks**
⊞ BeatBooks.com, 32 St Paul's View, 15 Amwell Street, London, EC1R 1UP Tel: 020 7278 5034 sclanders@beatbooks.com www.beatbooks.com

**Beaulieu Autojumble**
⊞ Beaulieu Autojumble, www.beaulieu.co.uk

**Below Stairs**
⊞ Below Stairs, 103 High Street, Hungerford, Berkshire, RG17 0NB Tel: 01488 682317 hofgartner@belowstairs.co.uk www.belowstairs.co.uk

**Bentley's**
⚒ Bentley's Fine Art Auctioneers, The Old Granary, Waterloo Road, Cranbrook, Kent, TN17 3JQ Tel: 01580 715857 BentleysKent@aol.com www.bentleysfineartauctioneers.co.uk

**Beth**
⊞ Beth, GO 43-44 Alfies Antique Market, 13-25 Church Street, Marylebone, London, NW8 8DT Tel: 020 7723 5613 or 0777 613 6003

**Beverley**
⊞ Beverley, 30 Church Street, Marylebone, London, NW8 8EP Tel: 020 7262 1576 or 07776136003

**Biblion**
⊞ Biblion, Grays Antique Market, 1-7 Davies Mews, London, W1K 5AB Tel: 020 7629 1374 info@biblion.com www.biblionmayfair.com

**Black History Store**
⊞ Black History Store, 3550 Broad Street #F, Chamblee, GA 30341, U.S.A. Tel: 770 458 6316 sylturner@mindspring.com www.blackhistorystore.com

**Bloomsbury**
⚒ Bloomsbury Auctions, Bloomsbury House, 24 Maddox Street, London, W1S 1PP Tel: 020 7495 9494 info@bloomsburyauctions.com www.bloomsburyauctions.com

**Books Afloat**
⊞ Books Afloat, 66 Park Street, Weymouth, Dorset, DT4 7DE Tel: 01305 779774

**Boom Interiors**
⊞ Boom Interiors, 115-117 Regents Park Road, Primrose Hill, London, NW1 8UR Tel: 020 7722 6622 or 07973 114 396 info@boominteriors.com www.boominteriors.com

**Bourbon-Hanby**
⊞ Bourbon-Hanby Arcade Antiques & Interiors, 151 Sydney Street, Chelsea, London, SW3 6NT Tel: 0870 1423403 www.bourbonhanby.co.uk www.antiqueschelsea.co.uk

**Bourton Bears**
⊞ Bourton Bears Tel: 01993 824756 help@bourtonbears.com www.bourtonbears.com

**Box of Porcelain**
⊞ Box of Porcelain, 51d Icen Way, Dorchester, Dorset, DT1 1EW Tel: 01305 267110 RLunn@BoxOfPorcelain.com www.boxofporcelain.com

**Brackley Antiques**
⊞ The Brackley Antique Cellar, Drayman's Walk, Brackley, Northamptonshire, NN13 6BE Tel: 01280 841841 antiquecellar@tesco.net

**Bradley Gent**
⊞ Bradley Gent Tel: 07711 158005 www.antiques-shop.co.uk

**Bread & Roses**
⊞ Bread & Roses Tel: 01926 817342

**Brenda Kimber & John Lewis**
⊞ Brenda Kimber & John Lewis, The Victoria Centre, 3-4 Victoria Road, Saltaire, Shipley, West Yorkshire Tel: 01274 611478 or 01482 442265

**Britannia**
⊞ Britannia, Grays Antique Market, Stand 101, 58 Davies Street, London, W1Y 1AR Tel: 020 7629 6772 britannia@grays.clara.net

**British Collectibles**
⊞ British Collectibles, 917 Chicago Avenue, Evanston, Illinois 60202, U.S.A. Tel: 800 634 0431 kevin@britishcollectibles.com sheila@britishcollectibles.com britcol@msn.com
*Photographer David Doty*

**British Notes**
⊞† British Notes, P.O. Box 257, Sutton, Surrey, SM3 9WW Tel: 020 8641 3224 pamwestbritnotes@aol.com www.britishnotes.co.uk

**Budd Auctions**
⚒† Graham Budd Auctions Ltd, P.O. BOX 47519, London, N14 6XD Tel: 020 8366 2525 or 07974 113394 gb@grahambuddauctions.co.uk www.grahambuddauctions.co.uk

**Cabinet of Curiosities**

**Camera House**
⊞ Camera House, 65 Oakworth Hall, Oakworth, Keighley, West Yorkshire, BD22 7HZ Tel: 01535 642333 colin@the-camera-house.co.uk www.the-camera-house.co.uk

**Candice Horley**
⊞ Candice Horley Antiques Tel: 01883 716056 or 0705 0044855 cjhorleyantiques@aol.com

**Canterbury Auctions**
⚒ Canterbury Auction Galleries, 40 Station Road West, Canterbury, Kent, CT2 8AN Tel: 01227 763337 auctions@thecanterburyauctiongalleries.com www.thecanterburyauctiongalleries.com

**Castlegate**
⊞ Castlegate Antiques Centre, 55 Castlegate, Newark, Nottinghamshire, NG24 1BE Tel: 01636 700076 or 07860 843739

**Chameleon**
⊞ Chameleon Fine Lighting, 223 East 59th Street, New York, NY 10022, U.S.A. Tel: 212 355 6300 mail@chameleon59.com www.chameleon59.com

**Charles Tomlinson**
⊞ Charles Tomlinson, Chester Tel: 01244 318395 charlestomlinson@tiscali.co.uk

**Charterhouse**
⚒ The Long Street Salerooms, Sherborne, Dorset, DT9 3BS Tel: 01935 812277 enquiry@charterhouse-auctions.co.uk www.charterhouse-auctions.co.uk

**Glass etc**
⊞ Glass etc, 18–22 Rope Walk, Rye, East Sussex, TN31 7NA
Tel: 01797 226600
decanterman@freezone.co.uk www.decanterman.com

**Glazed Over**
⊞ Glazed Over Tel: 0773 2789114

**Glenda Antique Dolls**
⊞ Glenda - Antique Dolls, A18-A19 Grays Antique Market,
Davies Mews, London, W1Y 2LP
Tel: 020 8367 2441/020 7629 7034
glenda@glenda-antiquedolls.com
www.glenda-antiquedolls.com

**Gloucester Antiques**
⊞ Antiques Centre Gloucester, 1 Severn Road,
The Historic Docks, Gloucester, GL1 2LE Tel: 01452 529716
www.antiques.center.com

**Gloucester Toy Mart**
⊞ Gloucester Toy Mart, Ground Floor, Antique Centre Gloucester,
Severn Road, Old Docks, Gloucester, GL1 2LE
Tel: 07973 768452

**Godfrey Wallem**
⊞ Godfrey Wallem Tel: 07970 497 801

**Gorringes (L)**
⚒ Gorringes, 15 North Street, Lewes, East Sussex, BN7 2PD
Tel: 01273 478221
clientservices@gorringes.co.uk www.gorringes.co.uk

**Goss & Crested Club**
The Goss & Crested China Club & Museum, incorporating Milestone
Publications, 62 Murray Road, Horndean, Hampshire, PO8 9JL
Tel: (023) 9259 7440
info@gosschinaclub.demon.co.uk
www.gosscrestedchina.co.uk

**Graham Cooley**
⊞ Graham Cooley Tel: 07968 722269

**Grimes Militaria**
⊞ Grimes Militaria, 13 Lower Park Row, Bristol, Somerset, BS1 5BN
Tel: 0117 929 8205

**GWR Auctions**
⚒†Gloucestershire Worcestershire Railwayana Auctions LLP,
The Willows, Badsey Road, Evesham, Worcestershire, WR11 7PA
Tel: 01386 421324 or 01684 773487
master@gwra.co.uk www.gwra.co.uk

**Halcyon** see Jean Sears

**Hans's Vintage Fountain Pens**
⊞ Hans's Vintage Fountain Pens
Tel: 01323 765398 or 07850 771183
HSeiringer@aol.com www.hanspens.com

**Hardy's Collectables**

**Harry Poster**
⊞ Harry Poster, 1310 Second Street, Fair Lawn, NJ 07410, U.S.A.
tvs@harryposter.com www.harryposter.com

**Hayman & Hayman**
⊞ Hayman & Hayman, Stand D5 Antiquarius, 135 Kings Road,
London, SW3 4PW Tel: 020 7351 6568 or 07742 987715
georgina@haymanframes.co.uk www.haymanframes.co.uk

**Hazle Ceramics**
⚒ Hazle Ceramics Limited, 33-35 Barleylands Craft Centre,
Barleylands Road, Billericay, Essex, CM11 2UD Tel: 01268 270892
hazle@hazle.com www.hazle.com

**Heanor Antiques**
⊞ Heanor Antiques Centre, 1–3 Ilkeston Road, Heanor,
Derbyshire, DE75 7AE Tel: 01773 531181/762783
sales@heanorantiquescentre.co.uk www.heanorantiquescentre.co.uk

**Heirloom Antiques**

**Hemswell Antique Centre**
⊞† Hemswell Antique Centre, Caenby Corner Estate, Hemswell Cliff,
Gainsborough, Lincolnshire, DN21 5TJ Tel: 01427 668389
enquiries@hemswell-antiques.com www.hemswell-antiques.com

**Henry Aldridge**
⚒ Henry Aldridge & Son Auctions, Unit 1 Bath Road Business
Centre, Devizes, Wiltshire, SN10 1XA Tel: 01380 729199
andrew@henry-aldridge.co.uk www.henry-aldridge.co.uk

**Heritage**
⚒ Heritage Auction Galleries, 3500 Maple Avenue, 17th Floor,
Dallas, Texas 75219-3941, U.S.A.
Tel: 214 528 3500/800 872 6467
bid@HeritageAuctions.com www.HeritageAuctions.com

**hi+lo modern**
⊞ hi+lo modern www.hiandlomodern.com

**High Street Retro**
⊞ High Street Retro, 39 High Street, Old Town, Hastings,
East Sussex, TN34 3ER Tel: 01424 460068
www.highstreetretro.co.uk

**Home & Colonial**
⊞ Home & Colonial, 134 High Street, Berkhamsted,
Hertfordshire, HP4 3AT Tel: 01442 877007
homeandcolonial@btinternet.com www.homeandcolonial.co.uk

**Hope & Glory**
⊞ Hope & Glory, 131A Kensington Church Street, London,
W8 7LP Tel: 020 7727 8424

**Houghton Antiques**
⊞ Houghton Antiques, Houghton, Cambridgeshire
Tel: 01480 461887 or 07803 716842

**Humbleyard**
⊞ Humbleyard Fine Art, Unit 32 Admiral Vernon Arcade,
Portobello Road, London, W11 2DY
Tel: 01362 637793 or 07836 349416

**Hunt Auctions**
⚒ Hunt Auctions, Inc., 75 E. Uwchlan Avenue, Suite 130, Exton,
Pennsylvania 19341, U.S.A. Tel: 610 524 0822
info@huntauctions.com www.huntauctions.com

**Islwyn Watkins**
⊞ Islwyn Watkins, Offa's Dyke Antique Centre, 4 High Street,
Knighton, Powys, LD7 1AT, Wales Tel: 01547 520145

**J & J's**
⊞ J & J's, Paragon Antiquities, Antiques & Collectors Market,
3 Bladud Buildings, The Paragon, Bath, Somerset, BA1 5LS
Tel: 01225 463715

**J & M Collectables**
⊞ J & M Collectables Tel: 01580 891657 or 077135 23573
jandmcollectables@tinyonline.co.uk

**J & S Haley**
⊞† John & Simon Haley, 89 Northgate, North Bridge, Halifax,
Yorkshire, HX1 1XF Tel: 01422 360434
collectorsoldtoy@aol.com www.collectorsoldtoyshop.com

**J. Costello**
⊞ J. Costello Tel: 02476 269905
johncost@ntlworld.com

**J R & S J Symes**
⊞ J.R & S.J Symes of Bristol Tel: 0117 9501074

**Jam Jar**
⊞ Jam Jar Tel: 078896 17593

**James Bond Toys**
⊞ James Bond Toys Tel: 01942 511912 or 07788 596077
bond@007lotus.co.uk www.jamesbondtoys.co.uk

**James D Julia**
⚒ James D Julia, Inc., P O Box 830, Rte.201 Skowhegan Road,
Fairfield, ME 04937, U.S.A. Tel: 207 453 7125
jjulia@juliaauctions.com www.juliaauctions.com

**James Hardwick**
⊞ James Hardwick
Tel: 07768 667 986 popshopuk@aol.com

**James Strang**
⊞ James Strang
Tel: 01334 472 566 or 07950 490088
james@mod-i.com www.mod-i.com

**Jane Wicks**
⊞ Jane Wicks Kitchenalia, 'Country Ways', Strand Quay, Rye, East Sussex, TN31 7AY Tel: 01424 713635 or 07754 308269
janes_kitchen@hotmail.com

**Jean Sears**
⊞ Jean Sears, Halcyon, Unit 170 Station Mill Antique Centre, Station Road, Chipping Norton, Oxfordshire, OX7 5HX
Tel: 01608 644563

**Jessie's Button Box**
⊞ Jessie's Button Box, Bartlett Street Antique Centre, Bath, Somerset, BA1 5DY Tel: 0117 929 9065

**Jim Bullock Militaria**
⊞† Jim Bullock Militaria, P.O. Box 217, Romsey, Hampshire, SO51 5XL Tel: 01794 516455
jim@jimbullockmilitaria.com
www.jimbullockmilitaria.com

**Jim Call**
⊞ Jim Call, Broomfield, Colorado, U.S.A.
tribalam@all2easy.net
www.3Gsmilkbottles.com www.milkbottleworld.com

**John English**
⊞ John English Gifts, 6 Prices Arcade (closed during Feb), Picadilly, London, SW1Y 6DS Tel: 020 7437 2082
brian@johnenglishgifts.com www.johnenglishgifts.com

**John Smart**
⊞ John Smart, 26 Halford Road, Attleborough, NR17 2JF
Tel: 01953 456107

**Jonathan Harris**
⊞ Jonathan Harris Studio Glass Ltd, Woodland House, 24 Peregrine Way, Apley Castle, Telford, Shropshire, TF1 6TH
Tel: 01952 246381/588441
jonathan@jhstudioglass.com www.jhstudioglass.com

**Junktion**
⊞† Junktion, The Old Railway Station, New Bolingbroke, Boston, Lincolnshire, PE22 7LB Tel: 01205 480068 or 07836 345491
junktionantiques@hotmail.com

**Just Glass**
⊞ Just Glass, Cross House, Market Place, Alston, Cumbria, CA9 3HS Tel: 01434 381263 or 0783 3994948

**Just Jewellery**
⊞ Just Jewellery Tel: 01926 854745

**K & M Antiques**
⊞ K & M Antiques, 369-370 Grays Antique Market, 58 Davies Street, London, W1K 5LP Tel: 020 7491 4310 or 07787 565 505 Kandmantiques@aol.com

**KARS Unlimited**
⊞ KARS Unlimited, P.O. Box 895340, Leesburg, FL 34789-5340, U.S.A. Tel: 352 365 0229
karsunltd@aol.com www.kars-unlimited.com

**Katherine Higgins**

**KCS Ceramics**
⊞ KCS Ceramics International, Mrs Karen Parker
Tel: 020 8384 8981
karen@kcsceramics.co.uk www.kcsceramics.co.uk

**Kevin Ward**
⊞ Kevin Ward Tel: 01733 765548

**Kingston Antiques**
⊞ Kingston Antiques Centre, 29-31 London Road, Kingston-upon-Thames, Surrey, KT2 6ND
Tel: 020 8549 2004/3839
enquiries@kingstonantiquescentre.co.uk
www.kingstonantiquescentre.co.uk

**Kit Barry Ephemera**
⊞ Kit Barry Ephemera & Supplies, Courtesy Ruby Lane, 74 Cotton Mill Hill, #A252, Brattleboro, VT 05301, U.S.A.

**Knick Knack Nook**
⊞ The Knick Knack Nook, Courtesy Ruby Lane, W. Pratt Boulevard, Chicago, IL 60626, U.S.A. Tel: 773 274 9511
www.knickknacknook.com

**La Femme**
⊞ La Femme Tel: 07971 844279
jewels@joancorder.freeserve.co.uk

**Le Boudoir Collectables**
⊞ Le Boudoir Collectables, The Basement, George Street Antique Centre, 8 Edgar Buildings, Bath, Somerset, BA1 2EE
Tel: 01225 311061 or 07974 918630
www.le-boudoir-online.com

**Lewis Antiques**
⊞ Lewis Antiques & Interiors Tel: 07764 576106
sandie.lewis@blueyonder.co.uk

**Limelight**
⊞ Limelight Movie Art, 135 King's Road, Chelsea, London, SW3 4PW Tel: 020 7751 5584
info@limelightmovieart.com www.limelightmovieart.com

**Linda Bee**
⊞ Linda Bee Art Deco, Stand L18-21, Grays Antique Market, 1-7 Davies Mews, London, W1Y 1AR
Tel: 020 7629 5921

**Locke & England**
⚒ Locke & England, 18 Guy Street, Leamington Spa, Warwickshire, CV32 4RT Tel: 01926 889100
info@leauction.co.uk www.auctions-online.com/locke

**Lolli Dollies**
⊞ Lolli Dollies Online, 8 Athol Terrace, Dover, Kent, CT16 1LT
contact@lolli-dollies-online.co.uk
www.lolli-dollies-online.co.uk

**London Cigarette Card Co**
⊞† London Cigarette Card Co Ltd, Sutton Road, Somerton, Somerset, TA11 6QP Tel: 01458 273452
cards@londoncigcard.co.uk www.londoncigcard.co.uk

**Long Street Antiques**
⊞ Long Street Antiques, Stamford House, 14 Long Street, Tetbury, Gloucestershire, GL8 8AQ Tel: 01666 500850
longstantiques@aol.com www.longstreetantiques.co.uk

**Losch's**
⊞ The Losch's, Ubierstrasse 7, 53173 Bonn, Germany
Tel: (0) 228 368 0 398
www.the-loschs.com

**Luna**
⊞ Luna, 139 Lower Parliament Street, Nottingham, NG1 1EE
Tel: 0115 924 3267
info@luna-online.co.uk www.luna-online.co.uk

**M&C Cards**
⊞ M&C Cards, Unit 30/32 Antique Centre, Severn Road, Gloucester, GL1 2LE Tel: 01452 506361
www.mandccards.co.uk

**Made**
⊞ Made by the People for the People Ltd, Apex House, 2 Slivester Road, Hackney, London, E8 1EP Tel: 020 8510 5699
enquiries@made.uk.com www.made.uk.com

**Magic Toy Box**
⊞ The Magic Toy Box, 210 Havant Road, Drayton, Portsmouth, Hampshire, PO6 2EH Tel: 02392 221307
magictoybox@btinternet.com www.magictoybox.co.uk
www.sindy-dolls.co.uk

**Malcolm Welch**
⊞ Malcolm Welch Antiques, Wild Jebbett, Pudding Bag Lane, Thurlaston, Nr Rugby, Warwickshire, CV23 9JZ
Tel: 01788 810 616 www.rb33.co.uk

**Manfred Schotten**
⊞ Manfred Schotten, 109 High Street, Burford, Oxfordshire, OX18 4RG Tel: 01993 822302
sport@schotten.com www.schotten.com

**Marlene Evans**
⊞ Marlene Evans, Headrow Antiques Centre, Headrow Centre, Leeds, Yorkshire Tel: 0113 245 5344

**Marsh-McNamara**
⊞ Marsh-McNamara Tel: 07790 759162

**Martin's Antiques**
⊞ Martin's Antiques & Collectibles
Jackiem743710633@aol.com
www.martinsantiquescollectibles.co.uk

**Mary's Memories**
⊞ Mary's Memories, Courtesy TIAS.com, P.O. Box 2342,
Centreville, VA 20122, U.S.A. mcmonet@hughes.net
www.tias.com/stores/mm

**Mastro Auctions**
⚒ Mastro Auctions, 7900 South Madison Street, Burr Ridge,
Illinois 60527, U.S.A. Tel: 630 472 1200
jmarren@mastroauctions.com www.mastroauctions.com

**Maxwells**
⚒ Maxwells, 133A Woodford Road, Woodford,
Cheshire, SK7 1QD Tel: 0161 439 5182
www.maxwells-auctioneers.co.uk

**Memories Collectors Shop**
⊞ Memories Collectors Shop, 130-132 Brent Street,
Hendon, London, NW4 2DR Tel: 020 8203 1500
dave@ppv.uk.com www.memoriespostcards.co.uk

**Metropolis Toys**
⊞ Metropolis Toys, 31 Derby Street, Burton on Trent,
Staffordshire, DE14 2LD Tel: 01283 740400
chris@metropolistoys.co.uk www.metropolistoys.co.uk

**Mia Cartwright**
⊞ Mia Cartwright Tel: 07956 440260 mia.cartwright@virgin.net

**Michael D Long**
⊞ Michael D Long Ltd, 96-98 Derby Road,
Nottingham, NG1 5FB Tel: 0115 941 3307
sales@michaeldlong.com www.michaeldlong.com

**Michael Saffell**
⊞ Michael Saffell Antiques, 3 Walcot Buildings, London Road,
Bath, Somerset, BA1 6AD Tel: 01225 315857
michael.saffell@virgin.net

**Mike Weedon**
⊞ Mike Weedon, 7 Camden Passage, Islington, London, N1 8EA
Tel: 020 7226 5319 or 020 7609 6826
info@mikeweedonantiques.com
www.mikeweedonantiques.com

**Militaryman**
⊞ Militaryman Tel: 01473 274367
militaryman@peace41.fsnet.co.uk
www.dinkycollector.com

**Mimi Fifi**
⊞ Mimi Fifi, 27 Pembridge Road, Notting Hill Gate,
London, W11 3HG Tel: 020 7243 3154
info@mimififi.com www.mimififi.com

**ModCats**
⊞ ModCats.com info@modcats.com
www.modcats.com

**Modern Warehouse**
⊞ The Modern Warehouse, 243b Victoria Park Road,
London, E9 Tel: 020 8986 0740, 07747 758852 or 07930 304361
info@themodernwarehouse.com
www.themodernwarehouse.com

**Moorcroft Antiques**
⊞ Moorcroft Antiques, 33 Rookery Close, Bodicote, Banbury,
Oxfordshire, OX15 4BA Tel: 01295 255910
www.moorcroftantiques.webstall.net

**Mr A Harris**
⊞ Mr A Harris Tel: 020 8207 1569 or 07960 811260

**Muir Hewitt**
⊞ Muir Hewitt Art Deco Originals, Redbrick Mill,
218 Bradford Road, Batley, West Yorkshire, WF17 6JF
Tel: 01924 458800 or 07813 685990
muirhewitt@hotmail.com
www.muirhewitt.com

**Murray Cards**
⊞ Murray Cards (International) Ltd, 51 Watford Way,
Hendon Central, London, NW4 3JH Tel: 020 8202 5688
murraycards@ukbusiness.com www.murraycard.com/

**Murrays' Antiques**
⊞ Murray's Antiques & Collectables Tel: 01202 823870

**My Gigi's Treasures**
⊞ My Gigi's Treasures, Courtesy TIAS.com,
517 Spring Gardens Court, Birmingham, AL 35217, U.S.A.
hsmith2@bham.rr.com www.tias.com/stores/rabasa

**Myott Collectors Club**
Myott Collectors Club, P.O. Box 110, Sutton, Surrey, SM3 9YQ
Tel: 07986 437 904 martin@setforthenet.com
www.myottcollectorsclub.com

**New 2 You**
⊞ New 2 You, Cinque Ports Street, Rye, East Sussex, TN31 7AD
Tel: 01797 226379 or 07903 464716
ruthforrest@hotmail.co.uk

**Newark Antiques**
⊞ Newark Antiques Warehouse Ltd, Old Kelham Road,
Newark, Nottinghamshire, NG24 1BX
Tel: 01636 674869/07974 429185
enquiries@newarkantiques.co.uk www.newarkantiques.co.uk

**Nigel Williams Rare Books**
⊞ Nigel Williams Rare Books, 25 Cecil Court,
London, WC2N 4EZ Tel: 020 7836 7757
nigel@nigelwilliams.com www.nigelwilliams.com

**Noble Gold**
⊞ Noble Gold Ltd Tel: 01275 464152
james.cole1@btinternet.com

**Offa's Dyke**
⊞ Offa's Dyke Antique Centre, 4 High Street, Knighton, Powys,
LD7 1AT, Wales Tel: 01547 528635/520145

**Old Ironmongers**
⊞ The Old Ironmongers Antiques Centre, 5 Burford Street,
Lechlade, Gloucestershire, GL7 3AP Tel: 01367 252397

**Old Tackle Box**
⊞ The Old Tackle Box, P.O. Box 55, High Street, Cranbrook, Kent,
TN17 3ZU Tel: 01580 713979 or 07729 278 293
tackle.box@virgin.net

**Oldnautibits**
⊞ Oldnautibits, P.O. Box 67, Langport, Somerset, TA10 9WJ
Tel: 01458 241816 or 07947 277833
geoff.pringle@oldnautibits.com www.oldnautibits.com

**On The Air**
⊞† On The Air, The Vintage Technology Centre, The Highway,
Hawarden (Nr Chester), Deeside, Cheshire, CH5 3DN
Tel: 01244 530300 or 07778 767734
www.vintageradio.co.uk

**Onslow's Auctions**
⚒†Onslow's Auctions Ltd, The Coach House, Manor Road,
Stourpaine, Blandford Forum, Dorset, DT8 8TQ
Tel: 01258 488838 onslowauctions@btinternet.com

**Orchard Books**
⊞ Orchard Books, The Watts Publishing Group (a division of
Hachette Children's Books) 338 Euston Road, London, NW1 3BH
Tel: 020 7873 6000
www.orchardbooks.co.uk

**Otford Centre**
⊞ Otford Antiques & Collectors Centre, 26-28 High Street,
Otford, Kent, TN14 5PQ Tel: 01959 522025
info@otfordantiques.co.uk www.otfordantiques.co.uk

**Outernational**
⊞ Outernational, Germany info@outernational.info
www.outernational.info

**Pantiles Spa Antiques**
⊞ Pantiles Spa Antiques, 4, 5, 6 Union House,
The Pantiles, Tunbridge Wells, Kent, TN4 8HE
Tel: 01892 541377 psa.wells@btinternet.com
www.antiques-tun-wells-kent.co.uk

**Pascoe**
⊞ Pascoe & Company, 253 SW 22nd Avenue, Miami, Florida 33135, U.S.A. Tel: 800 872 0195/305 643 2550 mike@pascoeandcompany.com www.pascoeandcompany.com

**P B A Galleries**
⊞ PBA Galleries, 133 Kearny Street, 4th Floor, San Francisco, California 94108, U.S.A. Tel: 415 989 2665 www.pbagalleries.com

**PennyMachines**
⊞ PennyMachines.co.uk, 50 Charlemont Road, Walsall, West Midlands, WS5 3NQ Tel: 01922 621888 david@pennymachines.co.uk

**Penrith Farmers' & Kidd's**
⚒ Penrith Farmers' & Kidd's plc, Skirsgill Salerooms, Penrith, Cumbria, CA11 0DN Tel: 01768 890781 info@pfkauctions.co.uk www.pfkauctions.co.uk

**Pepe Tozzo**
⊞ Pepe Tozzo pepe@tozzo.co.uk

**Peter Campbell**
⊞ Peter Campbell Antiques, 59 Bath Road, Atworth, Nr. Melksham, Wiltshire, SN12 8JY Tel: 01225 709742

**Peter Harrington**
⊞ Peter Harrington, 100 Fulham Road, London, SW3 6HS Tel: 020 7591 0220/0330 www.peter-harrington-books.com

**phil-comics**
⊞ phil-comics auctions, P.O. Box 3433, Brighton, East Sussex, BN50 9JA Tel: 01273 673462 or 07739 844703 phil@phil-comics.com www.phil-comics.com

**Philip Knighton**
⊞ Philip Knighton, 1c South Street, Wellington, Somerset, TA21 8NS Tel: 01823 661618 philip.knighton@btconnect.com

**Piccadilly Antiques**
⊞ Piccadilly Antiques, 280 High Street, Batheaston, Bath, Somerset, BA1 7RA Tel: 01225 851494 or 07785 966132 piccadillyantiques@ukonline.co.uk

**Pineapple Ice Bucket**
⊞ Pineapple Ice Bucket, The Retro Room @ Squirrels Antiques, Lyndhurst Road, Brockenhurst, Hampshire, SO42 7RL retro_pineapple@msn.com www.pineappleicebucket.co.uk

**Pollyanna**
⊞ Pollyanna, 34 High Street, Arundel, West Sussex, BN18 9AB Tel: 01903 885198 or 07949903457

**Poole Room**
⊞ The Poole Room info@pooleroom.co.uk www.pooleroom.co.uk

**Postcard Club**
Postcard Club of Great Britain, Est 1960, c/o Mrs D. Brennan, 34 Harper House, St James Crescent, London, SW9 7LW Tel: 020 7771 9404

**Prop Store**
⊞† The Prop Store of London www.propstore.com

**Pure Imagination**
⊞ P.O. Box 140, South Shields, Tyne & Wear, NE33 3WU Tel: 0191 4169090 or 0771 5054919 www.pureimaginations.co.uk

**Q & C Militaria**
⊞ Q & C Militaria, 22 Suffolk Road, Cheltenham, Gloucestershire, GL50 2AQ Tel: 01242 519815 or 07778 613977 qcmilitaria@btconnect.com www.qcmilitaria.com

**Quay Centre**
⊞ Quay Centre, Topsham, Nr Exeter, Devon, EX3 0JA Tel: 01392 874006 office@quayantiques.com www.quayantiques.com

**R B Farley**
⊞ R.B. Farley Tel: 01323 848285 grahamfar1ey@aol.com

**Racing Stuff**
⊞ Racing Stuff, P.O. Box 127, Bicester, Oxfordshire, OX26 2WL Tel: 07779 925537 www.racingstuff.piczo.com

**Rago Arts & Auction Center**
⚒ Rago Arts & Auction Center, 333 North Main Street, Lambertville, New Jersey 08530, U.S.A. Tel: 609 397 9374 info@ragoarts.com www.ragoarts.com

**Reasons to be Cheerful**
⊞ Reasons to be Cheerful, Georgian Village, 30-31 Islington Green, London, N18 DU Tel: 0207 281 4600

**ReMemories**
⊞ ReMemories Antiques, 74 High Street, Tenterden, Kent, TN30 6AU Tel: 01580 763416

**Repsycho**
⊞ Repsycho, 85 Gloucester Road, Bishopston, Bristol, Gloucestershire, BS7 8AS Tel: 0117 983 0007

**Retro Centre**
⊞ Retro Centre Tel: 0118 950 7224 al@retro-centre.co.uk www.retro-centre.co.uk

**Retro2Go**
⊞ Retro2Go, Courtesy Ruby Lane, P.O. Box 1171, Sault Ste, Marie, MI 49783, U.S.A.

**RetroArtGlass.com**
⊞ Retro Art Glass, California, U.S.A. Tel: 951 639 3032 www.retroartglass.com

**Retrobrick**
⊞ Retrobrick www.retrobrick.com

**retroselect**
⊞ www.retroselect.com info@retroselect.com

**Richard Twort**
⊞ Richard Twort Tel: 01934 612439 or 07711 939789 walls@mirage-interiors.com

**Richard Wallis Antiks**
⊞ Richard Wallis Antiks Tel: 020 8529 1749 www.richardwallisantiks.com

**Rin Tin Tin**
⊞ Rin Tin Tin, 34 North Road, Brighton, East Sussex, BN1 1YB Tel: 01273 672424 rick@rintintin.freeserve.co.uk

**Robert Mills**
⊞ Robert Mills Ltd, Narroways Road, Eastville, Bristol, Somerset, BS2 9XB Tel: 0117 955 6542 info@rmills.co.uk www.rmills.co.uk

**Robert Mullin**
⊞ Robert Mullin, The Wee Web, 61 (Flat 2), Rosevale Terrace, Edinburgh, EH6 8AN, Scotland Tel: 0131 467 7147 contact@theweeweb.co.uk www.theweeweb.co.uk

**Roger Harris**
⊞ Roger Harris, Saturdays at:Stall A12-A13 Roger's Arcade, 65 Portobello Road, London, W11 Tel: 020 8747 8545 or 07885 723 433 antiques@rogerharris.tv

**Rokit (B)**
⊞ Rokit Ltd, 101 & 107 Brick Lane, London, E1 6SE Tel: 020 7375 3864

**Rosebery's**
⚒ Rosebery's Auctioneers & Valuers, 74/76 Knights Hill, London, SE27 0JD Tel: 020 8761 2522 info@roseberys.co.uk www.roseberys.co.uk

**Roy Laycock**
⊞ Roy Laycock Tel: 01430 860313

**Royal Mint Collectors' Club**
Royal Mint Collectors' Club, P.O. Box 500, Pontyclun, CF1 1HA Tel: 0845 6088300 www.royalmint.com
*Images Crown copyright*

**Ruskin Decorative Arts**
⊞ Ruskin Decorative Arts, 5 Talbot Court, Stow-on-the-Wold, Gloucestershire, GL54 1DP Tel: 01451 832254 william.anne@ruskindecarts.co.uk

**S&D Postcards**
⊞ S&D Postcards, Bartlett Street Antique Centre, 5-10 Bartlett Street, Bath, Somerset, BA1 2QZ Tel: 07979 506415 wndvd@aol.com

**Scherazade**
⊞ Scherazade Tel: 01708 641117 or 07855 383996 scherz1@yahoo.com

**Schmidt Museum**
Schmidt Museum of Coca-Cola Memorabilia, 109 Buffalo Creek Dr., Elizabethtown, KY 42701-7518, U.S.A. Tel: 270 234 1100 schmidtmuseum@yahoo.com www.schmidtmuseum.com

**Scottish Antique & Arts**
⊞ Scottish Antique & Arts Centre, Carse of Cambus, Doune, Perthshire, FK16 6HG, Scotland Tel: 01786 841203 sales@scottish-antiques.com www.scottish-antiques.com

**Scottish Antique & Arts**
⊞ Scottish Antique & Arts Centre, Abernyte, Perthshire, PH14 9SJ, Scotland Tel: 01828 686401 sales@scottish-antiques.com www.scottish-antiques.com

**Scottow Antiques**
⊞ Scottow Antiques, Green Street Green, Orpington, Kent Tel: 07860 795909

**Sherwood Golf Antiques**
⊞ Sherwood Golf Antiques Tel: 07968 848448 sherwoodgolf@btinternet.com

**Shibusa Gallery**
⊞ The Shibusa Gallery, Sub Post Office, Rear of 14 Dunyeats Road, Broadstone, Dorset, BH18 8AB Tel: 07931 298584 david@shibusa-gallery.co.uk www.shibusa-gallery.co.uk

**Signature Connection**
⊞ Signature Connection Tel: 07919 092991 steve@thesignatureconnection.co.uk www.thesignatureconnection.co.uk

**Silversnow Antiques**
⊞ Silversnow Antiques and More, Courtesy TIAS.com www.tias.com/stores/silsnow

**Skinner**
🔨 Skinner Inc., The Heritage On The Garden, 63 Park Plaza, Boston, MA 02116, U.S.A. Tel: 617 350 5400 www.skinnerinc.com

**Skip & Janie Smithson**
⊞ Skip & Janie Smithson Antiques Tel: 01754 810265 or 07831 399180 smithsonantiques@hotmail.com

**Soldiers of Rye**
⊞ Soldiers of Rye, 105 High Street, Rye, East Sussex Tel: 0777 2791756 rameses@supanet.com www.rameses.supanet.com

**Sotheby's (NY)**
🔨 Sotheby's, 1334 York Avenue at 72nd St, New York, NY 10021, U.S.A. Tel: 212 606 7000 www.sothebys.com

**Sotheby's (S)**
🔨 Sotheby's, Summers Place, Billingshurst, West Sussex, RH14 9AD Tel: 01403 833500 www.sothebys.com

**Sparkle Moore**
⊞ Sparkle Moore, Alfies Antique Market, G100 & G116 Ground Floor, 13-25 Church Street, Marylebone, London, NW8 8DT Tel: 020 7724 8984 or 07958 515614 sparkle.moore@virgin.net www.sparklemoore.com

**Special Auction Services**
🔨† Special Auction Services, Kennetholme, Midgham, Reading, Berkshire, RG7 5UX Tel: 0118 971 2949 www.specialauctionservices.com

**Spinna Disc Records**
⊞ Spinna Disc Records, 2B Union Street, Aldershot, Hants, GU11 1EG Tel: 01252 327261 sales@spinnadiscrecords.com www.spinnadiscrecords.com

**Sporting Antiques**
⊞ Sporting Antiques, 9 Church St, St Ives, Cambridgeshire, PE27 6DG Tel: 01480 463891 or 07831 274774 johnlambden@sportingantiques.co.uk www.sportingantiques.co.uk

**Steinberg & Tolkien**
⊞ Steinberg & Tolkien Vintage & Designer Clothing, 193 Kings Road, London, SW3 5EB Tel: 020 7376 3660

**Steptoes Dog**
⊞† Steptoes Dog Antiques Tel: 07731475164 steptoes.dog@virgin.net www.steptoesantiques.co.uk

**Steve Blackham**
⊞ Steve Blackham Tel: 01302 849256

**Steven Bishop**
⊞ Steven Bishop Antiques & Decorative Arts Tel: 07761563095 meridian34all@btinternet.com www.meridiangallery.co.uk

**Sue Killinger**
⊞ Sue Killinger Antiques Tel: 01494 862975 or 07836684815

**Sue Wilde**
⊞ Sue Wilde at Wildewear Tel: 01395 577966 compacts@wildewear.co.uk www.wildewear.co.uk

**Swan at Tetsworth**
⊞ The Swan at Tetsworth, High Street, Tetsworth, Nr Thame, Oxfordshire, OX9 7AB Tel: 01844 281777 antiques@theswan.co.uk www.theswan.co.uk

**Sweet Memories**
⊞ Sweet Memories Vinyl Records UK www.vinylrecords.co.uk

**Sweetbriar Gallery**
⊞† Sweetbriar Gallery Ltd., 29 Beechview Road, Kingsley, Frodsham, Cheshire, WA6 8DF Tel: 01928 788225 sales@sweetbriar.co.uk www.sweetbriar.co.uk www.sweetbriarartglass.co.uk

**Sworders**
🔨 Sworders, 14 Cambridge Road, Stansted Mountfitchet, Essex, CM24 8BZ Tel: 01279 817778 auctions@sworder.co.uk www.sworder.co.uk

**Symes of Bristol** see J.R. & S.J.Symes

**Teddy Bears of Witney**
⊞† Teddy Bears of Witney, 99 High Street, Witney, Oxfordshire, OX28 6HY Tel: 01993 706616 bears@witneybears.co.uk www.teddybears.co.uk

**Telephone Lines**
⊞† Telephone Lines Ltd, 304 High Street, Cheltenham, Gloucestershire, GL50 3JF Tel: 01242 583699 info@telephonelines.net www.telephonelines.net

**Tenterden Antiques**
⊞ Tenterden Antiques Centre, 66-66A High Street, Tenterden, Kent, TN30 6AU Tel: 01580 765655/765885

**Tenterden Silver Vaults**
⊞ Tenterden Antiques & Silver Vaults, 66 High Street, Tenterden, Kent, TN30 6AU Tel: 01580 765885

**Tin Shop**
⊞ The Tin Shop, Market Vaults, Scarborough, N. Yorkshire, YO11 1EU Tel: 01723 351089 www.tinshop.co.uk

## Tin Tin
⊞ Tin Tin Collectables, G38-42 Alfies's Antique Market, 13-25 Church Street, Marylebone, London, NW8 8DT Tel: 020 7258 1305 leslie@tintincollectables.com www.tintincollectables.com

## Tintern Antiques
⊞ Tintern Antiques, The Olde Bakehouse, Monmouth Road, Tintern, NP16 6SE, Wales Tel: 01291 689705

## Tony Durante
⊞† Tony Durante, Alfie's Antique Market, Unit G047-G048 Ground Floor, 13–25 Church Street, London, NW8 8DT Tel: 020 7723 0449 or 07989 446569 durantetony@hotmail.com

## Tony Horsley
⊞† Tony Horsley, P.O. Box 3127, Brighton, East Sussex, BN1 5SS Tel: 01273 550770

## Top Banana
⊞ The Top Banana Antiques Mall, 1 New Church Street, Tetbury, Gloucestershire, GL8 8DS Tel: 0871 288 1102 info@topbananaantiques.com www.topbananaantiques.com

## Totally Teapots
Totally Teapots, The Novelty Teapot Collectors Club, Vince McDonald, Euxton, Chorley, Lancashire, PR7 6EY Tel: 01257 450366 vince@totallyteapots.com www.totallyteapots.com

## Toydreams
⊞ Toydreams sales@toydreams.co.uk www.toydreams.co.uk

## Toys & Hobbies
⊞ Toys & Hobbies Tel: 0161 794 5360 toysandhobbies@btinternet.com www.toysandhobbies.net

## Turn On Lighting
⊞ Turn On Lighting, Antique Lighting Specialists, 116/118 Islington High St, Camden Passage, Islington, London, N1 8EG Tel: 020 7359 7616

## Tussie Mussies
⊞ Tussie Mussies, The Old Stables, 2b East Cross, Tenterden, Kent, TN30 6AD Tel: 01580 766244 tussiemussies@btinternet.com www.tussiemussies.co.uk

## Twinkled
⊞ Twinkled, 1.5 Kingly Court, Carnaby Street, London, W1B 5PW Tel: 020 7734 1978 info@twinkled.net www.twinkled.net

## Upstairs Downstairs
⊞ Upstairs Downstairs, 40 Market Place, Devizes, Wiltshire, SN10 1JG Tel: 01380 730266 or 07974 074220 devizesantiques@btconnect.com

## Van Sabben
⚒ Van Sabben Poster Auctions, Appelsteeg 1-B, NL-1621 BD, Hoorn, Netherlands Tel: 31 (0)229 268203 uboersma@vansabbenauctions.nl www.vansabbenauctions.nl

## Vanessa Turner
⊞ Vanessa Turner Tel: 07770 851136 vanessa.turner@ipba-uk.co.uk

## Vault Auctions
⚒ Vault Auctions Ltd, P.O. Box 257, South Norwood, London, SE25 6JN Tel: 01342 300 900 contact@vaultauctions.com www.vaultauctions.com

## Vectis
⚒† Vectis Auctions Ltd and Vectis Direct, Fleck Way, Thornaby, Stockton-on-Tees, Cleveland, TS17 9JZ Tel: 01642 750616 and 01642 764455 admin@vectis.co.uk and admin@vectisdirect.co.uk www.vectis.co.uk www.vectisdirect.co.uk

## Vetta Decorative Arts
⊞ Vetta Decorative Arts, P.O. Box 247, Oxford, OX1 5XH Tel: 0780 905 4969 vettaatam@aol.com

## VicMart.com
⊞ VicMart.com info@vicmart.com www.vicmart.com

## Vintage Modes
⊞ Vintage Modes, Grays Antique Markets, 1-7 Davies Mews, London, W1 Tel: 020 7409 0400 www.vintagemodes.co.uk

## Vintage & Rare Guitars
⊞ Vintage & Rare Guitars (Bath) Ltd, 7-8 Saville Row, Bath, Somerset, BA1 2QP Tel: 01225 330 888 enquiries@vintageandrareguitars.com www.vintageandrareguitars.com

## Vintage & Rare Guitars
⊞ Vintage & Rare Guitars (London), 6 Denmark Street, London, WC2H 8LX Tel: 020 7240 7500 enquiries@vintageandrareguitars.com www.vintageandrareguitars.com

## Vintage Pens
⊞ Vintage Pens, P.O. Box 41452, Providence, RI 02940-1452, U.S.A. Tel: 401 351 7607 pen.info@vintagepens.com www.vintagepens.com

## Vintage Swank
⊞ Vintage Swank, 212 East Main Street, Front Royal, VA 22630, U.S.A. Tel: 540 636 0069 info@vintageswank.com www.vintageswank.com

## Vintage Toybox
⊞ Vintage Toybox, Gainsborough, Lincolnshire contact@vintagetoybox.xo.uk www.vintagetoybox.co.uk

## Vintage Toys
⊞ Vintage Toys Tel: 01993 840064

## Wallis & Wallis
⚒ Wallis & Wallis, West Street Auction Galleries, Lewes, East Sussex, BN7 2NJ Tel: 01273 480208 auctions@wallisandwallis.co.uk grb@wallisandwallis.co.uk www.wallisandwallis.co.uk

## Wardrobe
⊞ Wardrobe, 51 Upper North Street, Brighton, East Sussex, BN1 3FH Tel: 01273 202201 www.decoratif.co.uk
*Costume jewellery courtesy of Philip Parfitt*

## Wellers Auctioneers
⚒ Wellers Auctioneers, 70/70a Guildford Street, Chertsey, Surrey, KT16 9BB Tel: 01932 568678 auctions@wellersauctions.com www.wellersauctions.com

## Wenderton Antiques
⊞ Wenderton Antiques Tel: 01227 720295 (by appt only)

## Wheels of Steel
⊞ Wheels of Steel, Grays Antique Market, Stand A12-13, Unit B10 Basement, 1-7 Davies Mews, London, W1Y 2LP Tel: 020 7629 2813

## Williams Amusements
⊞ Williams Amusements Ltd, Bluebird House, Povey Cross Road, Horley, Surrey, RH6 0AG Tel: 01293 782222 or 07970 736486 sales@williams-amusements.co.uk www.williams-amusements.co.uk

## Wonderful World of Animation
⊞ Wonderful World of Animation, 9517 Culver Blvd, Culver City, CA 90232, U.S.A. Tel: 310 836 4992 gallery@animationartgallery.com www.wonderfulworldofanimation.com

## Woodville Antiques
⊞ Woodville Antiques, The Street, Hamstreet, Ashford, Kent, TN26 2HG Tel: 01233 732981 woodvilleantiques@yahoo.co.uk

## Woolley & Wallis
⚒ Woolley & Wallis, Salisbury Salerooms, 51-61 Castle Street, Salisbury, Wiltshire, SP1 3SU Tel: 01722 424500/411854 enquiries@woolleyandwallis.co.uk www.woolleyandwallis.co.uk

## Worcester Antiques
⊞ Worcester Antiques Centre, Reindeer Court, Mealcheapen Street, Worcester, WR1 4DF Tel: 01905 610680 info@worcesterantiquecentre.com www.worcesterantiquecentre.com

## Yew Tree Antiques
⊞ Yew Tree Antiques, Woburn Abbey Antiques Centre, Woburn, Bedfordshire, MK17 9WA Tel: 01525 872514

# INDEX TO ADVERTISERS

# INDEX

**Bold** page numbers refer to information and pointer boxes